Frank G. Jennings
Executive Director
Library Club of America
and

Charles J. Calitri
Benjamin Franklin High School
New York City

STORIES

Harcourt, Brace & World, Inc.
New York   Chicago   San Francisco   Atlanta   Dallas

Copyrights and Acknowledgments

The authors thank the publishers and copyright holders for their permission to use the selections reprinted in this book: THE AMERICAN-SCANDINAVIAN FOUNDATION—"The Father" by Björnstjerne Björnson, copyright The American-Scandinavian Foundation. APPLETON-CENTURY-CROFTS, INC.—"Bill's Little Girl" from *Yellow Gentians and Blue* by Zona Gale, copyright, 1927, D. Appleton & Company, reprinted by permission of the publishers, Appleton-Century-Crofts, Inc. ROBERT K. BINGHAM—"The Unpopular Passenger," originally in *The Reporter*, February 2, 1954. BRANDT AND BRANDT—"The Quiet Man" by Maurice Walsh, copyright, 1933, by The Curtis Publishing Company; "The Most Dangerous Game" by Richard Connell, copyright, 1924, by Richard Connell, copyright renewed, 1952, by Louise Fox Connell; "Nightmare Number Three" from *Selected Works of Stephen Vincent Benét*, Rinehart & Company, copyright, 1935, by Stephen Vincent Benét; "Nancy Hanks" by Rosemary Benét from *A Book of Americans*, Rinehart & Company, copyright, 1933, by Rosemary and Stephen Vincent Benét; "Recuerdo" from *Collected Lyrics of Edna St. Vincent Millay*, Harper & Brothers, copyright, 1919, 1947, by Edna St. Vincent Millay. FLOYD DELL—"The Blanket," originally in *Collier's*. DOUBLEDAY & COMPANY, INC.—"After Twenty Years" from *The Four Million* by O. Henry, copyright 1904 by Doubleday & Company, Inc.; "Those Two Boys" from *Tobogganing on Parnassus* by Franklin P. Adams, copyright 1911 by Doubleday & Company, Inc. ERNST, CANE & BERNER—"Romance" from *Peace, It's Wonderful* by William Saroyan, published by the Starling Press-Modern Age Books, Inc., copyright, 1939, by William Saroyan, reprinted by permission of the author. BARTHOLD FLES (literary agent)—"The New Kid" by Murray Heyert, published in *Harper's* Magazine, June 1944. HARCOURT, BRACE AND COMPANY, INC.—"The Sniper" from *Spring Sowing* by Liam O'Flaherty; "A Girl from the Queer People" from *Remembrance Rock* by Carl Sandburg, copyright, 1948, by Harcourt, Brace and Company, Inc.; "Nancy," copyright, 1948, by Elizabeth Enright, reprinted from her volume *The Moment Before the Rain*; "A Time of Learning," copyright, 1946, by Jessamyn West, reprinted from her volume, *Love, Death, And The Ladies' Drill Team*. HARPER & BROTHERS—"The Duchess and the Smugs" from *A Wreath for the Enemy* by Pamela Frankau, copyright, 1952, by Pamela Frankau. HENRY HOLT AND COMPANY, INC.—"When I Was One-and-Twenty" from *A Shropshire Lad* by A. E. Housman, copyright, 1924, by Henry Holt and Company; "Happiness" from *Chicago Poems* by Carl Sandburg, copyright, 1916, by Henry Holt and Company, copyright, 1944, by Carl Sandburg; "An Epitaph" from *Collected Poems 1901–1918* by Walter de la Mare, copyright, 1920, by Henry Holt and Company, copyright, 1948, by Walter de la Mare; "Fire and Ice" from *New Hampshire* by Robert Frost, copyright, 1923, by Henry Holt and Company, copyright, 1951, by Robert Frost, all reprinted by permission of the publishers. ALFRED A. KNOPF, INC.—"Paul's Case" from *Youth and the Bright Medusa* by Willa Cather, copyright 1905, 1932 by Willa Cather; "The Great Automatic Grammatisator" by Roald Dahl, copyright 1953 by Roald Dahl; "Mario and the Magician" from *Stories of Three Decades* by Thomas Mann, copyright 1931, 1936 by Alfred A. Knopf, Inc., all reprinted by permission of Alfred A. Knopf, Inc. LITTLE, BROWN & COMPANY—"The Brain Is Wider Than the Sky" from *Poems by Emily Dickinson*, edited by Martha Dickinson Bianchi and Alfred Leete Hampson. THE MACMILLAN COMPANY—"The Man He Killed" from *Collected Poems* by Thomas Hardy, copyright, 1925, by The Macmillan Company; "The Song of the Old Mother" from *Collected Poems* by William Butler Yeats, copyright 1934 by The Macmillan Company, both reprinted by permission of The Macmillan Company. HAROLD MATSON COMPANY—"The Golden Kite, the Silver Wind" by Ray Bradbury, copyright 1953 by Epoch Associates; "Thus I Refute Beelzy" by John Collier, originally in *The Atlantic Monthly*, copyright 1940 by John Collier, both reprinted by permission of Harold Matson Company. HAROLD OBER ASSOCIATES—"Snake Dance" by Corey Ford, originally in *Liberty* Magazine, copyright 1934 by Corey Ford, reprinted by permission of Harold Ober Associates. RANDOM HOUSE, INC.—"Barn Burning" from *Collected Stories of William Faulkner*, copyright 1939 by William Faulkner, reprinted by permission of Random House, Inc. RINEHART & COMPANY, INC.—"The Answer" by Phillip Wylie, copyright, 1955, by Curtis Publishing Company, reprinted by permission of Rinehart & Company, Inc., New York, publishers. SIDNEY SATENSTEIN—"My First Two Women" copyright, 1956, by Nadine Gordimer, reprinted from her volume *Six Feet of the Country* by permission of Simon and Schuster, Inc. CHARLES SCRIBNER'S SONS—"Haircut" copyright 1925, 1953, by Ellis A. Lardner, reprinted from *Roundup* by Ring Lardner; "Bernice Bobs Her Hair," copyright 1920, 1948, by The Curtis Publishing Company, from *Flappers and Philosophers* by F. Scott Fitzgerald; "The Undefeated" from *Men Without Women* by Ernest Hemingway, copyright 1927 by Charles Scribner's Sons, 1955 by Ernest Hemingway, all used by permission of Charles Scribner's Sons. THE VIKING PRESS, INC.—"Piano" from *Collected Poems* by D. H. Lawrence, copyright 1929 by Jonathan Cape & Harrison Smith; "The Dreamers" from *Collected Poems* by Siegfried Sassoon, copyright 1918 by E. P. Dutton & Co., 1946 by Siegfried Sassoon; "Molly Morgan" from *The Pastures of Heaven* by John Steinbeck, copyright 1932 by John Steinbeck; "The Rocking-Horse Winner" from *The Portable D. H. Lawrence*, copyright 1933 by the Estate of D. H. Lawrence, all reprinted by permission of The Viking Press, Inc.

Contents

PART 1 STORIES OF IMPACT

*Many stories are accompanied by poems
related in tone, feeling, or theme.*

PART 2   STORIES OF DEPTH

PART 3 *STORIES TO THINK ABOUT*

Part 1

STORIES OF IMPACT

Part 1

The Sniper

THE LONG June twilight faded into night. Dublin lay enveloped in darkness but for the dim light of the moon that shone through fleecy clouds, casting a pale light as of approaching dawn over the streets and the dark waters of the Liffey. Around the beleaguered Four Courts the heavy guns roared. Here and there through the city, machine guns and rifles broke the silence of the night, spasmodically, like dogs barking on lone farms. Republicans and Free Staters were waging civil war.

On a roof top near O'Connell Bridge, a Republican sniper lay watching. Beside him lay his rifle and over his shoulders were slung a pair of field glasses. His face was the face of a student, thin and ascetic, but his eyes had the cold gleam of the fanatic. They were deep and thoughtful, the eyes of a man who is used to looking at death.

He was eating a sandwich hungrily. He had eaten nothing since morning. He had been too excited to eat. He finished the sandwich, and, taking a flask of whisky from his pocket, he took a short draught. Then he returned the flask to his pocket. He paused for a moment, considering whether he should risk a smoke. It was dangerous. The flash might be seen in the darkness, and there were enemies watching. He decided to take the risk.

Placing a cigarette between his lips, he struck a match, inhaled the smoke hurriedly and put out the light. Almost immediately, a bullet flattened itself against the parapet of the roof. The sniper took another whiff and put out the cigarette. Then he swore softly and crawled away to the left.

Cautiously he raised himself and peered over the parapet. There was a flash and a bullet whizzed over his head. He dropped immediately. He had seen the flash. It came from the opposite side of the street.

He rolled over the roof to a chimney stack in the rear, and slowly drew himself up behind it, until his eyes were level with the top of the parapet. There was nothing to be seen—just the dim outline of the opposite housetop against the blue sky. His enemy was under cover.

Just then an armored car came across the bridge and advanced slowly up the street. It stopped on the opposite side of the street, fifty yards ahead. The sniper could hear the dull panting of the motor. His heart beat faster. It was an enemy car. He wanted to fire, but he knew it was useless. His bullets would never pierce the steel that covered the gray monster.

Then round the corner of a side street came an old woman, her head covered by a tattered shawl. She began to talk to the man in the turret of the car. She was pointing to the roof where the sniper lay. An informer.

The turret opened. A man's head and shoulders appeared, looking toward the sniper. The sniper raised his rifle and fired. The head fell heavily on the turret wall. The woman darted toward the side street. The sniper fired again. The woman whirled round and fell with a shriek into the gutter.

Suddenly from the opposite roof a shot rang out and the sniper dropped his rifle with a curse. The rifle clattered to the roof. The sniper thought the noise would wake the dead. He stopped to pick the rifle up. He couldn't lift it. His forearm was dead. "I'm hit," he muttered.

Dropping flat onto the roof, he crawled back to the parapet. With his left hand he felt the injured right forearm. The blood was oozing through the sleeve of his coat. There was no pain—just a deadened sensation, as if the arm had been cut off.

Quickly he drew his knife from his pocket, opened it on the breastwork of the parapet, and ripped open the sleeve. There was a small hole where the bullet had entered. On the other side there was no hole. The bullet had lodged in the bone. It must have fractured it. He bent the arm below the wound. The arm bent back easily. He ground his teeth to overcome the pain.

Then taking out his field dressing, he ripped open the packet with his knife. He broke the neck of the iodine bottle and let the bitter fluid drip into the wound. A paroxysm of pain swept through him. He placed the cotton wadding over the wound and wrapped the dressing over it. He tied the ends with his teeth.

Then he lay still against the parapet, and, closing his eyes, he made an effort of will to overcome the pain.

In the street beneath all was still. The armored car had retired speedily over the bridge, with the machine gunner's head hanging lifeless over the turret. The woman's corpse lay still in the gutter.

The sniper lay still for a long time nursing his wounded arm and planning escape. Morning must not find him wounded on the roof. The enemy on the opposite roof covered his escape. He must kill that enemy and he could not use his rifle. He had only a revolver to do it. Then he thought of a plan.

Taking off his cap, he placed it over the muzzle of his rifle. Then he pushed the rifle slowly upward over the parapet, until the cap was visible from the opposite side of the street. Almost immediately there was a report, and a bullet pierced the center of the cap. The sniper slanted the rifle forward. The cap slipped down into the street. Then catching the rifle in the middle, the sniper dropped his left hand over the roof and let it hang, lifelessly. After a few moments he let the rifle drop to the street. Then he sank to the roof, dragging his hand with him.

Crawling quickly to the left, he peered up at the corner of the roof. His ruse had succeeded. The other sniper, seeing the cap and rifle fall, thought that he had killed his man. He was now standing before a row of chimney pots, looking across, with his head clearly silhouetted against the western sky.

The Republican sniper smiled and lifted his revolver above the edge of the parapet. The distance was about fifty yards—a hard shot in the dim light, and his right arm was paining him like a thousand devils. He took a steady aim. His hand trembled with eagerness. Pressing his lips together, he took a deep breath through his nostrils and fired. He was almost deafened with the report and his arm shook with the recoil.

Then when the smoke cleared he peered across and uttered a cry of joy. His enemy had been hit. He was reeling over the parapet in his death agony. He struggled to keep his feet, but he was slowly falling forward, as if in a dream. The rifle fell from his grasp, hit the parapet, fell over, bounded off the pole of a barber's shop beneath and then clattered on the pavement.

Then the dying man on the roof crumpled up and fell forward. The body turned over and over in space and hit the ground with a dull thud. Then it lay still.

The sniper looked at his enemy falling and he shuddered. The lust of battle died in him. He became bitten by remorse. The sweat stood out in beads on his forehead. Weakened by his wound and the long summer day of fasting and watching on the roof, he revolted from the sight of the shattered mass of his dead enemy. His teeth chattered, he began to gibber to himself, cursing the war, cursing himself, cursing everybody.

He looked at the smoking revolver in his hand, and with an oath he hurled it to the roof at his feet. The revolver went off with the concussion and the bullet whizzed past the sniper's head. He was frightened back to his senses by the shock. His nerves steadied. The cloud of fear scattered from his mind and he laughed.

Taking the whisky flask from his pocket, he emptied it at a draught. He felt reckless under the influence of the spirit. He decided to leave the roof now and look for his company commander, to report. Everywhere around was quiet. There was not much danger in going through the streets. He picked up his revolver and put it in his pocket. Then he crawled down through the skylight to the house underneath.

When the sniper reached the laneway on the street level, he felt a sudden curiosity as to the identity of the enemy sniper whom he had killed. He decided that he was a good shot, whoever he was. He wondered did he know him. Perhaps he had been in his own company before the split in the army. He decided to risk going over to have a look at him. He peered around the corner into O'Connell Street. In the upper part of the street there was heavy firing, but around here all was quiet.

The sniper darted across the street. A machine gun tore up the ground around him with a hail of bullets, but he escaped. He threw himself face downward beside the corpse. The machine gun stopped.

Then the sniper turned over the dead body and looked into his brother's face.

The Man He Killed

THOMAS HARDY

"Had he and I but met
By some old ancient inn,
We should have sat us down to wet
Right many a nipperkin!

"But ranged as infantry,
And staring face to face,
I shot at him as he at me,
And killed him in his place.

"I shot him dead because—
Because he was my foe,
Just so: my foe of course he was;
That's clear enough; although

"He thought he'd 'list, perhaps,
Off-hand-like—just as I—
Was out of work—had sold his traps—
No other reason why.

"Yes; quaint and curious war is!
You shoot a fellow down
You'd treat, if met where any bar is
Or help to half-a-crown."

Bill's Little Girl

BILL WAS thirty when his wife died, and little Minna was four. Bill's carpenter shop was in the yard of his house, so he thought that he could keep up his home for Minna and himself. All day while he worked at his bench, she played in the yard, and when he was obliged to be absent for a few hours, the woman next door looked after her. Bill could cook a little, coffee and bacon and fried potatoes and flapjacks, and he found bananas and sardines and crackers useful. When the woman next door said this was not the diet for four-year-olds, he asked her to teach him to cook oatmeal and vegetables, and though he always burned the dishes in which he cooked these things, he cooked them every day. He swept, all but the corners, and he dusted, dabbed at every object; and he complained that after he had cleaned the windows he could not see out as well as he could before. He washed and patched Minna's little garments and mended her doll. He found a kitten

for her so that she wouldn't be lonely. At night he heard her say her prayer, kneeling in the middle of the floor with her hands folded, and speaking like lightning. If he forgot the prayer, he either woke her up, or else he made her say it the first thing next morning. He himself used to try to pray: "Lord, make me do right by her if you see me doing wrong." On Sundays he took her to church and sat listening with his head on one side, trying to understand, and giving Minna peppermints when she rustled. He stopped work for a day and took her to the Sunday school picnic. "Her mother would of," he explained. When Minna was old enough to go to kindergarten, Bill used to take her morning or afternoon, and he would call for her. Once he dressed himself in his best clothes and went to visit the school. "I think her mother would of," he told the teacher, diffidently. But he could make little of the colored paper and the designs and the games, and he did not go again. "There's some things I can't be any help to her with," he thought.

Minna was six when Bill fell ill. On a May afternoon he went to a doctor. When he came home he sat in his shop for a long time and did nothing. The sun was beaming through the window in bright squares. He was not going to get well. It might be that he had six months. . . . He could hear Minna singing to her doll.

When she came to kiss him that night, he made an excuse, for he must never kiss her now. He held her at arm's length, looked in her eyes, said: "Minna's a big girl now. She doesn't want papa to kiss her." But her lip curled and she turned away sorrowful, so the next day Bill went to another doctor to make sure. The other doctor made him sure.

He tried to think what to do. He had a sister in Nebraska, but she was a tired woman. His wife had a brother in the city, but he was a man of many words. And little Minna . . . there were things known to her which he himself did not know—matters of fairies and the words of songs. He wished that he could hear of somebody who would understand her. And he had only six months. . . .

Then the woman next door told him bluntly that he ought not to have the child there, and him coughing as he was; and he knew that his decision was already upon him.

One whole night he thought. Then he advertised in a city paper:

A man with a few months to live would like nice people to adopt his little girl, six, blue eyes, curls. References required.

They came in a limousine, as he had hoped that they would come. Their clothes were as he had hoped. They had with them a little girl who cried: "Is this my little sister?" On which the woman in the smart frock said sharply:

"Now then, you do as mama tells you and keep out of this or we'll leave you here and take this darling little girl away with us."

So Bill looked at this woman and said steadily that he had now other plans for his little girl. He watched the great blue car roll away. "For the land sake!" said the woman next door when she heard. "You done her out of a fortune. You hadn't the right—a man in your health." And when other cars came, and he let them go, this woman told her husband that Bill ought most certainly to be reported to the authorities.

The man and woman who walked into Bill's shop one morning were still mourning their own little girl. The woman was not sad—only sorrowful, and the man, who was tender of her, was a carpenter. In a blooming of his hope and his dread, Bill said to them: "You're the ones." When they asked: "How long before we can have her?" Bill said: "One day more."

That day he spent in the shop. It was summer and Minna was playing in the yard. He could hear the words of her songs. He cooked their supper and while she ate, he watched. When he had tucked her in her bed, he stood in the dark hearing her breathing. "I'm a little girl tonight—kiss me," she had said, but he shook his head. "A big girl, a big girl," he told her.

When they came for her the next morning, he had her ready and her little garments were ready, washed and mended, and he had mended her doll. "Minna's never been for a visit!" he told her buoyantly. And when she ran toward him, "A big girl, a big girl," he reminded her.

He stood and watched the man and woman walking down the street with Minna between them. They had brought her a little blue parasol in case the parting should be hard. This parasol Minna held bobbing above her head, and she was so absorbed in looking up at the blue silk that she did not remember to turn and wave her hand.

Nancy Hanks

ROSEMARY BENÉT

If Nancy Hanks
Came back as a ghost,
Seeking news
Of what she loved most,
She'd ask first,
"Where's my son?
What's happened to Abe?
What's he done?"

"Poor little Abe
Left all alone
Except for Tom,
Who's a rolling stone;
He was only nine
The year I died.
I remember still
How hard he cried."

"Scraping along
In a little shack
With hardly a shirt
To cover his back,
And a prairie wind
To blow him down,
Or pinching times
If he went to town."

"You wouldn't know
About my son?
Did he grow tall?
Did he have fun?
Did he learn to read?
Did he get to town?
Do you know his name?
Did he get on?"

Romance

WOULD YOU rather sit on this side or would you rather sit on the other side? the redcap said.

Hmm? the young man said.

This side is all right? the redcap said.

Oh, the young man said. Sure.

He gave the redcap a dime. The redcap accepted the small thin coin and folded the young man's coat and placed it on the seat.

Some people like one side, he said, and some like the other.

What? the young man said.

The redcap didn't know if he ought to go into detail, about some people being used to and preferring certain things in the landscape looking out of the train from one side, and others wanting to get both sides of the landscape all the way down and back, preferring one side going down, usually the shady side, but in some cases the opposite, where a lady liked sunlight or had read it was healthy, and the other side coming up, but he imagined it would take too long to explain everything, especially in view of the fact that he wasn't feeling real well and all morning hadn't been able to give that impression of being on excellent terms with everybody which pleased him so much.

I mean, he said, it's no more than what anybody wants, I guess.

The redcap figured the young man was a clerk who was going to have a little Sunday holiday, riding in a train from a big city to a little one, going and coming the same day, but what he didn't understand was why the young man seemed so lost, or, as the saying is, dead to the world. The boy was young, not perhaps a college graduate, more likely a boy who'd gone through high school and gotten a job in an office somewhere, maybe twenty-three years old, and perhaps in love. Anyhow, the redcap thought, the young man looked to be somebody who might at any moment fall in love, without much urging. He had that sad or dreamy look of the potential adorer of something in soft and colorful cloth with long hair and smooth skin.

The young man came to an almost violent awakening which very nearly upset the redcap.

Oh, he said, I've been sort of daydreaming.

He wiggled the fingers of his right hand near his head, or where people imagined one daydreamed.

Have I given you a tip? he said.

The redcap felt embarrassed.

Yes, sir, he said.

The young man wiggled the fingers of his left hand before his face.

I very often forget what I'm doing, he said, until long afterwards— sometimes years. May I ask how much I gave you?

The redcap couldn't figure it out at all. If the young man was being funny or trying to work some sort of racket, it was just too bad because the redcap wasn't born yesterday. The young man had given him a dime and if the young man came out with the argument that he had given the redcap some such ridiculous coin as a five-dollar gold piece the redcap would simply hold his ground and say, this is all you gave me—this dime.

You gave me a dime, he said.

I'm sorry, the young man said; here.

He gave the redcap another dime.

Thank you, sir, the redcap said.

Were you saying something while we were coming down the aisle? the young man said.

Nothing important, the redcap said. I was only saying how some folks liked to sit on one side and others on the other.

Oh, the young man said. Is this side all right?

Yes, it is, the redcap said. Unless of course you prefer not getting the sunshine.

No, the young man said, I kind of like the sunshine.

It's a fine day too, the redcap said.

The young man looked out the window as if at the day. There was nothing but trains to see, but he looked out the window as if he were looking to see how fine a day it was.

The sun don't get in here where it's covered up, the redcap said, but no sooner than you get out of here into the open you'll be running into a lot of sunshine. Most California folks get tired of it and get over on the other side. You from New York?

There was nothing about the young man to suggest that he was from New York or for that matter from anywhere else either, but the redcap wondered where the young man was from, so he asked.

No, the young man said, I've never been out of California.

The redcap was in no hurry, although there was considerable activity everywhere, people piling into the car, other redcaps rushing about, helping with bags, and hurrying away. Nevertheless, he lingered and carried on a conversation. There was a girl across the aisle who was listening to the conversation and the redcap fancied he and the young man were cutting quite a figure with her, one way or another. It was charming conversation, in the best of spirits, and, although between men in different stations of life, full of that fraternal feeling which is characteristic of westerners and Americans.

I've never been out of California myself, the redcap said.

You'd think you'd be the sort of man to travel a good deal, the young man said.

Yes, you would at that, the redcap said. Working on trains, or leastways near them, on and off most of my life since I was eighteen, which was thirty years ago, but it's true, I haven't set foot outside the boundary lines of this state. I've met a lot of travelers though, he added.

I wouldn't mind getting to New York some day, the young man said.

I don't blame a young man like you for wanting to get to New York, the redcap said. New York sure must be an interesting place down around in there.

Biggest city in the world, the young man said.

It sure is, the redcap said, and then he made as if to go, dragging himself away as it were, going away with tremendous regret.

Well, he said, have a pleasant journey.

Thanks. the young man said.

The redcap left the car. The young man looked out the window and then turned just in time to notice that the girl across the aisle was looking at him and was swiftly turning her head away, and he himself, so as not to embarrass her, swiftly continued turning his head so that something almost happened to his neck. Almost instantly he brought his head all the way back to where it had been, near the window, looking out, and felt an awful eagerness to look at the girl again and at the same time a wonderful sense of at last beginning to go places, in more ways than one, such as meeting people like her and marrying one of them and settling down in a house somewhere.

He didn't look at the girl again, though, for some time but kept wanting to very eagerly, so that finally when he did look at her he was embarrassed and blushed and gulped and tried very hard to smile but just couldn't quite make it. The girl just couldn't make it either.

That happened after they'd been moving along for more than ten minutes, the train rolling out among the hills and rattling pleasantly and making everything everywhere seem pleasant and full of wonderful potentialities, such as romance and a good deal of good humor and easygoing naturalness, especially insofar as meeting her and being friendly and pleasant and little by little getting to know her and falling in love.

They saw one another again after about seven minutes more, and then again after four minutes, and then they saw one another more steadily by pretending to be looking at the landscape on the other side, and finally they just kept seeing one another steadily for a long time, watching the landscape.

At last the young man said, are you from New York?

He didn't know what he was saying. He felt foolish and unlike young men in movies who do such things on trains.

Yes, I am, the girl said.

What? the young man said.

Didn't you ask if I was from New York? the girl said.

Oh, the young man said. Yes, I did.

Well, the girl said, I am.

I didn't know you were from New York, the young man said.

I know you didn't, the girl said.

The young man tried very hard to smile the way they smiled in pictures.

How did you know? he said.

Oh, I don't know, the girl said. Are you going to Sacramento?

Yes, I am, the young man said. Are you?

Yes, I am, the girl said.

What are you doing so far from home? the young man said.

New York isn't my home, the girl said. I was born there, but I've been living in San Francisco most of my life.

So have I most of mine, the young man said. In fact all of it.

I've lived in San Francisco practically all of my life too, the girl said, with the possible exception of them few months in New York.

Is that all the time you lived in New York? the young man said.

Yes, the girl said, only them first five months right after I was born in New York.

I was born in San Francisco, the young man said. There's lots of room on these two seats, he said with great effort. Wouldn't you like to sit over here and get the sun?

All right, the girl said.

She stepped across the aisle and sat across from the young man.

I just thought I'd go down to Sacramento on the special Sunday rate, the young man said.

I've been to Sacramento three times, the girl said.

The young man began to feel very happy. The sun was strong and warm and the girl was wonderful. Unless he was badly mistaken, or unless he got fired Monday morning, or unless America got into a war and he had to become a soldier and go away and get himself killed, he had a hunch some day he would go to work and get acquainted with the girl and marry her and settle down.

He sat back in the sunlight while the train rattled along and smiled romantically at the girl, getting ready for the romance.

Recuerdo

EDNA ST. VINCENT MILLAY

We were very tired, we were very merry—
We had gone back and forth all night on the ferry.
It was bare and bright, and smelled like a stable—
But we looked into a fire, we leaned across a table,
We lay on a hill-top underneath the moon;
And the whistles kept blowing, and the dawn came soon.

We were very tired, we were very merry—
We had gone back and forth all night on the ferry;
And you ate an apple, and I ate a pear,
From a dozen of each we had bought somewhere;
And the sky went wan, and the wind came cold,
And the sun rose dripping, a bucketful of gold.

We were very tired, we were very merry—
We had gone back and forth all night on the ferry.
We hailed, "Good morrow, mother!" to a shawl-covered head,
And bought a morning paper, which neither of us read;
And she wept, "God bless you!" for the apples and the pears,
And we gave her all our money but our subway fares.

The Blanket

PETEY HADN'T really believed that Dad would be doing it—sending Granddad away. "Away" was what they were calling it. Not until now could he believe it of Dad.

But here was the blanket that Dad had that day bought for him, and in the morning he'd be going away. And this was the last evening they'd be having together. Dad was off seeing that girl he was to marry. He'd not be back till late, and they could sit up and talk.

It was a fine September night, with a silver moon riding high over the gully. When they'd washed up the supper dishes they went out on the shanty porch, the old man and the bit of a boy, taking their chairs. "I'll get me fiddle," said the old man, "and play ye some of the old tunes." But instead of the fiddle he brought out the blanket. It was a big, double blanket, red, with black cross stripes.

"Now, isn't that a fine blanket!" said the old man, smoothing it over his knees. "And isn't your fa-

ther a kind man to be giving the old fellow a blanket like that to go away with? It cost something, it did—look at the wool of it! And warm it will be these cold winter nights to come. There'll be few blankets there the equal of this one!"

It was like Granddad to be saying that. He was trying to make it easier. He'd pretended all along it was he that was wanting to go away to the great brick building—the government place, where he'd be with so many other old fellows having the best of everything. . . . But Petey hadn't believed Dad would really do it, until this night when he brought home the blanket.

"Oh, yes, it's a fine blanket," said Petey, and got up and went into the shanty. He wasn't the kind to cry, and, besides, he was too old for that, being eleven. He'd just come in to fetch Granddad's fiddle.

The blanket slid to the floor as the old man took the fiddle and stood up. It was the last night they'd be having together. There wasn't any need to say, "Play all the old tunes." Granddad tuned up for a minute, and then said, "This is one you'll like to remember."

The silver moon was high overhead, and there was a gentle breeze playing down the gully. He'd never be hearing Granddad play like this again. It was as well Dad was moving into that new house, away from here. He'd not want, Petey wouldn't, to sit here on the old porch of fine evenings, with Granddad gone.

The tune changed. "Here's something gayer." Petey sat and stared out over the gully. Dad would marry that girl. Yes, that girl who'd kissed him and slobbered over him, saying she'd try to be a good mother to him, and all. . . . His chair creaked as he involuntarily gave his body a painful twist.

The tune stopped suddenly, and Granddad said: "It's a poor tune, except to be dancing to." And then: "It's a fine girl your father's going to marry. He'll be feeling young again, with a pretty wife like that. And what would an old fellow like me be doing around their house, getting in the way, an old nuisance, what with my talk of aches and pains! And then there'll be babies coming, and I'd not want to be there to hear them crying at all hours. It's best that I take myself off, like I'm doing. One more tune or two, and then we'll be going to bed to get some sleep against the morning, when I'll pack up my fine

blanket and take my leave. Listen to this, will you? It's a bit sad, but a fine tune for a night like this."

They didn't hear the two people coming down the gully path, Dad and the pretty girl with the hard, bright face like a china doll's. But they heard her laugh, right by the porch, and the tune stopped on a wrong, high, startled note. Dad didn't say anything, but the girl came forward and spoke to Granddad prettily: "I'll not be seeing you leave in the morning, so I came over to say good-by."

"It's kind of you," said Granddad, with his eyes cast down; and then, seeing the blanket at his feet, he stooped to pick it up. "And will you look at this," he said in embarrassment, "the fine blanket my son has given me to go away with!"

"Yes," she said, "it's a fine blanket." She felt of the wool, and repeated in surprise, "A fine blanket—I'll say it is!" She turned to Dad, and said to him coldly, "It cost something, that."

He cleared his throat, and said defensively, "I wanted him to have the best. . . ."

The girl stood there, still intent on the blanket. "It's double, too," she said reproachfully to Dad.

"Yes," said Granddad, "it's double—a fine blanket for an old fellow to be going away with."

The boy went abruptly into the shanty. He was looking for something. He could hear that girl reproaching Dad, and Dad becoming angry in his slow way. And now she was suddenly going away in a huff. . . . As Petey came out, she turned and called back, "All the same, he doesn't need a double blanket!" And she ran up the gully path.

Dad was looking after her uncertainly.

"Oh, she's right," said the boy coldly. "Here, Dad"—and he held out a pair of scissors. "Cut the blanket in two."

Both of them stared at the boy, startled. "Cut it in two, I tell you, Dad!" he cried out. "And keep the other half!"

"That's not a bad idea," said Granddad gently. "I don't need so much of a blanket."

"Yes," said the boy harshly, "a single blanket's enough for an old man when he's sent away. We'll save the other half, Dad; it will come in handy later."

"Now, what do you mean by that?" asked Dad.

"I mean," said the boy slowly, "that I'll give it to you, Dad—when you're old and I'm sending you—away."

There was a silence, and then Dad went over to Granddad and stood before him, not speaking. But Granddad understood, for he put out a hand and laid it on Dad's shoulder. Petey was watching them. And he heard Granddad whisper, "It's all right, son—I knew you didn't mean it. . . ." And then Petey cried.

But it didn't matter—because they were all three crying together.

The Song of the Old Mother

WILLIAM BUTLER YEATS

I rise in the dawn, and I kneel and blow
Till the seed of the fire flicker and glow.
And then I must scrub, and bake, and sweep,
Till the stars are beginning to blink and peep;
But the young lie long and dream in their bed
Of the matching of ribbons, the blue and the red,
And their day goes over in idleness,
And they sigh if the wind but lift a tress.
While I must work, because I am old
And the seed of the fire gets feeble and cold.

Snake Dance

"HELLO. That you, Mom? . . . Oh, I'm sorry, operator, I thought I was connected with . . . No, I'm trying to get long-distance . . . What? Centerville, Ohio, twelve ring five, I told that other operator . . . What? . . . I *am* holding it."

He fished nervously in his pocket for a pack of cigarettes, pulled one cigarette out of the pack with his thumb and forefinger, and stuck it swiftly between his lips. He glanced at his watch and scowled. The game had been over for a half hour. The snake dance would be coming down the street this way any minute now. With his free hand he tore a match from the paper safe, and propped the telephone receiver for a moment between shoulder and ear while he struck the match on the flap. As he put the match to the tip of the cigarette, a thin voice rasped vaguely inside the receiver, and he whipped out the match.

"Hello. Mom? . . . Oh, I'm sorry," he mumbled. "How much?" He took a handful of silver from his pocket and began to drop the coins into the slot of the pay telephone. He could hear someone speaking above the echoing reverberations inside the phone.

"What? Oh, Mom? Hello, Mom. This is Jerry. I say, this is—Can you hear me now? . . . Sure, I can hear you fine . . . Sure, I'm all right. I'm fine. And you? . . . That's fine.

"Mom"—and his voice seemed to falter for a fraction of a second. Then: "How is he? Is there any change?"

There was a tiny silence.

"Oh." His voice was a little duller when he spoke again. "I see. Yeh. This afternoon, eh? And that other specialist, he said the same thing? Um-hmm . . . Oh, sure, sure. No, of course, Mom, there's nothing to worry about. No, I'm not worried; I only just called to find out if there was any change, that was all. . . . Did they say if he could ever—I mean, can he move his arms any yet?" He gulped. "Well, that doesn't mean anything, really . . . No, of course, all those things take time. Sure, a year, or maybe even less . . . What?"

He took a second cigarette out of his pocket and thrust it between his lips nervously. He lit it from the stub of the first one and ground out the stub beneath his heel.

"What money? Oh, you mean I sent you last week? Now, Mom," impatiently, "I told you all about that already in the letter, didn't I? . . . Sure it's a scholarship. I got it for playing football. And so naturally I didn't need all that money you and Pop had been saving up for me to go to college, and so I just thought maybe, with Pop being laid up now for a while and all . . .

"Where? Why, right here." He frowned. "No, this isn't exactly a dormitory; it's—I live here in the fraternity house, you see. Sure I'm in a fraternity. It's the one Pop wanted me to join, too, tell him . . . No, honest, Mom, it doesn't cost me a cent for my room. It's on account of my football."

He opened the folding door a little. He thought he could hear the band in the distance.

"Who, me? Homesick? Not so you'd notice it." He laughed. "I'm having the time of my life here. Everybody's so swell. I know practically everybody here at Dover already. They even all call me by my first name. Say, if you don't think I'm sitting pretty, you ought to see my fraternity house here." He gazed out through the glass door of the phone booth.

"Every night the fellows sit around and we drink beer and chew the fat till . . . Oh, no. No, Mom. Just beer. Or usually we just go down to Semple's for a milk shake . . . No, that's only the drugstore . . . No." He smiled slowly. "I promised you I wouldn't drink, Mom."

In the distance now he could hear the sound of the band approaching.

"Well, Mom, I gotta hang up now. The gang'll be here in a minute. We're having a celebration after the game today. We played Alvord—took 'em sixteen to nothing. . . . Sure I did, the whole game; you oughta seen me in there. I made two touchdowns. Everybody's going down to Semple's after the game, and I gotta be ready, because of course they'll all want me to be there too. Can you hear the band now?"

It was growing louder, and the eager voices in the snake dance could be heard above the brasses, chanting the score of the game in time with the band.

"Now, listen, Mom. One other little thing before they get here. Mom, see, I'm going to be sending you about ten or twelve dollars or so each week from now on until Pop is better. . . . No, Mom. Heck, I got plenty. Sure, they always fix you up with a soft job if you're a good enough player. The alumni do it. . . . Here they are now. Hear them?"

The band had halted outside.

Someone led a cheer.

"That's for me, Mom. . . . Sure. Didn't I practically win the game for them today? Hear that?" He kicked open the door of the phone booth.

He held the receiver toward the open door of the phone booth. They were calling, "Jerry!" "Hey, Jerry, hang up on that babe!"

"Hear that, Mom? Now goodby. And look, by the way, if you should ever happen to see Helen," he added carelessly, "tell her I'm sorry I couldn't ask her up to the freshman dance like I'd planned, but with the football season and my scholarship and all—Tell her, Mom. She—she didn't answer my last letter. O.K., Mom. Tell Pop everything's O.K., see? Now don't worry . . . 'By."

He replaced the receiver slowly on the hook and stared at the mouthpiece a moment. As he opened the door and stepped out of the booth, he could see his reflection for a moment in the tall mirror behind the soda fountain—the familiar white cap, the white jacket with "Semple's" stitched in red letters on the pocket. The crowd was lined along the soda fountain, shouting, "Jerry!" "Milk shake, Jerry!"

Thus I Refute Beelzy

"THERE GOES the tea bell," said Mrs. Carter. "I hope Simon hears it."

They looked out from the window of the drawing room. The long garden, agreeably neglected, ended in a waste plot. Here a little summer-house was passing close by beauty on its way to complete decay. This was Simon's retreat. It was almost completely screened by the tangled branches of the apple tree and the pear tree, planted too close together, as they always are in the suburbs. They caught a glimpse of him now and then, as he strutted up and down, mouthing and gesticulating, performing all the solemn mumbo-jumbo of small boys who spend long afternoons at the forgotten ends of long gardens.

"There he is, bless him!" said Betty.

"Playing his game," said Mrs. Carter. "He won't play with the other children any more. And if I go down there—the temper! And comes in tired out!"

"He doesn't have his sleep in the afternoons?" asked Betty.

"You know what Big Simon's ideas are," said Mrs. Carter. " 'Let him choose for himself,' he says. That's what he chooses, and he comes in as white as a sheet."

"Look! He's heard the bell," said Betty. The expression was justified, though the bell had ceased ringing a full minute ago. Small Simon stopped in his parade exactly as if its tinny dingle had at that moment reached his ear. They watched him perform certain ritual sweeps and scratchings with his little stick, and come lagging over the hot and flaggy grass toward the house.

Mrs. Carter led the way down to the playroom, or garden room, which was also the tea room for hot days. It had been the huge scullery of this tall Georgian house. Now the walls were cream-washed, there was coarse blue net in the windows, canvas-covered armchairs on the stone floor, and a reproduction of Van Gogh's "Sunflowers" over the mantelpiece.

Small Simon came drifting in, and accorded Betty a perfunctory greeting. His face was an almost perfect triangle, pointed at the chin, and he was paler than he should have been. "The little elf-child!" cried Betty.

Simon looked at her. "No," said he.

At that moment the door opened, and Mr. Carter came in, rubbing his hands. He was a dentist, and washed them before and after everything he did. "You!" said his wife. "Home already!"

"Not unwelcome, I hope," said Mr. Carter, nodding to Betty. "Two people canceled their appointments; I decided to come home. I said, I hope I am not unwelcome."

"Silly!" said his wife. "Of course not."

"Small Simon seems doubtful," continued Mr. Carter. "Small Simon, are you sorry to see me at tea with you?"

"No, Daddy."

"No, what?"

"No, Big Simon."

"That's right. Big Simon and Small Simon. That sounds more like friends, doesn't it? At one time little boys had to call their father 'sir.' If they forgot—a good spanking. On the bottom, Small Simon! On the bottom!" said Mr. Carter, washing his hands once more with his invisible soap and water.

The little boy turned crimson with shame or rage.

"But now, you see," said Betty, to help, "you can call your father whatever you like."

"And what," asked Mr. Carter, "has Small Simon been doing this afternoon? While Big Simon has been at work."

"Nothing," muttered his son.

"Then you have been bored," said Mr. Carter. "Learn from experience, Small Simon. Tomorrow, do something amusing, and you will not be bored. I want him to learn from experience, Betty. That is my way, the new way."

"I have learned," said the boy, speaking like an old, tired man, as little boys so often do.

"It would hardly seem so," said Mr. Carter, "if you sit on your behind all the afternoon, doing nothing. Had *my* father caught me doing nothing, I should not have sat very comfortably."

"He played," said Mrs. Carter.

"A bit," said the boy, shifting on his chair.

"Too much," said Mrs. Carter. "He comes in all nervy and dazed. He ought to have his rest."

"He is six," said her husband. "He is a reasonable being. He must choose for himself. But what game is this, Small Simon, that is worth getting nervy and dazed over? There are very few games as good as all that."

"It's nothing," said the boy.

"Oh, come," said his father. "We are friends, are we not? You can tell me. I was a Small Simon once, just like you, and played the same games you play. Of course there were no airplanes in those days. With whom do you play this fine game? Come on, we must all answer civil questions, or the world would never go round. With whom do you play?"

"Mr. Beelzy," said the boy, unable to resist.

"Mr. Beelzy?" said his father raising his eyebrows inquiringly at his wife.

"It's a game he makes up," said she.

"Not makes up!" cried the boy. "Fool!"

"That is telling stories," said his mother. "And rude as well. We had better talk of something different."

"No wonder he is rude," said Mr. Carter, "if you say he tells lies, and then insist on changing the subject. He tells you his fantasy: you implant a guilt feeling. What can you expect? A defense mechanism. Then you get a real lie."

"Like in *These Three*," said Betty. "Only different, of course. *She* was an unblushing little liar."

"I would have made her blush," said Mr. Carter, "in the proper part of her anatomy. But Small Simon is in the fantasy stage. Are you not, Small Simon? You just make things up."

"No, I don't," said the boy.

"You do," said his father. "And because you do, it is not too late to reason with you. There is no harm in a fantasy, old chap. There is no harm in a bit of make-believe. Only you have to know the difference between daydreams and real things,

or your brain will never grow. It will never be the brain of a Big Simon. So come on. Let us hear about this Mr. Beelzy of yours. Come on. What is he like?"

"He isn't like anything," said the boy.

"Like nothing on earth?" said his father. "That's a terrible fellow."

"I'm not frightened of him," said the child, smiling. "Not a bit."

"I should hope not," said his father. "If you were, you would be frightening yourself. I am always telling people, older people than you are, that they are just frightening themselves. Is he a funny man? Is he a giant?"

"Sometimes he is," said the little boy.

"Sometimes one thing, sometimes another," said his father. "Sounds pretty vague. Why can't you tell us just what he's like?"

"I love him," said the small boy. "He loves me."

"That's a big word," said Mr. Carter. "That might be better kept for real things, like Big Simon and Small Simon."

"He is real," said the boy, passionately. "He's not a fool. He's real."

"Listen," said his father. "When you go down the garden there's nobody there. Is there?"

"No," said the boy.

"Then you think of him, inside your head, and he comes."

"No," said Small Simon. "I have to make marks. On the ground. With my stick."

"That doesn't matter."

"Yes, it does."

"Small Simon, you are being obstinate," said Mr. Carter. "I am trying to explain something to you. I have been longer in the world than you have, so naturally I am older and wiser. I am explaining that Mr. Beelzy is a fantasy of yours. Do you hear? Do you understand?"

"Yes, Daddy."

"He is a game. He is a let's-pretend."

The little boy looked down at his plate, smiling resignedly.

"I hope you are listening to me," said his father. "All you have to do is to say, 'I have been playing a game of let's-pretend. With someone I make up, called Mr. Beelzy.' Then no one will say you tell lies, and you will know the difference between dreams and reality. Mr. Beelzy is a daydream."

The little boy still stared at his plate.

"He is sometimes there and sometimes not there," pursued Mr. Carter. "Sometimes he's like one thing, sometimes another. You can't really see him. Not as you see me. I am real. You can't touch him. You can touch me. I can touch you." Mr. Carter stretched out his big, white, dentist's hand, and took his little son by the nape of the neck. He stopped speaking for a moment and tightened his hand. The little boy sank his head still lower.

"Now you know the difference," said Mr. Carter, "between a pretend and a real thing. You and I are one

thing; he is another. Which is the pretend? Come on. Answer me. What is the pretend?"

"Big Simon and Small Simon," said the little boy.

"Don't!" cried Betty, and at once put her hand over her mouth, for why should a visitor cry "Don't!" when a father is explaining things in a scientific and modern way? Besides, it annoys the father.

"Well, my boy," said Mr. Carter, "I have said you must be allowed to learn from experience. Go upstairs. Right up to your room. You shall learn whether it is better to reason, or to be perverse and obstinate. Go up. I shall follow you."

"You are not going to beat the child?" cried Mrs. Carter.

"No," said the little boy. "Mr. Beelzy won't let him."

"Go on up with you!" shouted his father.

Small Simon stopped at the door. "He said he wouldn't let anyone hurt me," he whimpered. "He said he'd come like a lion, with wings on, and eat them up."

"You'll learn how real he is!" shouted his father after him. "If you can't learn it at one end, you shall learn it at the other. I'll have your breeches down. I shall finish my cup of tea first, however," said he to the two women.

Neither of them spoke. Mr. Carter finished his tea, and unhurriedly left the room, washing his hands with his invisible soap and water.

Mrs. Carter said nothing. Betty could think of nothing to say. She wanted to be talking for she was afraid of what they might hear.

Suddenly it came. It seemed to tear the air apart. "Good God!" she cried. "What was that? He's hurt him." She sprang out of her chair, her silly eyes flashing behind her glasses. "I'm going up there!" she cried, trembling.

"Yes, let us go up," said Mrs. Carter. "Let us go up. That was not Small Simon."

It was on the second-floor landing that they found the shoe, with the man's foot still in it, like that last morsel of a mouse which sometimes falls unnoticed from the side of the jaws of the cat.

The Father

THE MAN whose story is here to be told was the wealthiest and most influential person in his parish; his name was Thord Overaas. He appeared in the priest's study one day, tall and earnest.

"I have gotten a son," said he, "and I wish to present him for baptism."

"What shall his name be?"

"Finn—after my father."

"And the sponsors?"

They were mentioned, and proved to be the best men and women of Thord's relations in the parish.

"Is there anything else?" inquired the priest, and looked up.

The peasant hesitated a little.

"I should like very much to have him baptized by himself," said he, finally.

"That is to say on a weekday?"

"Next Saturday, at twelve o'clock, noon."

"Is there anything else?" inquired the priest.

"There is nothing else;" and the peasant twirled his cap, as though he were about to go.

Then the priest rose. "There is yet this, however," said he, and walking toward Thord, he took him by the hand and looked gravely into his eyes: "God grant that the child may become a blessing to you!"

One day sixteen years later, Thord stood once more in the priest's study.

"Really, you carry your age astonishingly well, Thord," said the priest; for he saw no change whatever in the man.

"That is because I have no troubles," replied Thord.

To this the priest said nothing, but after a while he asked: "What is your pleasure this evening?"

"I have come this evening about that son of mine who is to be confirmed tomorrow."

"He is a bright boy."

"I did not wish to pay the priest

27

until I heard what number the boy would have when he takes his place in church tomorrow."

"He will stand number one."

"So I have heard; and here are ten dollars for the priest."

"Is there anything else I can do for you?" inquired the priest, fixing his eyes on Thord.

"There is nothing else."

Thord went out.

Eight years more rolled by, and then one day a noise was heard outside of the priest's study, for many men were approaching, and at their head was Thord, who entered first.

The priest looked up and recognized him.

"You come well attended this evening, Thord," said he.

"I am here to request that the bans may be published for my son; he is about to marry Karen Storliden, daughter of Gudmund, who stands here beside me."

"Why, that is the richest girl in the parish."

"So they say," replied the peasant, stroking back his hair with one hand.

The priest sat a while as if in deep thought, then entered the names in his book, without making any comments, and the men wrote their signatures underneath. Thord laid three dollars on the table.

"One is all I am to have," said the priest.

"I know that very well; but he is my only child, I want to do it handsomely."

The priest took the money.

"This is now the third time, Thord, that you have come here on your son's account."

"But now I am through with him," said Thord, and folding up his pocketbook, he said farewell and walked away.

The men slowly followed him.

A fortnight later, the father and son were rowing across the lake, one calm, still day, to Storliden to make arrangements for the wedding.

"This thwart is not secure," said the son, and stood up to straighten the seat on which he was sitting.

At the same moment the board he was standing on slipped from under him; he threw out his arms, uttered a shriek, and fell overboard.

"Take hold of the oar!" shouted the father, springing to his feet and holding out the oar.

But when the son had made a couple of efforts he grew stiff.

"Wait a moment!" cried the father, and began to row toward his son. Then the son rolled over on his back, gave his father one long look, and sank.

Thord could scarcely believe it; he held the boat still, and stared at the spot where his son had gone down, as though he must surely come to the surface again. There rose some bubbles, then some more, and finally one large one that burst; and the lake lay there as smooth and bright as a mirror again.

For three days and three nights people saw the father rowing round and round the spot, without taking either food or sleep; he was dragging the lake for the body of his son. And toward morning of the third day he found it, and carried it in his arms up over the hills to his farm.

It might have been about a year from that day, when the priest, late one autumn evening, heard someone in the passage outside of the door, carefully trying to find the latch. The priest opened the door, and in walked a tall, thin man, with bowed form and white hair. The priest looked long at him before he recognized him. It was Thord.

"Are you out walking so late?" said the priest, and stood still in front of him.

"Ah, yes! It is late," said Thord, and took a seat.

The priest sat down also, as though waiting. A long, long silence followed. At last Thord said:

"I have something with me that I should like to give to the poor; I want it to be invested as a legacy in my son's name."

He rose, laid some money on the table, and sat down again. The priest counted it.

"It is a great deal of money," said he.

"It is half the price of my farm. I sold it today."

The priest sat in silence. At last he asked, but gently:

"What do you propose to do now, Thord?"

"Something better."

They sat for a while, Thord with downcast eyes, the priest with his eyes fixed on Thord. Presently the priest said, slowly and softly:

"I think your son has at last brought you a true blessing."

"Yes, I think so myself," said Thord, looking up, while two big tears coursed slowly down his cheeks.

---

*And the king was deeply moved, and went up
to the chamber over the gate, and wept: and as he
went, thus he said, "O my son Absalom,
my son, my son Absalom! Would God I had died
for thee, O Absalom, my son, my son!"*

II SAMUEL, XVIII, 33

ROBERT BINGHAM

The Unpopular Passenger

SNOW WAS falling out of the dark into the tiny cones of light under street lamps down below as the plane circled to land at Cleveland. When the hostess saw that I was awake and that my safety belt was already fastened, she smiled efficiently and moved on down the aisle, waking the other passengers and asking them to fasten their safety belts. I did not make the effort to return her smile but turned again to look down on the miniature suburbs below.

The young soldier sitting next to me stretched awake and looked out the window too. "Must be a late party at that house," he said, through a yawn. He pointed to where the lights were on in one half of a brick two-family house on a street of unlighted but otherwise identical brick two-family houses. Or somebody dying, was my first thought.

Being awake at three or four in the morning, sober and bored, waiting only for a certain time to elapse

or a certain distance to be traveled, reminded me inevitably of my own days and nights as a soldier, of an emptiness in which at last even the too familiar prospect of death loses its power to provoke emotion.

After hovering uncertainly in the air, the plane settled clumsily on the ground, stumbled to a stop, and then waddled into the brightly lighted area round the terminal building, wheezing and gasping. "One hour and forty-five minutes late," declared a resonant bass voice several seats behind me. "I told them we'd be there at a decent hour, but at this rate we won't be there before dawn." Several other passengers glanced at their wrist watches.

Those of us who were getting off at Cleveland stood in the aisle, and while I waited behind a woman with yellowish-white hair who was pointing at things she wanted her husband to pass down from the luggage rack, I was pushed abruptly against my seat by a short, fat man wearing a broad-brimmed blue hat that fitted down very far on his head. He also pushed the woman in front of me, and with an exaggerated cry of alarm she let herself fall back into the seat from which she had just arisen. A thin fox scarf had fallen onto the floor and lay there staring up at its mistress with eyes of orange bead. The woman snatched the animal to her and shook it violently. "Really!" she said indignantly, glaring back down the aisle at her assailant, who by this time had forced his way through the other passengers to be the first one out of the plane when the door was opened. Then she glared at her husband, a small man with steel-rimmed glasses, who averted his eyes and reached for a patent-leather hatbox. "Really!" the woman said again, this time loud enough for everyone in the plane to hear. "Some people just have no consideration."

When I left the plane I found the man in the big hat blocking my way at the bottom of the portable stairway. He was breathing heavily. "Hey, there, Miss Hostess!" he shouted past me up at the door of the plane. "I got to make a phone call." He coughed and turned his head to spit. "So where's the phone?" His face was made up of four round and very nearly equal bulbs of flesh—a forehead, two cheeks, and a nose. Under this last bulb a large lower lip hung down, wet and open.

The hostess suggested that if he would follow the other passengers to the terminal building he would find public telephones in the lobby. After glancing suspiciously through the screen of soft, dry snow in the direction she had pointed, he wheeled himself around and trotted awkwardly away on his short legs.

"And not one word of thanks, you'll notice," said the woman with the yellowish-white hair, clutching the bright-eyed fox firmly about her throat.

Even though the short, fat man had run all the way, I got to the terminal building almost as soon as he did. "Hey, there, Johnny!" he shouted to a uniformed pilot. "I got to make a phone call." He snapped his plump fingers impatiently. Looking down on the man in the big hat, the pilot permitted his mustache to twitch several times before he jerked his thumb contemptuously over his shoulder and paraded away.

Just outside the only booth that was free, two men had set down their briefcases and were going through their pockets for change, but the man in the big hat dived right between them toward the booth. "Just a minute there, my friend," said one of the men, taking hold of the intruder's elbow. It was the same resonant bass voice I had heard on the plane.

"I got to make a phone call," said the man in the big hat, weaving himself free of the taller man's grip and working his way into the booth.

"Oh, you got to make a phone call, have you?" the man with the deep voice mimicked. "Well, listen, my friend, I got to make a phone call too, and I was here first."

The man in the big hat drew in his breath and seemed about to speak, but instead he broke the grip on his elbow with a sudden snap and slammed the collapsible door of the booth shut behind him.

His mouth held open as if in speechless amazement, the man with the deep voice turned to his companion for confirmation of what he had just seen.

"How come you let him get away with that?" said the other man, stuttering slightly. The man with the deep voice stared angrily into the booth but said nothing. The voice from the booth, alternatingly threatening and pleading, was loud but indistinct. He might have been speaking in a foreign language.

The snack bar and the magazine stand were boarded over for the night, and so I stood outside near the limousine that would take me to downtown Cleveland and waited for the baggage to be brought around. The night was cold: I felt the walls of my nostrils sticking together, and the snow groaned and complained under my feet. Both the lights and the sounds of the airport were dimmed by the thickly falling snow.

Out of the dark a crowd loomed up upon me. There were five passengers, a man in a leather jacket whom I took to be the driver of the limousine, and two porters pulling a baggage cart. The passengers were all talking to the whole crowd at the same time, as if they were old friends or relatives who had just met after a long separation instead of strangers who had arrived in a large city by chance on the same plane.

One of the passengers—it was the man with a slight stutter—said, "I still don't see why you let him get away with it." He held the right front door of the limousine so that his companion would have to sit in the middle.

"He knocked me down, I tell you," said the woman with the fox scarf. "What do you mean, why did *I* let him get away with it?" said the man with the deep voice. "You were standing right there. Why didn't you do something?"

"Well, for one thing," said the other man sarcastically, "it was you that wanted to use the phone, not me."

"Oh, what's the use?" said the man with the deep voice, accepting the inside seat. "It never does any good with people like that. They never change."

"You're absolutely right," said the woman with the fox scarf, employing elaborate gestures to arrange herself in the middle of the back seat. Her husband got in next to her, and I, not noticing the folded jump seats, sat down on the other side of her. The soldier took the jump seat in front of her husband,

and the other two men were in the front.

"I wonder what he was in such a hurry to get to that phone for," said the soldier. He spoke in a flat nasal drawl.

"Business," said the man with the deep voice. "With those people it's always business." He held up a gloved hand and rubbed his thumb and forefinger together.

"And then you never can tell," said the soldier. "He might have had something on his mind."

"And did you notice the way he treated that sweet little hostess?" the woman interrupted. "Did you notice, dear?" Her husband cleared his throat. "With those people it's always self, self, self," she went on. "They have no human consideration for anyone whatsoever."

"Oh, I knew one or two of them that was all right," said the soldier. The man with the deep voice hummed skeptically.

After watching the porters stow our luggage in the trunk, the driver had gone back to the terminal building, and for a while we awaited his return in silence. We felt rather than heard the heavy rhythm of the limousine's motor. Both men in the front seat were smoking cigars, and the soldier and the woman lighted cigarettes. The stale air nauseated me, and at last I lowered my window about five or six inches. The woman, who had been smoking rapidly and nervously, stiffened beside me. "The snow seems to be coming in the windows," she pro-

nounced mincingly. She sucked in a mouthful of smoke and expelled it immediately with a small explosion. Both men in the front seat turned around and watched me as I cranked up the window. Since leaving the plane, the woman had drawn an incongruously wide line across her mouth with lipstick. In the pale green light that came to us, filtered through snow from the terminal building, her mouth looked purple. "Really!" she muttered.

The man with the deep voice kept turning around to stare back at the terminal building, and we waited in silence once more. Tired as I was, I did not even look forward to sleeping. For me the tedium was almost entirely devoid of interest, appetite, or emotion. It was meaningless time, empty time, and the only thing I felt at all was a weak hatred for the other passengers.

"I wonder what keeps us waiting so long," said the soldier.

"Can't somebody do something?" the woman demanded resentfully.

The man with the deep voice stubbed his cigar out in the ash tray and devoted himself for several minutes to staring back at the terminal building before he gave it up and lighted another cigar. "I should never have let him get away with it," he said softly. The motor was running all the time.

Finally there were voices, and we all looked to see who was coming. The driver was walking rapidly toward the limousine carrying a small aluminum suitcase, and trotting along beside him, looking up into his face earnestly, came the short, fat man in the big hat.

"So that's who kept us waiting so long," said the woman, settling back triumphantly. "So that's who it is," said the soldier. The man with the slight stutter grunted. "No human consideration for anyone else whatsoever," the woman reminded us.

After the trunk had been slammed shut behind us, the driver opened the door beside me, pulled up the second jump seat, and stood back to let the last passenger get in. But before the short, fat man got in, he examined the driver's face carefully. "And I could get a cab right away?" he said.

"Yes, yes, you could get a cab right away," said the driver, his tone suggesting that he had already answered the same question many times.

The man who had delayed our departure peered into the dark limousine suspiciously before tak-

ing his place on the jump seat in front of me. Only the stutterer met the newcomer's eyes, and then he looked expectantly at his companion. But the man with the deep voice was staring straight through the windshield in front of him. Nobody said a word.

The driver got in and we started on our way, with one loose chain clanking tiresomely against a fender above the soft sound the tires made pressing down against the dry snow. The short, fat man sat sideways in his seat, his face almost pressed against the glass. At first I thought that he was merely watching the view, trying to get a glimpse through the windows of houses where for some reason there happened to be people still up at that late hour. But each time the limousine passed under a street lamp, as it did with rhythmic regularity, I could see that he was weeping, biting his large lower lip cruelly in an effort to control his trembling, contorted features.

A Girl from the Queer People

ON SEPTEMBER 16, 1620, on the day the *Mayflower* sailed from Plymouth for America, twelve-year-old Remember Spong found a corner where she said to herself, "I like it alone here. I can tell myself what I wish and no one will hear my wish and it will be a secret between Me and Myself and when the wish comes true, then Me will say to Myself, 'That was pretty to be wishing.'"

Along the wharf went sailors, passengers, idlers, onlookers, helpers, bustling to and fro with last-minute cargo, belongings, repairs, materials for the *Mayflower* voyage. Visitors, idlers, onlookers, some for mere curiosity, ambled or stood around, some just gaping and daydreaming. A few, saying farewell with anxious faces, favored the ship, its people and their hopes. Others wore scowls of contempt or smiles of amusement at the foolhardiness of these queer people setting out for nowhere to do nothing worth

the time and effort of respectable persons.

John and Mary Spong had brought Remember to the wharf after an early morning visit to say farewell and Godspeed to the boys Freeborn and Oliver. Remember put her arms around each of her brothers, kissed them with tears, hugged and kissed Angus Smith and his wife saying she knew they would take good care of her brothers. Then Remember had run out of the house, to wait outside for her father and mother, the parting not easy for her.

John and Mary had gone up the gangplank with things for use on the voyage, telling Remember to go play a while on the wharf. She had asked that. Before the ship sailed they would be back for her, join with her in walking English soil for perhaps the last time in their lives. And Remember with glad feet had strolled, run, skipped. Her feet took her away from the crowd to a wharf shed filled with cargo, ship junk, and salvage. With the shed between her and the crowd, she stood looking at the sea, then toward the town of Plymouth, then ships at anchor, enjoying her meditations, finding a cozy quiet and loneliness about it. "I can tell myself what I wish and no one will hear my wish and it will be a secret between Me and Myself and when the wish comes true then Me will say to Myself, 'That was pretty to be wishing.'"

She had her mother's dreaminess at times. On the human-packed ships the faces and voices gave her small chance for her kind of dreaminess. To the sea, to the town, to the ships at anchor, her eyes turned. She felt rich. The quiet of the spaces and slants of the morning sun on the town, the ships, the sea, wrapped her in dreaminess. "I clear forgot you, Tamia," she broke her mood, speaking to what she held tucked in her right arm, a bright yellow kitten with black spots on its haunches. "Now you make wishes like I do, Tamia, and after any of them come true you tell me of it."

Of a sudden came voices hailing her, calling at her. From around the corner of the shed came five boys, glee in their voices and mischief on their faces. The four smaller seemed twelve to fourteen years in age, the tall one perhaps sixteen. A small pretty mouth he had, the tall one, the leader, black silk stockings, a short black velvet waistcoat, long blond curls falling to the shoulders.

They formed a half-circle around her where she stood between two small empty beer barrels. Remember met the flashing light brown eyes of the leader, met on his face a look of overstressed importance as though he had waited this chance to show his quality, his leadership, to himself and to his four young followers.

"You are sailing on the ship *Mayflower* today?"

"Yes."

"And ye knew not we had been seeking you?"

Remember shrank. Her eyes roved the five for a breach to run through swiftly. They had her hemmed in and cornered.

"Why should you be seeking me?"

"We know all there is need to be known of you." The small pretty mouth spoke loftily, the eyebrows lifting, the light brown eyes screwing to a slit. "The queer people, we call you. A pack of fanatics, my father calls you, and my mother holds you to be a shameless set of busybodies and troublemakers and she hopes the ship will sink with all of you when you get far enough from land so you can see no land. England is not good enough for you. You hate our churches. You detest our prayer book. You mislike our faces. So you must flee to be rid of our church, our prayer book, our faces."

He paused, bent toward the right, then the left, as though studying her ears. "What excellent white ears stand forth from your excellent head! Yet they are evil ears accustomed to hearing evil preached. What if we should cut off your ear on this side," as he pinched her right ear, "and then," as he pinched her left ear, "this other one?"

Remember felt herself tremble from head to toe. Her dry lips she moistened with moving them over and under each other. She began to speak and the words stuck on the tongue at the roof of her mouth. With another effort the words came. "Do you know what you do? Let me be. Let me go to my father and mother, who wait for me on the ship. I would give answers if I could think the answers for you. I have heard it many times those who measure out evil to me I should measure out good in return."

"So you have." And the leader's eyes left her for a moment and swept along the faces of his four open-eyed and admiring companions. "So you have. Truly those are pretty ears." He held her two ears with his hands and spoke with sarcasm and plainly with a vehemence of feeling caught from association with elders passionate in their hate of Dissenters from the Established Church order and methodical in their ways of dealing with heresy. "Pretty ears. And they hear no evil. And they listen to good doctrine only, yea, yea." His mock gaiety rose on a tone near laughter. "Have you seen the man now here with two ears missing? They were cut off. By the law they were cut off.

When his hands feel for his ears, he finds they are not there and he asks, 'Why did I lose my ears?' Then he remembers his ears heard too much evil and his tongue spouted the evil he heard. He may give thanks they did not slit his nose, seeing the high manner of his proud nose. Now your pretty ears —" His hands let go her ears, he paused. Remember, though fearing she would crush the yellow kitten under her arm, made a dash, trying to break through their line, first at one place, then at two more places. At each place they stopped her, pushed her back between the two small empty beer barrels. She stood scared and mute as he went on: "We leave you soon now, after we give you your lesson according to law. What do you say? Why is your tongue tied? You can talk. Your people talk. Your people talk, talk, talk. Make us a speech."

Remember, her wits coming back in part, stroking Tamia, spoke rather as though to herself than to them. "You hate me. And why do you hate me? For my thoughts? And what do you know of my thoughts? I came to this quiet place to wish, not to think. And how have my little wishes and thoughts ever touched you, ever harmed you?"

"You dispute well. You devote your days to argument and your lives to dispute, I have heard my good father say. We will leave you. We will go." His tone was casual as though each thing done was of the moment, each move of sudden impulse and prompting. "Now before we go, suppose I spit in your face. Your ears you can keep though mayhap"—and he paused with a malicious, steady gaze—"mayhap you will speak and make yourself known if we spit in your face."

He stooped and set one of the empty beer barrels on end and commanded, "Mount and stand there." Two of them lifted her up on the barrel as he mounted the other barrel and faced her. He swung a short piece of thick-tarred rope, swinging it so near her face that she drew back to escape it as he was saying, "Now I will show you we have mercy. I shall not lash you with this rope. Many of your people have tasted this but I shall not touch you with it." Again he swung it swiftly within an inch of her face. Remember, still clutching the kitten Tamia, leaped off the barrel, tried for escape, but they caught her. She wrestled and wriggled to get away but they put her back on the barrel.

The leader went on with his mockery. "I shall not lash you, though your people deserve lashing, all of you." He took out a fisherman's knife, opened a long sawtooth blade for gutting fish, brandished it toward Remember. "We shall not harm your ears, your nose." He closed the knife, put it away back in a pocket. "And yet how would it be if I should spit in your face and you tried to wipe it off and you should find you never could wipe it off and the shame of

it would be there on your face for life and whatever you might forget you could never forget our compliments to you and your people, how would it be?"

His face brightened with what he regarded as a whimsical smile. "At least you will speak enough to tell us what is the name of your kitten."

Her shoulders hunched forward and a little dreamlike, Remember drew her left hand across her mouth and face as though perhaps cleansing it of spittle.

"You scare easy, you queer people."

Two boys echoed, "Queer people, queer people," two others in a timebeat as though marching to drums, "Queer—queer, queer—queer." And the small pretty boy mouth framed in blond curls snapped words like a whiplash: "Speak and give the name of your dirty yellow kitten."

"Mesopotamia."

"You say the name Mesopotamia? That long name for that little dirty scared kitten?"

Weakly and shrinkingly, "Tamia for short."

"Who would have believed it? Tamia for short! And now before we go, how would it be if I spit in your face so you will not forget us when your ship is on the sea or when your ship arrives in America if God does not punish you by sending you to the bottom of the sea?" And the small whiplash boy mouth snarled, "Speak now." He leaned toward her, his teeth shining, his lips twisting.

Remember and her tormentors had been fascinated by the ingenuity, wild words, garrulity, and fury that piled one shame on another. None of them had seen a boy of perhaps fourteen years who had come near and stood listening. Now this newcomer could no longer stand still and listen. He leaped forward, threw all the weight of his body he could bring into the shove of his right foot against the barrel the leader was mounted on. The blond curls, black velvet, and silk stockings tumbled to the ground sprawling. The pretty boy picked himself up, and somewhat dizzy rubbed sore spots on his buttocks and shoulders.

The newcomer swung an ax handle, circling it in all directions, doing a mad club dance as he whirled and howled, once narrowly missing the blond curls by just the margin he meant to miss. From his wild face showing all its front teeth came a howling curse. "Get away from her, you dirty dogs, you lousy rats. If you don't get away from this girl I'll break your skulls, I'll kill you, I'll knock your bones loose, I'll mash your noses flat on your bloody faces."

The leader and his four followers wondered what had happened and stood dazed, awaiting they knew not what. The followers would have run if the leader had said the word or had himself run.

The newcomer's war dance with an ax handle had ended. But he stood wide-eyed, every muscle tensed, his body swaying as he held the club over his right shoulder ready to swing, leap, and swing again. His eyes ranged the four small ones, then turned straight to the light brown eyes of the leader and the small pretty mouth, and now talking cool, loud and slow: "If one of you takes a step this way, you'll go down with your head broken."

Two of the small followers slowly began walking away. The other two nodded their heads toward the leader as though it was time to be going. The leader looked at the piece of tarred rope in his hand. His fingers loosened and it fell to the groun⌐. Not yet out of his daze, dusting off spots that came from his sudden fall off the barrel, he moved away, mumbling to the followers who were leading him away. "We do not have time for this poor fool out of his right mind."

The newcomer walked with Remember along the wharf so alive with all the last errands of a ship leaving for a long voyage. She thanked him and said she could not speak enough thanks. He asked why she had left the wharf for the shed.

"To be alone once after being on ships so long—and to wish."

"And even your wish to be alone —you can't have that little wish."

Remember said, "Was there need for thee to take the name of the Lord in vain as thee did?"

"Did I? They would not believe me lest I spoke as though I came from the Head Demon of Hell. And I was not myself. I was out of my head when I ran in swinging this ax handle I found in the shed."

She spoke thanks again to him. Her eyes enjoyed his eyes and ranged over his face and shoulders. She tingled with more than admiration for him.

They came to the gangplank of the *Mayflower*. She must go up on the ship.

"Let me hold the yellow kitten once."

He stroked the fur, touched his fingers to the black spots on its haunches, and called it by name, "Mesopotamia—and Tamia for short."

They shook hands and said Godspeed with their faces very near each other, both of them bashful.

Remember ran up the gangplank, waved to him from the deck and he waved back. Then she held Mesopotamia high as her arms could reach and the boy waved to Meso-potamia, turned, walked farther away, and looked back to see Remember with her upstretched arms swaying the yellow kitten to and fro. The boy watched her, suddenly swung his ax handle breaking two imaginary heads, threw a kiss first with one hand and then the other to the girl and the kitten, turned and ran fast as his feet would take him. She saw him climb into a one-horse cart with a man who took the reins and they drove off and faded up a Plymouth street.

At supper in a little farm cottage near Plymouth that evening the boy told his mother what he had seen and done at the wharf. Later that evening she tucked a blanket around him in his pallet of rushes on the floor and kissed him good night, and he told her more, ending, "The name of the yellow kitten was Mesopotamia and for short Tamia."

"And the girl's name?"

"She didn't tell me."

"And the name of the ship?"

"I don't remember."

The Golden Kite, the Silver Wind

"IN THE SHAPE of a *pig?*" cried the Mandarin.

"In the shape of a pig," said the messenger, and departed.

"Oh, what an evil day in an evil year," cried the Mandarin. "The town of Kwan-Si, beyond the hill, was very small in my childhood. Now it has grown so large that at last they are building a wall."

"But why should a wall two miles away make my good father sad and angry all within the hour?" asked his daughter quietly.

"They build their wall," said the Mandarin, "in the shape of a pig! Do you see? Our own city wall is built in the shape of an orange. That pig will devour us, greedily!"

"Ah."

They both sat thinking.

Life was full of symbols and omens. Demons lurked everywhere, Death swam in the wetness of an eye, the turn of a gull's wing meant rain, a fan held *so,* the tilt of a roof, and, yes, even a city wall was of immense importance. Travelers and tourists, caravans, musicians, artists, coming upon these two towns, equally judging the portents, would say, "The city shaped like an orange? No! I will enter the city shaped like a pig and prosper, eating all, growing fat with good luck and prosperity!"

The Mandarin wept. "All is lost! These symbols and signs terrify. Our city will come on evil days."

"Then," said the daughter, "call in your stonemasons and temple builders. I will whisper from behind the silken screen and you will know the words."

The old man clapped his hands despairingly. "Ho, stonemasons! Ho, builders of towns and palaces!"

The men who knew marble and granite and onyx and quartz came quickly. The Mandarin faced them most uneasily, himself waiting for a whisper from the silken screen behind his throne. At last the whisper came.

"I have called you here," said the whisper.

"I have called you here," said the Mandarin aloud, "because our city is shaped like an orange, and the vile city of Kwan-Si has this day shaped theirs like a ravenous pig—"

Here the stonemasons groaned and wept. Death rattled his cane in the outer courtyard. Poverty made a sound like a wet cough in the shadows of the room.

"And so," said the whisper, said the Mandarin, "you raisers of walls must go bearing trowels and rocks and change the shape of *our* city!"

The architects and masons gasped. The Mandarin himself gasped at what he had said. The whisper whispered. The Mandarin went on: "And you will change our walls into a club which may beat the pig and drive it off!"

The stonemasons rose up, shouting. Even the Mandarin, delighted at the words from his mouth, applauded, stood down from his throne. "Quick!" he cried. "To work!"

When his men had gone, smiling and bustling, the Mandarin turned with great love to the silken screen. "Daughter," he whispered, "I will embrace you." There was no reply. He stepped around the screen, and she was gone.

Such modesty, he thought. She has slipped away and left me with a triumph, as if it were mine.

The news spread through the city; the Mandarin was acclaimed. Everyone carried stone to the walls. Fireworks were set off and the demons of death and poverty did not linger, as all worked together. At the end of the month the wall had been changed. It was now a mighty bludgeon with which to drive pigs, boars, even lions, far away. The Mandarin slept like a happy fox every night.

"I would like to see the Mandarin of Kwan-Si when the news is learned. Such pandemonium and hysteria; he will likely throw himself from a mountain! A little more of that wine, oh Daughter-who-thinks-like-a-son."

But the pleasure was like a winter flower; it died swiftly. That very afternoon the messenger rushed into the courtroom. "Oh, Mandarin, disease, early sorrow, avalanches, grasshopper plagues, and poisoned well water!"

The Mandarin trembled.

"The town of Kwan-Si," said the messenger, "which was built like a pig and which animal we drove away by changing our walls to a mighty stick, has now turned triumph to winter ashes. They have built their city's walls like a great bonfire to burn our stick!"

The Mandarin's heart sickened within him, like an autumn fruit upon an ancient tree. "Oh, gods! Travelers will spurn us. Tradesmen, reading the symbols, will turn from the stick, so easily destroyed, to the fire, which conquers all!"

"No," said a whisper like a snow-flake from behind the silken screen.

"No," said the startled Mandarin.

"Tell my stonemasons," said the whisper that was a falling drop of rain, "to build our walls in the shape of a shining lake."

The Mandarin said this aloud, his heart warmed.

"And with this lake of water," said the whisper and the old man, "we will quench the fire and put it out forever!"

The city turned out in joy to learn that once again they had been saved by the magnificent Emperor of ideas. They ran to the walls and built them nearer to this new vision, singing, not as loudly as before, of course, for they were tired, and not as quickly, for since it had taken a month to rebuild the wall the first time, they had had to neglect business and crops and therefore were somewhat weaker and poorer.

There then followed a succession of horrible and wonderful days, one in another like a nest of frightened boxes.

"Oh, Emperor," cried the messenger, "Kwan-Si has rebuilt their walls to resemble a mouth with which to drink all our lake!"

"Then," said the Emperor, standing very close to his silken screen, "build our walls like a needle to sew up that mouth!"

"Emperor!" screamed the messenger. "They make their walls like a sword to break your needle!"

The Emperor held, trembling, to the silken screen. "Then shift the stones to form a scabbard to sheathe that sword!"

"Mercy," wept the messenger the following morn, "they have worked all night and shaped their walls like lightning which will explode and destroy that sheath!"

Sickness spread in the city like a pack of evil dogs. Shops closed. The population, working now steadily for endless months upon the changing of the walls, resembled Death himself, clattering his white bones like musical instruments in the wind. Funerals began to appear in the streets, though it was the middle of summer, a time when all should be tending and harvesting. The Mandarin fell so ill that he had his bed drawn up by the silken screen and there he lay, miserably giving his architectural orders. The voice behind the screen was weak now, too, and faint, like the wind in the eaves.

"Kwan-Si is an eagle. Then our walls must be a net for that eagle. They are a sun to burn our net. Then we build a moon to eclipse their sun!"

Like a rusted machine, the city ground to a halt.

At last the whisper behind the screen cried out:

"In the name of the gods, send for Kwan-Si!"

Upon the last day of summer the

Mandarin Kwan-Si, very ill and withered away, was carried into our Mandarin's courtroom by four starving footmen. The two mandarins were propped up, facing each other. Their breaths fluttered like winter winds in their mouths. A voice said:

"Let us put an end to this."

The old men nodded.

"This cannot go on," said the faint voice. "Our people do nothing but rebuild our cities to a different shape every day, every hour. They have no time to hunt, to fish, to love, to be good to their ancestors and their ancestors' children."

"This I admit," said the mandarins of the towns of the Cage, the Moon, the Spear, the Fire, the Sword and this, that, and other things.

"Carry us into the sunlight," said the voice.

The old men were borne out under the sun and up a little hill. In the late summer breeze a few very thin children were flying dragon kites in all the colors of the sun, and frogs and grass, the color of the sea and the color of coins and wheat.

The first Mandarin's daughter stood by his bed.

"See," she said.

"Those are nothing but kites," said the two old men.

"But what is a kite on the ground?" she said. "It is nothing. What does it need to sustain it and make it beautiful and truly spiritual?"

"The wind, of course!" said the others.

"And what do the sky and the wind need to make *them* beautiful?"

"A kite, of course—many kites, to break the monotony, the sameness of the sky. Colored kites, flying!"

"So," said the Mandarin's daughter. "You, Kwan-Si, will make a last rebuilding of your town to resemble nothing more nor less than the wind. And we shall build like a golden kite. The wind will beautify the kite and carry it to wondrous heights. And the kite will break the sameness of the wind's existence and give it purpose and meaning. One without the other is nothing. Together, all will be beauty and co-operation and a long and enduring life."

Whereupon the two mandarins were so overjoyed that they took their first nourishment in days, momentarily were given strength, embraced, and lavished praise upon each other, called the Mandarin's daughter a boy, a man, a stone pillar, a warrior, and a true and unforgettable son. Almost immediately they parted and hurried to their towns, calling out and singing, weakly but happily.

And so, in time, the towns became the Town of Golden Kite and the Town of the Silver Wind. And harvestings were harvested and business tended again, and the flesh returned, and disease ran off like a frightened jackal. And on every night of the year the inhabitants in the Town of the Kite could hear the good clear wind sustaining them. And those in the Town of the Wind could hear the kite sing- ing, whispering, rising, and beauti- fying them.

"So be it," said the Mandarin in front of his silken screen.

The Brain Is Wider Than the Sky

EMILY DICKINSON

The brain is wider than the sky,
For, put them side by side,
The one the other will include
With ease, and you beside.

The brain is deeper than the sea,
For, hold them, blue to blue,
The one the other will absorb,
As sponges, buckets do.

The brain is just the weight of God,
For, lift them, pound for pound,
And they will differ, if they do,
As syllable from sound.

After Twenty Years

THE POLICEMAN on the beat moved up the avenue impressively. The impressiveness was habitual and not for show, for spectators were few. The time was barely ten o'clock at night, but chilly gusts of wind with a taste of rain in them had well nigh depeopled the streets.

Trying doors as he went, twirling his club with many intricate and artful movements, turning now and then to cast his watchful eye down the pacific thoroughfare, the officer, with his stalwart form and slight swagger, made a fine picture of a guardian of the peace. The vicinity was one that kept early hours. Now and then you might see the lights of a cigar store or of an all-night lunch counter; but the majority of the doors belonged to business places that had long since been closed.

When about midway of a certain block, the policeman suddenly slowed his walk. In the doorway of a darkened hardware store a man leaned, with an unlighted cigar in his mouth. As the policeman walked up to him, the man spoke up quickly.

"It's all right, officer," he said, reassuringly. "I'm just waiting for a friend. It's an appointment made twenty years ago. Sounds a little funny to you, doesn't it? Well, I'll explain if you'd like to make certain it's all straight. About that long ago there used to be a restaurant where this store stands—'Big Joe' Brady's restaurant."

"Until five years ago," said the policeman. "It was torn down then."

The man in the doorway struck a match and lit his cigar. The light showed a pale, square-jawed face with keen eyes, and a little white scar near his right eyebrow. His scarfpin was a large diamond, oddly set.

"Twenty years ago tonight," said the man, "I dined here at 'Big Joe' Brady's with Jimmy Wells, my best chum, and the finest chap in the world. He and I were raised here in New York, just like two brothers, together. I was eighteen and Jimmy was twenty. The next morning I was to start for the West to make my fortune. You couldn't have dragged Jimmy out of New York; he thought it was the only place on earth. Well, we agreed that night that we would meet here again exactly twenty years from that date and time, no matter what our conditions might be or from what distance we might have to come. We figured that in twenty years each of us ought to have our destiny worked out and our fortunes made, whatever they were going to be."

"It sounds pretty interesting," said the policeman. "Rather a long time between meets, though, it seems to me. Haven't you heard from your friend since you left?"

"Well, yes, for a time we corresponded," said the other. "But after a year or two we lost track of each other. You see, the West is a pretty big proposition, and I kept hustling around over it pretty lively. But I know Jimmy will meet me here if he's still alive, for he always was the truest, stanchest old chap in the world. He'll never forget. I came a thousand miles to stand in this door tonight, and it's worth it if my old partner turns up."

The waiting man pulled out a handsome watch, the lids of it set with small diamonds.

"Three minutes to ten," he announced. "It was exactly ten o'clock when we parted here at the restaurant door."

"Did pretty well out West, didn't you?" asked the policeman.

"You bet! I hope Jimmy has done half as well. He was a kind of plodder, though, good fellow as he was. I've had to compete with some of the sharpest wits going to get my pile. A man gets in a groove in New York. It takes the West to put a razor-edge on him."

The policeman twirled his club and took a step or two.

"I'll be on my way. Hope your friend comes around all right. Going to call time on him sharp?"

"I should say not!" said the other. "I'll give him half an hour at least. If Jimmy is alive on earth he'll be here by that time. So long, officer."

"Good-night, sir," said the policeman, passing on along his beat, trying doors as he went.

There was now a fine, cold drizzle falling, and the wind had risen from its uncertain puffs into a steady blow. The few foot passengers astir in that quarter hurried dismally and silently along with coat collars turned high and pocketed hands. And in the door of the hardware store the man who had come a thousand miles to fill an appointment, uncertain almost to absurdity, with the friend of his youth, smoked his cigar and waited.

About twenty minutes he waited, and then a tall man in a long overcoat, with collar turned up to his ears, hurried across from the opposite side of the street. He went directly to the waiting man.

"Is that you, Bob?" he asked, doubtfully.

"Is that you, Jimmy Wells?" cried the man in the door.

"Bless my heart!" exclaimed the new arrival, grasping both the other's hands with his own. "It's Bob, sure as fate. I was certain I'd find you here if you were still in existence. Well, well, well!—twenty years is a long time. The old restaurant's gone, Bob; I wish it had lasted, so we could have had another dinner there. How has the West treated you, old man?"

"Bully; it has given me everything I asked it for. You've changed lots, Jimmy. I never thought you were so tall by two or three inches."

"Oh, I grew a bit after I was twenty."

"Doing well in New York, Jimmy?"

"Moderately. I have a position in one of the city departments. Come on, Bob; we'll go around to a place I know of, and have a good long talk about old times."

The two men started up the street, arm in arm. The man from the West, his egotism enlarged by success, was beginning to outline the history of his career. The other, submerged in his overcoat, listened with interest.

At the corner stood a drugstore, brilliant with electric lights. When they came into this glare each of them turned simultaneously to gaze upon the other's face.

The man from the West stopped suddenly and released his arm.

"You're not Jimmy Wells," he snapped. "Twenty years is a long time, but not long enough to change a man's nose from a Roman to a pug."

"It sometimes changes a good man into a bad one," said the tall man. "You've been under arrest for ten minutes, 'Silky' Bob. Chicago thinks you may have dropped over our way and wires us she wants to have a chat with you. Going quietly, are you? That's sensible. Now, before we go to the station here's a note I was asked to hand to you. You may read it here at the window. It's from Patrolman Wells."

The man from the West unfolded the little piece of paper handed him. His hand was steady when he began to read, but it trembled a little by the time he had finished. The note was rather short.

Bob: I was at the appointed place on time. When you struck the match to light your cigar I saw it was the face of the man wanted in Chicago. Somehow I couldn't do it myself, so I went around and got a plain-clothes man to do the job.

JIMMY.

Those Two Boys

FRANKLIN P. ADAMS

When Bill was a lad he was terribly bad
  He worried his parents a lot;
He'd lie and he'd swear and pull little girls' hair;
  His boyhood was naught but a blot.

At play and in school he would fracture each rule—
  In mischief from autumn to spring;
And the villagers knew when to manhood he grew
  He would never amount to a thing.

When Jim was a child he was not very wild;
  He was known as a good little boy;
He was honest and bright and the teachers' delight—
  To his father and mother a joy.

All the neighbors were sure that his virtue'd endure,
  That his life would be free of a spot;
They were certain that Jim had a great head on him
  And that Jim would amount to a lot.

And Jim grew to manhood and honor and fame
  And bears a good name;
While Bill is shut up in a dark prison cell—
  You never can tell.

STEPHEN CRANE

The Upturned Face

"WHAT WILL we do now?" said the adjutant, troubled and excited.

"Bury him," said Timothy Lean.

The two officers looked down close to their toes where lay the body of their comrade. The face was chalk-blue; gleaming eyes stared at the sky. Over the two upright figures was a windy sound of bullets, and on the top of the hill Lean's prostrate company of Spitzbergen infantry was firing measured volleys.

"Don't you think it would be better—" began the adjutant. "We might leave him until tomorrow."

"No," said Lean. "I can't hold that post an hour longer. I've got to fall back, and we've got to bury old Bill."

"Of course," said the adjutant, at once. "Your men got entrenching tools?"

Lean shouted back to his little line, and two men came slowly, one with a pick, one with a shovel. They started in the direction of the Rostina sharpshooters. Bullets cracked

near their ears. "Dig here," said Lean gruffly. The men, thus caused to lower their glances to the turf, became hurried and frightened, merely because they could not look to see whence the bullets came. The dull beat of the pick striking the earth sounded amid the swift snap of close bullets. Presently the other private began to shovel.

"I suppose," said the adjutant, slowly, "we'd better search his clothes for—things."

Lean nodded. Together in curious abstraction they looked at the body. Then Lean stirred his shoulders suddenly, arousing himself.

"Yes," he said, "we'd better see what he's got." He dropped to his knees, and his hands approached the body of the dead officer. But his hands wavered over the buttons of the tunic. The first button was brick-red with drying blood, and he did not seem to dare touch it.

"Go on," said the adjutant, hoarsely.

Lean stretched his wooden hand,

and his fingers fumbled the blood-stained buttons. At last he rose with ghastly face. He had gathered a watch, a whistle, a pipe, a tobacco-pouch, a handkerchief, a little case of cards and papers. He looked at the adjutant. There was a silence. The adjutant was feeling that he had been a coward to make Lean do all the grisly business.

"Well," said Lean, "that's all, I think. You have his sword and revolver?"

"Yes," said the adjutant, his face working, and then he burst out in a sudden strange fury at the two privates. "Why don't you hurry up with that grave? What are you doing, anyhow? Hurry, do you hear? I never saw such stupid—"

Even as he cried out in his passion the two men were laboring for their lives. Ever overhead the bullets were spitting.

The grave was finished. It was not a masterpiece—a poor little shallow thing. Lean and the adjutant again looked at each other in a curious silent communication.

Suddenly the adjutant croaked out a weird laugh. It was a terrible laugh, which had its origin in that part of the mind which is first moved by the singing of the nerves. "Well," he said humorously to Lean, "I suppose we had best tumble him in."

"Yes," said Lean. The two privates stood waiting, bent over their implements. "I suppose," said Lean, "it would be better if we laid him in ourselves."

"Yes," said the adjutant. Then, apparently remembering that he had made Lean search the body, he stooped with great fortitude and took hold of the dead officer's clothing. Lean joined him. Both were particular that their fingers should not feel the corpse. They tugged away; the corpse lifted, heaved, toppled, flopped into the grave, and the two officers, straightening, looked again at each other—they were always looking at each other. They sighed with relief.

The adjutant said, "I suppose we should—we should say something. Do you know the service, Tim?"

"They don't read the service until the grave is filled in," said Lean, pressing his lips to an academic expression.

"Don't they?" said the adjutant, shocked that he had made the mistake. "Oh well," he cried, suddenly, "let us—let us say something—while he can hear us."

"All right," said Lean. "Do you know the service?"

"I can't remember a line of it," said the adjutant.

Lean was extremely dubious. "I can repeat two lines, but—"

"Well, do it." said the adjutant. "Go as far as you can. That's better than nothing. And the beasts have got our range exactly."

Lean looked at his two men. "Attention," he barked. The privates came to attention with a click, looking much aggrieved. The adjutant lowered his helmet to his knee. Lean, bareheaded, stood over the grave. The Rostina sharpshooters fired briskly.

"O Father, our friend has sunk in the deep waters of death, but his spirit has leaped toward Thee as the bubble rises from the lips of the drowning. Perceive, we beseech, O Father, the little flying bubble, and—"

Lean, although husky and ashamed, had suffered no hesitation up to this point, but he stopped with a hopeless feeling and looked at the corpse.

The adjutant moved uneasily. "And from Thy superb heights—" he began, and then he too came to an end.

"And from Thy superb heights," said Lean.

The adjutant suddenly remembered a phrase in the back of the Spitzbergen burial service, and he exploited it with the triumphant manner of a man who has recalled everything, and can go on.

"O God, have mercy—"

"O God, have mercy—" said Lean.

"Mercy," repeated the adjutant, in quick failure.

"Mercy," said Lean. And then he was moved by some violence of feeling, for he turned upon his two men and tigerishly said, "Throw the dirt in."

The fire of the Rostina sharpshooters was accurate and continuous.

One of the aggrieved privates came forward with his shovel. He lifted his first shovel-load of earth, and for a moment of inexplicable hesitation it was held poised above this corpse, which from its chalk-blue face looked keenly out from the grave. Then the soldier emptied his shovel on—on the feet.

Timothy Lean felt as if tons had been swiftly lifted off his forehead. He had felt that perhaps the private might empty the shovel on—on the face. It had been emptied on the feet. There was a great point gained there—ha, ha!—the first shovelful had been emptied on the feet. How satisfactory!

The adjutant began to babble. "Well, of course—a man we've messed with all these years—impossible—you can't, you know, leave your intimate friends rotting on the field. Go on, for God's sake, and shovel, you."

The man with the shovel suddenly ducked, grabbed his left arm with his right hand, and looked at his officer for orders. Lean picked the shovel from the ground. "Go to the rear," he said to the wounded man. He also addressed the other private. "You get under cover, too; I'll finish this business."

The wounded man scrambled hard still for the top of the ridge without devoting any glances to the direction from whence the bullets came, and the other man followed at an equal pace; but he was different, in that he looked back anxiously three times.

This is merely the way—often—of the hit and unhit.

Timothy Lean filled the shovel, hesitated, and then, in a movement which was like a gesture of abhorrence, he flung the dirt into the grave, and as it landed it made a sound—plop. Lean suddenly stopped and mopped his brow—a tired laborer.

"Perhaps we have been wrong," said the adjutant. His glance wavered stupidly. "It might have been better if we hadn't buried him just at this time. Of course, if we advance tomorrow the body would have been—"

"Damn you," said Lean, "shut your mouth." He was not the senior officer.

He again filled the shovel and flung the earth. Always the earth made that sound—plop. For a space Lean worked frantically, like a man digging himself out of danger.

Soon there was nothing to be seen but the chalk-blue face. Lean filled the shovel. "Good God," he cried to the adjutant. "Why didn't you turn him somehow when you put him in? This—" Then Lean began to stutter.

The adjutant understood. He was pale to the lips. "Go on, man," he cried, beseechingly, almost in a shout.

Lean swung back the shovel. It went forward in a pendulum curve. When the earth landed it made a sound—plop.

Dreamers

SIEGFRIED SASSOON

Soldiers are citizens of death's gray land,
  Drawing no dividend from time's tomorrows.
In the great hour of destiny they stand;
  Each with his feuds, and jealousies and sorrows.
Soldiers are sworn to action; they must win
  Some flaming, fatal climax with their lives.
Soldiers are dreamers; when the guns begin
  They think of firelit homes, clean beds, and wives.

I see them in foul dug-outs, gnawed by rats,
  And in ruined trenches, lashed by rain.
Dreaming of things they did with balls and bats,
  And mocked by hopeless longing to regain
Bank-holidays, and picture shows, and spats,
  And going to the office on the train.

Part 2

STORIES OF DEPTH

The New Kid

By the time Marty ran up the stairs, past the dentist's office, where it smelled like the time his father was in the hospital, past the fresh paint smell, where the new kid lived, past the garlic smell from the Italians in 2D; and waited for Mommer to open the door; and threw his schoolbooks on top of the old newspapers that were piled on the sewing machine in the hall; and drank his glass of milk ("How many times must I tell you not to gulp! Are you going to stop gulping like that or must I smack your face!"); and set the empty glass in the sink under the faucet; and changed into his brown keds; and put trees into his school shoes ("How many times must I talk to you! God in Heaven—when will you learn to take care of your clothes and not make me follow you around like this!"); and ran downstairs again, past the garlic and the paint and the hospital smells; by the time he got into the street and looked breathlessly around him, it

was too late. The fellows were all out there, all ready for a game, and just waiting for Eddie Deakes to finish chalking a base against the curb.

Running up the street with all his might, Marty could see that the game would start any minute now. Out in the gutter Paulie Dahler was tossing high ones to Ray-Ray Stickerling, whose father was a bus driver and sometimes gave the fellows transfers so they could ride free. The rest were sitting on the curb, waiting for Eddie to finish making the base and listening to Gelberg, who was a Jew, explain what it meant to be bar-mizvah'd, like he was going to be next month.

They did not look up as Marty galloped up to them all out of breath. Eddie finished making his base and after looking at it critically a moment, with his head on one side, moved down toward the sewer that was home plate and began drawing a scoreboard alongside it. With his nose running from excitement Marty trotted over to him.

"Just going to play with two bases?" he said, wiping his nose on the sleeve of his lumber jacket, and hoping with all his might that Eddie would think he had been there all the while and was waiting for a game like all the other fellows.

Eddie raised his head and saw that it was Marty. He gave Marty a shove. "Why don't you watch where you're walking?" he said. "Can't you see I'm making a scoreboard!"

He bent over again and with his chalk repaired the lines that Marty had smudged with his sneakers. Marty hopped around alongside him, taking care to keep his feet off the chalked box. "Gimme a game, Eddie?" he said.

"What are you asking me for?" Eddie said, without looking up. "It ain't my game."

"Aw, come on, Eddie. I'll get even on you!" Marty said.

"Ask Gelberg. It's his game," Eddie said, straightening himself and shoving his chalk into his pants pocket. He trotted suddenly into the middle of the street and ran sideways a few feet. "Here go!" he hollered. "All the way!"

From his place up near the corner Paulie Dahler heaved the ball high into the air, higher than the telephone wires. Eddie took a step back, then a step forward, then back again, and got under it.

Marty bent his knees like a catcher, pounded his fist into his palm as though he were wearing a mitt, and held out his hands. "Here go, Eddie!" he hollered. "Here go!"

Holding the ball in his hand, and without answering him, Eddie walked toward the curb, where the rest of the fellows were gathered around Gelberg. Marty straightened his knees, put down his hands, and sniffling his nose, trotted after Eddie.

"All right, I'll choose Gelberg for sides," Eddie said.

Gelberg heaved himself off the curb and put on his punchball glove, which was one of his mother's old kid gloves, with the fingers and thumb cut off short. "Odds, once takes it," he said.

After a couple of preparatory swings of their arms they matched fingers. Gelberg won. He chose Albie Newbauer. Eddie looked around him and took Wally Reinhard. Gelberg took Ray-Ray Stickerling. Eddie took Wally Reinhard's brother, Howey.

Marty hopped around on the edge of the group. "Hey, Gelberg," he hollered, in a high voice. "Gimme a game, will you?"

"I got Arnie," Gelberg said.

Eddie looked around him again. "All right, I got Paulie Dahler."

They counted their men. "Choose you for up first," Gelberg said. Feeling as though he were going to cry, Marty watched them as they swung their arms, stuck out their fingers. This time Eddie won. Gelberg gathered his men around him and they trotted into the street to take up positions on the field. They hollered "Here go!" threw the ball from first to second, then out into the field, and back again to Gelberg in the pitcher's box.

Marty ran over to him. "Gimme a game, will you, Gelberg?"

"We're all choosed up," Gelberg said, heaving a high one to Arnie out in center field.

Marty wiped his nose on his sleeve. "Come on, gimme a game. Didn't I let you lose my Spaulding Hi-Bouncer down the sewer once?"

"Want to give the kid a game?" Gelberg called to Eddie, who was seated on the curb, figuring out his batting order with his men.

"Aw, we got the sides all choosed up!" Eddie said.

Marty stuck out his lower lip and wished that he would not have to cry. "You give Howey Reinhard a game!" he said, pointing at Howey sitting on the curb next to Eddie. "He can't play any better than me!"

"Yeah," Howey yelled, swinging back his arm as though he were going to punch Marty in the jaw. "You couldn't hit the side of the house!"

"Yeah, I can play better than you any day!" Marty hollered.

"You can play left outside!" Howey said, looking around to see how the joke went over.

"Yeah, I'll get even on you!" Marty hollered, hoping that maybe they would get worried and give him a game after all.

With a fierce expression on his face, as if to indicate that he was through joking and now meant se-rious business, Howey sprang up from the curb and sent him staggering with a shove. Marty tried to duck, but Howey smacked him across the side of the head. Flinging his arms up about his ears Marty scrambled down the street; for no reason at all Paulie Dahler booted him in the pants as he went by.

"I'll get even on you!" Marty yelled, when he was out of reach. With a sudden movement of his legs Howey pretended to rush at him. Almost falling over himself in panic Marty dashed toward the house, but stopped, feeling ashamed, when he saw that Howey had only wanted to make him run.

For a while he stood there on the curb, wary and ready to dive into the house the instant any of the fellows made a move toward him. But presently he saw that the game was beginning, and that none of them was paying any more attention to him. He crept toward them again, and seating himself on the curb a little distance away, watched the game start. For a moment he thought of breaking it up, rushing up to the scoreboard and smudging it with his sneakers before anyone could stop him, and then dashing into the house before they caught him. Or grabbing the ball when it came near him and flinging it down the sewer. But he decided not to; the fellows would catch him in the end, smack him and make another scoreboard or get another ball, and then he would never get a game.

Every minute feeling more and

more like crying, he sat there on the curb, his elbow on his knee, his chin in his palm, and tried to think where he could get another fellow, so that they could give him a game and still have even sides. Then he lifted his chin from his palm and saw that the new kid was sitting out on the stoop in front of the house, chewing something and gazing toward the game; and all at once the feeling that he was going to cry disappeared. He sprang up from the curb.

"Hey, Gelberg!" he hollered. "If I get the new kid for even sides can I get a game?"

Without waiting for an answer he dashed down the street toward the stoop where the new kid was sitting.

"Hey, fellow!" he shouted. "Want a game? Want a game of punchball?"

He could see now that what the new kid was eating was a slice of rye bread covered with apple sauce. He could see, too, that the new kid was smaller than he was, and had a narrow face and a large nose with a few little freckles across the bridge. He was wearing Boy Scout pants and a brown woolen pullover, and on the back of his head was a skullcap made from the crown of a man's felt hat, the edge turned up and cut into sharp points that were ornamented with brass paper clips.

All out of breath he stopped in front of the new kid. "What do you say?" he hollered. "Want a game?"

The new kid looked at him and

took another bite of rye bread. "I don't know," he said, with his mouth full of bread, turning to take another look at the fellows in the street. "I guess I got to go to the store soon."

"You don't have to go to the store right away, do you?" Marty said, in a high voice.

The new kid swallowed his bread and continued looking up toward the game. "I got to stay in front of the house in case my mother calls me."

"Maybe she won't call you for a while," Marty said. He could see that the inning was ending, that they would be starting a new inning in a minute, and his legs twitched with impatience.

"I don't know," the new kid said, still looking up at the game. "Anyway, I got my good shoes on."

"Aw, I bet you can't even play punchball!" cried Marty.

The new kid looked at him with his lower lip stuck out. "Yeah, I can so play! Only I got to go to the store!"

Once more he looked undecidedly up toward the game. Marty could see that the inning was over now. He turned pleadingly to the new kid.

"You can hear her if she calls you, can't you? Can't you play just till she calls you? Come on, can't you?"

Putting the last of his rye bread into his mouth, the new kid got up from the stoop. "Well, when she calls me—" he said, brushing off the seat of his pants with his hand, "when she calls me I got to quit and go to the store."

As fast as he could run Marty dashed up the street with the new kid trailing after him. "Hey, I got another man for even sides!" he yelled. "Gimme a game now? I got another man!"

The fellows looked at the new kid coming up the street behind Marty.

"You new on the block?" Howey Reinhard asked, eying the Boy Scout pants, as Marty and the new kid came up to them.

"You any good?" Gelberg demanded, bouncing the ball at his feet and looking at the skullcap ornamented with brass paper clips. "Can you hit?"

"Come on!" Marty said. He wished that they would just give him a game and not start asking a lot of questions. "I got another man for even sides, didn't I?"

"Aw, we got the game started already!" Ray-Ray Stickerling hollered.

Marty sniffled his nose, which was beginning to run again, and looked at him as fiercely as he was able. "It ain't your game!" he yelled. "It's Gelberg's game! Ain't it your game, Gelberg?"

Gelberg gave him a shove. "No one said you weren't going to get a game!" With a last bounce of his ball he turned to Eddie, who was looking the new kid over carefully.

"All right, Eddie. I'll take the new kid and you can have Marty."

Eddie drew his arm back as though he were going to hit him. "Like fun! Why don't you take Marty, if you're so wise?"

"I won the choose-up!" Gelberg hollered.

"Yeah, that was before! I'm not taking Marty!"

"I won the choose-up, didn't I?"

"Well, you got to choose up again for the new kid!"

Marty watched them as they stood up to each other, each eying the other suspiciously, and swung their arms to choose. Eddie won. "Cheating shows!" he yelled, seizing the new kid by the arm, and pulling him into the group on his side.

Trying to look like the ball players he had seen the time his father had taken him to the Polo Grounds, Marty ran into the outfield and took the position near the curb that Gelberg had selected for him. He tried not to feel bad because Eddie had taken the new kid, that no one knew anything about, how he could hit, or anything; and that he had had to go to the loser of the choose-up. As soon as he was out in the field he leaned forward, with his hands propped on his knees, and hollered: "All right, all right, these guys can't hit!" Then he straightened up and pounded his fist into his palm as though he were wearing a fielder's glove and shouted: "Serve it to them on a silver platter, Gelberg! These guys are just a bunch of fan artists!" He propped his hands on his knees again, like a big-leaguer, but all the while he felt unhappy, not nearly the way he should have felt, now that they had finally given him a game. He hoped that they would hit to him, and he would make one-handed catches over his head, run way out with his back to the ball and spear them blind, or run in with all his might and pick them right off the tops of his shoes.

A little nervous chill ran through his back as he saw Paulie Dahler get up to hit. On Gelberg's second toss Paulie stepped in and sent the ball sailing into the air. A panic seized Marty as he saw it coming at him. He took a step nervously forward, then backward, then forward again, trying as hard as he could to judge the ball. It smacked into his cupped palms, bounced out and dribbled toward the curb. He scrambled after it, hearing them shouting at him, and feeling himself getting more scared every instant. He kicked the ball with his sneaker, got his hand on it, and straightening himself in a fever of fright, heaved it with all his strength at Ray-Ray on first. The moment the ball left his hand he knew he had done the wrong thing. Paulie was already on his way to second; and besides, the throw was wild. Ray-Ray leaped into the air, his arms flung up, but it was way over his head, bouncing beyond him on the sidewalk and almost hitting a woman who was jouncing a baby carriage at the door of the apartment house opposite.

With his heart beating the same way it did whenever anyone chased him, Marty watched Paulie gallop across the plate. He sniffled his nose, which was beginning to run again, and felt like crying.

"Holy Moses!" he heard Gelberg yell. "What do you want, a basket? Can't you hold on to them once in a while?"

"Aw, the sun was in my eyes!" Marty said.

"You wait until you want another game!" Gelberg shouted.

Breathing hard, Ray-Ray got back on first and tossed the ball to Gelberg. "Whose side are you on anyway?" he hollered.

Eddie Deakes put his hands to his mouth like a megaphone. "Attaboy, Marty!" he yelled. "Having you out there is like having another man on our side!"

The other fellows on the curb laughed, and Howey Reinhard made them laugh harder by pretending to catch a fly ball with the sun in his eyes, staggering around the street with his eyes screwed up and his hands cupped like a sissy, so that the wrists touched and the palms were widely separated.

No longer shouting or punching his fist into his palm, Marty took his place out in the field again. He stood there, feeling like crying, and wished that he hadn't dropped that ball, or thrown it over Ray-Ray's head. Then, without knowing why, he looked up to see whether the new kid was laughing at him like all the rest. But the new kid was sitting a little off by himself at one end of the row of fellows on the curb, and with a serious expression on his face gnawed at the skin at the side of his thumbnail. Marty began to wonder if the new kid was any good or not. He saw him sitting there, with the serious look on his face, his ears sticking out, not joking like the other fellows, and from nowhere the thought leaped into Marty's head that maybe the new kid was no good. He looked at the skinny legs, the Boy Scout pants, and the mama's boy shoes and all at once he began to hope that Eddie would send the new kid in to hit, so that he could know right away whether he was any good or not.

But Wally Reinhard was up next. He fouled out on one of Gelberg's twirls, and after him Howey popped up to Albie Newbauer and Eddie was out on first. The fellows ran in to watch Eddie chalk up Paulie's run on the scoreboard alongside the sewer. They were still beefing and hollering at Marty for dropping that ball, but he pretended he did not hear them and sat down on the curb to watch the new kid out in the field.

He was over near the curb, playing in closer than Paulie Dahler. Marty could see that he was not hollering "Here go!" or "All the way!" like the others, but merely stood there with that serious expression on his face and watched them throw the ball around. He held one leg bent at the ankle, so

that the side of his shoe rested on the pavement, his belly was stuck out, and he chewed the skin at the side of his thumbnail.

Gelberg got up to bat. Standing in the pitcher's box, Eddie turned around and motioned his men to lay out. The new kid looked around him to see what the other fellows did, took a few steps backward, and then, with his belly stuck out again, went on chewing his thumb.

Marty felt his heart begin to beat hard. He watched Gelberg stand up to the plate and contemptuously fling back the first few pitches.

"Come on, gimme one like I like!" Gelberg hollered.

"What's the matter! You afraid to reach for them?" Eddie yelled.

"Just pitch them to me, that's all!" Gelberg said.

Eddie lobbed one in that bounced shoulder high. With a little sideways skip Gelberg lammed into it.

The ball sailed down toward the new kid. Feeling his heart begin to beat harder, Marty saw him take a hurried step backward, and at the same moment fling his hands before his face and duck his head. The ball landed beyond him and bounded up on the sidewalk. For an instant the new kid hesitated, then he was galloping after it, clattering across the pavement in his polished shoes.

Swinging his arms in mock haste, Gelberg breezed across the plate. "Get a basket!" he hollered over his shoulder. "Get a basket!"

Marty let his nose run without

bothering to sniffle. He jumped up from the curb and curved his hands around his mouth like a megaphone. "He's scared of the ball!" he yelled at the top of his lungs. "He's scared of the ball! That's what he is, scared of the ball!"

The new kid tossed the ball back to Eddie. "I wasn't scared!" he said, moistening his lips with his tongue. "I wasn't scared! I just couldn't see it coming!"

With an expression of despair on his face Eddie shook his head. "Holy Moses! If you can't see the ball why do you try to play punchball?" He bounced the ball hard at his feet and motioned Gelberg to send in his next batter. Arnie got up from the curb and wiping his hands on his pants walked toward the plate.

Marty felt his heart pounding in his chest. He hopped up and down with excitement and seizing Gelberg by the arm pointed at the new kid.

"You see him duck?" he yelled. "He's scared of the ball, that's what he is!" He hardly knew where to turn first. He rushed up to Ray-Ray, who was sitting on the curb making marks on the asphalt with the heel of his sneaker. "The new kid's scared to stop a ball! You see him duck!"

The new kid looked toward Marty and wet his lips with his tongue. "Yeah," he yelled, "didn't you muff one that was right in your hands?"

He was looking at Marty with a sore expression on his face, and his lower lip stuck out; and a sinking feeling went through Marty, a sudden sick feeling that maybe he had started something he would be sorry for. Behind him on the curb he could hear the fellows sniggering in that way they did when they picked on him. In the pitcher's box Eddie let out a loud cackling laugh.

"Yeah, the new kid's got your number!"

"The sun was in my eyes!" Marty said. He could feel his face getting red, and in the field the fellows were laughing. A wave of self-pity flowed through him.

"What are you picking on me for!" he yelled, in a high voice. "The sun was so in my eyes. Anyway, I ain't no yellowbelly! I wasn't scared of the ball!"

The instant he said it he was sorry. He sniffled his nose uneasily as he saw Gelberg look at Ray-Ray. For an instant he thought of running into the house before anything happened. But instead he just stood there, sniffling his nose and feeling his heart beating, fast and heavy.

"You hear what he called you?" Paulie Dahler yelled at the new kid.

"You're not going to let him get away with calling you a yellowbelly, are you?" Eddie said, looking at the new kid.

The new kid wet his lips with his tongue and looked at Marty. "I wasn't scared!" he said. He shifted the soles of his new-looking shoes on the pavement. "I wasn't scared!

I just couldn't see it coming, that's all!"

Eddie was walking toward the new kid now, bouncing the ball slowly in front of him as he walked. In a sudden panic Marty looked back toward the house where old lady Kipnis lived. She always broke up fights; maybe she would break up this one; maybe she wouldn't even let it get started. But she wasn't out on her porch. He sniffled his nose, and with all his might hoped that the kid's mother would call him to go to the store.

"Any kid that lets himself be called a yellowbelly must be a yellowbelly!" Albie Newbauer said, looking around him for approval.

"Yeah," Gelberg said. "I wouldn't let anyone call me a yellowbelly."

With a sudden shove Eddie sent the new kid scrambling forward toward Marty. He tried to check himself by stiffening his body and twisting to one side, but it was no use. Before he could recover his balance another shove made him stagger forward.

Marty sniffled his nose and looked at the kid's face close in front of him. It seemed as big as the faces he saw in the movies; and he could see that the kid's nose was beginning to run just like his own; and he could see in the corner of his mouth a crumb of the rye bread he had eaten on the stoop. For a moment the kid's eyes looked squarely into Marty's, so that he could see the little dark specks in the colored part around the pupil. Then the

glance slipped away to one side; and all at once Marty had a feeling that the new kid was afraid of him.

"You gonna let him get away with calling you a yellowbelly?" he heard Eddie say. From the way it sounded he knew that the fellows were on his side now. He stuck out his jaw and waited for the new kid to answer.

"I got to go to the store!" the new kid said. There was a scared look on his face and he took a step back from Marty.

Paulie Dahler got behind him and shoved him against Marty. Although he tried not to, Marty couldn't help flinging his arms up before his face. But the new kid only backed away and kept his arms at his sides. A fierce excitement went through Marty as he saw how scared the look on the kid's face was. He thrust his chest up against the new kid.

"Yellowbelly!" he hollered, making his voice sound tough. "Scared of the ball!"

The new kid backed nervously away, and there was a look on his face as though he wanted to cry.

"Yeah, he's scared!" Eddie yelled.

"Slam him, Marty!" Wally Reinhard hollered. "The kid's scared of you!"

"Aw, sock the yellowbelly!" Marty heard Gelberg say, and he smacked the kid as hard as he could on the shoulder. The kid screwed up his face to keep from crying, and tried to back through the fellows ringed around him.

"Lemme alone!" he yelled.

Marty looked at him fiercely, with his jaw thrust forward, and felt his heart beating. He smacked the kid again, making him stagger against Arnie in back of him.

"Yeah, yellowbelly!" Marty hollered, feeling how the fellows were on his side, and how scared the new kid was. He began smacking him again and again on the shoulder.

"Three, six, nine, a bottle of wine, I can fight you any old time!" he yelled. With each word he smacked the kid on the shoulder or arm. At the last word he swung with all his strength. He meant to hit the kid on the shoulder, but at the last instant, even while his arm was swinging, something compelled him to change his aim; his fist caught the kid on the mouth with a hard, wet, socking sound. The shock of his knuckles against the kid's mouth, and that sound of it, made Marty want to hit him again and again. He put his head down and began swinging wildly, hitting the new kid without any aim on the head and shoulders and arms.

The new kid buried his head in his arms and began to cry. "Lemme alone!" he yelled. He tried to rush through the fellows crowded around him.

With all his might Marty smacked him on the side of the head. Rushing up behind him Arnie smacked him too. Paulie Dahler shoved the skullcap, with its paper clip ornaments, over the kid's eyes; and as he went by Gelberg booted him in the pants.

Crying and clutching his cap the new kid scampered over to the curb out of reach.

"I'll get even on you!" he cried.

With a fierce expression on his face Marty made a sudden movement of his legs and pretended to rush at him. The kid threw his arms about his head and darted down the street toward the house. When he saw that Marty was not coming after him he sat down on the stoop; and Marty could see him rubbing his knuckles against his mouth.

Howey Reinhard was making fun of the new kid, scampering up and down the pavement with his arms wrapped around his head and hollering, "Lemme alone! Lemme alone!" The fellows laughed, and although he was breathing hard, and his hand hurt from hitting the kid, Marty had to laugh too.

"You see him duck when that ball came at him?" he panted at Paulie Dahler.

Paulie shook his head. "Boy, just wait until we get the yellowbelly in the schoolyard!"

"And on Halloween," Gelberg said. "Wait until we get him on Halloween with our flour stockings!" He gave Marty a little shove and made as though he were whirling an imaginary flour stocking around his head.

Standing there in the middle of the street, Marty suddenly thought of Halloween, of the winter and snowballs, of the schoolyard. He saw himself whirling a flour stocking around his head and rushing at the new kid, who scampered in terror before him hollering, "Lemme alone! Lemme alone!" As clearly as if it were in the movies, he saw himself flinging snowballs and the new kid backed into a corner of the schoolyard, with his hands over his face. Before he knew what he was doing, Marty turned fiercely toward the stoop where the new kid was still sitting, rubbing his mouth and crying.

"Hey, yellowbelly!" Marty hollered; and he pretended he was going to rush at the kid.

Almost falling over himself in fright the new kid scrambled inside the house. Marty stood in the middle of the street and sniffled his nose. He shook his fist at the empty doorway.

"You see him run?" he yelled, so loud that it made his throat hurt. "Boy, you see him run?" He stood there shaking his fist, although the new kid was no longer there to see him. He could hardly wait for the winter, for Halloween, or the very next day in the schoolyard.

The Undefeated

MANUEL GARCIA climbed the stairs to Don Miguel Retana's office. He set down his suitcase and knocked on the door. There was no answer. Manuel, standing in the hallway, felt there was someone in the room. He felt it through the door.

"Retana," he said, listening.

There was no answer.

He's there, all right, Manuel thought.

"Retana," he said and banged the door.

"Who's there?" said someone in the office.

"Me, Manolo," Manuel said.

"What do you want?" asked the voice.

"I want to work," Manuel said.

Something in the door clicked several times and it swung open. Manuel went in, carrying his suitcase.

A little man sat behind a desk at the far side of the room. Over his head was a bull's head, stuffed by a Madrid taxidermist; on the walls were framed photographs and bull-fight posters.

The little man sat looking at Manuel.

"I thought they'd kill you," he said.

Manuel knocked with his knuckles on the desk. The little man sat looking at him across the desk.

"How many corridas you had this year?" Retana asked.

"One," he answered.

"Just that one?" the little man asked.

"That's all."

"I read about it in the papers," Retana said. He leaned back in the chair and looked at Manuel.

Manuel looked up at the stuffed bull. He had seen it often before. He felt a certain family interest in it. It had killed his brother, the promising one, about nine years ago. Manuel remembered the day. There was a brass plate on the oak shield the bull's head was mounted on. Manuel could not read it, but he imagined it was in memory of his brother. Well, he had been a good kid.

The plate said: "The Bull 'Mariposa' of the Duke of Veragua, which accepted 9 varas for 7 caballos, and caused the death of Antonio Garcia, Novillero, April 27, 1909."

Retana saw him looking at the stuffed bull's head.

"The lot the Duke sent me for Sunday will make a scandal," he said. "They're all bad in the legs. What do they say about them at the Café?"

"I don't know," Manuel said. "I just got in."

"Yes," Retana said. "You still have your bag."

He looked at Manuel, leaning back behind the big desk.

"Sit down," he said. "Take off your cap."

Manuel sat down; his cap off, his face was changed. He looked pale, and his coleta pinned forward on his head, so that it would not show under the cap, gave him a strange look.

"You don't look well," Retana said.

"I just got out of the hospital," Manuel said.

"I heard they'd cut your leg off," Retana said.

"No," said Manuel. "It got all right."

Retana leaned forward across the desk and pushed a wooden box of cigarettes toward Manuel.

"Have a cigarette," he said.

"Thanks."

Manuel lit it.

"Smoke?" he said, offering the match to Retana.

"No," Retana waved his hand, "I never smoke."

Retana watched him smoking.

"Why don't you get a job and go to work?" he said.

"I don't want to work," Manuel said. "I am a bullfighter."

"There aren't any bullfighters any more," Retana said.

"I'm a bullfighter," Manuel said.

"Yes, while you're in there," Retana said.

Manuel laughed.

Retana sat, saying nothing and looking at Manuel.

"I'll put you in a nocturnal if you want," Retana offered.

"When?" Manuel asked.

"Tomorrow night."

"I don't like to substitute for anybody," Manuel said. That was the way they all got killed. That was the way Salvator got killed. He tapped with his knuckles on the table.

"It's all I've got," Retana said.

"Why don't you put me on next week?" Manuel suggested.

"You wouldn't draw," Retana said. "All they want is Litri and Rubito and La Torre. Those kids are good."

"They'd come to see me get it," Manuel said, hopefully.

"No, they wouldn't. They don't know who you are any more."

"I've got a lot of stuff," Manuel said.

"I'm offering to put you on tomorrow night," Retana said. "You can work with young Hernandez and kill two novillos after the Charlots."

"Whose novillos?" Manuel asked.

"I don't know. Whatever stuff they've got in the corrals. What the veterinaries won't pass in the daytime."

"I don't like to substitute," Manuel said.

"You can take it or leave it," Retana said. He leaned forward over the papers. He was no longer interested. The appeal that Manuel had made to him for a moment when he thought of the old days was gone. He would like to get him to substitute for Larita because he could get him cheaply. He could get others cheaply too. He would like to help him though. Still he had given him the chance. It was up to him.

"How much do I get?" Manuel asked. He was still playing with the idea of refusing. But he knew he could not refuse.

"Two hundred and fifty pesetas," Retana said. He had thought of five hundred, but when he opened his mouth it said two hundred and fifty.

"You pay Villalta seven thousand," Manuel said.

"You're not Villalta," Retana said.

"I know it," Manuel said.

"He draws it, Manolo," Retana said in explanation.

"Sure," said Manuel. He stood up. "Give me three hundred, Retana."

"All right," Retana agreed. He reached in the drawer for a paper.

"Can I have fifty now?" Manuel asked.

"Sure," said Retana. He took a fifty-peseta note out of his pocketbook and laid it, spread out flat, on the table.

Manuel picked it up and put it in his pocket.

"What about a cuadrilla?" he asked.

"There's the boys that always work for me nights," Retana said. "They're all right."

"How about picadors?" Manuel asked.

"They're not much," Retana admitted.

"I've got to have one good pic," Manuel said.

"Get him then," Retana said. "Go and get him."

"Not out of this," Manuel said. "I'm not paying for any cuadrilla out of sixty duros."

Retana said nothing but looked at Manuel across the big desk.

"You know I've got to have one good pic," Manuel said.

Retana said nothing but looked at Manuel from a long way off.

"It isn't right," Manuel said.

Retana was still considering him, leaning back in his chair, considering him from a long way away.

"There're the regular pics," he offered.

"I know," Manuel said. "I know your regular pics."

Retana did not smile. Manuel knew it was over.

"All I want is an even break,"

Manuel said reasoningly. "When I go out there I want to be able to call my shots on the bull. It only takes one good picador."

He was talking to a man who was no longer listening.

"If you want something extra," Retana said, "go and get it. There will be a regular cuadrilla out there. Bring as many of your own pics as you want. The charlotada is over by 10:30."

"All right," Manuel said. "If that's the way you feel about it."

"That's the way," Retana said.

"I'll see you tomorrow night," Manuel said.

"I'll be out there," Retana said.

Manuel picked up his suitcase and went out.

"Shut the door," Retana called.

Manuel looked back. Retana was sitting forward looking at some papers. Manuel pulled the door tight until it clicked.

He went down the stairs and out of the door into the hot brightness of the street. It was very hot in the street and the light on the white buildings was sudden and hard on his eyes. He walked down the shady side of the steep street toward the Puerta del Sol. The shade felt solid and cool as running water. The heat came suddenly as he crossed the intersecting streets. Manuel saw no one he knew in all the people he passed.

Just before the Puerta del Sol he turned into a café.

It was quiet in the café. There were a few men sitting at tables against the wall. At one table four men played cards. Most of the men sat against the wall smoking, empty coffee cups and liqueur glasses before them on the tables. Manuel went through the long room to a small room in back. A man sat at a table in the corner asleep. Manuel sat down at one of the tables.

A waiter came in and stood beside Manuel's table.

"Have you seen Zurito?" Manuel asked him.

"He was in before lunch," the waiter answered. "He won't be back before five o'clock."

"Bring me some coffee and milk and a shot of the ordinary," Manuel said.

The waiter came back into the room carrying a tray with a big coffee glass and a liqueur glass on it. In his left hand he held a bottle of brandy. He swung these down to the table and a boy who had followed him poured coffee and milk into the glass from two shiny, spouted pots with long handles.

Manuel took off his cap and the waiter noticed his pigtail pinned forward on his head. He winked at the coffee-boy as he poured out the brandy into the little glass beside Manuel's coffee. The coffee-boy looked at Manuel's pale face curiously.

"You fighting here?" asked the waiter, corking up the bottle.

"Yes," Manuel said. "Tomorrow."

The waiter stood there, holding the bottle on one hip.

"You in the Charlie Chaplins?" he asked.

The coffee-boy looked away, embarrassed.

"No. In the ordinary."

"I thought they were going to have Chaves and Hernandez," the waiter said.

"No. Me and another."

"Who? Chaves or Hernandez?"

"Hernandez, I think."

"What's the matter with Chaves?"

"He got hurt."

"Where did you hear that?"

"Retana."

"Hey, Looie," the waiter called to the next room, "Chaves got cogida."

Manuel had taken the wrapper off the lumps of sugar and dropped them into his coffee. He stirred it and drank it down, sweet, hot, and warming in his empty stomach. He drank off the brandy.

"Give me another shot of that," he said to the waiter.

The waiter uncorked the bottle and poured the glass full, slopping another drink into the saucer. Another waiter had come up in front of the table. The coffee-boy was gone.

"Is Chaves hurt bad?" the second waiter asked Manuel.

"I don't know," Manuel said, "Retana didn't say."

"A lot he cares," the tall waiter said. Manuel had not seen him before. He must have just come up.

"If you stand in with Retana in this town, you're a made man," the tall waiter said. "If you aren't in

with him, you might just as well go out and shoot yourself."

"You said it," the other waiter who had come in said. "You said it then."

"You're right I said it," said the tall waiter. "I know what I'm talking about when I talk about that bird."

"Look what he's done for Villalta," the first waiter said.

"And that ain't all," the tall waiter said. "Look what he's done for Marcial Lalanda. Look what he's done for Nacional."

"You said it, kid," agreed the short waiter.

Manuel looked at them, standing talking in front of his table. He had drunk his second brandy. They had forgotten about him. They were not interested in him.

"Look at that bunch of camels," the tall waiter went on. "Did you ever see this Nacional II?"

"I seen him last Sunday, didn't I?" the original waiter said.

"He's a giraffe," the short waiter said.

"What did I tell you?" the tall waiter said. "Those are Retana's boys."

"Say, give me another shot of that," Manuel said. He had poured the brandy the waiter had slopped over in the saucer into his glass and drank it while they were talking.

The original waiter poured his glass full mechanically, and the three of them went out of the room talking.

In the far corner the man was still asleep, snoring slightly on the intaking breath, his head back against the wall.

Manuel drank his brandy. He felt sleepy himself. It was too hot to go out into the town. Besides there was nothing to do. He wanted to see Zurito. He would go to sleep while he waited. He kicked his suitcase under the table to be sure it was there. Perhaps it would be better to put it back under the seat, against the wall. He leaned down and shoved it under. Then he leaned forward on the table and went to sleep.

When he woke there was someone sitting across the table from him. It was a big man with a heavy brown face like an Indian. He had been sitting there some time. He had waved the waiter away and sat reading the paper and occasionally looking down at Manuel, asleep, his head on the table. He read the paper laboriously, forming the words with his lips as he read. When it tired him he looked at Manuel. He sat heavily in the chair, his black Cordoba hat tipped forward.

Manuel sat up and looked at him.

"Hello, Zurito," he said.

"Hello, kid," the big man said.

"I've been asleep." Manuel rubbed his forehead with the back of his fist.

"I thought maybe you were."

"How's everything?"

"Good. How is everything with you?"

"Not so good."

They were both silent. Zurito, the picador, looked at Manuel's white face. Manuel looked down at the picador's enormous hands folding the paper to put away in his pocket.

"I got a favor to ask you, Manos," Manuel said.

Manosduros was Zurito's nickname. He never heard it without thinking of his huge hands. He put them forward on the table self-consciously.

"Let's have a drink," he said.

"Sure," said Manuel.

The waiter came and went and came again. He went out of the room looking back at the two men at the table.

"What's the matter, Manolo?" Zurito set down his glass.

"Would you pic two bulls for me tomorrow night?" Manuel asked, looking up at Zurito across the table.

"No," said Zurito. "I'm not pic-ing."

Manuel looked down at his glass. He had expected that answer; now he had it. Well, he had it.

"I'm sorry, Manolo, but I'm not pic-ing." Zurito looked at his hands.

"That's all right," Manuel said.

"I'm too old," Zurito said.

"I just asked you," Manuel said.

"Is it the nocturnal tomorrow?"

"That's it. I figured if I had just one good pic, I could get away with it."

"How much are you getting?"

"Three hundred pesetas."

"I get more than that for pic-ing."

"I know," said Manuel. "I didn't have any right to ask you."

"What do you keep on doing it for?" Zurito asked. "Why don't you cut off your coleta, Manolo?"

"I don't know," Manuel said.

"You're pretty near as old as I am," Zurito said.

"I don't know," Manuel said. "I got to do it. If I can fix it so that I get an even break, that's all I want. I got to stick with it, Manos."

"No, you don't."

"Yes, I do. I've tried keeping away from it."

"I know how you feel. But it isn't right. You ought to get out and stay out."

"I can't do it. Besides, I've been going good lately."

Zurito looked at his face.

"You've been in the hospital."

"But I was going great when I got hurt."

Zurito said nothing. He tipped the cognac out of his saucer into his glass.

"The papers said they never saw a better faena," Manuel said.

Zurito looked at him.

"You know when I get going I'm good," Manuel said.

"You're too old," the picador said.

"No," said Manuel. "You're ten years older than I am."

"With me it's different."

"I'm not too old," Manuel said.

They sat silent, Manuel watching the picador's face.

"I was going great till I got hurt," Manuel offered.

"You ought to have seen me, Manos," Manuel said, reproachfully.

"I don't want to see you," Zurito said. "It makes me nervous."

"You haven't seen me lately."

"I've seen you plenty."

Zurito looked at Manuel, avoiding his eyes.

"You ought to quit it, Manolo."

"I can't," Manuel said. "I'm going good now, I tell you."

Zurito leaned forward, his hands on the table.

"Listen. I'll pic for you and if you don't go big tomorrow night, you'll quit. See? Will you do that?"

"Sure."

Zurito leaned back, relieved.

"You got to quit," he said. "No monkey business. You got to cut the coleta."

"I won't have to quit," Manuel said. "You watch me. I've got the stuff."

Zurito stood up. He felt tired from arguing.

"You got to quit," he said. "I'll cut your coleta myself."

"No, you won't," Manuel said. "You won't have a chance."

Zurito called the waiter.

"Come on," said Zurito. "Come on up to the house."

Manuel reached under the seat for his suitcase. He was happy. He knew Zurito would pic for him. He was the best picador living. It was all simple now.

"Come on up to the house and we'll eat," Zurito said.

Manuel stood in the patio de caballos waiting for the Charlie Chaplins to be over. Zurito stood beside him. Where they stood it was dark. The high door that led into the bull ring was shut. Above them they heard a shout, then another shout of laughter. Then there was silence. Manuel liked the smell of the stables about the patio de caballos. It smelled good in the dark. There was another roar from the arena and then applause, prolonged applause, going on and on.

"You ever seen these fellows?" Zurito asked, big and looming beside Manuel in the dark.

"No," Manuel said.

"They're pretty funny," Zurito said. He smiled to himself in the dark.

The high, double, tight-fitting door into the bull ring swung open and Manuel saw the ring in the hard light of the arc lights, the plaza, dark all the way around, rising high; around the edge of the ring were running and bowing two men dressed like tramps, followed by a third in the uniform of a hotel bellboy who stooped and picked up the hats and canes thrown down onto the sand and tossed them back up into the darkness.

The electric light went on in the patio.

"I'll climb onto one of those ponies while you collect the kids," Zurito said.

Behind them came the jingle of the mules, coming out to go into the arena and be hitched onto the dead bull.

The members of the cuadrilla, who had been watching the burlesque from the runway between the barrera and the seats, came walking back and stood in a group talking, under the electric light in the patio. A good-looking lad in a silver-and-orange suit came up to Manuel and smiled.

"I'm Hernandez," he said and put out his hand.

Manuel shook it.

"They're regular elephants we've got tonight," the boy said cheerfully.

"They're big ones with horns," Manuel agreed.

"You drew the worst lot," the boy said.

"That's all right," Manuel said. "The bigger they are, the more meat for the poor."

"Where did you get that one?" Hernandez grinned.

"That's an old one," Manuel said. "You line up your cuadrilla, so I can see what I've got."

"You've got some good kids," Hernandez said. He was very cheerful. He had been on twice before in nocturnals and was beginning to get a following in Madrid. He was happy the fight would start in a few minutes.

"Where are the pics?" Manuel asked.

"They're back in the corrals fighting about who gets the beautiful horses," Hernandez grinned.

The mules came through the gate in a rush, the whips snapping, bells jangling and the young bull ploughing a furrow of sand.

They formed up for the paseo as soon as the bull had gone through. Manuel and Hernandez stood in front. The youths of the cuadrillas were behind, their heavy capes furled over their arms. In back, the four picadors, mounted, holding their steel-tipped push-poles erect in the half-dark of the corral.

"It's a wonder Retana wouldn't give us enough light to see the horses by," one picador said.

"He knows we'll be happier if we don't get too good a look at these skins," another pic answered.

"This thing I'm on barely keeps me off the ground," the first picador said.

"Well, they're horses."

"Sure, they're horses."

They talked, sitting their gaunt horses in the dark.

Zurito said nothing. He had the only steady horse of the lot. He had tried him, wheeling him in the corrals and he responded to the bit and the spurs. He had taken the bandage off his right eye and cut the strings where they had tied his ears tight shut at the base. He was a good, solid horse, solid on his legs. That was all he needed. He intended to ride him all through the corrida. He had already, since he had mounted, sitting in the half-dark in the big, quilted saddle, waiting for the paseo, pic-ed through the whole corrida in his mind. The other picadors went on talking on both sides of him. He did not hear them.

The two matadors stood together in front of their three peones, their capes furled over their left arms in the same fashion. Manuel was thinking about the three lads in back of him. They were all three Madrileños, like Hernandez, boys about nineteen. One of them, a gypsy, serious, aloof, and dark-faced, he liked the look of. He turned.

"What's your name, kid?" he asked the gypsy.

"Fuentes," the gypsy said.

"That's a good name," Manuel said.

The gypsy smiled, showing his teeth.

"You take the bull and give him a little run when he comes out," Manuel said.

"All right," the gypsy said. His face was serious. He began to think about just what he would do.

"Here she goes," Manuel said to Hernandez.

"All right. We'll go."

Heads up, swinging with the music, their right arms swinging free, they stepped out, crossing the sanded arena under the arc lights, the cuadrillas opening out behind, the picadors riding after; behind came the bull-ring servants and the jingling mules. The crowd applauded Hernandez as they marched across the arena. Arrogant, swinging, they looked straight ahead as they marched.

They bowed before the president, and the procession broke up into its component parts. The bullfighters went over to the barrera and changed their heavy mantles for the light fighting capes. The mules went out. The picadors galloped jerkily around the ring, and two rode out the gate they had come in by. The servants swept the sand smooth.

Manuel drank a glass of water poured for him by one of Retana's deputies, who was acting as his manager and sword-handler. Hernandez came over from speaking with his own manager.

"You got a good hand, kid," Manuel complimented him.

"They like me," Hernandez said happily.

"How did the paseo go?" Manuel asked Retana's man.

"Like a wedding," said the handler. "Fine. You came out like Joselito and Belmonte."

Zurito rode by, a bulky equestrian statue. He wheeled his horse and faced him toward the toril on the far side of the ring where the bull would come out. It was strange under the arc light. He pic-ed in the hot afternoon sun for big money. He didn't like this arc-light business. He wished they would get started.

Manuel went up to him.

"Pic him, Manos," he said. "Cut him down to size for me."

"I'll pic him, kid." Zurito spat on the sand. "I'll make him jump out of the ring."

"Lean on him, Manos," Manuel said.

"I'll lean on him," Zurito said. "What's holding it up?"

"He's coming now," Manuel said.

Zurito sat there, his feet in the box-stirrups, his great legs in the buckskin-covered armor gripping the horse, the reins in his left hand, the long pic held in his right hand, his broad hat well down over his eyes to shade them from the lights, watching the distant door of the toril. His horse's ears quivered. Zurito patted him with his left hand.

The red door of the toril swung back and for a moment Zurito looked into the empty passageway far across the arena. Then the bull came out in a rush, skidding on his four legs as he came out under the lights, then charging in a gallop, moving softly in a fast gallop, silent except as he woofed through wide nostrils as he charged, glad to be free after the dark pen.

In the first row of seats, slightly bored, leaning forward to write on the cement wall in front of his knees, the substitute bullfight critic of *El Heraldo* scribbled: "Campagnero, Negro, 42, came out at 90 miles an hour with plenty of gas—"

Manuel, leaning against the barrera, watching the bull, waved his hand and the gypsy ran out, trailing his cape. The bull, in full gallop, pivoted and charged the cape, his head down, his tail rising. The gypsy moved in a zigzag, and as he passed, the bull caught sight of him and abandoned the cape to charge the man. The gyp sprinted and vaulted the red fence of the barrera as the bull struck it with his horns. He tossed into it twice with his horns, banging into the wood blindly.

The critic of *El Heraldo* lit a cigarette and tossed the match at the bull, then wrote in his notebook, "large and with enough horns to satisfy the cash customers, Campagnero showed a tendency to cut into the terrain of the bullfighters."

Manuel stepped out on the hard sand as the bull banged into the fence. Out of the corner of his eye he saw Zurito sitting the white horse close to the barrera, about a quarter of the way around the ring to the left. Manuel held the cape close in front of him, a fold in each hand, and shouted at the bull, "Huh! Huh!" The bull turned, seemed to brace against the fence as he charged in a scramble, driving into the cape as Manuel sidestepped, pivoted on his heels with the charge of the bull, and swung the cape just ahead of the horns. At the end of the swing he was facing the bull again and held the cape in the same position close in front of his body, and pivoted again as the bull recharged. Each time, as he swung, the crowd shouted.

Four times he swung with the bull, lifting the cape so it billowed full, and each time bringing the bull around to charge again. Then, at the end of the fifth swing, he held the cape against his hip and pivoted, so the cape swung out like a ballet dancer's skirt and wound the bull around himself like a belt, to step clear, leaving the bull facing Zurito on the white horse, come up and planted firm, the horse facing the bull, its ears forward, its lips nervous, Zurito, his hat over his eyes, leaning forward, the long pole sticking out before and behind in a sharp angle under his right arm, held halfway down, the triangular iron point facing the bull.

El Heraldo's second-string critic, drawing on his cigarette, his eyes on the bull, wrote: "The veteran Manolo designed a series of acceptable veronicas, ending in a very Belmontistic recorte that earned applause from the regulars, and we entered the tercio of the cavalry."

Zurito sat his horse, measuring the distance between the bull and the end of the pic. As he looked, the bull gathered himself together and charged, his eyes on the horse's chest. As he lowered his head to hook, Zurito sunk the point of the pic in the swelling hump of muscle above the bull's shoulder, leaned all his weight on the shaft, and with his left hand pulled the white horse into the air, front hoofs pawing, and swung him to the right as he pushed the bull under and through so the horns passed safely under the horse's belly and the horse came down, quivering, the bull's tail brushing his chest as he charged the cape Hernandez offered him.

Hernandez ran sideways, taking the bull out and away with the cape, toward the other picador. He fixed him with a swing of the cape, squarely facing the horse and rider, and stepped back. As the bull saw the horse he charged. The picador's lance slid along his back, and as the shock of the charge lifted the horse, the picador was already halfway out of the saddle, lifting his right leg clear as he missed with the lance and falling to the left side to keep the horse between him and the bull. The horse, lifted and gored, crashed over with the bull driving into him, the picador gave a shove with his boots against the horse and lay clear, waiting to be lifted and hauled away and put on his feet.

Manuel let the bull drive into the fallen horse; he was in no hurry, the picador was safe; besides, it did a picador like that good to worry. He'd stay on longer next time. Lousy pics! He looked across the sand at Zurito a little way out from the barrera, his horse rigid, waiting.

"Huh!" he called to the bull, "Tomar!" holding the cape in both hands so it would catch his eye. The bull detached himself from the horse and charged the cape, and Manuel, running sideways and holding the cape spread wide, stopped, swung on his heels, and brought the bull sharply around facing Zurito.

"Campagnero accepted a pair of varas for the death of one rosinante, with Hernandez and Manolo at the quites," *El Heraldo's* critic wrote. "He pressed on the iron and clearly showed he was no horse-lover. The veteran Zurito resurrected some of his old stuff with the pike-pole, notably the suerte—"

"Olé! Olé!" the man sitting beside him shouted. The shout was lost in the roar of the crowd, and he slapped the critic on the back. The critic looked up to see Zurito, directly below him, leaning far out over his horse, the length of the pic rising in a sharp angle under his armpit, holding the pic almost by the point, bearing down with all his weight, holding the bull off, the bull pushing and driving to get at the horse, and Zurito, far out, on top of him, holding him, holding him, and slowly pivoting the horse against the pressure, so that at last he was clear. Zurito felt the moment when the horse was clear and the bull could come past, and relaxed the absolute steel lock of his resistance, and the triangular steel point of the pic ripped in the bull's hump of shoulder muscle as he tore loose to find Hernandez's cape before his muzzle. He charged blindly into the cape and the boy took him out into the open arena.

Zurito sat patting his horse and looking at the bull charging the cape that Hernandez swung for him out under the bright light while the crowd shouted.

"You see that one?" he said to Manuel.

"It was a wonder," Manuel said.

"I got him that time," Zurito said. "Look at him now."

At the conclusion of a closely turned pass of the cape the bull slid to his knees. He was up at once, but far out across the sand Manuel and Zurito saw the shine of the pumping flow of blood, smooth against the black of the bull's shoulder.

"I got him that time," Zurito said.

"He's a good bull," Manuel said.

"If they gave me another shot at him, I'd kill him," Zurito said.

"They'll change the thirds on us," Manuel said.

"Look at him now," Zurito said.

"I got to go over there," Manuel said, and started on a run for the other side of the ring, where the monos were leading a horse out by the bridle toward the bull, whacking him on the legs with rods and all, in a procession, trying to get him toward the bull, who stood, dropping his head, pawing, unable to make up his mind to charge.

Zurito, sitting his horse, walking him toward the scene, not missing any detail, scowled.

Finally the bull charged, the horse leaders ran for the barrera, the picador hit too far back, and the bull got under the horse, lifted him, threw him onto his back.

Zurito watched. The monos, in their red shirts, running out to drag the picador clear. The picador, now on his feet, swearing and flopping his arms. Manuel and Hernandez standing ready with their capes. And the bull, the great, black bull, with a horse on his back, hooves dangling, the bridle caught in the horns. Black bull with a horse on his back, staggering short-legged, then arching his neck and lifting, thrusting, charging to slide the horse off, horse sliding down. Then the bull into a lunging charge at the cape Manuel spread for him.

The bull was slower now, Manuel felt. He was bleeding badly. There was a sheen of blood all down his flank.

Manuel offered him the cape again. There he came, eyes open, ugly, watching the cape. Manuel stepped to the side and raised his arms, tightening the cape ahead of the bull for the veronica.

Now he was facing the bull. Yes, his head was going down a little. He was carrying it lower. That was Zurito.

Manuel flopped the cape; there he comes; he side-stepped and swung in another veronica. He's shooting awfully accurately, he thought. He's had enough fight, so he's watching now. He's hunting now. Got his eye on me. But I always give him the cape.

He shook the cape at the bull; there he comes; he side-stepped. Awful close that time. I don't want to work that close to him.

The edge of the cape was wet with blood where it had swept along the bull's back as he went by.

All right, here's the last one.

Manuel, facing the bull, having turned with him each charge, offered the cape with his two hands. The bull looked at him. Eyes watching, horns straight forward, the bull looked at him, watching.

"Huh!" Manuel said, "Toro!" and leaning back, swung the cape forward. Here he comes. He side-stepped, swung the cape in back of him, and pivoted, so the bull followed a swirl of cape and then was left with nothing, fixed by the pass, dominated by the cape. Manuel swung the cape under his muzzle with one hand, to show the bull was fixed, and walked away.

There was no applause.

Manuel walked across the sand toward the barrera, while Zurito rode out of the ring. The trumpet had blown to change the act to the planting of the banderillos while Manuel had been working with the bull. He had not consciously noticed it. The monos were spreading canvas over the two dead horses and sprinkling sawdust around them.

Manuel came up to the barrera for a drink of water. Retana's man handed him the heavy porous jug.

Fuentes, the tall gypsy, was standing holding a pair of banderillos, holding them together, slim, red sticks, fish-hook points out. He looked at Manuel.

"Go on out there," Manuel said.

The gypsy trotted out. Manuel set down the jug and watched. He wiped his face with his handkerchief.

The critic of *El Heraldo* reached for the bottle of warm champagne that stood between his feet, took a drink, and finished his paragraph.

"—the aged Manolo rated no applause for a vulgar series of lances with the cape and we entered the third of the palings."

Alone in the center of the ring the bull stood, still fixed. Fuentes, tall, flat-backed, walking toward him arrogantly, his arms spread out, the two slim, red sticks, one in each hand, held by the fingers, points straight forward. Fuentes walked forward. Back of him and to one side was a peon with a cape. The bull looked at him and was no longer fixed.

His eyes watched Fuentes, now standing still. Now he leaned back, calling to him. Fuentes twitched the two banderillos and the light on the steel points caught the bull's eye.

His tail went up and he charged.

He came straight, his eyes on the man. Fuentes stood still, leaning back, the banderillos pointing forward. As the bull lowered his head to hook, Fuentes leaned backward, his arms came together and rose, his two hands touching, the banderillos two descending red lines, and leaning forward drove the points into the bull's shoulder, leaning far in over the bull's horns and pivoting on the two upright sticks, his legs tight together, his body curving to one side to let the bull pass.

"Olé!" from the crowd.

The bull was hooking wildly, jumping like a trout, all four feet off the ground. The red shafts of the banderillos tossed as he jumped.

Manuel, standing at the barrera, noticed that he looked always to the right.

"Tell him to drop the next pair on the right," he said to the kid who started to run out to Fuentes with the new banderillos.

A heavy hand fell on his shoulder. It was Zurito.

"How do you feel, kid?" he asked.

Manuel was watching the bull.

Zurito leaned forward on the barrera, leaning the weight of his body on his arms. Manuel turned to him.

"You're going good," Zurito said.

Manuel shook his head. He had nothing to do now until the next third. The gypsy was very good with the banderillos. The bull would come to him in the next third in good shape. He was a good bull. It had all been easy up to now. The final stuff with the sword was all he worried over. He did not really worry. He did not even think about it. But standing there he had a heavy sense of apprehension. He looked out at the bull, planning his faena, his work with the red cloth that was to reduce the bull, to make him manageable.

The gypsy was walking out toward the bull again, walking heel-and-toe, insultingly, like a ball-room dancer, the red shafts of the banderillos twitching with his walk. The bull watched him, not fixed now, hunting him, but waiting to get close enough so he could be sure of getting him, getting the horns into him.

As Fuentes walked forward the bull charged. Fuentes ran across the quarter of a circle as the bull charged and, as he passed running

backward, stopped, swung forward, rose on his toes, arm straight out, and sunk the banderillos straight down into the tight of the big shoulder muscles as the bull missed him.

The crowd were wild about it.

"That kid won't stay in this night stuff long," Retana's man said to Zurito.

"He's good," Zurito said.

"Watch him now."

They watched.

Fuentes was standing with his back against the barrera. Two of the cuadrilla were back of him, with their capes ready to flop over the fence to distract the bull.

The bull, with his tongue out, his barrel heaving, was watching the gypsy. He thought he had him now. Back against the red planks. Only a short charge away. The bull watched him.

The gypsy bent back, drew back his arms, the banderillos pointing at the bull. He called to the bull, stamped one foot. The bull was suspicious. He wanted the man. No more barbs in the shoulder.

Fuentes walked a little closer to the bull. Bent back. Called again. Somebody in the crowd shouted a warning.

"He's too close," Zurito said.

"Watch him," Retana's man said.

Leaning back, inciting the bull with the banderillos, Fuentes jumped, both feet off the ground. As he jumped the bull's tail rose and he charged. Fuentes came down on his toes, arms straight out, whole body arching forward, and drove the shafts straight down as he swung his body clear of the right horn.

The bull crashed into the barrera where the flopping capes had attracted his eye as he lost the man.

The gypsy came running along the barrera toward Manuel, taking the applause of the crowd. His vest was ripped where he had not quite cleared the point of the horn. He was happy about it, showing it to the spectators. He made the tour of the ring. Zurito saw him go by, smiling, pointing at his vest. He smiled.

Somebody else was planting the last pair of banderillos. Nobody was paying any attention.

Retana's man tucked a baton inside the red cloth of a muleta, folded the cloth over it, and handed it over the barrera to Manuel. He reached in the leather sword-case, took out a sword, and holding it by its leather scabbard, reached it over the fence to Manuel. Manuel pulled the blade out by the red hilt and the scabbard fell limp.

He looked at Zurito. The big man saw he was sweating.

"Now you get him, kid," Zurito said.

Manuel nodded.

"He's in good shape," Zurito said.

"Just like you want him," Retana's man assured him.

Manuel nodded.

The trumpeter, up under the roof, blew for the final act, and Manuel walked across the arena toward where, up in the dark boxes, the president must be.

In the front row of seats the substitute bullfight critic of *El Heraldo* took a long drink of the warm champagne. He had decided it was not worth while to write a running story and would write up the corrida back in the office. What was it anyway? Only a nocturnal. If he missed anything he would get it out of the morning papers. He took another drink of the champagne. He had a date at Maxim's at twelve. Who were these bullfighters anyway? Kids and bums. A bunch of bums. He put his pad of paper in his pocket and looked over toward Manuel, standing very much alone in the ring, gesturing with his hat in a salute toward a box he could not see high up in the dark plaza. Out in the ring the bull stood quiet, looking at nothing.

"I dedicate this bull to you, Mr. President, and to the public of Madrid, the most intelligent and generous of the world," was what Manuel was saying. It was a formula. He said it all. It was a little long for nocturnal use.

He bowed at the dark, straightened, tossed his hat over his shoulder, and, carrying the muleta in his left hand and the sword in his right, walked out toward the bull.

Manuel walked toward the bull. The bull looked at him; his eyes were quick. Manuel noticed the way the banderillos hung down on his left shoulder and the steady sheen of blood from Zurito's pic-ing. He noticed the way the bull's feet were. As he walked forward, holding the muleta in his left hand and the sword in his right, he watched the bull's feet. The bull could not charge without gathering his feet together. Now he stood square on them, dully.

Manuel walked toward him, watching his feet. This was all right. He could do this. He must work to get the bull's head down, so he could go in past the horns and kill him. He did not think about the sword, not about killing the bull. He thought about one thing at a time. The coming things oppressed him, though. Walking forward, watching the bull's feet, he saw successively his eyes, his wet muzzle, and the wide, forward-pointing spread of his horns. The bull had light circles about his eyes. His eyes watched Manuel. He felt he was going to get this little one with the white face.

Standing still now and spreading the red cloth of the muleta with the sword, pricking the point into the cloth so that the sword, now held in his left hand, spread the red flannel like the jib of a boat, Manuel noticed the points of the bull's horns. One of them was splintered from banging against the barrera. The other was sharp as a porcupine quill. Manuel noticed while spreading the muleta that the white base of the horn was stained red. While he noticed these things he did not lose sight of the bull's feet. The bull watched Manuel steadily.

He's on the defensive now. Ma-

nuel thought. He's reserving himself. I've got to bring him out of that and get his head down. Always get his head down. Zurito had his head down once, but he's come back. He'll bleed when I start him going and that will bring it down.

Holding the muleta, with the sword in his left hand widening it in front of him, he called to the bull.

The bull looked at him.

He leaned back insultingly and shook the widespread flannel.

The bull saw the muleta. It was a bright scarlet under the arc light. The bull's legs tightened.

Here he comes. Whoosh! Manuel turned as the bull came and raised the muleta so that it passed over the bull's horns and swept down his broad back from head to tail. The bull had gone clean up in the air with the charge. Manuel had not moved.

At the end of the pass the bull turned like a cat coming around a corner and faced Manuel.

He was on the offensive again. His heaviness was gone. Manuel noted the fresh blood shining down the black shoulder and dripping down the bull's leg. He drew the sword out of the muleta and held it in his right hand. The muleta held low down in his left hand, leaning toward the left, he called to the bull. The bull's legs tightened, his eyes on the muleta. Here he comes, Manuel thought. Yuh!

He swung with the charge, sweeping the muleta ahead of the bull, his feet firm, the sword following the curve, a point of light under the arcs.

The bull recharged as the pase natural finished and Manuel raised the muleta for a pase de pecho. Firmly planted, the bull came by his chest under the raised muleta. Manuel leaned his head back to avoid the clattering banderillo shafts. The hot, black bull body touched his chest as it passed.

Too close, Manuel thought. Zurito, leaning on the barrera, spoke rapidly to the gypsy, who trotted out toward Manuel with a cape. Zurito pulled his hat down low and looked out across the arena at Manuel.

Manuel was facing the bull again, the muleta held low and to the left. The bull's head was down as he watched the muleta.

"If it was Belmonte doing that stuff, they'd go crazy," Retana's man said.

Zurito said nothing. He was watching Manuel out in the center of the arena.

"Where did the boss dig this fellow up?" Retana's man asked.

"Out of the hospital," Zurito said.

"That's where he's going damn quick," Retana's man said.

Zurito turned on him.

"Knock on that," he said, pointing to the barrera.

"I was just kidding, man," Retana's man said.

"Knock on the wood."

Retana's man leaned forward and knocked three times on the barrera.

"Watch the faena," Zurito said.

Out in the center of the ring, under the lights, Manuel was kneeling, facing the bull, and as he raised the muleta in both hands the bull charged, tail up.

Manuel swung his body clear and, as the bull recharged, brought around the muleta in a half-circle that pulled the bull to his knees.

"Why, that one's a great bullfighter," Retana's man said.

"No, he's not," said Zurito.

Manuel stood up and, the muleta in his left hand, the sword in his right, acknowledged the applause from the dark plaza.

The bull had humped himself up from his knees and stood waiting, his head hung low.

Zurito spoke to two of the other lads of the cuadrilla and they ran out to stand back of Manuel with their capes. There were four men back of him now. Hernandez had followed him since he first came out with the muleta. Fuentes stood watching, his cape held against his body, tall, in repose, watching lazy-eyed. Now the two came up. Hernandez motioned them to stand one at each side. Manuel stood alone, facing the bull.

Manuel waved back the men with the capes. Stepping back cautiously, they saw his face was white and sweating.

Didn't they know enough to keep back? Did they want to catch the bull's eye with the capes after he was fixed and ready? He had enough to worry about without that kind of thing.

The bull was standing, his four feet square, looking at the muleta. Manuel furled the muleta in his left hand. The bull's eyes watched it. His body was heavy on his feet. He carried his head low, but not too low.

Manuel lifted the muleta at him. The bull did not move. Only his eyes watched.

He's all lead, Manuel thought. He's all square. He's framed right. He'll take it.

He thought in bullfight terms. Sometimes he had a thought and the particular piece of slang would not come into his mind and he could not realize the thought. His instincts and his knowledge worked automatically, and his brain worked slowly and in words. He knew all about bulls. He did not have to think about them. He just did the right thing. His eyes noted things and his body performed the necessary measures without thought. If he thought about it, he would be gone.

Now, facing the bull, he was conscious of many things at the same time. There were the horns, the one splintered, the other smoothly sharp, the need to profile himself toward the left horn, lance himself short and straight, lower the muleta so the bull would follow it, and, going in over the horns, put the sword all the way into a little spot about as big as a five-peseta piece straight in back of the neck, between the sharp pitch of the bull's shoulders. He must do all this and must then come out from between the horns. He was conscious he must do all this, but his only thought was in words: "Corto y derecho."

"Corto y derecho," he thought, furling the muleta. Short and straight. Corto y derecho, he drew the sword out of the muleta, profiled on the splintered left horn, dropped the muleta across his body, so his right hand with the sword on the level with his eye made the sign of the cross, and, rising on his toes, sighted along the dipping blade of the sword at the spot high up between the bull's shoulders.

Corto y derecho he launched himself on the bull.

There was a shock, and he felt himself go up in the air. He pushed on the sword as he went up and over, and it flew out of his hand. He hit the ground and the bull was on him. Manuel, lying on the ground, kicked at the bull's muzzle with his slippered feet. Kicking, kicking, the bull after him, missing him in his excitement, bumping him with his head, driving the horns into the sand. Kicking like a man keeping a ball in the air, Manuel kept the bull from getting a clean thrust at him.

Manuel felt the wind on his back from the capes flopping at the bull, and then the bull was gone, gone over him in a rush. Dark, as his belly went over. Not even stepped on.

Manuel stood up and picked up the muleta. Fuentes handed him the sword. It was bent where it had struck the shoulder blade. Manuel straightened it on his knee and ran toward the bull, standing now beside one of the dead horses. As he ran, his jacket flopped where it had been ripped under his armpit.

"Get him out of there," Manuel shouted to the gypsy. The bull had smelled the blood of the dead horse and ripped into the canvas-cover with his horns. He charged Fuentes' cape, with the canvas hanging from his splintered horn, and the crowd laughed. Out in the ring, he tossed his head to rid himself of the canvas. Hernandez, running up from behind him, grabbed the end of the canvas and neatly lifted it off the horn.

The bull followed it in a half-charge and stopped still. He was on the defensive again. Manuel was walking toward him with the sword and muleta. Manuel swung the muleta before him. The bull would not charge.

Manuel profiled toward the bull, sighting along the dipping blade of the sword. The bull was motionless, seemingly dead on his feet, incapable of another charge.

Manuel rose to his toes, sighting along the steel, and charged.

Again there was the shock and he felt himself being borne back in a rush, to strike hard on the sand. There was no chance of kicking this time. The bull was on top of him. Manuel lay as though dead, his head on his arms, and the bull bumped him. Bumped his back, bumped his face in the sand. He felt the horn go into the sand between his folded arms. The bull hit him in the small of the back. His face drove into the sand. The horn drove through one of his sleeves and the bull ripped it off. Manuel was tossed clear and the bull followed the capes.

Manuel got up, found the sword and muleta, tried the point of the sword with his thumb, and then ran toward the barrera for a new sword. Retana's man handed him the sword over the edge of the barrera.

"Wipe off your face," he said.

Manuel, running again toward the bull, wiped his bloody face with his handkerchief. He had not seen Zurito. Where was Zurito?

The cuadrilla had stepped away from the bull and waited with their capes. The bull stood, heavy and dull again after the action.

Manuel walked toward him with the muleta. He stopped and shook it. The bull did not respond. He passed it right and left, left and right before the bull's muzzle. The bull's eyes watched it and turned with the swing, but he would not charge. He was waiting for Manuel.

Manuel was worried. There was nothing to do but go in. Corto y derecho. He profiled close to the bull, crossed the muleta in front of his body, and charged. As he pushed in the sword, he jerked his body to the left to clear the horn. The bull passed him and the sword shot up in the air, twinkling under the arc lights, to fall red-hilted on the sand.

Manuel ran over and picked it up. It was bent and he straightened it over his knee.

As he came running toward the bull, fixed again now, he passed Hernandez standing with his cape

"He's all bone," the boy said encouragingly.

Manuel nodded, wiping his face. He put the bloody handkerchief in his pocket.

There was the bull. He was close to the barrera now. Damn him. Maybe he was all bone. Maybe there was not any place for the sword to go in. . . . He'd show them.

He tried a pass with the muleta and the bull did not move. Manuel chopped the muleta back and forth in front of the bull. Nothing doing.

He furled the muleta, drew the sword out, profiled, and drove in on the bull. He felt the sword buckle as he shoved it in, leaning his weight on it, and then it shot high in the air, end-over-ending into the crowd. Manuel had jerked clear as the sword jumped.

The first cushions thrown down out of the dark missed him. Then one hit him in the face, his bloody face looking toward the crowd. They were coming down fast. Spotting the sand. Somebody threw an empty champagne bottle from close range. It hit Manuel on the foot. He stood there watching the dark, where the things were coming from. Then something whished through the air and struck by him. Manuel leaned over and picked it

up. It was his sword. He straightened it over his knee and gestured with it to the crowd.

"Thank you," he said. "Thank you."

Oh, the dirty dogs! Dirty dogs! Oh, the lousy, dirty dogs! He kicked into a cushion as he ran.

There was the bull. The same as ever. All right, you dirty, lousy brute!

Manuel passed the muleta in front of the bull's black muzzle.

Nothing doing.

You won't! All right. He stepped close and jammed the sharp peak of the muleta into the bull's damp muzzle.

The bull was on him as he jumped back and as he tripped on a cushion he felt the horn go into him, into his side. He grabbed the horn with his two hands and rode backward, holding tight onto the place. The bull tossed him and he was clear. He lay still. It was all right. The bull was gone.

He got up coughing and feeling broken and gone. The dirty dogs!

"Give me the sword," he shouted. "Give me the stuff."

Fuentes came up with the muleta and the sword.

Hernandez put his arm around him.

"Go on to the infirmary, man," he said. "Don't be a fool."

"Get away from me," Manuel said. "Get away from me."

He twisted free. Hernandez shrugged his shoulders. Manuel ran toward the bull.

There was the bull standing, heavy, firmly planted.

All right, you brute! Manuel drew the sword out of the muleta, sighted with the same movement, and flung himself onto the bull. He felt the sword go in all the way. Right up to the guard. Four fingers and his thumb into the bull. The blood was hot on his knuckles, and he was on top of the bull.

The bull lurched with him as he lay on, and seemed to sink; then he was standing clear. He looked at the bull going down slowly over on his side, then suddenly four feet in the air.

Then he gestured at the crowd, his hand warm from the bull blood.

All right, you dogs! He wanted to say something, but he started to cough. It was hot and choking. He looked down for the muleta. He must go over and salute the president. . . . He was sitting down looking at something. It was the bull. His four feet up. Thick tongue out. Things crawling around on his belly and under his legs. Crawling where the hair was thin. . . . He started to get to his feet and commenced to cough. He sat down again, coughing. Somebody came and pushed him up.

They carried him across the ring to the infirmary, running with him across the sand, standing blocked at the gate as the mules came in, then around under the dark passageway, men grunting as they took him up the stairway, and then laid him down.

The doctor and two men in white were waiting for him. They laid him out on the table. They were cutting away his shirt. Manuel felt tired. His whole chest felt scalding inside. He started to cough and they held something to his mouth. Everybody was very busy.

There was an electric light in his eyes. He shut his eyes.

He heard someone coming very heavily up the stairs. Then he did not hear it. Then he heard a noise far off. That was the crowd. Well, somebody would have to kill his other bull. They had cut away all his shirt. The doctor smiled at him. There was Retana.

"Hello, Retana!" Manuel said. He could not hear his voice.

Retana smiled at him and said something. Manuel could not hear it.

Zurito stood beside the table, bending over where the doctor was working. He was in his picador clothes, without his hat.

Zurito said something to him. Manuel could not hear it.

Zurito was speaking to Retana. One of the men in white smiled and handed Retana a pair of scissors. Retana gave them to Zurito. Zurito said something to Manuel. He could not hear it.

To hell with this operating table. He'd been on plenty of operating tables before. He was not going to die. There would be a priest if he was going to die.

Zurito was saying something to him. Holding up the scissors.

That was it. They were going to cut off his coleta. They were going to cut off his pigtail.

Manuel sat up on the operating table. The doctor stepped back, angry. Someone grabbed him and held him.

"You couldn't do a thing like that, Manos," he said.

He heard suddenly, clearly, Zurito's voice.

"That's all right," Zurito said. "I won't do it. I was joking."

"I was going good," Manuel said. "I didn't have any luck. That was all."

Manuel lay back. They had put something over his face. It was all familiar. He inhaled deeply. He felt very tired. He was very, very tired. They took the thing away from his face.

"I was going good," Manuel said weakly. "I was going great."

Retana looked at Zurito and started for the door.

"I'll stay here with him," Zurito said.

Retana shrugged his shoulders.

Manuel opened his eyes and looked at Zurito.

"Wasn't I going good, Manos?" he asked, for confirmation.

"Sure," said Zurito. "You were going great."

The doctor's assistant put the cone over Manuel's face and he inhaled deeply. Zurito stood awkwardly, watching.

Invictus

WILLIAM ERNEST HENLEY

Out of the night that covers me,
Black as the Pit from pole to pole,
I thank whatever gods may be
For my unconquerable soul.

In the fell clutch of circumstance
I have not winced nor cried aloud.
Under the bludgeonings of chance
My head is bloody but unbowed.

Beyond this place of wrath and tears
  Looms but the Horror of the shade,
And yet the menace of the years
  Finds and shall find me, unafraid.

It matters not how strait the gate,
  How charged with punishments the scroll,
I am the master of my fate:
  I am the captain of my soul.

GUY DE MAUPASSANT

Translated by Ernest Boyd

The Necklace

SHE WAS ONE of those pretty and charming girls born, as though fate had blundered over her, into a family of artisans. She had no marriage portion, no expectations, no means of getting known, understood, loved, and wedded by a man of wealth and distinction; and she let herself be married off to a little clerk in the Ministry of Education.

Her tastes were simple because she had never been able to afford any other, but she was as unhappy as though she had married beneath her; for women have no caste or class, their beauty, grace, and charm serving them for birth or family. Their natural delicacy, their instinctive elegance, their nimbleness of wit, are their only mark of rank, and put the slum girl on a level with the highest lady in the land.

She suffered endlessly, feeling herself born for every delicacy and luxury. She suffered from the poorness of her house, from its mean walls, worn chairs, and ugly curtains. All these things, of which other women of her class would not even have been aware, tormented and insulted her. The sight of the little Breton girl who came to do the work in her little house aroused heart-broken regrets and hopeless dreams in her mind. She imagined silent antechambers, heavy with Oriental tapestries, lit by torches in lofty bronze sockets, with two tall footmen in knee-breeches sleeping in large arm-chairs, overcome by the heavy warmth of the stove. She imagined vast saloons hung with antique silks, exquisite pieces of furniture supporting priceless ornaments, and small, charming, perfumed rooms, created just for little parties of intimate friends, men who were famous and sought after, whose homage roused every other woman's envious longings.

When she sat down for dinner

92

at the round table covered with a three-days-old cloth, opposite her husband, who took the cover off the soup tureen and exclaimed delightedly: "Aha! Scotch broth! There's nothing better," she imagined delicate meals, gleaming silver, tapestries peopling the walls with folk of a past age and strange birds in faery forest; she imagined delicate food served in marvelous dishes, murmured gallantries, listened to with an inscrutable smile as one trifled with the rosy flesh of trout or wings of roast chicken.

She had no clothes, no jewels, nothing. And these were the only things she loved; she felt that she was made for them. She had longed so eagerly to charm, to be desired, to be wildly attractive and sought after.

She had a rich friend, an old school friend whom she refused to visit, because she suffered so keenly when she returned home. She would weep whole days, with grief, regret, despair, and misery.

One evening her husband came home with an exultant air, holding a large envelope in his hand.

"Here's something for you," he said.

Swiftly she tore the paper and drew out a printed card on which were these words: *The Minister of Education and Madame Ramponneau request the pleasure of the company of Monsieur and Madame Loisel at the Ministry on the evening of Monday, January the 18th.*

Instead of being delighted, as her husband hoped, she flung the invitation petulantly across the table, murmuring:

"What do you want me to do with this?"

"Why, darling, I thought you'd be pleased. You never go out, and this is a great occasion. I had tremendous trouble to get it. Everyone wants one; it's very select, and very few go to the clerks. You'll see all the really big people there."

She looked at him out of furious eyes, and said impatiently:

"And what do you suppose I am to wear at such an affair?"

He had not thought about it; he stammered, "Why, the dress you go to the theater in. It looks very nice, to me. . . ."

He stopped, stupefied and utterly at a loss when he saw that his wife was beginning to cry. Two large tears ran slowly down from the corners of her eyes toward the corners of her mouth.

"What's the matter with you? What's the matter with you?" he faltered.

But with a violent effort she overcame her grief and replied in a calm voice, wiping her wet cheeks.

"Nothing. Only I haven't a dress and so I can't go to this party. Give your invitation to some friend of yours whose wife will be turned out better than I shall."

He was heartbroken.

"Look here, Mathilde," he persisted. "What would be the cost of a suitable dress, which you could use on other occasions as well, something very simple?"

She thought for several seconds, reckoning up prices and also wondering for how large a sum she could ask without bringing upon herself an immediate refusal and an exclamation of horror from the careful-minded clerk.

At last she replied with some hesitation: "I don't know exactly, but I think I could do it on four hundred francs."

He grew slightly pale, for this was exactly the amount he had been saving for a gun, intending to get a little shooting next summer on the plain of Nanterre with some friends who went lark-shooting there on Sundays.

Nevertheless he said, "Very well. I'll give you four hundred francs. But try and get a really nice dress with the money."

The day of the party drew near, and Madame Loisel seemed sad, uneasy, and anxious. Her dress was ready, however. One evening her husband said to her, "What's the matter with you? You've been very odd for the last three days."

"I'm utterly miserable at not having any jewels, not a single stone, to wear," she replied. "I shall look absolutely no one. I would almost rather not go to the party."

"Wear flowers," he said. "They're very smart at this time of year. For ten francs you could get two or three gorgeous roses." She was not convinced.

"No . . . there's nothing so hu-

miliating as looking poor in the middle of a lot of rich women."

"How stupid you are!" exclaimed her husband. "Go and see Madame Forestier and ask her to lend you some jewels. You know her quite well enough for that."

She uttered a cry of delight.

"That's true. I never thought of it."

Next day she went to see her friend and told her her trouble.

Madame Forestier went to her dressing table, took up a large box, brought it to Madame Loisel, opened it, and said:

"Choose, my dear."

First she saw some bracelets, then a pearl necklace, then a Venetian cross in gold and gems, of exquisite workmanship. She tried the effect of the jewels before the mirror, hesitating, unable to make up her mind to leave them, to give them up. She kept on asking, "Haven't you anything else?"

"Yes. Look for yourself. I don't know what you would like best."

Suddenly she discovered, in a black satin case, a superb diamond necklace; her heart began to beat covetously. Her hands trembled as she lifted it. She fastened it round her neck, upon her high dress, and remained in ecstasy at sight of herself. Then, with hesitation, she asked in anguish, "Could you lend me this, just this alone?"

"Yes, of course."

She flung herself on her friend's breast, embraced her frenziedly, and went away with her treasure.

The day of the party arrived. Madame Loisel was a success. She was the prettiest woman present, elegant, graceful, smiling, and quite above herself with happiness. All the men stared at her, inquired her name, and asked to be introduced to her. All the under-secretaries of state were eager to waltz with her. The Minister noticed her.

She danced madly, ecstatically, drunk with pleasure, with no thought for anything, in the triumph of her beauty, in the pride of her success, in a cloud of happiness made up of this universal homage and admiration, of the desires she had aroused, of the completeness of a victory so dear to her feminine heart.

She left about four o'clock in the morning. Since midnight her husband had been dozing in a deserted little room, in company with three other men whose wives were having a good time.

He threw over her shoulders the garments he had brought for them to go home in, modest everyday clothes, whose poorness clashed with the beauty of the ball dress. She was conscious of this and was anxious to hurry away, so that she would not be noticed by the other women putting on their costly furs. Loisel restrained her.

"Wait a little. You'll catch cold in the open. I'm going to fetch a cab."

But she did not listen to him and rapidly descended the staircase. When they were out in the street they could not find a cab; they began to look for one, shouting at the drivers whom they saw passing in the distance.

They walked down toward the Seine, desperate and shivering. At last they found on the quay one of those old night-prowling carriages which are only to be seen in Paris after dark, as though they were ashamed of their shabbiness in the daylight.

It brought them to their door in Rue des Martyrs, and sadly they walked up to their own apartment. It was the end, for her. As for him, he was thinking that he must be at the office at ten.

She took off the garments in which she had wrapped her shoulders, so as to set herself in all her glory before the mirror. But suddenly she uttered a cry. The necklace was no longer around her neck!

"What's the matter with you?" asked her husband, already half undressed.

She turned toward him in the utmost distress.

"I . . . I . . . I've no longer got Madame Forestier's necklace. . . ."

He stared with astonishment. "What! . . . Impossible!"

They searched in the folds of her dress, in the folds of the coat, in the pockets, everywhere. They could not find it.

"Are you sure that you still had it on when you came away from the ball?" he asked.

"Yes, I touched it in the hall at the Ministry."

"But if you had lost it in the street, we should have heard it fall."

"Yes. Probably we should. Did you take the number of the cab?"

"No. You didn't notice it, did you?"

"No."

They stared at one another, dumbfounded. At last Loisel put on his clothes again.

"I'll go over all the ground we walked," he said, "and see if I can find it."

And he went out. She remained in her evening clothes, lacking strength to get into bed, huddled on a chair, without volition or power of thought.

Her husband returned about seven. He had found nothing.

He went to the police station, to the newspapers, to offer a reward to the cab companies, everywhere that a ray of hope impelled him.

She waited all day long, in the same state of bewilderment at this fearful catastrophe.

Loisel came home at night, his face lined and pale; he had discovered nothing.

"You must write your friend," he said, "and tell her that you've broken the clasp of her necklace and are getting it mended. That will give us time to look about us."

She wrote at his dictation.

By the end of a week they had lost all hope.

Loisel, who had aged five years, declared:

"We must see about replacing the diamonds."

Next day they took the box which had held the necklace and went to the jeweler whose name was inside. He consulted his books.

"It was not I who sold this necklace, madame; I must have merely supplied the clasp."

Then they went from jeweler to jeweler, searching for another necklace like the first, consulting their memories, both ill with remorse and anguish of mind.

In a shop at the Palais-Royal they found a string of diamonds which seemed to them exactly like the one they were looking for. It was worth forty thousand francs. They were allowed to have it for thirty-six thousand.

They begged the jeweler not to sell it for three days. And they arranged matters on the understanding that it would be taken back for thirty-four thousand francs, if the first one were found before the end of February.

Loisel possessed eighteen thousand francs left to him by his father. He intended to borrow the rest.

He did borrow it, getting a thousand from one man, five hundred from another, five louis here, three louis there. He gave notes of hand, entered into ruinous agreements, did business with usurers and the whole race of money-lenders. He mortgaged the whole remaining years of his existence, risked his signature without even knowing if he could honor it, and, appalled at the agonizing face of the future, at the black misery about to fall upon him, at the prospect of every possible physical privation and mortal torture, he went to get the new necklace and put down upon the jeweler's counter thirty-six thousand francs.

When Madame Loisel took back the necklace to Madame Forestier, the latter said to her in a chilly voice:

"You ought to have brought it back sooner; I might have needed it."

She did not, as her friend had feared, open the case. If she had noticed the substitution, what would she have thought? What would she have said? Would she not have taken her for a thief?

Madame Loisel came to know the ghastly life of abject poverty. Right from the start she played her part heroically. This fearful debt must be paid off. She would pay it. The servant was dismissed. They changed their apartment; they took a garret under the roof.

She came to know the heavy work of the house, the hateful duties of the kitchen. She washed the plates, wearing out her pink nails on the coarse pottery and the bottoms of pans. She washed the dirty linen, the shirts and dish cloths, and hung them out to dry on a string; every morning she took the dustbin down into the street and carried up the water, stopping on each landing to get her breath. And, clad like a poor woman, she went to the fruiterer, to the grocer, to the butcher, a basket on her arm, haggling, insulted, fighting for every wretched centime of her money.

Every month notes had to be paid off, others to be renewed, time to be gained.

Her husband worked in the evenings at putting straight a merchant's accounts, and often at night he did copying at three centimes a page.

And this life lasted ten years.

At the end of ten years everything was paid off, everything, the usurers' charges and the accumulation of superimposed interest.

Madame Loisel looked old now. She had become like all the other strong, hard, coarse women of poor households. Her hair was badly done, her skirts were awry, her hands were red. She spoke in a shrill voice, and the water slopped all over the floor when she scrubbed it. But sometimes, when her husband was at the office, she sat down by the window and thought of that evening long ago, of the ball at which she had been so beautiful and so much admired.

What would have happened if she had never lost those jewels? Who knows? Who knows? How strange life is, how fickle! How little is needed to ruin or to save!

One Sunday, as she had gone for a walk along the Champs Élysées to freshen herself after the labors of the week, she caught sight suddenly of a woman who was taking a child out for a walk. It was Madame Forestier, still young, still beautiful, still attractive.

Madame Loisel was conscious of some emotion. Should she speak to her? Yes, certainly. And now that she had paid, she would tell her all. Why not?

She went up to her. "Good morning, Jeanne."

The other did not recognize her, and was surprised at being thus familiarly addressed by a poor woman. "But . . . madame . . ." she stammered. "I don't know . . . you must be making a mistake."

"No . . . I am Mathilde Loisel."

Her friend uttered a cry. "Oh! . . . my poor Mathilde, how you have changed! . . ."

"Yes, I've had some hard times since I saw you last; and many sorrows . . . and all on your account."

"On my account! . . . How was that?"

"You remember the diamond necklace you lent me for the ball at the Ministry?"

"Yes. Well?"

"Well, I lost it."

"How could you? Why, you brought it back."

"I brought you another one just like it. And for the last ten years we have been paying for it. You realize it wasn't easy for us; we had no money . . . Well, it's paid for at last, and I'm mighty glad."

Madame Forestier had halted. "You say you bought a diamond necklace to replace mine?"

"Yes. You hadn't noticed it? They were very much alike." And she smiled in proud and innocent happiness.

Madame Forestier, deeply moved, took her two hands. "Oh, my poor Mathilde! But mine was imitation. It was worth at the very most only five hundred francs! . . ."

NATHANIEL HAWTHORNE

The Minister's Black Veil

A Parable

THE SEXTON stood in the porch of Milford meetinghouse, pulling busily at the bell rope. The old people of the village came stooping along the street. Children, with bright faces, tripped merrily beside their parents, or mimicked a graver gait, in the conscious dignity of their Sunday clothes. Spruce bachelors looked sidelong at the pretty maidens, and fancied that the Sabbath sunshine made them prettier than on weekdays. When the throng had mostly streamed into the porch, the sexton began to toll the bell, keeping his eye on the Reverend Mr. Hooper's door. The first glimpse of the clergyman's figure was the signal for the bell to cease its summons.

"But what has good Parson Hooper got upon his face?" cried the sexton in astonishment.

All within hearing immediately turned about, and beheld the semblance of Mr. Hooper, pacing slowly his meditative way toward the meetinghouse. With one accord they started, expressing more wonder than if some strange minister were coming to dust the cushions of Mr. Hooper's pulpit.

"Are you sure it is our parson?" inquired Goodman Gray of the sexton.

"Of a certainty it is good Mr. Hooper," replied the sexton. "He was to have exchanged pulpits with Parson Shute, of Westbury; but Parson Shute sent to excuse himself yesterday, being to preach a funeral sermon."

The cause of so much amazement may appear sufficiently slight. Mr. Hooper, a gentlemanly person, of about thirty, though still a bachelor, was dressed with due clerical neatness, as if a careful wife had starched his band, and brushed the weekly dust from his Sunday's garb. There was but one thing remarkable in his appearance. Swathed about his forehead, and hanging down over his face, so low as to be shaken by his breath, Mr. Hooper had on a black veil. On a nearer view it seemed to consist of two folds of crape, which entirely concealed his features, except the mouth and chin, but probably did not intercept his sight, further than to give a darkened aspect to all living and inanimate things. With this gloomy shade before him, good Mr. Hooper walked onward, at a slow and quiet pace, stooping somewhat, and looking on the ground, as is customary with abstracted men, yet nodding kindly to those of his parishioners who still waited on the meetinghouse steps. But so wonder-struck were they that his greeting hardly met with a return.

"I can't really feel as if good Mr. Hooper's face was behind that piece of crape," said the sexton.

"I don't like it," muttered an old woman, as she hobbled into the meetinghouse. "He has changed himself into something awful, only by hiding his face."

"Our parson has gone mad!" cried Goodman Gray, following him across the threshold.

A rumor of some unaccountable phenomenon had preceded Mr. Hooper into the meetinghouse, and set all the congregation astir. Few could refrain from twisting their heads toward the door; many stood upright, and turned directly about; while several little boys clambered upon the seats, and came down again with a terrible racket. There was a general bustle, a rustling of the women's gowns and shuffling of the men's feet, greatly at variance with that hushed repose which should attend the entrance of the minister. But Mr. Hooper appeared not to notice the perturbation of his people. He entered with an almost noiseless step, bent his head mildly to the pews on each side, and bowed as he passed his oldest parishioner, a white-haired great-grandsire, who occupied an armchair in the center of the aisle. It was strange to observe how slowly this venerable man became conscious of something singular in the appearance of his pastor. He seemed not fully to partake of the prevailing wonder, till Mr. Hooper had ascended the stairs, and showed himself in the pulpit, face to face with his congregation, except for the black veil. That mysterious emblem was never once withdrawn. It shook with his measured breath, as he gave out the psalm; it threw its obscurity between him and the holy page, as he read the Scriptures; and while he prayed, the veil lay heavily on his uplifted countenance. Did he seek to hide it from the dread Being whom he was addressing?

Such was the effect of this simple piece of crape, that more than one woman of delicate nerves was forced to leave the meetinghouse. Yet perhaps the pale-faced congregation was almost as fearful a sight to the minister, as his black veil to them.

Mr. Hooper had the reputation of a good preacher, but not an energetic one; he strove to win his people heavenward by mild, persuasive influences, rather than to drive them thither by the thunders of the Word. The sermon which he now delivered was marked by the same characteristics of style and manner as the general series of his pulpit oratory. But there was something, either in the sentiment of the discourse itself, or in the imagination of the auditors, which made it greatly the most powerful effort that they had ever heard from their pastor's lips. It was tinged, rather more darkly than usual, with the gentle gloom of Mr. Hooper's temperament. The subject had reference to secret sin, and those sad mysteries which we hide from our nearest and dearest, and would fain conceal from our own consciousness, even forgetting that the Omniscient can detect them. A subtle power was breathed into his words. Each member of the congregation, the most innocent girl, and the man of hardened breast, felt as if the preacher had crept upon them, behind his awful veil, and discovered their hoarded iniquity of deed or thought. Many spread their clasped hands on their bosoms. There was nothing terrible in what Mr. Hooper said, at least no violence; and yet, with every tremor of his melancholy voice, the hearers quaked. An unsought pathos came hand in hand with awe. So sensible were the audience of some unwonted attribute in their minister, that they longed for a breath of wind to blow aside the veil, almost believing that a stranger's visage would be discovered, though the form, gesture, and voice were those of Mr. Hooper.

At the close of the services, the people hurried out with indecorous confusion, eager to communicate their pent-up amazement, and conscious of lighter spirits the moment they lost sight of the black veil. Some gathered in little circles, huddled closely together, with their mouths all whispering in the center; some went homeward alone, wrapt in silent meditation; some talked loudly, and profaned the Sabbath day with ostentatious laughter. A few shook their sagacious heads, intimating that they could penetrate the mystery; while one or two affirmed that there was no mystery at all, but only that Mr. Hooper's eyes were so weakened by the midnight lamp, as to require a shade. After a brief interval, forth came good Mr. Hooper also, in the rear of his flock. Turning his veiled face from one group to another, he paid due reverence to the hoary heads, saluted the middle-aged with kind dignity as their friend and spiritual guide, greeted the young with mingled authority and love, and laid his hands on the little children's heads to bless them. Such was always his custom on the Sabbath day. Strange and bewildered looks repaid him for his courtesy. None, as on former occasions, aspired to the honor of walking by their pastor's side. Old Squire Saunders, doubtless by an accidental lapse of memory, neglected to invite

Mr. Hooper to his table, where the good clergyman had been wont to bless the food, almost every Sunday since his settlement. He returned, therefore, to the parsonage, and, at the moment of closing the door, was observed to look back upon the people, all of whom had their eyes fixed upon the minister. A sad smile gleamed faintly from beneath the black veil, and flickered about his mouth, glimmering as he disappeared.

"How strange," said a lady, "that a simple black veil, such as any woman might wear on her bonnet, should become such a terrible thing on Mr. Hooper's face!"

"Something must surely be amiss with Mr. Hooper's intellects," observed her husband, the physician of the village. "But the strangest part of the affair is the effect of this vagary, even on a sober-minded man like myself. The black veil, though it covers only our pastor's face, throws its influence over his whole person, and makes him ghostlike from head to foot. Do you not feel it so?"

"Truly do I," replied the lady; "and I would not be alone with him for the world. I wonder he is not afraid to be alone with himself!"

"Men sometimes are so," said her husband.

The afternoon service was attended with similar circumstances. At its conclusion, the bell tolled for the funeral of a young lady. The relatives and friends were assembled in the house, and the more distant acquaintances stood about the door, speaking of the good qualities of the deceased, when their talk was interrupted by the appearance of Mr. Hooper, still covered with his black veil. It was now an appropriate emblem. The clergyman stepped into the room where the corpse was laid, and bent over the coffin, to take a last farewell of his deceased parishioner. As he stooped, the veil hung straight down from his forehead, so that, if her eyelids had not been closed forever, the dead maiden might have seen his face. Could Mr. Hooper be fearful of her glance, that he so hastily caught back the black veil? A person who watched the interview between the dead and the living scrupled not to affirm, that, at the instant when the clergyman's features were disclosed, the corpse had slightly shuddered, rustling the shroud and muslin cap, though the countenance retained the composure of death. A superstitious old woman was the only witness of this prodigy. From the coffin Mr. Hooper passed into the chamber of the mourners, and thence to the head of the staircase, to make the funeral prayer. It was a tender and heart-dissolving prayer, full of sorrow, yet so imbued with celestial hopes, that the music of a heavenly harp, swept by the fingers of the dead, seemed faintly to be heard among the saddest accents of the minister. The people trembled, though they but darkly understood him when he prayed that they, and himself, and all of mortal race, might be read as he trusted this young maiden had been, for the dreadful hour that should snatch the veil from their faces. The bearers went heavily forth, and the mourners followed, saddening all the street, with the dead before them, and Mr. Hooper in his black veil behind.

"Why do you look back?" said one in the procession to his partner.

"I had a fancy," replied she, "that the minister and the maiden's spirit were walking hand in hand."

"And so had I, at the same moment," said the other.

That night, the handsomest couple in Milford village were to be joined in wedlock. Though reckoned a melancholy man, Mr. Hooper had a placid cheerfulness for such occasions, which often excited a sympathetic smile where livelier merriment would have been thrown away. There was no quality of his disposition which made him more beloved than this. The company at the wedding awaited his arrival with impatience, trusting that the strange awe, which had gathered over him throughout the day, would now be dispelled. But such was not the result. When Mr. Hooper came, the first thing that their eyes rested on was the same horrible black veil, which had added deeper gloom to the funeral, and could portend nothing but evil to the wedding. Such was its immediate effect on the guests that a cloud seemed to have rolled duskily

from beneath the black crape and dimmed the light of the candles. The bridal pair stood up before the minister. But the bride's cold fingers quivered in the tremulous hand of the bridegroom, and her deathlike paleness caused a whisper that the maiden who had been buried a few hours before was come from her grave to be married. If ever another wedding were so dismal, it was that famous one where they tolled the wedding knell. After performing the ceremony, Mr. Hooper raised a glass of wine to his lips, wishing happiness to the new-married couple in a strain of mild pleasantry that ought to have brightened the features of the guests, like a cheerful gleam from the hearth. At that instant, catching a glimpse of his figure in the looking glass, the black veil involved his own spirit in the horror with which it overwhelmed all others. His frame shuddered, his lips grew white, he spilt the untasted wine upon the carpet, and rushed forth into the darkness. For the Earth, too, had on her Black Veil.

The next day, the whole village of Milford talked of little else than Parson Hooper's black veil. That, and the mystery concealed behind it, supplied a topic for discussion between acquaintances meeting in the street, and good women gossiping at their open windows. It was the first item of news that the tavern-keeper told to his guests. The children babbled of it on their way to school. One imitative little imp covered his face with an old black handkerchief, thereby so affrighting his playmates that the panic seized himself, and he well-nigh lost his wits by his own waggery.

It was remarkable that of all the busybodies and impertinent people in the parish, not one ventured to put the plain question to Mr. Hooper, wherefore he did this thing. Hitherto, whenever there appeared the slightest call for such interference, he had never lacked advisers, nor shown himself averse to be guided by their judgment. If he erred at all, it was by so painful a degree of self-distrust, that even the mildest censure would lead him to consider an indifferent action as a crime. Yet, though so well acquainted with this amiable weakness, no individual among his parishioners chose to make the black veil a subject of friendly remonstrance. There was a feeling of dread, neither plainly confessed nor carefully concealed, which caused each to shift the responsibility upon another, till at length it was found expedient to send a deputation of the church, in order to deal with Mr. Hooper about the mystery, before it should grow into a scandal. Never did an embassy so ill discharge its duties. The minister received them with friendly courtesy, but remained silent, after they were seated, leaving to his visitors the whole burden of introducing their important business. The topic, it might be supposed, was obvious enough. There was the black veil

swathed round Mr. Hooper's forehead, and concealing every feature above his placid mouth, on which, at times, they could perceive the glimmering of a melancholy smile. But that piece of crape, to their imagination, seemed to hang down before his heart, the symbol of a fearful secret between him and them. Were the veil but cast aside, they might speak freely of it, but not till then. Thus they sat a considerable time, speechless, confused, and shrinking uneasily from Mr. Hooper's eye, which they felt to be fixed upon them with an invisible glance. Finally, the deputies returned abashed to their constituents, pronouncing the matter too weighty to be handled, except by a council of the churches, if, indeed, it might not require a general synod.

But there was one person in the village unappalled by the awe with which the black veil had impressed all besides herself. When the deputies returned without an explanation, or even venturing to demand one, she, with the calm energy of her character, determined to chase away the strange cloud that appeared to be settling round Mr. Hooper, every moment more darkly than before. As his plighted wife, it should be her privilege to know what the black veil concealed. At the minister's first visit, therefore, she entered upon the subject with a direct simplicity, which made the task easier both for him and her. After he had seated himself, she fixed her eyes steadfastly upon the veil, but could discern nothing of the dreadful gloom that had so over-awed the multitude; it was but a double fold of crape, hanging down from his forehead to his mouth, and slightly stirring with his breath.

"No," said she aloud, and smiling, "there is nothing terrible in this piece of crape, except that it hides a face which I am always glad to look upon. Come, good sir, let the sun shine from behind the cloud. First lay aside your black veil; then tell me why you put it on."

Mr. Hooper's smile glimmered faintly.

"There is an hour to come," said he, "when all of us shall cast aside our veils. Take it not amiss, beloved friend, if I wear this piece of crape till then."

"Your words are a mystery, too," returned the young lady. "Take away the veil from them, at least."

"Elizabeth, I will," said he, "so far as my vow may suffer me. Know, then, this veil is a type and a symbol, and I am bound to wear it ever, both in light and darkness, in solitude and before the gaze of multitudes, and as with strangers, so with my familiar friends. No mortal eye will see it withdrawn. This dismal shade must separate me from the world; even you, Elizabeth, can never come behind it!"

"What grievous affliction hath befallen you," she earnestly inquired, "that you should thus darken your eyes forever?"

"If it be a sign of mourning," replied Mr. Hooper, "I, perhaps, like most other mortals, have sorrows dark enough to be typified by a black veil."

"But what if the world will not believe that it is the type of an innocent sorrow?" urged Elizabeth. "Beloved and respected as you are, there may be whispers that you hide your face under the consciousness of secret sin. For the sake of your holy office, do away this scandal!"

The color rose into her cheeks as she intimated the nature of the rumors that were already abroad in the village. But Mr. Hooper's mildness did not forsake him. He even smiled again—that same sad smile, which always appeared like a faint glimmering of light, proceeding from the obscurity beneath the veil.

"If I hide my face for sorrow, there is cause enough," he merely replied; "and if I cover it for secret sin, what mortal might not do the same?"

And with this gentle, but unconquerable obstinacy did he resist her entreaties. At length Elizabeth sat silent. For a few moments she appeared lost in thought, considering, probably, what new methods might be tried to withdraw her lover from so dark a fantasy, which, if it had no other meaning, was perhaps a symptom of mental disease. Though of a firmer character than his own, the tears rolled down her cheeks. But, in an instant, as it were, a new feeling took the place of sorrow; her eyes were fixed insensibly on the black veil, when, like a sudden twilight in the air, its terrors fell around her. She arose, and stood trembling before him.

"And do you feel it then, at last?" said he mournfully.

She made no reply, but covered her eyes with her hand, and turned to leave the room. He rushed forward and caught her arm.

"Have patience with me, Elizabeth!" cried he, passionately. "Do not desert me, though this veil must be between us here on earth. Be mine, and hereafter there shall be no veil over my face, no darkness between our souls! It is but a mortal veil—it is not for eternity! O! you know not how lonely I am, and how frightened, to be alone behind my black veil. Do not leave me in this miserable obscurity forever!"

"Lift the veil but once, and look me in the face," said she.

"Never! It cannot be!" replied Mr. Hooper.

"Then farewell!" said Elizabeth.

She withdrew her arm from his grasp, and slowly departed, pausing at the door, to give one long shuddering gaze, that seemed almost to penetrate the mystery of the black veil. But, even amid his grief, Mr. Hooper smiled to think that only a material emblem had separated him from happiness, though the horrors which it shadowed forth must be drawn darkly between the fondest of lovers.

From that time no attempts were made to remove Mr. Hooper's black veil, or, by a direct appeal, to dis-cover the secret which it was supposed to hide. By persons who claimed a superiority to popular prejudice, it was reckoned more an eccentric whim, such as often mingles with the sober actions of men otherwise rational, and tinges them all with its own semblance of insanity. But with the multitude, good Mr. Hooper was irreparably a bugbear. He could not walk the street with any peace of mind, so conscious was he that the gentle and timid would turn aside to avoid him, and that others would make it a point of hardihood to throw themselves in his way. The impertinence of the latter class compelled him to give up his customary walk at sunset to the burial ground; for when he leaned pensively over the gate, there would always be faces behind the gravestones, peeping at his black veil. A fable went the rounds that the stare of the dead people drove him thence. It grieved him, to the very depth of his kind heart, to observe how the children fled from his approach, breaking up their merriest sports, while his melancholy figure was yet afar off. Their instinctive dread caused him to feel more strongly than aught else, that a preternatural horror was interwoven with the threads of the black crape. In truth, his own antipathy to the veil was known to be so great, that he never willingly passed before a mirror, nor stooped to drink at a still fountain, lest, in its peaceful bosom, he should be affrighted by himself. This was what gave plausibility to the whispers that Mr. Hooper's conscience tortured him for some great crime too horrible to be entirely concealed, or otherwise than so obscurely intimated. Thus, from beneath the black veil, there rolled a cloud into the sunshine, an ambiguity of sin or sorrow, which enveloped the poor minister, so that love or sympathy could never reach him. It was said that ghost and fiend consorted with him there. With self-shudderings and outward terrors, he walked continually in its shadow, groping darkly within his own soul, or gazing through a medium that saddened the whole world. Even the lawless wind, it was believed, respected his dreadful secret, and never blew aside the veil. But still good Mr. Hooper sadly smiled at the pale visages of the worldly throng as he passed by.

Among all its bad influences, the black veil had the one desirable effect of making its wearer a very efficient clergyman. By the aid of his mysterious emblem—for there was no other apparent cause—he became a man of awful power over souls that were in agony of sin. His converts always regarded him with a dread peculiar to themselves, affirming, though but figuratively, that, before he brought them to celestial light, they had been with him behind the black veil. Its gloom, indeed, enabled him to sympathize with all dark affections. Dying sinners cried aloud for Mr. Hooper, and would not yield their breath till he appeared; though ever, as he stooped to whisper consolation, they shuddered at the veiled face so near their own. Such were the terrors of the black veil, even when Death had bared his visage! Strangers came long distances to attend service at his church, with the mere idle purpose of gazing at his figure, because it was forbidden them to behold his face. But many were made to quake ere they departed! Once, during Governor Belcher's administration, Mr. Hooper was appointed to preach the election sermon. Covered with his black veil, he stood before the chief magistrate, the council, and the representatives, and wrought so deep an impression, that the legislative measures of that year were characterized by all the gloom and piety of our earliest ancestral sway.

In this manner Mr. Hooper spent a long life, irreproachable in outward act, yet shrouded in dismal suspicions; kind and loving, though unloved, and dimly feared; a man apart from men, shunned in their health and joy, but ever summoned to their aid in mortal anguish. As years wore on, shedding their snows above his sable veil, he acquired a name throughout the New England churches, and they called him Father Hooper. Nearly all his parishioners, who were of mature age when he was settled, had been borne away by many a funeral; he had one congregation in the church, and a more crowded one in the churchyard; and having wrought so late into the evening, and done his work so well, it was now good Father Hooper's turn to rest.

Several persons were visible by the shaded candlelight, in the death chamber of the old clergyman. Natural connections he had none. But there was the decorously grave, though unmoved physician, seeking only to mitigate the last pangs of the patient whom he could not save. There were the deacons, and other eminently pious members of his church. There, also, was the Reverend Mr. Clark, of Westbury, a young and zealous divine, who had ridden in haste to pray by the bedside of the expiring minister. There was the nurse, no hired handmaiden of death, but one whose calm affection had endured thus long in secrecy, in solitude, amid the chill of age, and would not perish, even at the dying hour. Who, but Elizabeth! And there lay the hoary head of good Father Hooper upon the death pillow, with the black veil still swathed about his brow, and reaching down over his face, so that each more difficult gasp of his faint breath caused it to stir. All through life that piece of crape had hung between him and the world; it had separated him from cheerful brotherhood and woman's love, and kept him in the saddest of all prisons, his own heart; and still it lay upon his face, as if to deepen the gloom of his darksome chamber, and shade him from the sunshine of eternity.

For some time previous, his mind had been confused, wavering doubtfully between the past and the present, and hovering forward, as it were, at intervals, into the indistinctness of the world to come. There had been feverish turns, which tossed him from side to side, and wore away what little strength he had. But in his most convulsive struggles, and in the wildest vagaries of his intellect, when no other thought retained its sober influence, he still showed an awful solicitude lest the black veil should slip aside. Even if his bewildered soul could have forgotten, there was a faithful woman at his pillow, who, with averted eyes, would have covered that aged face, which she had last beheld in the comeliness of manhood. At length the death-stricken old man lay quietly in the torpor of mental and bodily exhaustion, with an imperceptible pulse, and breath that grew fainter and fainter, except when a long, deep, and irregular inspiration seemed to prelude the flight of his spirit.

The minister of Westbury approached the bedside.

"Venerable Father Hooper," said he, "the moment of your release is at hand. Are you ready for the lifting of the veil that shuts in time from eternity?"

Father Hooper at first replied merely by a feeble motion of his head; then, apprehensive, perhaps, that his meaning might be doubtful, he exerted himself to speak.

"Yea," said he, in faint accents,

"my soul hath a patient weariness until that veil be lifted."

"And is it fitting," resumed the Reverend Mr. Clark, "that a man so given to prayer, of such a blameless example, holy in deed and thought, so far as mortal judgment may pronounce; is it fitting that a father in the church should leave a shadow on his memory, that may seem to blacken a life so pure? I pray you, my venerable brother, let not this thing be! Suffer us to be gladdened by your triumphant aspect as you go to your reward. Before the veil of eternity be lifted, let me cast aside this black veil from your face!"

And thus speaking the Reverend Mr. Clark bent forward to reveal the mystery of so many years. But, exerting a sudden energy, that made all the beholders stand aghast, Father Hooper snatched both his hands from beneath the bedclothes, and pressed them strongly on the black veil, resolute to struggle, if the minister of Westbury would contend with a dying man.

"Never!" cried the veiled clergyman. "On earth, never!"

"Dark old man!" exclaimed the affrighted minister, "with what horrible crime upon your soul are you now passing to the judgment?"

Father Hooper's breath heaved; it rattled in his throat; but, with a mighty effort, grasping forward with his hands, he caught hold of life, and held it back till he should speak. He even raised himself in bed; and there he sat, shivering with the arms of death around him, while the black veil hung down, awful, at that last moment, in the gathered terrors of a lifetime. And yet the faint, sad smile, so often there, now seemed to glimmer from its obscurity, and linger on Father Hooper's lips.

"Why do you tremble at me alone?" cried he, turning his veiled face round the circle of pale spectators. "Tremble also at each other! Have men avoided me, and women shown no pity, and children screamed and fled, only for my black veil? What, but the mystery which it obscurely typifies, has made this piece of crape so awful? When the friend shows his inmost heart to his friend; the lover to his best beloved; when man does not vainly shrink from the eye of his Creator, loathsomely treasuring up the secret of his sin; then deem me a monster, for the symbol beneath which I have lived, and die! I look around me, and, lo! on every visage a black veil."

While his auditors shrank from one another, in mutual affright, Father Hooper fell back upon his pillow, a veiled corpse, with a faint smile lingering on the lips. Still veiled, they laid him in his coffin, and a veiled corpse they bore him to the grave. The grass of many years has sprung up and withered on that grave, the burial stone is mossgrown, and good Mr. Hooper's face is dust; but awful is still the thought that it moldered beneath the black veil!

Nancy

FIONA FARMER was seven years old. Her mother was forty-six, her father was fifty-five, her nurse was sixty-one, and her grandmother and grandfather, with whom they were all spending the summer, had reached such altitudes of age that no one remembered what they were. From these great heights Fiona was loved and directed.

She wore her hair as her mother had worn it in 1914, braided tight and tied back in pretzel loops with big stiff ribbons. In winter she was the only girl at school to wear a flannel petticoat and underwear with sleeves. Her mother read her all the books she had loved in her childhood; *Rebecca of Sunnybrook Farm,* and *The Five Little Peppers,* and *Under the Lilacs.* Her grandmother read her the books *she* had loved as a child: Macé's *Fairy Tales,* and *Grimm's Fairy Tales,* and *The Princess and Curdie.* On this mixed diet of decorum and brutality Fiona was rapidly turning into a "quaint little creature." She

was a pensive child with large attentive eyes and rather elderly manners; all her play was quiet, accompanied at times by nothing noisier than a low continuous murmuring, so it was strange that the ranks of dolls on her nursery shelves were scalped, and eyeless, like the victims of a Sioux massacre.

"What on earth does she do to them?" her mother said to Nana, the nurse. "Why, when I was little my dollies were really like babies to me. I took such *care* of them, I *loved* them so. . . ."

"I honestly don't know, Mrs. Farmer," Nana said. "She'll be as quiet as a mouse in here for hours at a time, and then I'll come in and find all this—this destruction! It seems so unlike her!"

Fiona's grandmother reproached her quietly. "How would you like it if your dear mother pulled all your hair out of your head and broke your arms and legs? Your dolls are your little responsibilities, your *children* in a way. . . ."

Her admonishments though frequent were always mild. When Fiona scratched her head, or picked her nose, she would say: "That's not very pretty, dear, is it? We don't do those things, do we?" . . . She was a lofty, dignified, conventional lady, and she smelled like an old dictionary among whose pages many flowers have been dried and pressed. She taught Fiona how to make a sachet and a pomander ball and play parcheesi.

Fiona liked her grandfather the best. He was a man of wonderful patience and politeness; deaf as a post. Every morning she followed him out to the vegetable garden where, in his old loose button-down-the-front sweater and his white canvas golf hat that sagged in a ruffle around his head, he worked along the rows of beets and cabbages with his hoe and rake. Fiona followed at his heels, speaking ceaselessly; it did not matter to her that he never heard a word she said, she told him everything. Now and then he would stop, resting on his hoe handle, and look down at her appreciatively. "Well," he would say. "You're a pleasant little companion, aren't you?" Then he would reach out his old parched hand (he was so old that he never sweated any more) and give her a brittle tap or two on the shoulder or head, and he and Fiona would smile at each other out of a mutual feeling of benevolence.

Sooner or later, though, Nana's voice would begin to caw: "Fee-ona! Fee-ona!" and she would have to go back to the house to pick up her toys or change her dress or eat a meal, or some other dull thing.

Her grandparents' house was big and cool inside. All the rooms were full of greenish light reflected from the maple trees outdoors; the floors were dark and gleaming, the carpets had been taken up for the summer and the furniture had linen dresses on. There was no dust anywhere, not even in the corners of the empty fireplaces, for Cora and Mary, the maids who had been there for thirty years, spent their lives seeing that there was not.

Cora had arthritis, and on Sundays when Fiona had noon dinner with the whole family she marveled at the extreme slowness with which the maid moved about the table, like a running-down toy. Her face looked very still and concentrated then, relaxing only when she served Fiona, whispering: "Eat it all up now, dear, every bit, so I can tell Mary."

Oh food! People were always speaking of food to Fiona; the Sunday dinners were a trial to toil through. "Eat it all up, dear," and "Clean your plate" were phrases that were ugly in her ears.

After Sunday dinner everyone went to sleep for a while and the house droned with different pitches of snoring. Wearing nothing but a pink wrapper Fiona would lie on the big white bed while Nana sat in an armchair by the window rattling the Sunday paper. Out of doors the cicadas sounded hot as drills; the lazy air coming in the window brought a smell of grass, and Fiona wished that Nana would fall asleep so that she could get up and find something to play with, but Nana would not fall asleep.

But once she did.

Once on Sunday after the usual slow massive dinner, as Fiona lay in the extremity of boredom counting mosquito bites and listening to herself yawn, she heard another sound; a new one that might promise much. Quietly she raised herself to her elbows, hardly daring to believe, and saw that the impossible had happened at last. Nana lay in the armchair, abandoned, with her head thrown back and her hair coming down and her mouth wide open like that of a fish; a faint guttural sound came out of it each time she breathed.

A great light seemed to flood the room, and a voice from on high addressed Fiona: "Get up and dress, but do not put on your shoes. Carry them in your hand till you get outside, and close the front door quietly behind you."

Fiona got up at once, dressed with the silence and speed of light, and departed. The upstairs hall hummed and trumpeted with the noises of sleeping, no one heard her running down the stairs.

Out of doors it was bright and hot; she sat on the front step and put on her sandals with her heart galloping in her chest. Though old, the members of her family were

tall, their legs were long as ladders, and if they came after her they would surely catch her. Leaving the sandal straps unbuckled Fiona ran out of the gate and down the street, terrified and exhilarated. She ran till she was giddy and breathless, but when at last she stopped and looked behind her the street on which she found herself was still and empty; steeped in Sunday.

She walked for a long time. Her heart stopped racing and her breathing became comfortable again. Her fear, too, gave way to pleasure and pride. It was a beautiful afternoon. The street was very high with elms. The light that came through their roof of leaves was green and trembling like light through water. Fiona became a little crab crawling among the roots of seaweed. The parked cars were fishes which would eat her up, danger was everywhere. . . . She walked sideways, made claws out of her thumbs, hid behind trees, and felt that her eyes grew out on stems. But not for long. Suddenly, as sometimes happened, the fancy collapsed, betrayed her completely. There was no danger; the cars were cars only. Nothing was any better than real; in the end somebody would catch her and take her home or she would return of her own accord, driven by hunger or conscience, and everything would be as it had always been.

The houses sat back from their green laps of lawn, silent and substantial, regarding her like people wearing glasses. There was a smell of privet and hot asphalt in the still air; a boring smell. . . . Intolerable boredom amounting to anguish drove Fiona to turn abruptly and kick the iron palings of a fence that she was passing; a kick that hurt right through her shoe.

The big street came to an end finally at a small Civil War monument and branched out beyond it in three roads. She chose the right-hand one because there was a dog asleep on the sidewalk there, but when she got to him she saw the flies strolling up and down his face and he looked up at her balefully with a low ripple of sound in his throat and she hurried on.

This street had few trees; it was broader, and the houses, while farther apart, were shabbier. The afternoon sun was in her eyes, drawing her along the gilded road. The wind had sprung up, too, warm and lively, blowing from the west.

On the outskirts of the town she came upon her destination, though at first she did not realize it. For some time the wind had been bringing her great blasts of radio music; and she saw now that these had their source in a gray frame house that fairly trembled with melody. Though not small, this was the seediest of all the houses. It stood in the middle of a yard as full of tall grass as a field. There were paths through the field and bald patches where people had stamped and trampled, and many souvenirs abandoned and half grown over: a

rusted little wagon with no wheels, somebody's shoe, an old tire . . .

The house had a queer shape, fancy, but with everything coming off or breaking. Some of the shutters hung by one hinge only; the cupola on top was crooked and so was the porch from which half the palings were gone. The fence, too, had lost many of its pickets and stood propped against the tangle like a large comb with teeth missing; but it had kept its gate and hanging onto this and swinging slowly back and forth were three little girls. Fiona walked more slowly.

One of the girls had a bandanna tied tightly around her head but the other two regarded her from under untrimmed dusty bangs, like animals peering out from under ferns. The gate gave a long snarl of sound as they pushed it forward.

"Where are you going?" said the tallest one.

Fiona could not be sure of the tone of this question: was it a friendly or a hostile challenge? She moved still more slowly touching each picket with her forefinger.

"No place," she said guardedly.

"What's your name?" demanded the girl with the bandanna. She smelled of kerosene.

"Fiona Farmer," said Fiona.

"That's a funny name. My name's Darlene, and hers is Pearl, and *hers* is Merle. Nancy is a nice name."

Fiona saw that all of them were wearing red nail polish and asked a question of her own.

"Are you all three sisters?"

"Yes, and there's more of us. *Them,*" said Pearl, the tallest girl, jerking her head. "In the swing."

Beyond the house Fiona now saw for the first time an old double-rocker swing full of boys.

"There's Norman and Stanley and Earl," Darlene said. "And in the house we got a baby sister named Marilyn, and down to the picture theater we got a big sister named Deanna. Come on in."

"Will they let me swing in the swing?" said Fiona.

"Sure they will. *What* did you say your name was?"

"Fiona," she admitted. "Fiona Farmer."

"Gee," said Pearl.

"We'll call her Nancy," said Darlene, who, though younger, seemed to be a leader in her way. "Come on, Nancy, you wanna swing on the gate? Get off, Merle."

Merle got off obediently, sucking her thumb.

"I would like to swing in the *swing,*" Fiona said.

She came into the yard gazing up at the tipsy cupola. "Can you get up there into that kind of little tower?"

"Sure," said Darlene. "Come on up and we'll show you."

Fiona followed them through the interesting grass in which she now saw a broken doll, somebody's garter, somebody's hat, and many weathered corncobs and beer cans.

On the porch which swayed when they walked on it there were a tough-looking baby buggy, two sleds, a bent tricycle, a lot of chairs and boxes and bushel baskets and peck baskets and a baby pen and a wagon wheel and some kindling wood. The screen door was full of holes and instead of a doorknob there was a wooden thread spool to turn.

The noise of music was stunning as they went indoors; it kept the Mason jars ringing on the shelves. They walked right into it, into the thrilling heart of noise which was the kitchen, where a woman was sitting nursing a baby and shouting random conversation at an old, old woman with a beak nose.

The music ceased with a flourish and the radio announcer's tremendous tones replaced it, but this did not stop the shouted discourse of the woman with the baby. As the girls crossed the kitchen she turned for a moment to look at them, saw Fiona and said, "Who's she?"

"She's Nancy," called Darlene, against the radio.

"Who?"

"Nancy! She dropped in."

"That's Mom," Pearl said.

Fiona went over to the lady to shake her hand. She made her usual curtsy and said, "How do you do?"

Mom's hand felt limp and rather damp and startled. She was a big woman with a wide face and tired blue eyes.

"The old one's Gramma," Darlene said, so Fiona curtsied to the old lady too, and shook her hand which felt like a few twigs in a glove.

"And that's my father," Darlene added, a few seconds later when they had gone up the loud bare stairs to the next floor; Fiona peeked in the doorway of the dim strong-smelling room but all she saw of *him* was the soles of his socks and she heard him snoring.

"Just like at home," she said. "Sunday afternoon they all sleep."

"Heck, he sleeps all *day* on Sundays," Darlene said, and Fiona felt a little humiliated for her own father.

"This is Gramma's room." Pearl threw open the door. "She likes flowers."

The room was a jungle steeped in musky twilight. A vine of some kind had crawled all over the window and parts of the wall, and on the sill, the sash, the floor below, were pots and jars and coffee tins in which stout lusty plants were growing and flowering.

"How does she open the window at night?" Fiona wondered.

"*She* don't open no windows day or night," Darlene said. "Heck, she's *old,* she's gotta stay *warm.*"

They went up another flight of stairs, narrow steep ones, crowded with magazines and articles of clothing and decayed toys. "Up here's where we sleep," Darlene said. "Us girls, all of us except Marilyn. Pearl and me and Merle sleep in the big bed and Deanna she sleeps in the cot. This is the attic like."

The big bed was made of iron with the post knobs missing. It dipped in the middle like a hammock and there, Fiona knew, the little girls would lie at night, dumped together in a tangle, quarreling or giggling in whispers.

"Look at all the comic books!" she cried, and indeed they lay everywhere in tattered profusion, a drift of stained, disordered leaves.

"We got about a hundred or a thousand of 'em, I guess," Pearl said. "You want some?"

"Could I really, Pearl? Could you spare them?"

"*Atom Annie*'s a good one," Pearl said. "We got a lot about her, and here's one called *Hellray* that's real good, real scarey. Take these."

Fiona looked at them longingly. "I don't know if my mother—she doesn't like for me to have comics."

"Heck, why not?"

"Well, maybe this time she won't mind," Fiona said, taking the books, determined that everything would be all right for once. "Thank you very, very much, Darlene and Pearl."

"Here's the stairs to the lookout," Darlene said. "Get out of the way, Merle, you wait till last."

They climbed the ladder steps in the middle of the room, Pearl pushed open the trap door, and one by one they ascended into the tiny chamber.

It was a tipped little cubicle like a ship's cabin in stiff weather, and stiflingly hot. It seemed remote, high, cozy, and its four soiled windows showed four different views of the town faded and reduced as pictures in an old book. Flies buzzed and butted at the hot glass. Fiona felt disappointed when she saw the steeple of the church that stood across the street from her grandfather's house. She had not thought it was so near.

"Jump!" cried Darlene. They all began to jump, and the cupola jarred and trembled under the pounding.

"Won't it break?" cried Fiona, pounding with the rest. "Won't it fall off?"

"Naw, it won't break," Darlene called back. "It never did yet."

"But it might some day, though," shouted Pearl encouragingly.

It was fun to jump riotously and yell, as the tiny tower rocked and resounded.

There was an interruption from below.

"Get out of there!" bawled Mom up the stairs. "How many times I told you kids to stay down out of there! You want to get your backs broke? You want to get killed? You scram down!"

"Get out of the way, Merle, let Nancy go first," Pearl said.

Mom stood at the foot of the steps wearing the baby around her neck. Anxiety had made her furious. "That place ain't safe, you know that!" she cried. "How many times have I told you?" She gave Pearl a slap on the cheek and would have given one to Darlene, too, if Darlene had not bent her neck adroitly.

"You let me catch you up there one more time and I'll get your fa-

ther to lick you good!"

"Aw, climb a tree," said Darlene. Fiona was aghast. What would happen now?

But nothing happened. Merle still quietly sucked her thumb, Darlene and Pearl seemed cool and jaunty, and as they descended through the house Mom's anger dried up like dew.

"You kids want a snack?" she said. "You didn't eat since break-fast."

"Can Nancy stay?"

"Why sure, I guess. Why not?"

"Oh, thank you very, very much. . . ."

The kitchen, like the rest of the house, had a rich bold musty smell. It smelled of constant usage and memories of usage. It was crowded and crusted with objects: pots, pans, kettles, boxes, jars, cans, buckets, dippers. There were two alarm clocks, one lying on its side, and each asserting a different hour, and four big Coca-Cola calendars on the wall, none for the current year. The radio was still thundering music, and close beside it warming herself at the noise sat Gramma, dark as a crow, chewing and chewing on her empty gums.

The stove was named Ebony Gem, and behind it in a cardboard box there was something alive; something moved. . . .

"It's kittens," said Merle, remov-ing her thumb from her mouth and speaking for the first time. "Our cat had kittens."

"Oh, let me see!" Fiona knelt by

the box. There inside it lay a bland and happy group: mother cat with her yellow eyes half closed and her paws splayed out in pleasure; kittens lined up all along her, sucking.

Merle put out her little forefinger with its chipped red nail polish, stroking first one infant, then the next. "The black one's name is Blackie and the white one's name is Whitey and we call *this* one Butch because he's so . . ."

"My father usually drowns them, all but one," Darlene interrupted. She bent her kerchiefed head close to Fiona's, so that there was a blinding smell of kerosene. "Tomorrow probly," she whispered. "We don't tell Merle, it makes her feel so bad." Then she raised her voice. "She knows it's going to happen but she don't know when, huh, Merle?"

"You could take one, Nancy," Merle said, still gazing at the kittens. "You could keep it and be good to it."

"Do you mean honestly and truly?"

Fiona's joy was suffocating.

"Any one? Any one at all?"

"Except Butch," Darlene said. "We're going to keep him to help with the rats."

"Could I have Blackie? Really for keeps?"

Merle plucked the dark little thing from the mother as if she were plucking off a burr and gave it to Fiona.

"I can feel its little tiny heart," Fiona said. "I'll give it milk all the time and brush its fur and it can sleep in the doll cradle. Oh look at its ears, oh Merle, oh thank you!"

Shamed by gratitude Merle put her thumb back in her mouth and looked away.

"You kids get out from under my feet," Mom said. "Sit up to the table now, it's all ready. Come on Mama, come on *boys!*" She opened the screen door and put her head out, shouting so hard that great cords stood out on her neck.

They sat around the big table with its oilcloth cover, everything in easy reach: cereal in paper boxes, sugar, catsup. . . . They had cornflakes and milk, Swiss cheese sandwiches with catsup, cream soda in bottles, and little cakes out of a box with pink and green beads on them. Fiona ate everything.

"Nancy eats good, don't she, Mom?" Darlene said.

"I never had catsup before," said Fiona. "My, it certainly is delicious, isn't it?"

The table was a family battlefield. Fiona had never seen anything like it in her life. Stanley and Norman threw pieces of sandwich at each other, Earl took one of Merle's cakes and Merle cried and Mom slapped Earl; Darlene stole big swigs from Pearl's soda bottle, was loudly accused and loudly defended herself.

"You kids shut up," Mom said, eating over Marilyn's head and giving her occasional bits of cake dipped in tea. Gramma was the only quiet one; she sat bent over, all wrapped and absorbed in her old age, gazing into her cup as she drank from it with a long purring sound. Blackie was quiet too, asleep in Fiona's lap. She kept one hand on his little velvet back.

Mom pointed at Fiona with her spoon. "Looks like Margaret O'Brien used to, don't she? The ribbons and all."

"Margaret who?" said Fiona.

"O'Brien, *you* know, the kid in the movies," Darlene said.

"Oh, I never go to movies," said Fiona. "I'm not allowed."

"Not allowed!" cried Darlene incredulously. "Heck, we go all the time, don't we, Mom? Even Deanna goes. We could take Nancy with us sometimes, couldn't we, Mom?"

"Maybe, if her folks say yes."

"Oh if I went with *you* it would be all right, I'm sure," cried Fiona joyously. Drunk with noise, strange flavors, gifts, and new friendship, she really believed this.

Afterward, still with catsup on their upper lips, they went out doors to play hide-and-seek.

"You be her partner, Stanley," ordered Darlene, who was "it." "You kind of look after her, she don't know our places to hide."

Then she hid her eyes with her arm, cast herself against a tree like a girl in grief, and began to count out loud.

"The cellar," hissed Stanley, grabbing Fiona's hand. He was a big eight-year-old boy, and still clutching the kitten Fiona ran with him willingly, hesitating only for a second at sight of the dark abyss.

On the steps were many cans and beer crates, but Stanley led her safely down among these and into the black deep tunnel beyond. Fiona could feel that there were solid things all around them; probably more boxes, more beer crates, but she could see nothing. Stanley's hand was warm and firm, it just fitted hers, and she liked having him lead her.

"We can stop now," he said, "but keep quiet."

Darlene could still be heard, faintly. Her counting voice sounded deserted and defiant: *"Ninety-*five, *ninety-*six, *ninety-*seven" . . . The blackness throbbed and shimmered and the air had a dense aged smell.

"Coming, ready or not!" called the faraway defiant voice.

"We're safe here anyways," Stanley said. "She won't come down *here,* she's scared to." He laughed silently and gave Fiona's hand a squeeze. "There's rats down here."

"Oh no, oh no! Oh, Stanley, let's go up again," cried Fiona, tears of panic in her voice.

But Stanley held onto her hand. "You going to be a sissy too?" he demanded. "We got the *cat,* ain't we?"

Fiona strained the tiny kitten to her chest. Her heart was banging terribly and she wanted to cry but she would not. All around the rats were closing in, large as dogs and smiling strangely; smiling like people. She almost sobbed when Stanley said, "Now we can go, hurry up, and keep still!"

They were the first ones back.

For a long time they played and Stanley always was her partner. He knew the best places to hide: up in the boughs of a pear tree, under the porch steps, and flat on their stomachs under the folded-back cellar door. Darlene was "it" till she caught Merle and Merle was "it" for hours. Fiona got spiderwebs in her mouth and gnats up her nose, tore her dress, scraped her knee, lost one hair ribbon, and gave the other to Merle, who had admired it.

When they were through with hide-and-seek they all got into the rocker swing and played gangsters. The swing leapt to and fro, to and fro, screaming wildly at the joints; surely it would break, and soon! That was the thrilling thing about this place: so many features of it— the tower, the swing, the porch— trembled at the edge of ruin, hung by a thread above the fatal plunge.

Earl and Stanley and Norman leaned over the back of one of the seats firing at the enemy. "Step on it, you guys," yelled Stanley, "they got a gat!"

"They got a rod!" yelled Norman. "They got a lotta rods!"

"What's a rod?" cried Fiona. "What's a gat?"

"Guns he means," Darlene told her. "Rods and gats is guns."

"Shoot 'em, Stanley," yelled Fiona. "With your gat, shoot the eyes out of 'em!"

Clutching the clawing kitten to her collarbone, her hair in her open mouth, she bawled encouragement to them. The swing accelerated ever more wildly: soon it would take off entirely, depart from its hinges, fly through the air, burn a hole through the sky! . . .

"Fee-ona Farmer!"

The cry was loud enough to be heard above all sounds of war and wind and radio music.

Beside the swing stood Nana, so tall, so highly charged with hurry and emotion, that the children stopped their play at once.

"Who's she?" Stanley asked.

"She's my nurse," Fiona murmured.

"Your nurse! What's the matter, are you sick?"

"No . . . she just—takes care of me."

"Takes *care* of you!"

"You get out of that swing and come this in-stant!"

Having struck the bottom of disgrace, Fiona stepped down and slowly went to Nana. From the swing the others watched as still as children posing for a photograph.

"Put down that cat and come at once."

"Oh no!" Fiona said. "It's mine, they gave it to me."

"Put. Down. That. Cat."

Darlene came to stand beside Fiona. "But we did give it to her, we want for her to have it."

Nana struck the kitten from Fiona's arms. "You will not take that creature home! It's filthy, it has fleas!"

"Oh my kitty!" shrieked Fiona,

diving after Blackie, but Nana caught her wrist.

"You come!"

Fiona pulled, struggled, cast a glare of anguish at all the rapt photograph-faces in the swing.

"You should be punished. You should be whipped. Whipped!" Nana whistled the cruel words; Nana, who was never cruel! Her fingers on Fiona's wrist were hard.

"Let me say good-by to them, Nana, let me say good-by to their *mother!* You said I should *always* say good-by to the mother!"

"Not this time, this time it doesn't matter," Nana said. "You're going straight home and into the tub. Heavens knows what you will have caught!" Upon Fiona's friends she turned a single brilliant glance like one cold flash from a lighthouse.

There was nothing to commend Fiona's departure; dragged by the hand, whimpering, she looked back at her friends in desperation. "Oh, Darlene!"

But it was easy to see that Darlene had detached herself. "Good-by, Nancy," she said, not without a certain pride. She did not smile or say anything else, but her attitude showed Fiona and Nana that she had no need for either of them, could not be hurt by them, and would not think of them again. As they went out the gate she turned her back and skipped away, and Fiona heard the rocker swing resume its screaming tempo.

Halfway home Nana's recrimina-tions began to modify, gradually becoming reproaches: "How could you have, Fiona, run away like that, why it's only by the grace of God I ever found you at all! And all the time I was half sick with worry I never said a word to your father and mother! I didn't want *them* to worry!"

Somewhere deep inside her Fiona understood exactly why Nana had said nothing to her parents, but she just kept on saying: "I want my kitty, I want my kitty."

Finally Nana said: "If you're a good girl maybe we'll get you another kitten."

"I don't want another, I want that one."

"Oh for pity's sakes, it had fleas; or worse. Anything belonging to the Fadgins would be bound to have—"

"Do *you* know them?"

"I know *about* them, everybody does. They're the dirtiest, the shiftlessest, the most down-at-the-heel tribe in this whole town!"

"They are not, they're nice, I love them!"

Nana relented a little. "Maybe it's hard not to be shiftless when you're that poor."

"*They* aren't poor. You should see all the things they've got! More than Grandmother's got in her whole house!"

"All right now, dearie, all right. We'll forget about it, shall we? It will be our secret and we'll never tell anyone because we don't want them to worry, do we? But you must promise me never, never to do such a thing again, hear?"

"I want my kitty," droned Fiona.

Her grandparents' house smelled cool and sweetish. There was a bowl of white and pink stock on the hall table and her grandmother's green linen parasol leaned in a corner among the pearly company of her grandfather's canes.

In the shaded living room Fiona saw her mother knitting and her grandmother at the piano playing the same kind of music she always played, with the loose rings clicking on her fingers.

"Is that my baby?" called her mother—but Nana answered hastily, "I'm getting her right into her bath, Mrs. Farmer. She's sim-ply fil-thy."

Upstairs Nana went in to run the water in the tub. Fiona kicked off one sandal, then the other. A terrible pain took hold of her; it began in her mind and spread down to her stomach. She had never been homesick before and did not know what ailed her: she knew only that she wanted to sleep at night in a big twanging bed full of children and to eat meals at a crowded table where people threw bread at each other and drank pop. She wanted Stanley's hand to guide her and Darlene's voice to teach her and Blackie's purr to throb against her chest. . . .

Beyond the window she saw her grandfather's wilted golf hat bobbing among the cornstalks and es-

caped again, running on bare feet down the back stairs and out of doors across the billowing lawn which seemed to be colliding with the trees and sky and shadows, all flooded and dazzled with tears. Blindly she flung open the garden gate and pushed her way through the green-paper corn forest to her grandfather who dropped his hoe and held out his arms when he saw her face.

"Come here now," he said in his gentle deaf voice. "Well, well, this won't do, no it won't, not at all. Come sit here with Grandpa, sit here in the arbor. Did you hurt yourself?"

He led her to the seat under the green grape trellis where he sometimes rested from the hot sun. He put his arm around her shoulders, offering himself as a support for grief, and Fiona howled against his waistcoat till the wet tweed chapped her cheek and there was not a tear left in her. He did not interrupt or ask questions but kept patting her shoulder in a sort of sympathetic accompaniment to her sobs, which he could not hear but which he felt. What's the cause of it all, he wondered. A broken toy? A scolding? Children's tragedies, he thought, children's little tragedies: there are bigger ones in store for you, Fiona, a world of them. The thought did not move him deeply; everyone must suffer, but for an instant he was not sorry to be old.

Fiona leaned against him and after a while between the hiccups left from sobbing she could hear the ancient heart inside his chest tick-tocking steadily, as tranquil and unhurried as he was himself. All the wild performance of her sorrow had not quickened its tempo by a single beat, and this for some reason was a comfort.

The sound of her grandmother's music, sugary and elegant, came sparkling from the house, and upstairs in the bedroom or the hall Nana began to call. "Fee-ona?" she cried. "Oh, Fee-*ona*?" There was a hint of panic in her voice, now, but no response came from under the green trellis: Feona's grandfather could not hear the calling, and Fiona, for the time being, did not choose to answer.

Happiness

CARL SANDBURG

I asked professors who teach the meaning of life to tell me what is happiness.

And I went to famous executives who boss the work of thousands of men.

They all shook their heads and gave me a smile as though I was trying to fool with them.

And then one Sunday afternoon I wandered out along the Desplaines River

And I saw a crowd of Hungarians under the trees with their women and children and a keg of beer and an accordion.

The Great Automatic Grammatisator

"WELL KNIPE, my boy. Now that it's all finished, I just called you in to tell you I think you've done a fine job."

Adolph Knipe stood still in front of Mr. Bohlen's desk. There seemed to be no enthusiasm in him at all.

"Aren't you pleased?"

"Oh yes, Mr. Bohlen."

"Did you see what the papers said this morning?"

"No sir, I didn't."

The man behind the desk pulled a folded newspaper toward him, and began to read: "The building of the great automatic computing engine, ordered by the government some time ago, is now complete. It is probably the fastest electronic calculating machine in the world today. Its function is to satisfy the ever-increasing need of science, industry, and administration for rapid mathematical calculation which, in the past, by traditional methods,

would have been physically impossible, or would have required more time than the problems justified. The speed with which the new engine works, said Mr. John Bohlen, head of the firm of electrical engineers mainly responsible for its construction, may be grasped by the fact that it can provide the correct answer in five seconds to a problem that would occupy a mathematician for a month. In three minutes, it can produce a calculation that by hand (if it were possible) would fill half a million sheets of foolscap paper. The automatic computing engine uses pulses of electricity, generated at the rate of a million a second, to solve all calculations that resolve themselves into addition, subtraction, multiplication, and division. For practical purposes there is no limit to what it can do . . ."

Mr. Bohlen glanced up at the

long, melancholy face of the younger man. "Aren't you proud, Knipe? Aren't you pleased?"

"Of course, Mr. Bohlen."

"I don't think I have to remind you that your own contribution, especially to the original plans, was an important one. In fact, I might go so far as to say that without you and some of your ideas, this project might still be on the drawing boards today."

Adolph Knipe moved his feet on the carpet, and he watched the two small white hands of his chief, the nervous fingers playing with a paper clip, unbending it, straightening out the hairpin curves. He didn't like the man's hands. He didn't like his face either, with the tiny mouth and the narrow purple-colored lips. It was unpleasant the way only the lower lip moved when he talked.

"Is anything bothering you, Knipe? Anything on your mind?"

"Oh no, Mr. Bohlen. No."

"How would you like to take a week's holiday? Do you good. You've earned it."

"Oh, I don't know, sir."

The older man waited, watching this tall, thin person who stood so sloppily before him. He was a difficult boy. Why couldn't he stand up straight? Always drooping and untidy, with spots on his jacket, and hair falling all over his face.

"I'd like you to take a holiday, Knipe. You need it."

"All right, sir. If you wish."

"Take a week. Two weeks if you like. Go somewhere warm. Get some sunshine. Swim. Relax. Sleep. Then come back, and we'll have another talk about the future."

Adolph Knipe went home by bus to his two-room apartment. He threw his coat on the sofa, poured himself a drink of stout, and sat down in front of the typewriter that was on the table. Mr. Bohlen was right. Of course he was right. Except that he didn't know the half of it. He probably thought it was a woman. Whenever a young man gets depressed, everybody thinks it's a woman.

He leaned forward and began to read through the half-finished sheet of typing still in the machine. It was headed "A Narrow Escape," and it began *"The night was dark and stormy, the wind whistled in the trees, the rain poured down like cats and dogs . . ."*

Adolph Knipe took a sip of stout, tasting the malty-bitter flavor, feeling the trickle of cold liquid as it traveled down his throat and settled in the top of his stomach, cool at first, then spreading and becoming warm, making a little area of warmness inside him. To the devil with Mr. John Bohlen anyway. And to the devil with the great electrical computing machine. . . .

At exactly that moment, his eyes and mouth began slowly to open, in a sort of wonder, and slowly he raised his head and became still, absolutely motionless, gazing at the wall opposite with this look that was more perhaps of astonishment than of wonder, but quite fixed now, unmoving, and remaining thus for forty, fifty, sixty seconds. Then gradually (the head still motionless), a subtle change spreading over the face, astonishment becoming pleasure, very slight at first, only around the corners of the mouth, increasingly gradually, spreading out until at last the whole face was open wide and shining with extreme delight. It was the first time Adolph Knipe had smiled in many, many months.

"Of course," he said, speaking aloud, "it's completely ridiculous." Again he smiled, raising his upper lip and baring his teeth in a queerly sensual manner.

"It's a delicious idea, but so impracticable it doesn't really bear thinking about at all."

From then on, Adolph Knipe began to think about nothing else. The idea fascinated him enormously, at first because it gave him a promise—however remote—of revenging himself in a most fiendish manner upon his greatest enemies. From this angle alone, he toyed idly with it for perhaps ten or fifteen minutes; then all at once he found himself examining it quite seriously as a practical possibility. He took paper and made some preliminary notes. But he didn't get far. He found himself, almost immediately, up against the old truth that a machine, however ingenious, is incapable of original thought. It can handle no problems except those

that resolve themselves into mathematical terms—problems that contain one, and only one, correct answer.

This was a stumper. There didn't seem any way around it. A machine cannot have a brain. On the other hand, it *can* have a memory, can it not? Their own electronic calculator had a marvelous memory. Simply by converting electric pulses, through a column of mercury, into supersonic waves, it could store away at least a thousand numbers at a time, extracting any one of them at the precise moment it was needed. Would it not be possible, therefore, on this principle, to build a memory section of almost unlimited size?

Now what about that?

Then suddenly, he was struck by a powerful but simple little truth, and it was this: *That English grammar is governed by rules that are almost mathematical in their strictness!* Given the words, and given the sense of what is to be said, then there is only one correct order in which those words can be arranged.

No, he thought, that isn't quite accurate. In many sentences there are several alternative positions for words and phrases, all of which may be grammatically correct. But what of it? The theory itself is basically true. Therefore, it stands to reason that an engine built along the lines of the electric computer could be adjusted to arrange words (instead of numbers) in their right order according to the rules of grammar.

Give it the verbs, the nouns, the adjectives, the pronouns, store them in the memory section as a vocabulary, and arrange for them to be extracted as required. Then feed it with plots and leave it to write the sentences.

There was no stopping Knipe now. He went to work immediately, and there followed during the next few days a period of intense labor. The living room became littered with sheets of paper: formulae and calculations; lists of words, thousands and thousands of words; the plots of stories, curiously broken up and subdivided; huge extracts from *Roget's Thesaurus;* pages filled with the first names of men and women; hundreds of surnames taken from the telephone directory; intricate drawings of wires and circuits and switches and thermionic valves; drawings of machines that could punch holes of different shapes in little cards, and of a strange electrical typewriter that could type ten thousand words a minute. Also, a kind of control panel with a series of small push buttons, each one labeled with the name of a famous American magazine.

He was working in a mood of exultation, prowling around the room amidst this littering of paper, rubbing his hands together, talking out loud to himself; and sometimes, with a sly curl of the nose, he would mutter a series of murderous imprecations in which the word "editor" seemed always to be present. On the fifteenth day of continuous work, he collected the papers into two large folders which he carried —almost at a run—to the offices of John Bohlen Inc., electrical engineers.

Mr. Bohlen was pleased to see him back.

"Well Knipe, good gracious me, you look a hundred per cent better. You have a good holiday? Where'd you go?"

He's just as ugly and untidy as ever, Mr. Bohlen thought. Why doesn't he stand up straight? He looks like a bent stick. "You look a hundred per cent better, my boy." I wonder what he's grinning about. Every time I see him, his ears seem to have got larger.

Adolph Knipe placed the folders on the desk. "Look, Mr. Bohlen!" he cried. "Look at these!"

Then he poured out his story. He opened the folders and pushed the plans in front of the astonished little man. He talked for over an hour, explaining everything, and when he had finished, he stepped back, breathless, flushed, waiting for the verdict.

"You know what I think, Knipe? I think you're nuts." Careful now, Mr. Bohlen told himself. Treat him carefully. He's valuable, this one is. If only he didn't look so awful, with that long horse face and the big teeth. The fellow had ears as big as rhubarb leaves.

"But Mr. Bohlen! It'll work! I've proved to you it'll work! You can't deny that!"

"Take it easy now, Knipe. Take it easy, and listen to me." Adolph Knipe watched his man, disliking him more every second.

"This idea," Mr. Bohlen's lower lip was saying, "is very ingenious— I might almost say brilliant—and it only goes to confirm my high opinion of your abilities, Knipe. But don't take it too seriously. After all, my boy, what possible use can it be to us? Who on earth wants a machine for writing stories? And where's the money in it, anyway? Just tell me that."

"May I sit down, sir?"

"Sure, take a seat."

Adolph Knipe seated himself on the edge of a chair. The older man watched him with alert brown eyes, wondering what was coming now.

"I would like to explain something, Mr. Bohlen, if I may, about how I came to do all this."

"Go right ahead, Knipe." He would have to be humored a little now, Mr. Bohlen told himself. The boy was really valuable—a sort of genius, almost—worth his weight in gold to the firm. Just look at these papers here. Darndest thing you ever saw. Astonishing piece of work. Quite useless, of course. No commercial value. But it proved again the boy's ability.

"It's a sort of confession, I suppose, Mr. Bohlen. I think it explains why I've always been so . . . so kind of worried."

"You tell me anything you want, Knipe. I'm here to help you—you know that."

The young man clasped his hands together tight on his lap, hugging himself with his elbows. It seemed as though suddenly he was feeling very cold.

"You see, Mr. Bohlen, to tell the honest truth, I don't really care much for my work here. I know I'm good at it and all that sort of thing, but my heart's not in it. It's not what I want to do most."

Up went Mr. Bohlen's eyebrows, quick like a spring. His whole body became very still.

"You see, sir, all my life I've wanted to be a writer."

"A writer!"

"Yes, Mr. Bohlen. You may not believe it, but every bit of spare time I've had, I've spent writing stories. In the last ten years I've written hundreds, literally hundreds of short stories. Five hundred and sixty-six, to be precise. Approximately one a week."

"Good heavens, man! What on earth did you do that for?"

"All I know, sir, is I have the urge."

"What sort of urge?"

"The creative urge, Mr. Bohlen." Every time he looked up he saw Mr. Bohlen's lips. They were growing thinner and thinner, more and more purple.

"And may I ask you what you do with these stories, Knipe?"

"Well sir, that's the trouble. No one will buy them. Each time I finish one, I send it out on the rounds. It goes to one magazine after another. That's all that happens,

Mr. Bohlen, and they simply send them back. It's very depressing."

Mr. Bohlen relaxed. "I can see quite well how you feel, my boy." His voice was dripping with sympathy. "We all go through it one time or another in our lives. But now—now that you've had proof—positive proof—from the experts themselves, from the editors, that your stories are—what shall I say—rather unsuccessful, it's time to leave off. Forget it, my boy. Just forget all about it."

"No, Mr. Bohlen! No! That's not true! I *know* my stories are good. My heavens, when you compare them with the stuff some of those magazines print—oh my word, Mr. Bohlen!—the sloppy, boring stuff that you see in the magazines week after week—why, it drives me mad!"

"Now wait a minute, my boy . . ."

"Do you ever read the magazines, Mr. Bohlen?"

"You'll pardon me, Knipe, but what's all this got to do with your machine?"

"Everything, Mr. Bohlen, absolutely everything! What I want to tell you is, I've made a study of the magazines, and it seems that each one tends to have its own particular type of story. The writers—the successful ones—know this, and they write accordingly."

"Just a minute, my boy. Calm yourself down, will you. I don't think all this is getting us anywhere."

"*Please,* Mr. Bohlen, hear me through. It's all terribly important." He paused to catch his breath. He was properly worked up now, throwing his hands around as he talked. The long, toothy face, with the big ears on either side, simply shone with enthusiasm, and there was an excess of saliva in his mouth which caused him to speak his words wet. "So you see, on my machine, by having an adjustable co-ordinator between the 'plot-memory' section and the 'word-memory' section, I am able to produce any type of story I desire simply by pressing the required button."

"Yes, I know, Knipe, I know. This is all very interesting, but what's the point of it?"

"Just this, Mr. Bohlen. The market is limited. We've got to be able to produce the right stuff, at the right time, whenever we want it. It's a matter of business, that's all. I'm looking at it from *your* point of view now—as a commercial proposition."

"My dear boy, it can't possibly be a commercial proposition—ever. You know as well as I do what it costs to build one of these machines."

"Yes sir, I do. But with due respect, I don't believe you know what the magazines pay writers for stories."

"What do they pay?"

"Anything up to twenty-five hundred dollars. It probably averages around a thousand."

Mr. Bohlen jumped.

"Yes *sir,* it's true."

"Absolutely impossible, Knipe! Ridiculous!"

"No sir, it's true."

"You mean to sit there and tell me that these magazines pay out money like that to a man for . . . just for scribbling off a story! Good heavens, Knipe! Whatever next! Writers must all be millionaires!"

"That's exactly it, Mr. Bohlen! That's where the machine comes in. Listen a minute, sir, while I tell you some more. I've got it all worked out. The big magazines are carrying approximately three fiction stories in each issue. Now, take the fifteen most important magazines—the ones paying the most money. A few of them are monthlies, but most of them come out every week. All right. That makes, let us say, around forty big money stories being bought each week. That's forty thousand dollars. So with our machine—when we get it working properly—we can collar nearly the whole of this market!"

"My dear boy, you're mad!"

"No sir, honestly, it's true what I say. Don't you see that with volume alone we'll completely overwhelm them! This machine can produce a five-thousand word story, all typed and ready for despatch, in thirty seconds. How can the writers compete with that? I ask you, Mr. Bohlen, *how?*"

At that point, Adolph Knipe noticed a slight change in the man's expression, an extra brightness in the eyes, the nostrils distending, the whole face becoming still, almost rigid. Quickly, he continued. "Nowadays, Mr. Bohlen, the handmade article hasn't a hope. It can't possibly compete with mass-production, especially in this country—you know that. Carpets . . . chairs . . . shoes . . . bricks . . . crockery . . . anything you like to mention—they're all made by machinery now. The quality may be inferior, but that doesn't matter. It's the cost of production that counts. And stories—well—they're just another product, like carpets or chairs, and no one cares how you produce them so long as you deliver the goods. We'll sell them wholesale, Mr. Bohlen! We'll undercut every writer in the country! We'll corner the market!"

Mr. Bohlen edged up straighter in his chair. He was leaning forward now, both elbows on the desk, the face alert, the small brown eyes resting on the speaker.

"I still think it's impracticable, Knipe."

"Forty thousand a week!" cried Adolph Knipe. "And if we halve the price, making it twenty thousand a week, that's still a million a year!" And softly he added, "You didn't get any million a year for building the old electronic calculator, did you, Mr. Bohlen?"

"But seriously now, Knipe. D'you really think they'd buy them?"

"Listen, Mr. Bohlen. Who on earth is going to want custom-made stories when they can get the other kind at half the price? It stands to reason, doesn't it?"

"And how will you sell them? Who will you say has written them?"

"We'll set up our own literary agency, and we'll distribute them through that. And we'll invent all the names we want for the writers."

"I don't like it, Knipe. To me, that smacks of trickery, does it not?"

"And another thing, Mr. Bohlen. There's all manner of valuable by-products once you've got started. Take advertising, for example. Beer manufacturers and people like that are willing to pay good money these days if famous writers will lend their names to their products. Why, my heavens, Mr. Bohlen! This isn't any children's plaything we're talking about. It's big business."

"Don't get too ambitious, my boy."

"And another thing. There isn't any reason why we shouldn't put *your* name, Mr. Bohlen, on some of the better stories, if you wished it."

"My goodness, Knipe. What should I want that for?"

"I don't know, sir, except that some writers get to be very much respected—like Mr. Erle Gardner or Kathleen Norris, for example. We've got to have names, and I was certainly thinking of using my own on one or two stories, just to help out."

"A writer, eh?" Mr. Bohlen said, musing. "Well, it would surely surprise them over at the club when they saw my name in the magazines—the good magazines."

"That's right, Mr. Bohlen."

For a moment, a dreamy, far-away look came into Mr. Bohlen's eyes, and he smiled. Then he stirred himself and began leafing through the plans that lay before him.

"One thing I don't quite understand, Knipe. Where do the plots come from? The machine can't possibly invent plots."

"We feed those in, sir. That's no problem at all. Everyone has plots. There's three or four hundred of them written down in that folder there on your left. Feed them straight into the 'plot-memory' section of the machine."

"Go on."

"There are many other little refinements too, Mr. Bohlen. You'll see them all when you study the plans carefully. For example, there's a trick that nearly every writer uses, of inserting at least one long, obscure word into each story. This makes the reader think that the man is very wise and clever. So I have the machine do the same thing. There'll be a whole stack of long words stored away just for this purpose."

"Where?"

"In the 'word-memory' section," he said, epexegetically.

Through most of that day the two men discussed the possibilities of the new engine. In the end, Mr. Bohlen said he would have to think about it some more. The next morning, he was quietly enthusiastic. Within a week, he was completely sold on the idea.

"What we'll have to do, Knipe, is to say that we're merely building another mathematical calculator, but of a new type. That'll keep the secret."

"Exactly, Mr. Bohlen."

And in six months the machine was completed. It was housed in a separate brick building at the back of the premises, and now that it was ready for action, no one was allowed near it excepting Mr. Bohlen and Adolph Knipe.

It was an exciting moment when the two men—the one, short, plump, breviped—the other tall, thin, and toothy—stood in the corridor before the control panel and got ready to run off the first story. All around them were walls dividing up into many small corridors, and the walls were covered with wiring and plugs and switches and huge glass valves. They were both nervous, Mr. Bohlen hopping from one foot to the other, quite unable to keep still.

"Which button?" Adolph Knipe asked, eying a row of small white discs that resembled the keys of a typewriter. "You choose, Mr. Bohlen. Lots of magazines to pick from—*Saturday Evening Post, Collier's, Ladies' Home Journal*—any one you like."

"Goodness me, boy! How do I know?" He was jumping up and down like a man with hives.

"Mr. Bohlen," Adolph Knipe said gravely, "do you realize that at this moment, with your little finger alone, you have it in your power to become the most versatile writer on this continent?"

"Listen Knipe, just get on with it, will you please—and cut out the preliminaries."

"Okay, Mr. Bohlen. Then we'll make it . . . let me see—this one. How's that?" He extended one finger and pressed down a button with the name *Today's Woman* printed across it in diminutive black type. There was a sharp click, and when he took his finger away, the button remained down, below the level of the others.

"So much for the selection," he said. "Now—here we go!" He reached up and pulled a switch on the panel. Immediately, the room was filled with a loud humming noise, and a crackling of electric sparks, and the jingle of many, tiny, quickly-moving levers; and almost in the same instant, sheets of quarto paper began sliding out from a slot to the right of the control panel and dropping into a basket below. They came out quick, one sheet a second, and in less than half a minute it was all over. The sheets stopped coming.

"That's it!" Adolph Knipe cried. "There's your story!"

They grabbed the sheets and began to read. The first one they picked up started as follows: "Aifkjmbsaoegwcztpplnvoqudskigt&,fuhpekanvbertyuiolkjhgfdsazxcvbnm,peruitrehdjkgmvnb,wmsuy . . ." They looked at the others. The style was roughly similar in all of them. Mr. Bohlen began to shout. The younger man tried to calm him down.

"It's all right, sir. Really it is. It only needs a little adjustment. We've got a connection wrong somewhere, that's all. You must remember, Mr. Bohlen, there's over a million feet of wiring in this room. You can't expect everything to be right the first time."

"It'll never work," Mr. Bohlen said.

"Be patient, sir. Be patient."

Adolph Knipe set out to discover the fault, and in four days time he announced that all was ready for the next try.

"It'll never work," Mr. Bohlen said. "I know it'll never work."

Knipe smiled and pressed the selector button marked *Reader's Digest*. Then he pulled the switch, and again the strange, exciting, humming sound filled the room. One page of typescript flew out of the slot into the basket.

"Where's the rest?" Mr. Bohlen cried. "It's stopped! It's gone wrong!"

"No sir, it hasn't. It's exactly right. It's for the *Digest*, don't you see?"

This time, it began: "Fewpeople yetknowthatarevolutionarynewcure hasbeendiscoveredwhichmaywellbri ngpermanentrelieftosufferersofthe mostdreadeddiseaseofourtime . . ." And so on.

"It's gibberish!" Mr. Bohlen shouted.

"No sir, it's fine. Can't you see?

It's simply that she's not breaking up the words. That's an easy adjustment. But the story's there. Look, Mr. Bohlen, look! It's all there except that the words are joined together."

And indeed it was.

On the next try a few days later, everything was perfect, even the punctuation. The first story they ran off, for a famous women's magazine, was a solid, plotty story of a boy who wanted to better himself with his rich employer. This boy arranged, so the story went, for a friend to hold up the rich man's daughter on a dark night when she was driving home. Then the boy himself, happening by, knocked the gun out of his friend's hand and rescued the girl. The girl was grateful. But the father was suspicious. He questioned the boy sharply. The boy broke down and confessed. Then the father, instead of kicking him out of the house, said that he admired the boy's resourcefulness. The girl admired his honesty—and his looks. The father promised to make him head of the Accounts Department. The girl married him.

"It's tremendous, Mr. Bohlen! It's exactly right!"

"Seems a bit sloppy to me, my boy."

"No sir, it's a seller, a real seller!"

In his excitement, Adolph Knipe promptly ran off six more stories in as many minutes. All of them—except one, which for some reason came out a trifle lurid—seemed entirely satisfactory.

Mr. Bohlen was now mollified. He agreed to set up a literary agency in an office downtown, and to put Knipe in charge. In a couple of weeks, this was accomplished. Then Knipe mailed out the first dozen stories. He put his own name to four of them, Mr. Bohlen's to one, and for the others he simply invented names.

Five of these stories were promptly accepted. The one with Mr. Bohlen's name on it was turned down with a letter from the fiction editor saying, "This is a skilful job, but in our opinion it doesn't quite come off. We would like to see more of this writer's work . . ." Adolph Knipe took a cab out to the factory and ran off another story for the same magazine. He again put Mr. Bohlen's name to it, and mailed it out immediately. That one they bought.

The money started pouring in. Knipe slowly and carefully stepped up the output, and in six months' time he was delivering thirty stories a week, and selling about half.

He began to make a name for himself in literary circles as a prolific and successful writer. So did Mr. Bohlen; but not quite such a good name, although he didn't know it. At the same time, Knipe was building up a dozen or more fictitious persons as promising young authors. Everything was going fine.

At this point it was decided to adapt the machine for writing novels as well as stories. Mr. Bohlen, thirsting now for greater honors in the literary world, insisted that Knipe go to work at once on this prodigious task.

"I want to do a novel," he kept saying. "I want to do a novel."

"And so you will, sir. And so you will. But please be patient. This is a very complicated adjustment I have to make."

"Everyone tells me I ought to do a novel," Mr. Bohlen cried. "All sorts of publishers are chasing after me day and night begging me to stop fooling around with stories and do something really important instead. A novel's the only thing that counts—that's what they say."

"We're all going to do novels," Knipe told him. "Just as many as we want. But please be patient."

"Now listen to me, Knipe. What I'm going to do is a *serious* novel, something that'll make 'em sit up and take notice. I've been getting rather tired of the sort of stories you've been putting my name to lately. As a matter of fact, I'm none too sure you haven't been trying to make a monkey out of me."

"A monkey, Mr. Bohlen?"

"Keeping all the best ones for yourself, that's what you've been doing."

"Oh no, Mr. Bohlen! No!"

"So this time I'm going to make darn sure I write a high-class, intelligent book. You understand that."

"Look, Mr. Bohlen. With the sort of switchboard I'm rigging up, you'll be able to write any sort of book you want."

And this was true, for within another couple of months, the genius of Adolph Knipe had not only adapted the machine for novel writing, but had constructed a marvelous new control system which enabled the author to pre-select literally any type of plot and any style of writing he desired. There were so many dials and levers on the thing, it looked like the instrument panel of some enormous airplane.

First, by depressing one of a series of master buttons, the writer made his primary decision: historical, satirical, philosophical, political, romantic, erotic, humorous, or straight. Then, from the second row (the basic buttons) he chose his theme: army life, pioneer days, civil war, world war, racial problem, wild west, country life, childhood memories, seafaring, the sea bottom, and many, many more. The third row of buttons gave a choice of literary style: classical, whimsical, racy, Hemingway, Faulkner, Joyce, feminine, and so on. The fourth row was for characters, the fifth for wordage—and so on and so on—ten long rows of pre-selector buttons.

But that wasn't all. Control had also to be exercised during the actual writing process (which took about fifteen minutes per novel), and to do this the author had to sit, as it were, in the driver's seat, and pull (or push) a battery of labeled stops, as on an organ. By so doing, he was able continually to modulate or merge fifty different and variable qualities such as tension, surprise, humor, pathos, and mystery. Numerous dials and gauges on the dashboard itself told him throughout exactly how far along he was with his work.

Finally, there was the question of "passion." From a careful study of the books at the top of the bestseller lists for the past year, Adolph Knipe had decided that this was the most important ingredient of all—a magical catalyst that somehow or other could transform the dullest novel into a howling success—at any rate financially. But Knipe also knew that passion was powerful, heady stuff, and must be prudently dispensed—the right proportions at the right moments; and to ensure this, he had devised an independent control consisting of two sensitive sliding adjustors operated by foot-pedals, similar to the throttle and brake in a car. One pedal governed the percentage of passion to be injected, the other regulated its intensity. There was no doubt, of course —and this was the only drawback —that the writing of a novel by the Knipe method was going to be rather like flying a plane and driving a car and playing an organ all at the same time, but this did not trouble the inventor. When all was ready, he proudly escorted Mr. Bohlen into the machine house and began to explain the operating procedure for the new wonder.

"Good heavens, Knipe! I'll never be able to do all that! Confound it, man, it'd be easier to write the thing by hand!"

"You'll soon get used to it, Mr. Bohlen, I promise you. In a week or two, you'll be doing it without really thinking. It's just like learning to drive."

Well, it wasn't quite as easy as that, but after many hours of practice, Mr. Bohlen began to get the hang of it, and finally, late one evening, he told Knipe to make ready for running off the first novel. It was a tense moment, with the fat little man crouching nervously in the driver's seat, and the tall toothy Knipe fussing excitedly around him.

"I intend to write an important novel, Knipe."

"I'm sure you will, sir. I'm sure you will."

With one finger, Mr. Bohlen carefully pressed the necessary pre-selector buttons:

Master button—*satirical*
Subject—*racial problem*
Style—*classical*
Characters—*six men, four women, one infant*
Length—*fifteen chapters.*

At the same time he had his eye particularly upon three organ stops marked *power, mystery, profundity.*

"Are you ready, sir?"

"Yes, yes, I'm ready."

Knipe pulled the switch. The great engine hummed. There was a deep whirring sound from the oiled movement of fifty thousand cogs and rods and levers; then came the drumming of the rapid electrical typewriter, setting up a shrill, almost intolerable clatter. Out into the basket flew the typewritten pages—one every two seconds. But what with the noise and the excitement, and having to play upon the stops, and watch the chapter-counter and the pace-indicator and the passion-gauge, Mr. Bohlen began to panic. He reacted in precisely the way a learner driver does in a car—by pressing both feet hard down on the pedals and keeping them there until the thing stopped.

"Congratulations on your first novel," Knipe said, picking up the great bundle of typed pages from the basket.

Little pearls of sweat were oozing out all over Mr. Bohlen's face. "It sure was hard work, my boy."

"But you got it done, sir. You got it done."

"Let me see it, Knipe. How does it read?"

He started to go through the first chapter, passing each finished page to the younger man.

"Good heavens, Knipe! What's this!" Mr. Bohlen's thin purple fish-lip was moving slightly as it mouthed the words, his cheeks were beginning slowly to inflate.

"But look here, Knipe! This is outrageous!"

"I must say it's a bit ripe, sir."

"*Ripe!* It's perfectly revolting! I can't possibly put my name to this!"

"Quite right, sir. Quite right."

"Knipe! Is this some nasty trick you've been playing on me?"

"Oh no, sir! No!"

"It certainly looks like it."

"You don't think, Mr. Bohlen, that you mightn't have been pressing a little hard on the passion-control pedals, do you?"

"My dear boy, how should *I* know?"

"Why don't you try another?"

So Mr. Bohlen ran off a second novel, and this time it went according to plan.

Within a week, the manuscript had been read and accepted by an enthusiastic publisher. Knipe followed with one in his own name, then made a dozen more for good measure. In no time at all, Adolph Knipe's Literary Agency had become famous for its large stable of promising young novelists. And once again the money started rolling in.

It was at this stage that young Knipe began to display a real talent for big business.

"See here, Mr. Bohlen," he said. "We still got too much competition. Why don't we just absorb all the other writers in the country?"

Mr. Bohlen, who now sported a bottle-green velvet jacket and allowed his hair to cover two-thirds of his ears, was quite content with things the way they were. "Don't know what you mean, my boy. You can't just absorb writers."

"Of course you can, sir. Exactly like Rockefeller did with his oil companies. Simply buy 'em out, and if they won't sell, squeeze 'em out. It's easy!"

"Careful now, Knipe. Be careful."

"I've got a list here, sir, of fifty of the most successful writers in the country, and what I intend to do is offer each one of them a lifetime contract with pay. All *they* have to do is undertake never to write another word; and, of course, to let us use their names on our own stuff. How about that?"

"They'll never agree."

"You don't know writers, Mr. Bohlen. You watch and see."

"What about that creative urge, Knipe?"

"It's bunk! All they're really interested in is the money—just like everybody else."

In the end, Mr. Bohlen reluctantly agreed to give it a try, and Knipe, with his list of writers in his pocket, went off in a large chauffeur-driven Cadillac to make his calls.

He journeyed first to the man at the top of the list, a very great and wonderful writer, and he had no trouble getting into the house. He told his story and produced a suitcase full of sample novels, and a contract for the man to sign which guaranteed him so much a year for life. The man listened politely, decided he was dealing with a lunatic, gave him a drink, then firmly showed him to the door.

The second writer on the list, when he saw Knipe was serious, actually attacked him with a large metal paperweight, and the inventor had to flee down the garden followed by such a torrent of abuse and obscenity as he had never heard before.

But it took more than this to discourage Adolph Knipe. He was disappointed but not dismayed, and off he went in his big car to seek his next client. This one was a female, famous and popular, whose fat romantic books sold by the million across the country. She received Knipe graciously, gave him tea, and listened attentively to his story.

"It all sounds very fascinating," she said. "But of course I find it a little hard to believe."

"Madam," Knipe answered. "Come with me and see it with your own eyes. My car awaits you."

So off they went, and in due course, the astonished lady was ushered into the machine house where the wonder was kept. Eagerly, Knipe explained its workings, and after a while he even permitted her to sit in the driver's seat and practice with the buttons.

"All right," he said suddenly, "You want to do a book now?"

"Oh yes!" she cried. "Please!"

She was very competent and seemed to know exactly what she wanted. She made her own pre-selections, then ran off a long, romantic, passion-filled novel. She read through the first chapter and became so enthusiastic that she signed up on the spot.

"That's one of them out of the way," Knipe said to Mr. Bohlen afterwards. "A pretty big one too."

"Nice work, my boy."

"And you know *why* she signed?"

"Why?"

"It wasn't the money. She's got plenty of that."

"Then why?"

Knipe grinned, lifting his lip and baring a long pale upper gum. "Simply because she saw the machine-made stuff was better than her own."

Thereafter, Knipe wisely decided to concentrate only upon mediocrity. Anything better than that—and there were so few it didn't matter much—was apparently not quite so easy to seduce.

In the end, after several months of work, he had persuaded something like seventy per cent of the writers on his list to sign the contract. He found that the older ones, those who were running out of ideas and had taken to drink, were the easiest to handle. The younger people were more troublesome. They were apt to become abusive, sometimes violent when he approached them; and more than once Knipe was slightly injured on his rounds.

But on the whole, it was a satisfactory beginning. This last year—the first full year of the machine's operation—it was estimated that at least one-half of all the novels and stories published in the English language were produced by Adolph Knipe upon the Great Automatic Grammatisator.

Does this surprise you?

I doubt it.

And worse is yet to come. Today, as the secret spreads, many more are hurrying to tie up with Mr.

Knipe. And all the time the screw turns tighter for those who hesitate to sign their names.

This very moment, as I sit here listening to the howling of my nine starving children in the other room, I can feel my own hand creeping closer and closer to that golden contract that lies over on the other side of the desk.

Give us strength, oh Lord, to let our children starve.

Nightmare Number Three

STEPHEN VINCENT BENÉT

We had expected everything but revolt
And I kind of wonder myself when they started thinking—
But there's no dice in that now.
      I've heard fellows say
They must have planned it for years and maybe they did.
Looking back, you can find little incidents here and there,
Like the concrete-mixer in Jersey eating the wop
Or the roto press that printed "Fiddle-dee-dee!"
In a three-color process all over Senator Sloop,
Just as he was making a speech. The thing about that
Was, how could it walk upstairs? But it was upstairs,
Clicking and mumbling in the Senate Chamber.
They had to knock out the wall to take it away
And the wrecking-crew said it grinned.
        It was only the best
Machines, of course, the superhuman machines,
The ones we'd built to be better than flesh and bone,
But the cars were in it, of course . . .
       and they hunted us
Like rabbits through the cramped streets on that Bloody Monday,
The Madison Avenue busses leading the charge.
The busses were pretty bad—but I'll not forget
The smash of glass when the Duesenberg left the show-room
And pinned three brokers to the Racquet Club steps,
Or the long howl of the horns when they saw the men run,
When they saw them looking for holes in the solid ground. . . .

I guess they were tired of being ridden in,
And stopped and started by pygmies for silly ends,
Of wrapping cheap cigarettes and bad chocolate bars,

Collecting nickels and waving platinum hair,
And letting six million people live in a town.
I guess it was that. I guess they got tired of us
And the whole smell of human hands.

                    But it was a shock
  To climb sixteen flights of stairs to Art Zuckow's office
(Nobody took the elevators twice)
And find him strangled to death in a nest of telephones,
The octopus-tendrils waving over his head,
And a sort of quiet humming filling the air. . . .
Do they eat? . . . There was red. . . . But I did not stop to look.
And it's lonely, here on the roof.

                    For a while I thought
That window-cleaner would make it, and keep me company.
But they got him with his own hoist at the sixteenth floor
And dragged him in with a squeal.
You see, they co-operate. Well, we taught them that,
And it's fair enough, I suppose. You see, we built them.
We taught them to think for themselves.
It was bound to come. You can see it was bound to come.
And it won't be so bad, in the country. I hate to think
Of the reapers, running wild in the Kansas fields,
And the transport planes like hawks on a chickenyard,
But the horses might help. We might make a deal with the horses.
At least you've more chance, out there.

                    And they need us too.
They're bound to realize that when they once calm down.
They'll need oil and spare parts and adjustments and tuning up.
Slaves? Well, in a way, you know, we were slaves before.
There won't be so much real difference—honest there won't.
(I wish I hadn't looked into that beauty-parlor
And seen what was happening there.
But those are female machines and a bit high-strung.)
Oh, we'll settle down. We'll arrange it. We'll compromise.
It wouldn't make sense to wipe out the whole human race.
Why, I bet if I went to my old Plymouth now
(Of course, you'd have to do it the tactful way)
And said, "Look here! Who got you the swell French horn?"
He wouldn't turn me over to those police cars.
At least I don't think he would.

                    Oh, it's going to be jake.
There won't be so much real difference—honest, there won't—

And I'd go down in a minute and take my chance—
I'm a good American and I always liked them—
Except for one small detail that bothers me
And that's the food proposition. Because you see,
The concrete-mixer may have made a mistake,
And it looks like just high spirits.
But, if it's got so they like the flavor . . . well . . .

MAURICE WALSH

The Quiet Man

Shawn Kelvin, a blithe young lad of twenty, went to the States to seek his fortune. And fifteen years thereafter he returned to his native Kerry, his blitheness sobered and his youth dried to the core, and whether he had made his fortune or whether he had not, no one could be knowing for certain. For he was a quiet man, not given to talking about himself and the things he had done. A quiet man, under middle size, with strong shoulders and deep-set blue eyes below brows darker than his dark hair—that was Shawn Kelvin. One shoulder had a trick of hunching slightly higher than the other, and some folks said that came from a habit he had of shielding his eyes in the glare of an open-hearth furnace in a place called Pittsburgh, while others said it used to be a way he had of guarding his chin that time he was a sort of sparring-partner punching bag at a boxing camp.

Shawn Kelvin came home and found that he was the last of the Kelvins, and that the farm of his forefathers had added its few acres to the ranch of Big Liam O'Grady, of Moyvalla. Shawn took no action to recover his land, though O'Grady had got it meanly. He had had enough of fighting, and all he wanted now was peace. He quietly went amongst the old and kindly friends and quietly looked about him for the place and peace he wanted; and when the time came, quietly produced the money for a neat, handy, small farm on the first warm shoulder of Knockanore Hill below the rolling curves of heather. It was not a big place but it was in good heart, and it got all the sun that was going; and, best of all, it suited Shawn to the tiptop notch of contentment; for it held the peace that tuned to his quietness, and it commanded the widest view in all Ireland—vale and mountain and the lifting green plain of the Atlantic Sea.

There, in a four-roomed, lime-washed, thatched cottage, Shawn made his life, and, though his friends hinted his needs and obligations, no thought came to him of bringing a wife into the place. Yet Fate had the thought and the dream in her loom for him. One middling imitation of a man he had to do chores for him, an ex-navy pensioner handy enough about house and byre, but with no relish for the sustained work of the field —and, indeed, as long as he kept house and byre shipshape, he found Shawn an easy master.

Shawn himself was no drudge toiler. He knew all about drudgery and the way it wears out a man's soul. He plowed a little and sowed a little, and at the end of a furrow he would lean on the handles of the cultivator, wipe his brow, if it needed wiping, and lose himself for whole minutes in the great green curve of the sea out there beyond the high black portals of Shannon mouth. And sometimes of an evening he would see, under the glory of the sky, the faint smoke smudge of an American liner. Then he would smile to himself—a pitying smile—thinking of the poor devils, with dreams of fortune luring them, going out to sweat in Ironville or to stand in a breadline. All these things were behind Shawn forever.

Market days he would go down and across to Listowel town, seven miles, to do his bartering; and in the long evenings, slowly slipping into the endless summer gloaming, his friends used to climb the winding lane to see him. Only the real

friends came that long road, and they were welcome—fighting men who had been out in the "Sixteen"; Matt Tobin the thresher, the schoolmaster, the young curate—men like that. A stone jar of malt whisky would appear on the table, and there would be a haze of smoke and a maze of warm, friendly disagreements.

"Shawn, old son," one of them might hint, "aren't you sometimes terrible lonely?"

"Never!" might retort Shawn derisively. "Why?"

"Nothing but the daylight and the wind and the sun setting with the wrath o' God."

"Just that! Well?"

"But after stirring times beyond in the States—"

"Ay! Tell me, fine man, have you ever seen a furnace in full blast?"

"A great sight."

"Great surely! But if I could jump you into a steel foundry this minute, you would be sure that God had judged you faithfully into the very hob of hell."

And then they would laugh and have another small one from the stone jar.

And on Sundays Shawn used to go to church, three miles down to the gray chapel above the black cliffs of Doon Bay. There Fate laid lure for him.

Sitting quietly on his wooden bench or kneeling on the dusty footboard, he would fix his steadfast, deep-set eyes on the vestmented celebrant and say his prayers slowly, or go into that strange trance, beyond dreams and visions, where the soul is almost at one with the unknowable.

But after a time, Shawn's eyes no longer fixed themselves on the celebrant. They went no farther than two seats ahead. A girl sat there, Sunday after Sunday she sat in front of him, and Sunday after Sunday his first casual admiration grew warmer.

She had a white nape to her neck and short red hair above it, and Shawn liked the color and wave of that flame. And he liked the set of her shoulders and the way the white neck had of leaning a little forward and she at her prayers—or her dreams. And the service over, Shawn used to stay in his seat so that he might get one quick but sure look at her face as she passed out. And he liked her face, too—the wide-set gray eyes, cheekbones firmly curved, clean-molded lips, austere yet sensitive. And he smiled pityingly at himself that one of her name should make his pulses stir—for she was an O'Grady.

One person, only, in the crowded chapel noted Shawn's look and the thought behind the look. Not the girl. Her brother, Big Liam O'Grady of Moyvalla, the very man who as good as stole the Kelvin acres. And that man smiled to himself, too—the ugly, contemptuous smile that was his by nature—and, after another habit he had, he tucked away his bit of knowledge in

mind corner against a day when it might come in useful for his own purposes.

The girl's name was Ellen—Ellen O'Grady. But in truth she was no longer a girl. She was past her first youth into that second one that has no definite ending. She might be thirty—she was no less—but there was not a lad in the countryside would say she was past her prime. The poise of her and the firm set of her bones below clean skin saved her from the fading of mere prettiness. Though she had been sought in marriage more than once, she had accepted no one, or rather, had not been allowed to encourage anyone. Her brother saw to that.

Big Liam O'Grady was a great raw-boned, sandy-haired man, with the strength of an ox and a heart no bigger than a sour apple. An overbearing man given to berserk rages. Though he was a churchgoer by habit, the true god of that man was Money—red gold, shining silver, dull copper—the trinity that he worshiped in degree. He and his sister Ellen lived on the big ranch farm of Moyvalla, and Ellen was his housekeeper and maid of all work. She was a careful housekeeper, a good cook, a notable baker, and she demanded no wage. All that suited Big Liam splendidly, and so she remained single—a wasted woman.

Big Liam himself was not a marrying man. There were not many spinsters with a dowry big enough to tempt him, and the few there were had acquired expensive tastes —a convent education, the deplorable art of hitting jazz out of a piano, the damnable vice of cigarette smoking, the purse-emptying craze for motor cars—such things.

But in due time, the dowry and the place—with a woman tied to them—came under his nose, and Big Liam was no longer tardy. His neighbor, James Carey, died in March and left his fine farm and all on it to his widow, a youngish woman without children, a woman with a hard name for saving pennies. Big Liam looked once at Kathy Carey and looked many times at her broad acres. Both pleased him. He took the steps required by tradition. In the very first week of the following Shrovetide, he sent an accredited emissary to open formal negotiations, and that emissary came back within the hour.

"My soul," said he, "but she is the quick one! I hadn't ten words out of me when she was down my throat. 'I am in no hurry,' says she, 'to come wife to a house with another woman at the fire corner. When Ellen is in a place of her own, I will listen to what Liam O'Grady has to say.'"

"She will, I say!" Big Liam stopped. "She will so."

There, now, was the right time to recall Shawn Kelvin and the look in his eyes. Big Liam's mind corner promptly delivered up its memory. He smiled knowingly and contemptuously. Shawn Kelvin daring to cast sheep's eyes at an O'Grady! The undersized chicken heart, who took the loss of the Kelvin acres lying down! The little Yankee runt hidden away on the shelf of Knockanore! But what of it? The required dowry would be conveniently small, and the girl would never go hungry, anyway. There was Big Liam O'Grady, far descended from many chieftains.

The very next market day at Listowel he sought out Shawn Kelvin and placed a huge, sandy-haired hand on the shoulder that hunched to meet it.

"Shawn Kelvin, a word with you! Come and have a drink."

Shawn hesitated. "Very well," he said then. He did not care for O'Grady, but he would hurt no man's feelings.

They went across to Sullivan's bar and had a drink, and Shawn paid for it. And Big Liam came directly to his subject—almost patronizingly, as if he were conferring a favor.

"I want to see Ellen settled in a place of her own," said he.

Shawn's heart lifted into his throat and stayed there. But that steadfast face with the steadfast eyes gave no sign and, moreover, he could not say a word with his heart where it was.

"Your place is small," went on the big man, "but it is handy, and no load of debt on it, as I hear. Not much of a dowry ever came to Knockanore, and not much of a dowry can I be giving with Ellen. Say two hundred pounds at the end of harvest, if prices improve. What do you say, Shawn Kelvin?"

Shawn swallowed his heart, and his voice came slow and cool: "What does Ellen say?"

"I haven't asked her," said Big Liam. "But what would she say, blast it?"

"Whatever she says, she will say it herself, not you, Big Liam."

But what could Ellen say? She looked within her own heart and found it empty; she looked at the granite crag of her brother's face and contemplated herself a slowly withering spinster at his fire corner; she looked up at the swell of Knockanore Hill and saw the white cottage among the green small fields below the warm brown of the heather. Oh, but the sun would shine up there in the lengthening spring day and pleasant breezes blow in sultry summer; and finally she looked at Shawn Kelvin, that firmly built, small man with the clean face and lustrous eyes below steadfast brow. She said a prayer to her God and sank head and shoulders in a resignation more pitiful than tears, more proud than the pride of chieftains. Romance? Welladay!

Shawn was far from satisfied with that resigned acceptance, but then was not the time to press for a warmer one. He knew the brother's wizened soul, guessed at the girl's clean one, and saw that she was doomed beyond hope to a fireside sordidly bought for her. Let it be his own fireside then. There were many worse ones—and God was good.

Ellen O'Grady married Shawn Kelvin. One small statement; and it holds the risk of tragedy, the chance of happiness, the probability of mere endurance—choices wide as the world.

But Big Liam O'Grady, for all his resolute promptness, did not win Kathy Carey to wife. She, foolishly enough, took to husband her own cattleman, a gay night rambler, who gave her the devil's own time and a share of happiness in the bygoing. For the first time, Big Liam discovered how mordant the wit of his neighbors could be, and to contempt for Shawn Kelvin he now added an unreasoning dislike.

Shawn Kelvin had got his precious, red-haired woman under his own roof now. He had no illusions about her feelings for him. On himself, and on himself only, lay the task of molding her into a wife and lover. Darkly, deeply, subtly, away out of sight, with gentleness, with restraint, with a consideration beyond kenning, that molding must be done, and she that was being molded must never know. He hardly knew, himself.

First he turned his attention to material things. He hired a small servant maid to help her with the housework. Then he acquired a rubber-tired tub cart and a half-bred gelding with a reaching knee action. And on market days, husband and wife used to bowl down to Listowel, do their selling and their buying, and bowl smoothly home again, their groceries in the well of the cart and a bundle of second-hand American magazines on the seat at Ellen's side. And in the nights, before the year turned, with the wind from the plains of the Atlantic keening above the chimney, they would sit at either side of the flaming peat fire, and he would read aloud strange and almost unbelievable things out of the high-colored magazines. Stories, sometimes, wholly unbelievable.

Ellen would sit and listen and smile, and go on with her knitting or her sewing; and after a time it was sewing she was at mostly—small things. And when the reading was done, they would sit and talk quietly in their own quiet way. For they were both quiet. Woman though she was, she got Shawn to do most of the talking. It could be that she, too, was probing and seeking, unwrapping the man's soul to feel the texture thereof, surveying the marvel of his life as he spread it diffidently before her. He had a patient, slow, vivid way of picturing for her the things he had seen and felt. He made her see the glare of molten metal, lambent yet searing, made her feel the sucking heat, made her hear the clang; she could see the roped square under the dazzle of the hooded arcs with the curling smoke layer above it, understand the explosive restraint of the game, thrill when he showed her how to stiffen wrist for the final

devastating right hook. And often enough the stories were humorous, and Ellen would chuckle, or stare, or throw back her red, lovely curls in laughter. It was grand to make her laugh.

Shawn's friends, in some hesitation at first, came in ones and twos up the slope to see them. But Ellen welcomed them with her smile that was shy and, at the same time, frank, and her table was loaded for them with scones and crumpets and cream cakes and heather honey; and at the right time it was she herself that brought forth the decanter of whisky—no longer the half-empty stone jar—and the polished glasses. Shawn was proud as sin of her. She would sit then and listen to their discussions and be forever surprised at the knowledgeable man her husband was—the way he would discuss war and politics and the making of songs, the turn of speech that summed up a man or a situation. And sometimes she would put in a word or two and he listened too, and they would look to see if her smile commended them, and be a little chastened by the wisdom of that smile—the age-old smile of the matriarch from whom they were all descended. In no time at all, Matt Tobin the thresher, who used to think, "Poor old Shawn! Lucky she was to get him," would whisper to the schoolmaster: "Herrin's alive! That fellow's luck would astonish nations."

Women, in the outside world, begin by loving their husbands; and then, if Fate is kind, they grow to admire them; and, if Fate is not unkind, may descend no lower than liking and enduring. And there is the end of lawful romance. Look now at Ellen O'Grady. She came up to the shelf of Knockanore and in her heart was only a nucleus of fear in a great emptiness, and that nucleus might grow into horror and disgust. But, glory of God, she, for reason piled on reason, presently found herself admiring Shawn Kelvin; and with or without reason, a quiet liking came to her for this quiet man who was so gentle and considerate; and then, one great heart-stirring dark o'night, she found herself fallen head and heels in love with her own husband. There is the sort of love that endures, but the road to it is a mighty chancy one.

A woman, loving her husband, may or may not be proud of him, but she will fight like a tiger if anyone, barring herself, belittles him. And there was one man that belittled Shawn Kelvin. Her brother, Big Liam O'Grady. At fair or market or chapel that dour giant designed not to hide his contempt and dislike. Ellen knew why. He had lost a wife and farm; he had lost in herself a frugally cheap housekeeper; he had been made the butt of a sly humor; and for these mishaps, in some twisted way, he blamed Shawn. But—and there came in the contempt—the little Yankee runt, who dared say nothing about the lost Kelvin acres,

would not now have the gall or guts to demand the dowry that was due. Lucky the hound to steal an O'Grady to hungry Knockanore! Let him be satisfied with that luck!

One evening before a market day, Ellen spoke to her husband: "Has Big Liam paid you my dowry yet, Shawn?"

"Sure there's no hurry, girl," said Shawn.

"Have you ever asked him?"

"I have not. I am not looking for your dowry, Ellen."

"And Big Liam could never understand that." Her voice firmed. "You will ask him tomorrow."

"Very well so, *agrah*," agreed Shawn easily.

And the next day, in that quiet diffident way of his, he asked Big Liam. But Big Liam was brusque and blunt. He had no loose money and Kelvin would have to wait till he had. "Ask me again, Shawneen," he finished, his face in a mocking smile, and turning on his heel, he plowed his great shoulders through the crowded market.

His voice had been carelessly loud and people had heard. They laughed and talked amongst themselves. "Begogs! The devil's own boy, Big Liam! What a pup to sell! Stealing the land and keeping a grip on the fortune! Ay, and a dangerous fellow, mind you, the same Big Liam! He would smash little Shawn at the wind of a word. And devil the bit his Yankee sparring tricks would help him!"

A friend of Shawn's, Matt Tobin

the thresher, heard that and lifted his voice: "I would like to be there the day Shawn Kelvin loses his temper."

"A bad day for poor Shawn!"

"It might then," said Matt Tobin, "but I would come from the other end of Kerry to see the badness that would be in it for someone."

Shawn had moved away with his wife, not heeding or not hearing.

"You see, Ellen?" he said in some discomfort. "The times are hard on the big ranchers, and we don't need the money, anyway."

"Do you think Big Liam does?" Her voice had a cut in it. "He could buy you and all Knockanore and be only on the fringe of his hoard. You will ask him again."

"But, girl dear, I never wanted a dowry with you."

She liked him to say that, but far better would she like to win for him the respect and admiration that was his due. She must do that now at all costs. Shawn, drawing back now, would be the butt of his fellow men.

"You foolish lad! Big Liam would never understand your feelings, with money at stake." She smiled and a pang went through Shawn's breast. For the smile was the smile of an O'Grady, and he could not be sure whether the contempt in it was for himself or for her brother.

Shawn asked Big Liam again, unhappy in his asking, but also dimly comprehending his woman's object. And Shawn asked again a third

time. The issue was become a famous one now. Men talked about it, and women too. Bets were made on it. At fair or market, if Shawn was seen approaching Big Liam, men edged closer and women edged away. Some day the big fellow would grow tired of being asked, and in one of his terrible rages half kill the little lad as he had half killed other men. A great shame! Here and there, a man advised Shawn to give up asking and put the matter in a lawyer's hands. "I couldn't do that," was Shawn's only answer. Strangely enough, none of these prudent advisers were amongst Shawn's close friends. His friends frowned and said little, but they were always about, and always amongst them was Matt Tobin.

The day at last came when Big Liam grew tired of being asked. That was the big October cattle fair at Listowel, and he had sold twenty head of fat Polled Angus beeves at a good price. He was a hard dealer and it was late in the day before he settled at his own figure, so that the banks were closed and he was not able to make a lodgment. He had, then, a great roll of bills in an inner vest pocket when he saw Shawn and Ellen coming across to where he was bargaining with Matt Tobin for a week's threshing. Besides, the day being dank, he had had a drink or two more than was good for him and the whisky had loosened his tongue and whatever he had of discretion. By the powers!—it was time and past time to deal once and for all with this little gadfly of a fellow, to show him up before the whole market. He strode to meet Shawn, and people got out of his savage way and edged in behind to lose nothing of this dangerous game.

He caught Shawn by the hunched shoulder—a rending grip—and bent down to grin in his face.

"What is it, little fellow? Don't be ashamed to ask!"

Matt Tobin was probably the only one there to notice the ease with which Shawn wrenched his shoulder free, and Matt Tobin's eyes brightened. But Shawn did nothing further and said no word. His deep-set eyes gazed steadily at the big man.

The big man showed his teeth mockingly. "Go on, you whelp! What do you want?"

"You know, O'Grady."

"I do. Listen, Shawneen!" Again he brought his handclap on the little man's shoulder. "Listen, Shawneen! If I had a dowry to give my sister, 'tis not a little shrimp like you would get her!"

His great hand gripped and he flung Shawn backwards as if he were only the image of a man filled with chaff.

Shawn went backwards, but he did not fall. He gathered himself like a spring, feet under him, arms half-raised, head forward into hunched shoulder. But as quickly as the spring coiled, as quickly it slackened, and he turned away to his wife. She was there facing him, tense and keen, her face pale and set, and a gleam of the race in her eyes.

"Woman, woman!" he said in his deep voice. "Why would you and I shame ourselves like this?"

"Shame!" she cried. "Will you let him shame you now?"

"But your own brother, Ellen—before them all?"

"And he cheating you—"

"Glory of God!" His voice was distressed. "What is his dirty money to me? Are you an O'Grady, after all?"

That stung her and she stung him back in one final effort. She placed a hand below her breast and looked close into his face. Her voice was low and bitter, and only he heard: "I am an O'Grady. It is a great pity that the father of this my son is a Kelvin and a coward."

The bosses of Shawn Kelvin's cheekbones were like hard marble, but his voice was as soft as a dove's.

"Is that the way of it? Let us be going home then, in the name of God!"

He took her arm, but she shook his hand off; nevertheless, she walked at his side, head up, through the people that made way for them. Her brother mocked them with his great, laughing bellow.

"That fixes the pair of them!" he cried, brushed a man who laughed with him out of his way, and strode off through the fair.

There was talk then—plenty of it. "Murder, but Shawn had a narrow squeak that time! Did you see the way he flung him? I wager he'll give Big Liam a wide road after this. And he by way of being a boxer! That's a pound you owe me, Matt Tobin."

"I'll pay it," said Matt Tobin, and that is all he said. He stood wide-legged, looking at the ground, his hand ruefully rubbing the back of his head and dismay and gloom on his face. His friend had failed him in the face of the people.

Shawn and Ellen went home in their tub cart and had not a single word or glance for each other on the road. And all that evening, at table or fireside, a heart-sickening silence held them in its grip. And all that night they lay side by side, still and mute. There was only one subject that possessed them and on that they dared speak no longer. They slept little. Ellen, her heart desolate, lay on her side, staring into the dark, grieving for what she had said and unable to unsay it. Shawn, on his back, contemplated things with a cold clarity. He realized that he was at the fork of life and that a finger pointed unmistakably. He must risk the very shattering of all happiness, he must do a thing so final and decisive that, once done, it could never again be questioned. Before morning, he came to his decision, and it was bitter as gall. He cursed himself. "Oh, you fool! You might have known that you should never have taken an O'Grady without breaking the O'Gradys."

He got up early in the morning at his usual hour and went out, as usual, to his morning chores—re-

bedding and foddering the cattle, rubbing down the half-breed, helping the servant maid with the milk in the creaming pans—and, as usual, he came in to his breakfast, and ate it unhungrily and silently, which was not usual. But, thereafter he again went out to the stable, harnessed his gelding and hitched him to the tub cart. Then he returned to the kitchen and spoke for the first time.

"Ellen, will you come with me down to see your brother?"

She hesitated, her hands thrown wide in a helpless, hopeless gesture. "Little use you going to see my brother, Shawn. 'Tis I should go and—and not come back."

"Don't blame me now or later, Ellen. It has been put on me and the thing I am going to do is the only thing to be done. Will you come?"

"Very well," she agreed tonelessly. "I will be ready in a minute."

And they went the four miles down into the vale to the big farmhouse of Moyvalla. They drove into the great square of cobbled yard and found it empty.

On one side of the square was the long, low, lime-washed dwelling house; on the other, fifty yards away, the two-storied line of steadings with a wide arch in the middle; and through the arch came the purr and zoom of a threshing machine. Shawn tied the half-breed to the wheel of a farm cart and, with Ellen, approached the house.

A slattern servant girl leaned over

the kitchen half-door and pointed through the arch. The master was out beyond in the haggard—the rickyard—and would she run across for him?

"Never mind, *achara*," said Shawn, "I'll get him. . . . Ellen, will you go in and wait?"

"No," said Ellen, "I'll come with you." She knew her brother.

As they went through the arch, the purr and zoom grew louder and, turning the corner, they walked into the midst of the activity. A long double row of cone-pointed corn-stacks stretched across the yard and, between them, Matt Tobin's portable threshing machine was busy. The smooth-flying, eight-foot driving wheel made a sleepy purr and the black driving belt ran with a sag and heave to the red-painted thresher. Up there on the platform, bare-armed men were feeding the flying drum with loosened sheaves, their hands moving in a rhythmic sway. As the toothed drum bit at the corn sheaves, it made an angry snarl that changed and slowed into a satisfied zoom. The wide convey-ing belt was carrying the golden straw up a steep incline to where other men were building a long rick; still more men were attending to the corn shoots, shoulders bend-ing under the weight of the sacks as they ambled across to the gran-ary. Matt Tobin himself bent at the face of his engine, feeding the fire box with sods of hard black peat. There were not less than two score men about the place, for, as was the custom, all Big Liam's friends and neighbors were giving him a hand with the threshing—"the day in harvest."

Big Liam came round the flank of the engine and swore. He was in his shirt sleeves, and his great fore-arms were covered with sandy hair.

"Look who's here!"

He was in the worst of tempers this morning. The stale dregs of yesterday's whisky were still with him, and he was in the humor that, as they say, would make a dog bite its father. He took two slow strides and halted, feet apart and head truculently forward.

"What is it this time?" he shouted. That was the un-Irish wel-come he gave his sister and her hus-band.

Shawn and Ellen came forward steadily, and, as they came, Matt Tobin slowly throttled down his engine. Big Liam heard the change of pitch and looked angrily over his shoulder.

"What do you mean, Tobin? Get on with the work!"

"Big Liam, this is my engine, and if you don't like it, you can leave it!" And at that he drove the throt-tle shut and the purr of the flywheel slowly sank.

"We will see in a minute," threat-ened Big Liam, and turned to the two now near at hand.

"What is it?" he growled.

"A private word with you. I won't keep you long." Shawn was calm and cold.

"You will not—on a busy morn-

ing," sneered the big man. "There
is no need for private words between me and Shawn Kelvin."

"There is need," urged Shawn.
"It will be best for us all if you hear
what I have to say in your own
house."

"Or here on my own land. Out
with it! I don't care who hears!"

Shawn looked round him. Up on
the thresher, up on the straw rick,
men leaned idle on fork handles
and looked down at him; from here
and there about the stackyard, men
moved in to see, as it might be,
what had caused the stoppage, but
only really interested in the two
brothers-in-law. He was in the
midst of Clan O'Grady, for they
were mostly O'Grady men—big,
strong, blond men, rough, confi-
dent, proud of their breed. Matt
Tobin was the only man he could
call a friend. Many of the others
were not unfriendly, but all had
contempt in their eyes, or, what was
worse, pity. Very well! Since he
had to prove himself, it was fitting
that he do it here amongst the
O'Grady men.

Shawn brought his eyes back to
Big Liam—deep, steadfast eyes that
did not waver. "O'Grady," said he—
and he no longer hid his contempt
—"you set a great store by money."

"No harm in that. You do it yourself, Shawneen."

"Take it so! I will play that game
with you, as long as you like. You
would bargain your sister and
cheat; I will sell my soul. Listen,
you big brute! You owe me two

hundred pounds. Will you pay it?"
There was an iron quality in his
voice that was somewhat awesome.
The big man, about to start forward
overbearingly, restrained himself to
a brutal playfulness.

"I will pay it when I am ready."

"Today."

"No; nor tomorrow."

"Right. If you break your bargain,
I break mine."

"What's that?" shouted Big
Liam.

"If you keep your two hundred
pounds, you keep your sister."

"What is it?" shouted Big Liam
again, his voice breaking in astonishment. "What is that you say?"

"You heard me. Here is your
sister Ellen! Keep her!"

He was completely astounded out
of his truculence. "You can't do
that!"

"It is done," said Shawn.

Ellen O'Grady had been quiet as
a statue at Shawn's side, but now,
slow like doom, she faced him. She
leaned forward and looked into his
eyes and saw the pain behind the
strength.

"To the mother of your son,
Shawn Kelvin?" she whispered that
gently to him.

His voice came cold as a stone
out of a stone face: "In the face of
God. Let Him judge me."

"I know—I know!" That was all
she said, and walked quietly across
to where Matt Tobin stood at the
face of his engine.

Matt Tobin placed hand on her
arm. "Give him time, *acolleen*," he

whispered urgently. "Give him his own time. He's slow but he's deadly as a tiger when he moves."

Big Liam was no fool. He knew exactly how far he could go. There was no use, at this juncture, in crushing the runt under a great fist. There was some force in the little fellow that defied dragooning. Whatever people might think of Kelvin, public opinion would be dead against himself. Worse, his inward vision saw eyes leering in derision, mouths open in laughter. The scandal on his name would not be bounded by the four seas of Erin. He must change his stance while he had time. These thoughts passed through his mind while he thudded the ground three times with ironshod heel. Now he threw up his head and bellowed his laugh.

"You fool! I was only making fun of you. What are your dirty few pounds to the likes of me? Stay where you are."

He turned, strode furiously away, and disappeared through the arch.

Shawn Kelvin was left alone in that wide ring of men. The hands had come down off the ricks and thresher to see closer. Now they moved back and aside, looked at one another, lifted eyebrows, looked at Shawn Kelvin, frowned and shook their heads. They knew Big Liam. They knew that, yielding up the money, his savagery would break out into something little short of killing. They waited, most of them, to prevent that savagery going too far.

Shawn Kelvin did not look at anyone. He stood still as a rock, his hands deep in his pockets, one shoulder hunched forward, his eyes on the ground and his face strangely calm. He seemed the least perturbed man there. Matt Tobin held Ellen's arm in a steadying grip and whispered in her ear: "God is good, I tell you."

Big Liam was back in two minutes. He strode straight to Shawn and halted within a pace of him.

"Look, Shawneen!" In his raised hand was a crumpled bundle of greasy bank notes. "Here is your money. Take it, and then see what will happen to you. Take it!" He thrust it into Shawn's hand. "Count it. Make sure you have it all—and then I will kick you out of this haggard—and look"—he thrust forward a hairy fist—"if ever I see your face again, I will drive that through it. Count it, you spawn!"

Shawn did not count it. Instead he crumpled it into a ball in his strong fingers. Then he turned on his heel and walked, with surprising slowness, to the face of the engine. He gestured with one hand to Matt Tobin, but it was Ellen, quick as a flash, who obeyed the gesture. Though the hot bar scorched her hand, she jerked open the door of the fire box and the leaping peat flames whispered out at her. And forthwith, Shawn Kelvin, with one easy sweep, threw the crumpled ball of notes into the heart of the flame. The whisper lifted one tone and one scrap of burned paper floated out of the funnel top. That was all the fuss the fire made of its work.

But there was fuss enough outside.

Big Liam O'Grady gave one mighty shout. No, it was more an anguished scream than a shout:

"My money! My good money!"

He gave two furious bounds forward, his great arms raised to crush and kill. But his hands never touched the small man.

"You dumb ox!" said Shawn Kelvin between his teeth. That strong, hunched shoulder moved a little, but no one there could follow the terrific drive of that hooked right arm. The smack of bone on bone was sharp as whip crack, and Big Liam stopped dead, went back on his heel, swayed a moment and staggered back three paces.

"Now and forever! Man of the Kelvins!" roared Matt Tobin.

But Big Liam was a man of iron. That blow should have laid him on his back—blows like it had tied men to the ground for the full count. But Big Liam only shook his head, grunted like a boar, and drove in at the little man. And the little man, instead of circling away, drove in at him, compact of power.

The men of the O'Gradys saw then an exhibition that they had not knowledge enough to appreciate fully. Thousands had paid as much as ten dollars each to see the great Tiger Kelvin in action, his footwork, his timing, his hitting; and never was his action more devastating than now. He was a thunderbolt on two feet and the big man a glutton.

Big Liam never touched Shawn with clenched fist. He did not know how. Shawn, actually forty pounds lighter, drove him by sheer hitting across the yard.

Men for the first time saw a two-hundred-pound man knocked clean off his feet by a body blow. They saw for the first time the deadly restraint and explosion of skill.

Shawn set out to demolish his enemy in the briefest space of time, and it took him five minutes to do it. Five, six, eight times he knocked the big man down, and the big man came again, staggering, slavering, raving, vainly trying to rend and smash. But at last he stood swaying and clawing helplessly, and Shawn finished him with his terrible double hit—left below the breastbone and right under the jaw.

Big Liam lifted on his toes and fell flat on his back. He did not even kick as he lay.

Shawn did not waste a glance at the fallen giant. He swung full circle on the O'Grady men and his voice of iron challenged them:

"I am Shawn Kelvin, of Knockanore Hill. Is there an O'Grady amongst you thinks himself a better man? Come then."

His face was deep-carved stone, his great chest lifted, the air whistled through his nostrils; his deep-set flashing eyes dared them.

No man came.

He swung around then and

walked straight to his wife. He halted before her.

His face was still of stone, but his voice quivered and had in it all the dramatic force of the Celt.

"Mother of my son, will you come home with me?"

She lifted to the appeal, voice and eye:

"Is it so you ask me, Shawn Kelvin?"

His face of stone quivered at last. "As my wife only—Ellen Kelvin!"

"Very well, heart's treasure." She caught his arm in both of hers. "Let us be going home."

"In the name of God," he finished for her.

And she went with him, proud as the morning, out of that place. But a woman, she would have the last word.

"Mother of God!" she cried. "The trouble I had to make a man of him!"

"God Almighty did that for him before you were born," said Matt Tobin softly.

The True Knight

STEPHEN HAWES

For knighthood is not in the feats of war,
As for to fight in quarrel right or wrong,
But in a cause which truth cannot defer:
He ought himself for to make sure and strong,
Justice to keep mixt with mercy among:
And no quarrel a knight ought to take
But for a truth, or for the common's sake.

JESSAMYN WEST

A Time of Learning

EMMETT MAGUIRE, hitching Old Clay to the buckboard, was suddenly convinced of folly. He became too sorrowful to slide the thin tail through the crupper, too pensive to buckle a hame strap. He stood in the sallow, early morning light gazing about the farmyard. Fool, he asked himself, where'll you find anything like this?

Just then, as he renounced it, the whole landscape so altered that he felt that for the first time in his nineteen years he was seeing it truly. All the familiar paraphernalia of the farm seemed suddenly to detach themselves from their background, move nearer him, become luminous and significant.

Amos, the blue-nosed mule, stood out against the sulphur-colored sky like sculpture. Emmett could not take his eyes from him. Now he was leaving—he had, in fact, moved heaven and earth to get away—and what did he really know of Amos? He had consigned himself to dab-

bling and traveling when he might have stayed home and learned, got to the bottom of mules. Against the morning sky, streaked now like a ripening Baldwin, Amos's head hung more heavy and knowledgeable than the rock of ages. Would there be any wisdom in the next county equal to what Amos had?

In the moment of leave-taking Emmett doubted it. Leaving, what could he expect? Girls and fritterings. No doubt sleep with the swine at the last, too, he supposed. But he felt as bound to move on as the prodigal himself, and for a better reason.

A sign and house painter soon paints himself out in his own neighborhood. All who incline toward paint and have money to pay for it come finally either to the end of the houses and sheds and outhouses needing a new coat or to the end of their money. All who care to have their fences decorated with signs for Hi-John Compelling Powder

156

have them so decorated. Then the painter moves on or puts down his brush.

"Having trouble?" Emmett's father came from behind the buckboard, where with Emmett's mother he had been stowing away a round leather box of clean collars.

"No trouble," said Emmett, pulling the long switch tail on through. "I was thinking."

He was thinking, if they shed a tear, I'll have to unhitch, unpack, stay forever. But he was mistaken. Had his father laid a hand on the bridle, or his mother clung to him, he would have been off, as determined and set in his leave-taking as he had been in his preparation to go. But the leave-taking was seemly, no tears shed or protestations made. As he drove away, the known objects continued to move toward him, become big with the brightness and urgency of the willfully rejected.

His parents saw him depart, untransformed: their dear son, artist and thinker, Emmett. Though those were words they had never been permitted to say to him.

Once, in the barn, his father had come upon a picture of Emmett's painting. He had stared at it a long time. It was a big, empty picture with great reaches of unoccupied cardboard. Except for the front of a house, an expanse of white siding dazzling in sunlight, there was almost nothing in the picture at all: shallow wooden steps ascended to a partially open door; beyond the door on the dark floor boards and deep in shadow lay something crumpled, a piece of goods, a ribbon perhaps, and beyond that a naked, retreating heel.

Emmett's father would have enriched the picture with many more objects: set pots of flowers on the steps, put a window next the door and a face at the window. Still empty and unembellished as the picture was, it had a certain power. He had found himself wondering about it: about that heel, more yellow than pink, about its haste, its alarm. Then he had noticed that there was a shadow across the steps, that near the house someone, stock-still, stood and watched. Listened, too, perhaps.

But when he had said to Emmett, who came in and found him staring, "Son, you're an artist," Emmett had taken the corn knife he had in his hand, and cut the picture to shreds.

"Don't call me that," he told his father. "Never say that. I can't learn. I'm a house and sign painter."

He was a house painter, or a barn or shed painter when he could find houses and barns and sheds to paint; but in Bucklin County he was treading upon the heels of a competitor. Emmett regarded with scorn the wash of murky green that marked the man's progress. A color not fit to set to the side of a hen house, he thought, not good enough for any privy I'd paint. He thanked

God for his contract and painted signs.

He had known for some time that he was being watched. That didn't trouble him. It was almost as if the eyes that followed the movements of his hand gave it added force. It was talk that troubled.

"What's 'Crossing and Un-Crossing Powder'?"

"I don't know," Emmett said, painting on.

"Would you make a sign for what you don't know?"

"Yes," said Emmett, "I would."

"I wouldn't."

Emmett said nothing.

"What's 'David the Fearless Floor Wash'?"

Emmett set his brush in the can of linseed oil, turned away from the granite rock on which he was lettering freehand.

"What's a kid who stands asking questions while you're trying to work?" he asked.

The boy was big but round, round as an apple, and his round black eyes were swallowing the lettering like quagmire.

"A nuisance," Emmett told him, shortly.

"What's the sign for?" the boy asked, as if he hadn't heard.

"Make people buy the stuff."

"How can they buy it if they don't know what it is?"

"You couldn't buy if you knew. You haven't got any money."

The boy's pants were tight, his pockets taut, his hands fat; still he managed to squeeze a quarter up to the air.

"All right," said Emmett. "Read that and be quiet." He tossed him the Occult Supplies Catalogue, turned back to his painting.

"Bat's Blood Oil," the boy said and Emmett could hear him moistly swallowing.

"Shut up," said Emmett, "or I'll take it away from you."

The boy shut up. Except for the swallowing he didn't make another sound until the sign was finished. The minute Emmett stepped away from the boulder to judge his completed work, he began again. "Which would you buy," he asked, "Graveyard Dust or Oriental Lover's Powder?"

"Graveyard Dust," said Emmett.

"Not me," said the boy. He pushed his quarter to the surface again. "I'll take three packages Oriental Lover's Powder."

"I don't sell the stuff," Emmett told him. "I just paint the signs. You write them," he pointed to the catalogue, "to get the powders."

"Have you got a pencil so's I could write it down?" the boy asked.

Emmett tore a sheet from the little notebook he carried, handed it and a pencil to the boy.

"What do you figure to do with it?" he asked, watching the boy, who wrote with his tongue as well as his fingers.

The boy looked up, but a sudden film came over his eyes. "None of your business," he said.

"That's right," said Emmett, "it isn't."

He took back the pencil and began to collect his gear.

"That your horse and rig by the bridge?"

"Yes," said Emmett.

"I'll help you carry your paints."

Emmett handed him a bucket. "Watch your step," he advised. "That's valuable."

The boy planted his bare feet as carefully as if walking through nettles. He looked over the amount of material in the back of the buckboard. "Takes an awful lot of paint to paint signs," he said.

"I paint houses, too," Emmett told him.

"Barns?" asked the boy.

"Sure," Emmett said.

"We got a barn to be painted."

"Who's we?"

"Us. My father. He wanted the other man to do it but Ivy said his paint looked like scum on a frog pond."

"Who's Ivy?" Emmett asked, thinking she'd picked the right word for it.

"My sister. But Ma said, 'There's things worse than scum, Miss Ivy.'"

"Don't your mother want the barn painted?"

"Oh, sure."

"I'll apply for the job," Emmett said. "You want to ride on home with me?"

They went by the river road. Red dust clung to the lush green growth that arched above their heads and Old Clay methodically lifted more

of it to their faces. Even in the gloom of red dust and green shadows the boy bent over the catalogue, reading or rereading, Emmett didn't know which, the wondrous items. Emmett himself was rehearsing a sales talk; reassuring himself, before he tried to convince others, that he was the man for the job.

When they turned away from the river, made for the open, rolling farm lands, Emmett asked the boy his name.

"Oral," he said, not looking up from his reading.

"Oral," Emmett repeated. "How do you spell that?"

Oral spelled it. "I'm named for a bird," he said, keeping his place in the catalogue with one finger. "A yellow, singing bird that sang where my mother used to live."

Emmett looked at the cannon-ball boy, his black eyes and white hair. "You're not very yellow, Oral," he said. "Can you sing?"

The boy didn't smile and he closed his catalogue. "No," he said, "nor lay eggs, neither."

"Excuse me, Oral," Emmett said.

There was no more talk for a time. Finally Oral said, "You're not very big for a man."

"Big enough," said Emmett.

"You ain't bad looking, though."

Emmett nodded his thanks.

"You got a girl?" Oral asked.

"No girl," Emmett said. "I'm off girls."

"Not me," said Oral. "I got two."

"You don't look very old to be having girls," Emmett told him.

"Old enough," said Oral and went back to his reading.

He roused to point out his home before they got there. It and its outbuildings were planted on a gentle rise of land, visible, as they approached, from every hilltop: a substantial brick house and a big weather-beaten, two-story barn. Three-story, it proved to be when they arrived, the hillside on the back having been scooped away to make room for stalls for the animals.

Oral's father, who was Oral expanded and coated with hoarfrost, heartily welcomed Emmett.

"I'm C. B. Lish," he said after Emmett had stated his own name and business, "and I'm pleased to make your acquaintance. The barn needs painting the worst way."

Emmett then delivered the rehearsed speech, speaking, as he thought right, of the quality of his paints: linseed base, lead content, color, time a coat would last; of his own work, skillful, experienced, painstaking. But C. B. Lish was reading.

"Candle Powder," he said wonderingly. "Now the way I always heard that was candle *power*."

"This is something different," Emmett explained, wishing the catalogue had never fallen into Lish hands. "This is a powder."

"Now, how," said C. B. Lish, "do you reckon they go about getting a Candle Powder? Grind 'em up?"

"I don't know," Emmett said. "I just paint the signs."

"Bible Bouquet Oil," he said reading on and sniffing as he read. "There's a concoction ought to be mighty sweet. You sell this, boy?"

"No, sir," Emmett said, "I don't. I'm a painter. I'd like to get the job painting your barn."

C. B. Lish was turning the pages. "Jinxers. Four inches tall."

"I don't sell that stuff," Emmett reminded him. "I paint."

C. B. Lish nodded, but didn't look up. "That's what you told me before. You walk on up to the house and talk to Emma and Ivy. They're the ones to decide."

Emmett never forgot the room he stepped into. After the summer dust and heat it was as if he had plunged into water, shadowed and cool. He closed his eyes once or twice as he would have done under water, to feel the coolness on his eyelids. The bricks, he supposed, were what made the room cool, the pulled blinds kept it dim.

The room was a kitchen because it had a stove in it: unlit, cool-looking, even, black and shiny like a stoat fresh from a shady wallow. But beside the kitchen furniture— the safe, the cabinet, the set table— there was much else in the room. There was a sofa, a small bird in a big wooden cage, a secretary whose space was about evenly divided between books and dishes, a diamond-shaped mirror with pegs for hats and coats at each corner. Beneath one of the pulled blinds, Emmett guessed, a prism was hanging, for onto the bleached floor boards fell shafts of multicolored lights.

And there was a girl in the room. Emmett saw her last of all. She stood in the darkest corner of the room, leaning against the sink, grating nutmeg on a pudding of some kind. Emmett could smell the vanilla, sweet and sharp, above the sweet muskiness of the nutmeg.

The girl looked up at Emmett, then grated away, not saying a word. Emmett prepared to speak, but could not for a minute. He knew what a beautiful girl should look like; he had often thought about it; he knew exactly what it took. So far as he could see, nothing was missing.

The girl had on a white dress. She curved in and she curved out. Her waist went in to a span as narrow and supple as a grapevine; elsewhere she had the fullness of the clusters. Her hair was like Oral's, but her eyes when she had looked up at Emmett were like the best milk-agates he had ever owned. O God, Emmett silently prayed, I thank thee for not letting me stay home and study mules.

She was a calm-looking girl, but seeing Emmett, she dropped the nutmeg, and the sound it made rolling along the bare floor boards brought him back to speech.

"Your nutmeg, Miss," said Emmett, getting it before it stopped rolling.

"Thank you," said the girl.

"I'm Emmett Maguire, house painter," Emmett told her.

"I'm pleased to meet you," said the girl. "I'm Miss Ivy Lish."

That night in the south upstairs chamber, a hot little room where a full-leafed chinaberry tree shut all the air from the single window, Emmett lay in a kind of trance. Sometimes he slept but more often he was awake, and every time he awakened he rejoiced as though he were Lazarus newly come to life. Sleeping, he dreamed of Ivy, but awake he thought of her. And, since he reckoned thinking to be one step nearer reality than dreaming, he hated to lose time in anything as second-hand as sleep.

He would awaken, wonder for a minute where he was, hear the leaves of the chinaberry tree moving outside his window with a watery ripple, say, "Ivy, Ivy." Inside himself he would feel a happiness so great it made him a little sick: a feeling like that he had tobogganing each winter on Sugar Slide, when at the final curve he always thought, I'll die this is so wonderful —joy and pain being at that point so delicately balanced.

Once he got out of his bed and laid the palms of both hands first against the west wall of his room, then against the east, telling himself as he did so, one inch of wood may be all that separates us. But all he heard as he stood, hands pressed to either wall, was a serene snoring: too delicate for Oral, probably C. B. Lish himself.

He had been in love before but

always unlucky, and never able to do much but suffer. Once with a girl who was engaged, who had bent down and kissed him twice on the eyelids, but would have no more to do with him; once with a girl whose father had promised to shoot any man or boy who came on the place, and Emmett, after hearing the first load of buckshot whistle past his legs, had never again been able to feel the same about her; the last time had been with a girl in Mercer, but before he had a horse of his own, and in the weeks when he had not been able to see her, she had met and married a coffee salesman.

But now he was lucky: in love and beneath the same roof with the girl he loved. And going to be beneath the same roof with her for two more weeks at the least. For the barn painting, if he did a good job, would take that long; and he intended doing not only a good job, but a job so wonderful people for miles around would marvel at it. He intended to paint the Lish barn as if it were a miniature, with every brush stroke being set on ivory.

The last time he awakened the summer night had ended. The air in the room had cooled and outside in the chinaberry tree the awakening birds were whetting their bills and stretching their throats.

I could paint her, Emmett thought. I see just how to do it, where she should stand, how turn her head. I would paint her in her

white dress, full length, a shadow at the base of her throat. In his hand he already felt the brush and the strokes it would make so that Ivy would stand curving in, curving out, alive upon cardboard. Alive with a reality beyond life because to her store of realness he would add all of his own.

There was nothing in the next week he did not do well. He was so filled with power and sureness he walked about his scaffolding as if gravity were a force from which he was exempt. He laid the brush against the barn each day in strokes so solid that the barn rose up clear and bright again, rebuilt, it almost seemed, as well as repainted.

At night, untired after the day's work, he washed first in turpentine and then in water, and talked with the family.

Privately, he said to C. B. Lish, "I'll paint the tool shed free if I can borrow your buggy, Sunday."

"What you want of the buggy?" Mr. Lish asked.

"I want to take Ivy to church."

Mr. Lish whistled. "So that's the way the wind blows."

"Yes, sir," said Emmett, "it is."

"Ivy's no churchgoer," Mr. Lish told him.

Emmett was taken aback. He had supposed all nice girls were churchgoers. He had no idea where else he could take a girl on Sunday, or what other entertainment she could want. Though he would never have denied that for himself coming and going would be the best part of it. Still this was Bucklin County, not home, and he hated a man who was set in his ways.

"Wherever she wants to go, I'll take her."

"The novelty of it," her father admitted, "might appeal to her."

Ivy said yes when he asked her, as if novelty had nothing to do with it.

Upon himself, upon Old Clay and the buggy, Emmett had done an amount of polishing just short of abrasion. A stroke or two more and varnish and hide, human and horse alike, would have given away. Tender and glittering, they drove churchward.

There was nothing Emmett could think of to say which did not seem too personal for words. His mind was filled with Ivy: her sweet, flowery smell, which it was probably wrong even to notice, let alone mention; the blue vein in her forehead; the way a fold of her full skirt lay across his shinbone, where its lightness weighed upon him like a burning glass.

They drove through heat waves rippling like lake water. Already the leaves hung downward, giving the sun only their sharp edges to taste. Old Clay was discolored by sweat and on the fence rails the birds rested with lifted wings.

"Ivy," said Emmett, "will you let me paint your picture?"

"Can you paint people, too?" Ivy asked. "Besides barns, I mean?"

"Yes," said Emmett, with sudden knowledge, "I can," and he used the word he had forbidden his father, "I'm an artist."

"Perhaps you would make me look funny," said Ivy.

"Funny," repeated Emmett. "What do you mean, funny?"

"Queer," Ivy told him. "Not pretty. Maybe you don't know how to paint well enough. Maybe you would make my eyes look funny. Eyes are very hard to paint."

"I know how to paint eyes," Emmett said. "I know how to paint all of a person. I would make you look the way you are, Ivy."

"How am I, Emmett?" asked Ivy.

"Beautiful," said Emmett, trembling with frankness.

From there on, the drive to church went by in a flash, the church time, too, though Ivy was unable to attend the services with Emmett. In the churchyard Arod Johnson had awaited her. His mother was sick, pining to see Ivy, and with Emmett's permission he would drive Ivy to his place, have her back by the time church was over. He was considerably later than that, and Emmett was sorry for Ivy cooped up with a sick old woman while he sat in the shaded churchyard. Still, he had been so deep in thought about his painting of her that he had not had time for much pity.

"Let's go home the long way," Ivy said when she got back.

They went home the long way through the hot afternoon.

"Tell me about my picture," Ivy said.

"I will paint you," Emmett said, "in the parlor bay window. I will push the lace curtain back so that on each side of the picture will be just their ripple. You will stand in your white dress before the clear glass and behind you will be the mock orange."

"How will I look?" asked Ivy.

"You will look," Emmett said slowly, seeing her like a white column budding for flowers—"fine."

"We came home the long way," Ivy told Oral, who was in the barnyard when they drove in. "We came home the long way and had to go slow because of the heat." She gave Emmett both her hands when he helped her from the buggy and walked at once to the house.

Oral helped with the unhitching.

"I reckon you seen Old Arod," he said.

"Arod Johnson?" asked Emmett.

"You know any other Arods?"

"No," said Emmett, "I don't. His mother was sick."

"She seems to be a mighty weak old lady," Oral told him, he himself leading Clay to the barn.

In the second week Emmett began work on the barn each morning at sunup. In that way he made time for his painting of Ivy. He had never supposed hand and brush could work so well together. It was as if the lines of Ivy's body flowed downward of themselves, through his arm and hand, and onto the

cardboard; it was as if her colors stained his fingers and he had only to touch his brush for them to be left where and as they should be.

"What do you think of while you paint?" Ivy asked.

He thought of very little. Then he was lost in the work; in the brush strokes, in the leaf-shaped shadows on the white dress, on the way Ivy's roundness and solidness were transferred by means of his skill so that in thin paint and upon a flat surface, still she was round and solid.

Afterward, when he was not painting, he thought: in later days the picture will hang in a special place in the house and I will say to visitors, that is my beautiful wife, Ivy Lish Maguire; and to the children I'll say, that is the first picture I ever painted of your mother. And I will never part with it, no matter what I should be offered for it.

"I would like my eyelashes made longer," said Ivy.

"No," said Emmett, "that would be wrong."

"Wrong?" said Ivy. "They are longer."

"But not looking at you," Emmett told her, "this way against the light."

If someone had told him, you have never said the word love, he would have been surprised. Everything he did said the word, every look, every tone, every gesture. He himself heard no other sound.

"Is it finished?" asked Ivy.

"One more day," said Emmett.

"Do you like it?"

"The eyelashes should be longer," said Ivy, but Emmett could tell by the way she stood looking at the picture, turning her head, smiling, that she liked it.

That night he worked until late on the barn and went early to bed. He lay in his upstairs bedroom listening to the chirr of summer insects, and thought, tomorrow night the picture will be finished and I will put, in one corner of the picture, my name, in the other, hers.

He was still awake when Oral came in, noisy in his unaccustomed shoes, and sat on the edge of his bed. Oral moved his feet back and forth across the floor boards, the bed squeaked as his weight shifted, a bird sang a note or two as if, awakening suddenly, it had mistaken the moonlight for dawn.

"Well, Oral?" asked Emmett.

"I got me a date with one of my girls," said Oral as if answering the question.

"Which one?" Emmett asked sleepily, not caring, thinking, he's got no one else to talk to about his girls.

"The best one," Oral said.

Emmett yawned silently, shut his eyes. The moonlight here in the corner, he thought, isn't strong enough for him to tell whether my eyes are open or shut.

"Two's too many," Oral said, "if you've got one good girl."

"One good girl's enough," Emmett agreed, smiling at Oral's wisdom. "How's the other one taking it?" he asked.

"She's down in the mouth," Oral admitted, "but she'll get over it."

"Sure," Emmett echoed out of his drowsiness, "they all get over it."

"Emmett," Oral asked, "who's that picture belong to, you or Ivy?"

"Ivy," Emmett said, wanting to say her name, though he had thought of the picture as theirs together.

"That's all right, then," Oral said getting off the bed.

"It's Ivy's and mine together," Emmett amended.

"She's given away your half too, then," Oral told him. "Both halves together to Arod Johnson."

Emmett sat up in bed. Oral was standing where the moonlight from the window fell across his broad and sorrowful face.

"I could've told you," he said, "but there wasn't ever a time when you'd hear to it."

"It's gone," he assured him, as Emmett got out of bed. "Wrapped in butcher paper and given away."

Emmett sat down again.

"My girl's waiting for me," Oral said. At the door he turned back. "Ivy's a born two-timer. You ain't the first."

For a long time after Oral left, Emmett sat on the edge of his bed. He felt numbed, beyond feeling anything, but when he stood up his hands and face were wet, and he saw that without knowing it he had been crying.

The thing to do, he decided, is to

get out, pack and leave. Get gone before I have to look on any of their faces again.

Outside, his carpetbag in his hand, he stood for a time in the barnyard. He could see that it was still early, a moonlit summer night, cooling off now so that the river mists were flowing up into the draws. He could hear the soft, slow movements of the animals in their stalls and once in awhile, as the air freshened, a slight fluttering of leaves.

Old Clay came quietly to the fence, hung his head across the top rail, and, with eyes glassy in the moonlight, looked at Emmett.

"Let's get out of here," Emmett said.

But when he saw the ladder and scaffolding still against the barn, and the unpainted section around the haymow door, he determined, stubbornly, to finish the job. "I'll not go and leave a stroke undone," he told Old Clay, as if his horse had argued with him about it.

Once he was on the scaffolding, brush in hand, another idea came to him: she took my picture and gave it away. I'll leave another here that can't be given away, and I'll paint her this time as she really is, so no eye can miss it.

He went down the ladder and brought up his other paints, and while he was doing this he was filled with hate and scorn, thinking I'll put her on the barn so that everyone can see what a slut looks like. But he could not do it.

He did not know which way it was: whether he was unable to paint and hate at the same time, or whether actually he would never be able to hate Ivy, no matter what she might do. Whichever way it was— whether the brush strokes took away his hate, or he was without real hate to begin with—he was painting a picture not much different from his first. And better, too, he knew; though whether on that surface, with the paints he had, it would show as much, he couldn't tell. There would be no rippling lace curtains in this picture because it would be Ivy herself, unobscured by any of his imaginings. He remembered what he had thought: a tower of white. And budding; and remembering, spat with disgust over the edge of the scaffolding.

From below someone whispered, "Look out for me," and there in the moonlight, gazing upward, was Oral.

"What you doing out this time of night?" Emmett asked.

"Getting home," Oral whispered, so that Emmett, answering, whispered too—though the house was far enough away to keep anyone from hearing. "You better get on to bed. You'll catch a strapping, staying out all night this way."

"Strapping," Oral scoffed. "I'm not sleeping in the house anyway," he said. "I'm sleeping in the haymow." He stood, stocky legs far apart, head thrown back so that his white hair shone in the moonlight like dandelion fuzz.

"What you painting her again for?" he whispered scornfully. "Whyn't you paint something nice for a change? Whyn't you paint something pretty up there? A big sunflower or a rooster?"

"Be quiet, can't you?" Emmett said. "This makes me feel better."

Oral went inside the barn and Emmett could hear him mounting the ladder into the haymow, then rustling about as he hollowed himself a place to sleep.

Long after Emmett had supposed him to be sleeping, he heard Oral's voice very near at hand as if he were speaking with his mouth close to a knothole or crack.

"Emmett?"

"What you want now, Oral?"

"Whyn't you get some of them powders, Emmett?"

"Powders?" asked Emmett.

"The ones from the catalogue. They work good Emmett." Oral's voice was filled with kindness.

"I didn't know they'd come."

"Oh, sure, they came. They're strong and good. I wish you'd try some, Emmett."

"No," Emmett told him, "they wouldn't work for me. No powder'll do me any good. I've just got to learn."

"Don't waste any more time on her," urged Oral. "Paint something nice. Paint a picture of a field of punkins."

"When I finish this," said Emmett, "I will."

The moon was still bright when he finished, but the stars had begun to dim and the sky's darkness was fading. He hitched and loaded his stuff into the buckboard, but before he drove away he stood looking up at his work.

"I can paint," he said looking at his picture of Ivy, forgetting Ivy herself.

He had driven down the slope from the house and up the first little rise when he heard a clear but controlled halooing behind him. Turning about, he saw that Oral had opened the door of the haymow so that his picture of Ivy was cut in two: a head, then where the upper part of her body should have been, the empty space of the open door, and below that the swelling white skirts.

"Emmett," Oral halooed quietly.

Emmett waved to show that he heard.

"You forgot your catalogue, Emmett."

"Keep it," Emmett called back. "You keep it, Oral. I can get another."

Their gentle voices carried on the quiet morning air. The last stars had faded and the river smell was fresh and sharp.

"Good-by, Emmett," Oral called as Emmett, waving, drove on.

For as long as Emmett could be seen, Oral stood in the open doorway, not waving, himself, but following the buckboard with his eyes until finally it topped a distant rise and dropped from sight.

When I Was One-and-Twenty

A. E. HOUSMAN

When I was one-and-twenty
I heard a wise man say,
"Give crowns and pounds and guineas
But not your heart away;
Give pearls away and rubies
But keep your fancy free."
But I was one-and-twenty,
No use to talk to me.

When I was one-and-twenty
I heard him say again,
"The heart out of the bosom
Was never given in vain;
'Tis paid with sighs a-plenty
And sold for endless rue."
And I am two-and-twenty,
And oh, 'tis true, 'tis true.

EDGAR ALLAN POE

The Cask of Amontillado

THE THOUSAND injuries of Fortunato I had borne as I best could, but when he ventured upon insult, I vowed revenge. You, who so well know the nature of my soul, will not suppose, however, that I gave utterance to a threat. *At length* I would be avenged; this was a point definitely settled—but the very definitiveness with which it was resolved precluded the idea of risk. I must not only punish, but punish with impunity. A wrong is unredressed when retribution overtakes its redresser. It is equally unredressed when the avenger fails to make himself felt as such to him who has done the wrong.

It must be understood that neither by word nor deed had I given Fortunato cause to doubt my good will. I continued, as was my wont, to smile in his face, and he did not perceive that my smile *now* was at the thought of his immolation.

He had a weak point—this Fortunato—although in other regards he was a man to be respected and even feared. He prided himself on his connoisseurship in wine. Few Italians have the true virtuoso spirit. For the most part their enthusiasm is adopted to suit the time and opportunity to practice imposture upon the British and Austrian millionaires. In painting and gemmary Fortunato, like his countrymen, was a quack, but in the matter of old wines he was sincere. In this respect I did not differ from him materially; I was skillful in the Italian vintages myself, and bought largely whenever I could.

It was about dusk, one evening during the supreme madness of the carnival season, that I encountered my friend. He accosted me with excessive warmth, for he had been drinking much. The man wore motley. He had on a tight-fitting parti-striped dress, and his head was surmounted by the conical cap and bells. I was so pleased to see him, that I thought I should never have done wringing his hand.

I said to him, "My dear Fortunato, you are luckily met. How remarkably well you are looking to-

169

day! But I have received a pipe of what passes for Amontillado, and I have my doubts."

"How?" said he, "Amontillado? A pipe? Impossible! And in the middle of the carnival?"

"I have my doubts," I replied, "and I was silly enough to pay the full Amontillado price without consulting you in the matter. You were not to be found, and I was fearful of losing a bargain."

"Amontillado!"

"I have my doubts."

"Amontillado!"

"And I must satisfy them."

"Amontillado!"

"As you are engaged, I am on my way to Luchesi. If any one has a critical turn, it is he. He will tell me—"

"Luchesi cannot tell Amontillado from sherry."

"And yet some fools will have it that his taste is a match for your own."

"Come, let us go."

"Whither?"

"To your vaults."

"My friend, no; I will not impose upon your good nature. I perceive you have an engagement. Luchesi—"

"I have no engagement; come."

"My friend, no. It is not the engagement, but the severe cold with which I perceive you are afflicted. The vaults are insufferably damp. They are encrusted with nitre."

"Let us go, nevertheless. The cold is merely nothing. Amontillado! You have been imposed upon; and

as for Luchesi, he cannot distinguish sherry from Amontillado."

Thus speaking, Fortunato possessed himself of my arm. Putting on a mask of black silk, and drawing a *roquelaure* closely about my person, I suffered him to hurry me to my palazzo.

There were no attendants at home; they had absconded to make merry in honor of the time. I had told them that I should not return until the morning, and had given them explicit orders not to stir from the house. These orders were sufficient, I well know, to insure their immediate disappearance, one and all, as soon as my back was turned.

I took from their sconces two flambeaux, and giving one to Fortunato, bowed him through several suites of rooms to the archway that led into the vaults. I passed down a long and winding staircase, requesting him to be cautious as he followed. We came at length to the foot of the descent, and stood together on the damp ground of the catacombs of the Montresors.

The gait of my friend was unsteady, and the bells upon his cap jingled as he strode.

"The pipe," said he.

"It is farther on," said I, "but observe the white web-work which gleams from these cavern walls."

He turned toward me, and looked into my eyes with two filmy orbs that distilled the rheum of intoxication.

"Nitre?" he asked, at length.

"Nitre," I replied. "How long

have you had that cough?"

"Ugh! ugh! ugh!—ugh! ugh! ugh!—ugh! ugh! ugh!—ugh! ugh! ugh!—ugh! ugh! ugh!"

My poor friend found it impossible to reply for many minutes.

"It is nothing," he said, at last.

"Come," I said, with decision, "we will go back; your health is precious. You are rich, respected, admired, beloved; you are happy, as once I was. You are a man to be missed. For me it is no matter. We will go back; you will be ill, and I cannot be responsible. Besides, there is Luchesi—"

"Enough," he said. "The cough is a mere nothing; it will not kill me. I shall not die of a cough."

"True—true," I replied, "and, indeed, I had no intention of alarming you unnecessarily—but you should use all proper caution. A draught of this Medoc will defend us from the damps."

Here I knocked off the neck of a bottle which I drew from a long row of its fellows that lay upon the mold.

"Drink," I said, presenting him the wine.

He raised it to his lips with a leer. He paused and nodded to me familiarly, while his bells jingled.

"I drink," he said, "to the buried that repose around us."

"And I to your long life."

He again took my arm, and we proceeded.

"These vaults," he said, "are extensive."

"The Montresors," I replied, "were a great and numerous family."

"I forget your arms."

"A huge human foot d'or, in a field azure; the foot crushes a serpent rampant whose fangs are imbedded in the heel."

"And the motto?"

"Nemo me impune lacessit." [1]

"Good!" he said.

The wine sparkled in his eyes and the bells jingled. My own fancy grew warm with the Medoc. We had passed through walls of piled bones, with casks and puncheons intermingling, into the inmost recesses of the catacombs. I paused again, and this time I made bold to seize Fortunato by an arm above the elbow.

"The nitre!" I said. "See, it increases. It hangs like moss upon the vaults. We are below the river's bed. The drops of moisture trickle among the bones. Come, we will go back ere it is too late. Your cough—"

"It is nothing," he said; "let us go on. But first, another draught of the Medoc." I broke and reached him a flagon of De Grâve. He emptied it at a breath. His eyes flashed with a fierce light. He laughed and threw the bottle upwards with a gesticulation I did not understand.

I looked at him in surprise. He repeated the movement—a grotesque one. "You do not comprehend?" he said.

"Not I," I replied.

[1] No one dare attack me with impunity (the motto of Scotland).

"Then you are not of the brother-hood."

"How?"

"You are not of the masons."

"Yes, yes," I said, "yes, yes."

"You? Impossible! A mason?"

"A mason," I replied.

"A sign," he said.

"It is this," I answered, produc-ing a trowel from beneath the folds of my *roquelaure.*

"You jest," he explained, recoil-ing a few paces. "But let us proceed to the Amontillado."

"Be it so," I said, replacing the tool beneath the cloak, and again offering him my arm. He leaned upon it heavily. We continued our route in search of the Amontillado. We passed through a range of low arches, descended, passed on, and descending again, arrived at a deep crypt, in which the foulness of the air caused our flambeaux rather to glow than flame.

At the most remote end of the crypt there appeared another less spacious. Its walls had been lined with human remains piled to the vault overhead, in the fashion of the great catacombs of Paris. Three sides of this interior crypt were still ornamented in this manner. From the fourth the bones had been thrown down, and lay promiscu-ously upon the earth, forming at one point a mound of some size. Within the wall thus exposed by the displacing of the bones, we per-ceived a still interior recess, in depth about four feet, in width three, in height six or seven. It seemed to

have been constructed for no espe-cial use within itself, but formed merely the interval between two of the colossal supports of the roof of the catacombs, and was backed by one of their circumscribing walls of solid granite.

It was in vain that Fortunato, uplifting his dull torch, endeavored to pry into the depths of the recess. Its termination the feeble light did not enable us to see.

"Proceed," I said. "Herein is the Amontillado. As for Luchesi—"

"He is an ignoramus," inter-rupted my friend, as he stepped un-steadily forward, while I followed immediately at his heels. In an in-stant he had reached the extremity of the niche, and finding his prog-ress arrested by the rock, stood stu-pidly bewildered. A moment more and I had fettered him to the gran-ite. In its surface were two iron staples, distant from each other about two feet, horizontally. From one of these depended a short chain, from the other a padlock. Throw-ing the links about his waist, it was but the work of a few seconds to secure it. He was too much as-tounded to resist. Withdrawing the key I stepped back from the recess.

"Pass your hand," I said, "over the wall; you cannot help feeling the nitre. Indeed it is *very* damp. Once more let me *implore* you to return. No? Then I must positively leave you. But I must first render you all the little attentions in my power."

"The Amontillado!" ejaculated

my friend, not yet recovered from his astonishment.

"True," I replied, "the Amontillado."

As I said these words I busied myself among the pile of bones of which I have before spoken. Throwing them aside, I soon uncovered a quantity of building-stone and mortar. With these materials and with the aid of my trowel, I began vigorously to wall up the entrance of the niche.

I had scarcely laid the first tier of the masonry when I discovered that the intoxication of Fortunato had in a great measure worn off. The earliest indication I had of this was a low moaning cry from the depth of the recess. It was *not* the cry of a drunken man. There was then a long and obstinate silence. I laid the second tier, and the third, and the fourth; and then I heard the furious vibrations of the chain. The noise lasted for several minutes, during which, that I might hearken to it with the more satisfaction, I ceased my labors and sat down upon the bones. When at last the clanking subsided, I resumed the trowel, and finished without interruption the fifth, the sixth, and the seventh tier. The wall was now nearly upon a level with my breast. I again paused, and holding the flambeaux over the masonwork, threw a few feeble rays upon the figure within.

A succession of loud and shrill screams, bursting suddenly from the throat of the chained form,

seemed to thrust me violently back. For a brief moment I hesitated—I trembled. Unsheathing my rapier, I began to grope with it about the recess; but the thought of an instant reassured me. I placed my hand upon the solid fabric of the catacombs, and felt satisfied. I reapproached the wall. I replied to the yells of him who clamored. I reechoed—I aided—I surpassed them in volume and in strength. I did this, and the clamorer grew still.

It was now midnight, and my task was drawing to a close. I had completed the eighth, the ninth, and the tenth tier. I had finished a portion of the last and the eleventh; there remained but a single stone to be fitted and plastered in. I struggled with its weight; I placed it partially in its destined position. But now there came from out the niche a low laugh that erected the hairs upon my head. It was succeeded by a sad voice, which I had difficulty in recognizing as that of the noble Fortunato. The voice said—

"Ha! ha! ha!—he! he!—a very good joke indeed—an excellent jest. We will have many a rich laugh about it at the palazzo—he! he! he! —over our wine—he! he! he!"

"The Amontillado!" I said.

"He! he! he!—he! he! he!—yes, the Amontillado. But is it not getting late? Will not they be awaiting us at the palazzo, the Lady Fortunato and the rest? Let us be gone."

"Yes," I said, "let us be gone."
"For the love of God, Montresor!"
"Yes," I said, "for the love of God!"
But to these words I hearkened in vain for a reply. I grew impatient. I called aloud, "Fortunato!"
No answer. I called again, "Fortunato!"
No answer still. I thrust a torch through the remaining aperture and let it fall within. There came forth in return only a jingling of the bells. My heart grew sick—on account of the dampness of the catacombs. I hastened to make an end of my labor. I forced the last stone into its position; I plastered it up. Against the new masonry I re-erected the old rampart of bones. For the half of a century no mortal has disturbed them. *In pace requiescat!*

A Poison Tree

I was angry with my friend:
I told my wrath, my wrath did end.
I was angry with my foe:
I told it not, my wrath did grow.

And I water'd it in fears,
Night and morning with my tears;
And I sunnèd it with smiles,
And with soft deceitful wiles,

And it grew both day and night,
Till it bore an apple bright;
And my foe beheld it shine,
And he knew that it was mine,

And into my garden stole
When the night had veil'd the pole:
In the morning glad I see
My foe outstretch'd beneath the tree.

The Most Dangerous Game

"Off there to the right—somewhere—is a large island," said Whitney. "It's rather a mystery—"

"What island is it?" Rainsford asked.

"The old charts call it 'Ship-Trap Island,'" Whitney replied. "A suggestive name, isn't it? Sailors have a curious dread of the place. I don't know why. Some superstition—"

"Can't see it," remarked Rainsford, trying to peer through the dank tropical night that was palpable as it pressed its thick warm blackness in upon the yacht.

"You've good eyes," said Whitney, with a laugh, "and I've seen you pick off a moose moving in the brown fall bush at four hundred yards, but even you can't see four miles or so through a moonless Caribbean night."

"Nor four yards," admitted Rainsford. "Ugh! It's like moist black velvet."

"It will be light enough in Rio," promised Whitney. "We should make it in a few days. I hope the jaguar guns have come from Pur-

dey's. We should have some good hunting up the Amazon. Great sport, hunting."

"The best sport in the world," agreed Rainsford.

"For the hunter," amended Whitney. "Not for the jaguar."

"Don't talk rot, Whitney," said Rainsford. "You're a big-game hunter, not a philosopher. Who cares how a jaguar feels?"

"Perhaps the jaguar does," observed Whitney.

"Bah! They've no understanding."

"Even so, I rather think they understand one thing—fear. The fear of pain and the fear of death."

"Nonsense," laughed Rainsford. "This hot weather is making you soft, Whitney. Be a realist. The world is made up of two classes—the hunters and the huntees. Luckily, you and I are hunters. Do you think we've passed that island yet?"

"I can't tell in the dark. I hope so."

"Why?" asked Rainsford.

"The place has a reputation—a bad one."

"Cannibals?" suggested Rainsford.

"Hardly. Even cannibals wouldn't live in such a God-forsaken place. But it's gotten into sailor lore, somehow. Didn't you notice that the crew's nerves seemed a bit jumpy today?"

"They were a bit strange, now you mention it. Even Captain Nielsen—"

"Yes, even that tough-minded old Swede, who'd go up to the devil himself and ask him for a light. Those fishy blue eyes held a look I never saw there before. All I could get out of him was: 'This place has an evil name among seafaring men, sir.' Then he said to me, very gravely: 'Don't you feel anything?'—as if the air about us was actually poisonous. Now, you mustn't laugh when I tell you this —I did feel something like a sudden chill.

"There was no breeze. The sea was as flat as a plate-glass window. We were drawing near the island then. What I felt was a—a mental chill; a sort of sudden dread."

"Pure imagination," said Rainsford. "One superstitious sailor can taint the whole ship's company with his fear."

"Maybe. But sometimes I think sailors have an extra sense that tells them when they are in danger. Sometimes I think evil is a tangible thing—with wave lengths, just as sound and light have. An evil place can, so to speak, broadcast vibrations of evil. Anyhow, I'm glad we're getting out of this zone. Well, I think I'll turn in now, Rainsford."

"I'm not sleepy," said Rainsford. "I'm going to smoke another pipe up on the after deck."

"Good night, then, Rainsford. See you at breakfast."

"Right. Good night, Whitney."

There was no sound in the night as Rainsford sat there but the muffled throb of the engine that drove the yacht swiftly through the darkness, and the swish and ripple of the wash of the propeller.

Rainsford, reclining in a steamer chair, indolently puffed on his favorite briar. The sensuous drowsiness of the night was on him. "It's so dark," he thought, "that I could sleep without closing my eyes; the night would be my eyelids—"

An abrupt sound startled him. Off to the right he heard it, and his ears, expert in such matters, could not be mistaken. Again he heard the sound, and again. Somewhere, off in the blackness, someone had fired a gun three times.

Rainsford sprang up and moved quickly to the rail, mystified. He strained his eyes in the direction from which the reports had come. but it was like trying to see through a blanket. He leaped upon the rail and balanced himself there, to get greater elevation; his pipe, striking a rope, was knocked from his mouth. He lunged for it; a short, hoarse cry came from his lips as he realized he had reached too far and had lost his balance. The cry was pinched off short as the blood-warm waters of the Caribbean Sea closed over his head.

He struggled up to the surface and tried to cry out, but the wash from the speeding yacht slapped him in the face and the salt water in his open mouth made him gag and strangle. Desperately he struck out with strong strokes after the receding lights of the yacht, but he stopped before he had swum fifty feet. A certain cool-headedness had come to him; it was not the first time he had been in a tight place. There was a chance that his cries could be heard by someone aboard the yacht, but that chance was slender, and grew more slender as the yacht raced on. He wrestled himself out of his clothes, and shouted with all his power. The lights of the yacht became faint and ever-vanishing fireflies; then they were blotted out entirely by the night.

Rainsford remembered the shots. They had come from the right, and doggedly he swam in that direction, swimming with slow, deliberate strokes, conserving his strength. For a seemingly endless time he fought the sea. He began to count his strokes; he could do possibly a hundred more and then—

Rainsford heard a sound. It came out of the darkness, a high screaming sound, the sound of an animal in an extremity of anguish and terror.

He did not recognize the animal that made the sound; he did not try to; with fresh vitality he swam toward the sound. He heard it again; then it was cut short by another noise, crisp, staccato.

"Pistol shot," muttered Rainsford, swimming on.

Ten minutes of determined effort brought another sound to his ears— the most welcome he had ever heard—the muttering and growling of the sea breaking on a rocky shore. He was almost on the rocks before he saw them; on a night less calm he would have been shattered against them. With his remaining strength he dragged himself from the swirling waters. Jagged crags appeared to jut up into the opaqueness; he forced himself upward, hand over hand. Gasping, his hands raw, he reached a flat place at the top. Dense jungle came down to the very edge of the cliffs. What perils that tangle of trees and underbrush might hold for him did not concern Rainsford just then. All he knew was that he was safe from his enemy, the sea, and that utter weariness was on him. He flung himself down at the jungle edge and tumbled headlong into the deepest sleep of his life.

When he opened his eyes he knew from the position of the sun that it was late in the afternoon. Sleep had given him new vigor; a sharp hunger was picking at him. He looked about him, almost cheerfully.

"Where there are pistol shots,

there are men. Where there are men, there is food," he thought. But what kind of men, he wondered, in so forbidding a place? An unbroken front of snarled and ragged jungle fringed the shore.

He saw no sign of a trail through the closely knit web of weeds and trees; it was easier to go along the shore, and Rainsford floundered along by the water. Not far from where he had landed, he stopped.

Some wounded thing, by the evidence, a large animal, had thrashed about in the underbrush; the jungle weeds were crushed down and the moss was lacerated; one patch of weeds was stained crimson. A small, glittering object not far away caught Rainsford's eye and he picked it up. It was an empty cartridge.

"A twenty-two," he remarked. "That's odd. It must have been a fairly large animal too. The hunter had his nerve with him to tackle it with a light gun. It's clear that the brute put up a fight. I suppose the first three shots I heard was when the hunter flushed his quarry and wounded it. The last shot was when he trailed it here and finished it."

He examined the ground closely and found what he had hoped to find—the print of hunting boots. They pointed along the cliff in the direction he had been going. Eagerly he hurried along, now slipping on a rotten log or a loose stone, but making headway; night was beginning to settle down on the island.

Bleak darkness was blacking out the sea and jungle when Rainsford sighted the lights. He came upon them as he turned a crook in the coast line, and his first thought was that he had come upon a village, for there were many lights. But as he forged along he saw to his great astonishment that all the lights were in one enormous building—a lofty structure with pointed towers plunging upward into the gloom. His eyes made out the shadowy outlines of a palatial chateau; it was set on a high bluff, and on three sides of it cliffs dived down to where the sea licked greedy lips in the shadows.

"Mirage," thought Rainsford. But it was no mirage, he found, when he opened the tall spiked iron gate. The stone steps were real enough; the massive door with a leering gargoyle for a knocker was real enough; yet above it all hung an air of unreality.

He lifted the knocker, and it creaked up stiffly, as if it had never before been used. He let it fall, and it startled him with its booming loudness. He thought he heard steps within; the door remained closed. Again Rainsford lifted the heavy knocker, and let it fall. The door opened then, opened as suddenly as if it were on a spring, and Rainsford stood blinking in the river of glaring gold light that poured out. The first thing Rainsford's eyes discerned was the largest man Rainsford had ever seen—a gigantic creature, solidly made and black-bearded to the waist. In his hand the man held a long-barreled revolver, and he was pointing it straight at Rainsford's heart.

Out of the snarl of beard two small eyes regarded Rainsford.

"Don't be alarmed," said Rainsford, with a smile which he hoped was disarming. "I'm no robber. I fell off a yacht. My name is Sanger Rainsford of New York City."

The menacing look in the eyes did not change. The revolver pointed as rigidly as if the giant were a statue. He gave no sign that he understood Rainsford's words, or that he had even heard them. He was dressed in uniform, a black uniform trimmed with gray astrakhan.

"I'm Sanger Rainsford of New York," Rainsford began again. "I fell off a yacht. I am hungry."

The man's only answer was to raise with his thumb the hammer of his revolver. Then Rainsford saw the man's free hand go to his forehead in a military salute, and he saw him click his heels together and stand at attention. Another man was coming down the broad marble steps, an erect, slender man in evening clothes. He advanced to Rainsford and held out his hand.

In a cultivated voice marked by a slight accent that gave it added precision and deliberateness, he said: "It is a very great pleasure and honor to welcome Mr. Sanger Rainsford, the celebrated hunter, to my home."

Automatically Rainsford shook the man's hand.

"I've read your book about hunting snow leopards in Tibet, you see," explained the man. "I am General Zaroff."

Rainsford's first impression was that the man was singularly handsome; his second was that there was an original, almost bizarre quality about the general's face. He was a tall man past middle age, for his hair was a vivid white; but his thick eyebrows and pointed military mustache were as black as the night from which Rainsford had come. His eyes, too, were black and very bright. He had high cheek bones, a sharp-cut nose, a spare, dark face, the face of a man used to giving orders, the face of an aristocrat. Turning to the giant in uniform, the general made a sign. The giant put away his pistol, saluted, withdrew.

"Ivan is an incredibly strong fellow," remarked the general, "but he has the misfortune to be deaf and dumb. A simple fellow, but, I'm afraid, like all his race, a bit of a savage."

"Is he Russian?"

"He is a Cossack," said the general, and his smile showed red lips and pointed teeth. "So am I.

"Come," he said, "we shouldn't be chatting here. We can talk later. Now you want clothes, food, rest. You shall have them. This is a most restful spot."

Ivan had reappeared, and the general spoke to him with lips that moved but gave forth no sound.

"Follow Ivan, if you please, Mr.

Rainsford," said the general. "I was about to have my dinner when you came. I'll wait for you. You'll find that my clothes will fit you, I think."

It was to a huge, beam-ceilinged bedroom with a canopied bed big enough for six men that Rainsford followed the silent giant. Ivan laid out an evening suit, and Rainsford, as he put it on, noticed that it came from a London tailor who ordinarily cut and sewed for none below the rank of duke.

The dining room to which Ivan conducted him was in many ways remarkable. There was a medieval magnificence about it; it suggested a baronial hall of feudal times with its oaken panels, its high ceiling, its vast refectory tables where twoscore men could sit down to eat. About the hall were the mounted heads of many animals—lions, tigers, elephants, moose, bears; larger or more perfect specimens Rainsford had never seen. At the great table the general was sitting, alone.

"You'll have a cocktail, Mr. Rainsford," he suggested. The cocktail was surpassingly good; and, Rainsford noted, the table appointments were of the finest—the linen, the crystal, the silver, the china.

They were eating borsch, the rich, red soup with whipped cream so dear to Russian palates. Half apologetically General Zaroff said: "We do our best to preserve the amenities of civilization here. Please forgive any lapses. We are well off the beaten track, you know. Do you think the champagne has suffered from its long ocean trip?"

"Not in the least," declared Rainsford. He was finding the general a most thoughtful and affable host, a true cosmopolite. But there was one small trait of the general's that made Rainsford uncomfortable. Whenever he looked up from his plate he found the general studying him, appraising him narrowly.

"Perhaps," said General Zaroff, "you were surprised that I recognized your name. You see, I read all books on hunting published in English, French, and Russian. I have but one passion in my life, Mr. Rainsford, and it is the hunt."

"You have some wonderful heads here," said Rainsford as he ate a particularly well cooked *filet mignon*. "That Cape buffalo is the largest I ever saw."

"Oh, that fellow. Yes, he was a monster."

"Did he charge you?"

"Hurled me against a tree," said the general. "Fractured my skull. But I got the brute."

"I've always thought," said Rainsford, "that the Cape buffalo is the most dangerous of all big game."

For a moment the general did not reply; he was smiling his curious red-lipped smile. Then he said slowly: "No. You are wrong, sir. The Cape buffalo is not the most dangerous big game." He sipped his wine. "Here in my preserve on this island," he said in the same slow tone, "I hunt more dangerous game."

Rainsford expressed his surprise. "Is there big game on this island?"

The general nodded. "The biggest."

"Really?"

"Oh, it isn't here naturally, of course. I have to stock the island."

"What have you imported, general?" Rainsford asked. "Tigers?"

The general smiled. "No," he said. "Hunting tigers ceased to interest me some years ago. I exhausted their possibilities, you see. No thrill left in tigers, no real danger. I live for danger, Mr. Rainsford."

The general took from his pocket a gold cigarette case and offered his guest a long black cigarette with a silver tip; it was perfumed and gave off a smell like incense.

"We will have some capital hunting, you and I," said the general. "I shall be most glad to have your society."

"But what game—" began Rainsford.

"I'll tell you," said the general. "You will be amused, I know. I think I may say, in all modesty, that I have done a rare thing. I have invented a new sensation. May I pour you another glass of port?"

"Thank you, general."

The general filled both glasses, and said: "God makes some men poets. Some He makes kings, some beggars. Me He made a hunter. My hand was made for the trigger, my father said. He was a very rich man with a quarter of a million acres in the Crimea, and he was an ardent sportsman. When I was only five years old he gave me a little gun, specially made in Moscow for me, to shoot sparrows with. When I shot some of his prize turkeys with it, he did not punish me; he complimented me on my marksmanship. I killed my first bear in the Caucasus when I was ten. My whole life has been one prolonged hunt. I went into the army—it was expected of noblemen's sons—and for a time commanded a division of Cossack cavalry, but my real interest was always the hunt. I have hunted every kind of game in every land. It would be impossible for me to tell you how many animals I have killed."

The general puffed at his cigarette.

"After the debacle in Russia I left the country, for it was imprudent for an officer of the Czar to stay there. Many noble Russians lost everything. I, luckily, had invested heavily in American securities, so I shall never have to open a tea room in Monte Carlo or drive a taxi in Paris. Naturally, I continued to hunt—grizzlies in your Rockies, crocodiles in the Ganges, rhinoceroses in East Africa. It was in Africa that the Cape buffalo hit me and laid me up for six months. As soon as I recovered I started for the Amazon to hunt jaguars, for I had heard they were unusually cunning. They weren't." The Cossack sighed. "They were no match at all for a hunter with his wits about him, and a high-powered rifle. I was bitterly disappointed. I was lying in my tent with a splitting headache one night when a terrible thought pushed its way into my mind. Hunting was beginning to bore me! And hunting, remember, had been my life. I have heard that in America businessmen often go to pieces when they give up the business that has been their life."

"Yes, that's so," said Rainsford.

The general smiled. "I had no wish to go to pieces," he said. "I must do something. Now, mine is an analytical mind, Mr. Rainsford. Doubtless that is why I enjoy the problems of the chase."

"No doubt, General Zaroff."

"So," continued the general, "I asked myself why the hunt no longer fascinated me. You are much younger than I am, Mr. Rainsford, and have not hunted as much, but you perhaps can guess the answer."

"What was it?"

"Simply this: hunting had ceased to be what you call 'a sporting proposition.' It had become too easy. I always got my quarry. Always. There is no greater bore than perfection."

The general lit a fresh cigarette.

"No animal had a chance with me any more. That is no boast; it is a mathematical certainty. The animal had nothing but his legs and his instinct. Instinct is no match for reason. When I thought of this it was a tragic moment for me, I can tell you."

Rainsford leaned across the table, absorbed in what his host was saying.

"It came to me as an inspiration what I must do," the general went on.

"And that was?"

The general smiled the quiet smile of one who has faced an obstacle and surmounted it with success. "I had to invent a new animal to hunt," he said.

"A new animal? You're joking."

"Not at all," said the general. "I never joke about hunting. I needed a new animal. I found one. So I bought this island, built this house, and here I do my hunting. The island is perfect for my purposes—there are jungles with a maze of trails in them, hills, swamps—"

"But the animal, General Zaroff?"

"Oh," said the general, "it supplies me with the most exciting hunting in the world. No other hunting compares with it for an instant. Every day I hunt, and I never grow bored now, for I have a quarry with which I can match my wits."

Rainsford's bewilderment showed in his face.

"I wanted the ideal animal to hunt," explained the general. "So I said: 'What are the attributes of an ideal quarry?' And the answer was, of course: 'It must have courage, cunning, and, above all, it must be able to reason.'"

"But no animal can reason," objected Rainsford.

"My dear fellow," said the general, "there is one that can."

"But you can't mean—" gasped Rainsford.

"And why not?"

"I can't believe you are serious, General Zaroff. This is a grisly joke."

"Why should I not be serious? I am speaking of hunting."

"Hunting? Good God, General Zaroff, what you speak of is murder."

The general laughed with entire good nature. He regarded Rainsford quizzically. "I refuse to believe that so modern and civilized a young man as you seem to be harbors romantic ideas about the value of human life. Surely your experiences in the war—"

"Did not make me condone cold-blooded murder," finished Rainsford stiffly.

Laughter shook the general. "How extraordinarily droll you are!" he said. "One does not expect nowadays to find a young man of the educated class, even in America, with such a naive, and, if I may say so, a mid-Victorian point of view. It's like finding a snuffbox in a limousine. Ah, well, doubtless you had Puritan ancestors. So many Americans appear to have had. I'll wager you'll forget your notions when you go hunting with me. You've a genuine new thrill in store for you, Mr. Rainsford."

"Thank you, I'm a hunter, not a murderer."

"Dear me," said the general, quite unruffled. "again that unpleas-ant word. But I think I can show you that your scruples are quite ill founded."

"Yes?"

"Life is for the strong, to be lived by the strong, and, if need be, taken by the strong. The weak of the world were put here to give the strong pleasure. I am strong. Why should I not use my gift? If I wish to hunt, why should I not? I hunt the scum of the earth—sailors from tramp ships—lascars, blacks, Chinese, whites, mongrels—a thoroughbred horse or hound is worth more than a score of them."

"But they are men," said Rainsford hotly.

"Precisely," said the general. "That is why I use them. It gives me pleasure. They can reason, after a fashion. So they are dangerous."

"But where do you get them?"

The general's left eyelid fluttered down in a wink. "This island is called Ship Trap," he answered. "Sometimes an angry god of the high seas sends them to me. Sometimes, when Providence is not so kind, I help Providence a bit. Come to the window with me."

Rainsford went to the window and looked out toward the sea.

"Watch! Out there!" exclaimed the general, pointing into the night. Rainsford's eyes saw only blackness, and then, as the general pressed a button, far out to sea Rainsford saw the flash of lights.

The general chuckled. "They indicate a channel," he said, "where there's none; giant rocks with razor edges crouch like a sea monster with wide-open jaws. They can crush a ship as easily as I crush this nut." He dropped a walnut on the hardwood floor and brought his heel grinding down on it. "Oh, yes," he said, casually, as if in answer to a question, "I have electricity. We try to be civilized here."

"Civilized? And you shoot down men?"

A trace of anger was in the general's black eyes, but it was there for but for a second, and he said, in his most pleasant manner: "Dear me, what a righteous young man you are! I assure you I do not do the thing you suggest. That would be barbarous. I treat these visitors with every consideration. They get plenty of good food and exercise. They get into splendid physical condition. You shall see for yourself tomorrow."

"What do you mean?"

"We'll visit my training school," smiled the general. "It's in the cellar. I have about a dozen pupils down there now. They're from the Spanish bark *San Lucar* that had the bad luck to go on the rocks out there. A very inferior lot, I regret to say. Poor specimens and more accustomed to the deck than to the jungle."

He raised his hand, and Ivan, who served as waiter, brought thick Turkish coffee. Rainsford, with an effort, held his tongue in check.

"It's a game, you see," pursued the general blandly. "I suggest to one of them that we go hunting. I give him a supply of food and an excellent hunting knife. I give him three hours' start. I am to follow, armed only with a pistol of the smallest caliber and range. If my quarry eludes me for three whole days, he wins the game. If I find him"—the general smiled—"he loses."

"Suppose he refuses to be hunted?"

"Oh," said the general, "I give him his option, of course. He need not play that game if he doesn't wish to. If he does not wish to hunt, I turn him over to Ivan. Ivan once had the honor of serving as official knouter to the Great White Czar, and he has his own ideas of sport. Invariably, Mr. Rainsford, invariably they choose the hunt."

"And if they win?"

The smile on the general's face widened. "To date I have not lost," he said. Then he added, hastily: "I don't wish you to think me a braggart, Mr. Rainsford. Many of them afford only the most elementary sort of problem. Occasionally I strike a tartar. One almost did win. I eventually had to use the dogs."

"The dogs?"

"This way, please. I'll show you."

The general steered Rainsford to a window. The lights from the windows sent a flickering illumination that made grotesque patterns on the courtyard below, and Rainsford could see moving about there a dozen or so huge black shapes; as they turned toward him, their eyes glittered greenly.

"A rather good lot, I think," observed the general. "They are let out at seven every night. If anyone should try to get into my house—or out of it—something extremely regrettable would occur to him." He hummed a snatch of song from the *Folies Bergère*.

"And now," said the general, "I want to show you my new collection of heads. Will you come with me to the library?"

"I hope," said Rainsford, "that you will excuse me tonight, General Zaroff. I'm really not feeling well."

"Ah, indeed?" the general inquired solicitously. "Well, I suppose that's only natural, after your long swim. You need a good, restful night's sleep. Tomorrow you'll feel like a new man, I'll wager. Then we'll hunt, eh? I've one rather promising prospect—" Rainsford was hurrying from the room.

"Sorry you can't go with me tonight," called the general. "I expect rather fair sport—a big, strong black. He looks resourceful—Well, good night, Mr. Rainsford; I hope you have a good night's rest."

The bed was good, and the pajamas of the softest silk, and he was tired in every fiber of his being, but nevertheless Rainsford could not quiet his brain with the opiate of sleep. He lay, eyes wide open. Once he thought he heard stealthy steps in the corridor outside his room. He sought to throw open the door; it would not open. He went to the window and looked out. His room

was high up in one of the towers. The lights of the chateau were out now, and it was dark and silent, but there was a fragment of sallow moon, and by its wan light he could see, dimly, the courtyard; there, weaving in and out in the pattern of shadow, were black, noiseless forms; the hounds heard him at the window and looked up, expectantly, with their green eyes. Rainsford went back to the bed and lay down. By many methods he tried to put himself to sleep. He had achieved a doze when, just as morning began to come, he heard, far off in the jungle, the faint report of a pistol.

General Zaroff did not appear until luncheon. He was dressed faultlessly in the tweeds of a country squire. He was solicitous about the state of Rainsford's health.

"As for me," sighed the general, "I do not feel so well. I am worried, Mr. Rainsford. Last night I detected traces of my old complaint."

To Rainsford's questioning glance the general said: "Ennui. Boredom."

Then, taking a second helping of crêpes suzette, the general explained: "The hunting was not good last night. The fellow lost his head. He made a straight trail that offered no problems at all. That's the trouble with these sailors; they have dull brains to begin with, and they do not know how to get about in the woods. They do excessively stupid and obvious things. It's most annoying. Will you have another glass of Chablis, Mr. Rainsford?"

"General," said Rainsford firmly, "I wish to leave this island at once."

The general raised his thickets of eyebrows; he seemed hurt. "But, my dear fellow," the general protested, "you've only just come. You've had no hunting—"

"I wish to go today," said Rainsford. He saw the dead black eyes of the general on him, studying him. General Zaroff's face suddenly brightened.

He filled Rainsford's glass with venerable Chablis from a dusty bottle.

"Tonight," said the general, "we will hunt—you and I."

Rainsford shook his head. "No, general," he said. "I will not hunt."

The general shrugged his shoulders and delicately ate a hothouse grape. "As you wish, my friend," he said. "The choice rests entirely with you. But may I not venture to suggest that you will find my idea of sport more diverting than Ivan's?"

He nodded toward the corner to where the giant stood, scowling, his thick arms crossed on his hogshead of chest.

"You don't mean—" cried Rainsford.

"My dear fellow," said the general, "have I not told you I always mean what I say about hunting? This is really an inspiration. I drink to a foeman worthy of my steel—at last." The general raised his glass, but Rainsford sat staring at him.

"You'll find this game worth playing," the general said enthusiastically. "Your brain against mine. Your woodcraft against mine. Your strength and stamina against mine. Outdoor chess! And the stake is not without value, eh?"

"And if I win—" began Rainsford huskily.

"I'll cheerfully acknowledge myself defeated if I do not find you by midnight of the third day," said General Zaroff. "My sloop will place you on the mainland near a town." The general read what Rainsford was thinking.

"Oh, you can trust me," said the Cossack. "I will give you my word as a gentleman and a sportsman. Of course you, in turn, must agree to say nothing of your visit here."

"I'll agree to nothing of the kind," said Rainsford.

"Oh," said the general, "in that case—But why discuss that now? Three days hence we can discuss it over a bottle of Veuve Cliquot, unless—"

The general sipped his wine.

Then a businesslike air animated him. "Ivan," he said to Rainsford, "will supply you with hunting clothes, food, a knife. I suggest you wear moccasins; they leave a poorer trail. I suggest, too, that you avoid the big swamp in the southeast corner of the island. We call it Death Swamp. There's quicksand there. One foolish fellow tried it. The deplorable part of it was that Lazarus followed him. You can imagine my feelings, Mr. Rainsford. I loved Lazarus; he was the finest hound in my pack. Well, I must beg you to excuse me now. I always take a siesta after lunch. You'll hardly have time for a nap, I fear. You'll want to start, no doubt. I shall not follow till dusk. Hunting at night is so much more exciting than by day, don't you think? *Au revoir,* Mr. Rainsford, *au revoir."* General Zaroff, with a deep, courtly bow, strolled from the room.

From another door came Ivan. Under one arm he carried khaki hunting clothes, a haversack of food, a leather sheath containing a long-bladed hunting knife; his right hand rested on a cocked revolver thrust in the crimson sash about his waist.

Rainsford had fought his way through the bush for two hours. "I must keep my nerve. I must keep my nerve," he said through tight teeth.

He had not been entirely clear-headed when the chateau gates snapped shut behind him. His whole idea at first was to put distance between himself and General Zaroff, and, to this end, he had plunged along, spurred on by the sharp rowels of something very like panic. Now he had got a grip on himself, had stopped, and was taking stock of himself and the situation. He saw that straight flight was futile; inevitably it would bring him face to face with the sea. He was in a picture with a frame of water, and his operations, clearly, must take place within that frame.

"I'll give him a trail to follow," muttered Rainsford, and he struck off from the rude path he had been following into the trackless wilderness. He executed a series of intricate loops; he doubled on his trail again and again, recalling all the lore of the fox hunt, and all the dodges of the fox. Night found him leg-weary, with hands and face lashed by the branches, on a thickly wooded ridge. He knew it would be insane to blunder on through the dark, even if he had the strength. His need for rest was imperative and he thought: "I have played the fox, now I must play the cat of the fable." A big tree with a thick trunk and outspread branches was near by, and, taking care to leave not the slightest mark, he climbed up into the crotch, and stretching out on one of the broad limbs, after a fashion, rested. Rest brought him new confidence and almost a feeling of security. Even so zealous a hunter as General Zaroff could not trace him there, he told himself; only the devil himself could follow that complicated trail through the jungle after dark. But, perhaps the general was a devil—

An apprehensive night crawled slowly by like a wounded snake, and sleep did not visit Rainsford, although the silence of a dead world was on the jungle. Toward morning when a dingy gray was varnishing the sky, the cry of some startled bird focused Rainsford's attention in that direction. Something was coming through the bush, coming slowly, carefully, coming by the same winding way Rainsford had come. He flattened himself down on the limb, and through a screen of leaves almost as thick as tapestry, he watched. . . That which was approaching was a man.

It was General Zaroff. He made his way along with his eyes fixed in utmost concentration on the ground before him. He paused, almost beneath the tree, dropped to his knees and studied the ground. Rainsford's impulse was to hurl himself down like a panther, but he saw that the general's right hand held something metallic—a small automatic pistol.

The hunter shook his head several times, as if he were puzzled. Then he straightened up and took from his case one of his black cigarettes; its pungent incenselike smoke floated up to Rainsford's nostrils.

Rainsford held his breath. The general's eyes had left the ground and were traveling inch by inch up the tree. Rainsford froze there, every muscle tensed for a spring. But the sharp eyes of the hunter stopped before they reached the limb where Rainsford lay; a smile spread over his brown face. Very deliberately he blew a smoke ring into the air; then he turned his back on the tree and walked carelessly away, back along the trail he had come. The swish of the underbrush against his hunting boots grew fainter and fainter.

The pent-up air burst hotly from Rainsford's lungs. His first thought made him feel sick and numb. The general could follow a trail through the woods at night; he could follow an extremely difficult trail; he must have uncanny powers; only by the merest chance had the Cossack failed to see his quarry.

Rainsford's second thought was even more terrible. It sent a shudder of cold horror through his whole being. Why had the general smiled? Why had he turned back?

Rainsford did not want to believe what his reason told him was true, but the truth was as evident as the sun that had by now pushed through the morning mists. The general was playing with him! The general was saving him for another day's sport! The Cossack was the cat; he was the mouse. Then it was that Rainsford knew the full meaning of terror.

"I will not lose my nerve. I will not."

He slid down from the tree, and struck off again into the woods. His face was set and he forced the machinery of his mind to function. Three hundred yards from his hiding place he stopped where a huge dead tree leaned precariously on a smaller, living one. Throwing off his sack of food, Rainsford took his knife from its sheath and began to work with all his energy.

The job was finished at last, and he threw himself down behind a fallen log a hundred feet away. He did not have to wait long. The cat was coming again to play with the mouse.

Following the trail with the sureness of a bloodhound came General Zaroff. Nothing escaped those searching black eyes, no crushed blade of grass, no bent twig, no mark, no matter how faint, in the moss. So intent was the Cossack on his stalking that he was upon the thing Rainsford had made before he saw it. His foot touched the protruding bough that was the trigger. Even as he touched it, the general sensed his danger and leaped back with the ability of an ape. But he was not quite quick enough; the dead tree, delicately adjusted to rest on the cut living one, crashed down and struck the general a glancing blow on the shoulder as it fell; but for his alertness, he must have been smashed beneath it. He staggered, but he did not fall; nor did he drop his revolver. He stood there, rubbing his injured shoulder, and Rainsford, with fear again gripping his heart, heard the general's mocking laugh ring through the jungle.

"Rainsford," called the general, "if you are within sound of my voice, as I suppose you are, let me congratulate you. Not many men know how to make a Malay mancatcher. Luckily, for me, I too have hunted in Malacca. You are proving interesting, Mr. Rainsford. I am going now to have my wound dressed; it's only a slight one. But I shall be back. I shall be back."

When the general, nursing his bruised shoulder, had gone, Rainsford took up his flight again. It was flight now, a desperate, hopeless flight, that carried him on for some hours. Dusk came, then darkness, and still he pressed on. The ground grew softer under his moccasins; the vegetation grew ranker, denser; insects bit him savagely. Then, as he stepped forward, his foot sank into the ooze. He tried to wrench it back, but the muck sucked viciously at his foot as if it were a giant leech. With a violent effort, he tore his feet loose. He knew where he was now. Death Swamp and its quicksand.

His hands were tight closed as if his nerve were something tangible that someone in the darkness was trying to tear from his grip. The softness of the earth had given him an idea. He stepped back from the quicksand a dozen feet or so and, like some huge prehistoric beaver, he began to dig.

Rainsford had dug himself in in France when a second's delay meant death. That had been a placid pastime compared to his digging now. The pit grew deeper; when it was above his shoulders, he climbed out and from some hard saplings cut stakes and sharpened them to a fine point. These stakes he planted in the bottom of the pit with the points sticking up. With flying fingers he wove a rough carpet of weeds and branches and with it he covered the mouth of the pit. Then, wet with sweat and aching with tiredness, he crouched behind the stump of a lightning-charred tree.

He knew his pursuer was coming; he heard the padding sound of feet on the soft earth, and the night breeze brought him the perfume of the general's cigarette. It seemed to Rainsford that the general was coming with unusual swiftness; he was not feeling his way along, foot by foot. Rainsford, crouching there, could not see the general, nor could he see the pit. He lived a year in a minute. Then he felt an impulse to cry aloud with joy, for he heard the sharp crackle of the breaking branches as the cover of the pit gave way; he heard the sharp scream of pain as the pointed stakes found their mark. He leaped up from his place of concealment. Then he cowered back. Three feet from the pit a man was standing, with an electric torch in his hand.

"You've done well, Rainsford," the voice of the general called. "Your Burmese tiger pit has claimed one of my best dogs. Again you score. I think, Mr. Rainsford, I'll see what you can do against my whole pack. I'm going home for a rest now. Thank you for a most amusing evening."

At daybreak Rainsford, lying near the swamp, was awakened by a sound that made him know that he had new things to learn about fear. It was a distant sound, faint and wavering, but he knew it. It was the baying of a pack of hounds.

Rainsford knew he could do one of two things. He could stay where he was and wait. That was suicide. He could flee. That was postponing the inevitable. For a moment he stood there, thinking. An idea that held a wild chance came to him, and, tightening his belt, he headed away from the swamp.

The baying of the hounds drew nearer, then still nearer, nearer, ever nearer. On a ridge Rainsford climbed a tree. Down a watercourse, not a quarter of a mile away, he could see the bush moving. Straining his eyes, he saw the lean figure of General Zaroff; just ahead of him Rainsford made out another figure whose wide shoulders surged through the tall jungle weeds; it was the giant Ivan, and he seemed pulled forward by some unseen force; Rainsford knew that Ivan must be holding the pack in leash.

They would be on him any minute now. His mind worked frantically. He thought of a native trick he had learned in Uganda. He slid down the tree. He caught hold of a springy young sapling and to it he fastened his hunting knife, with the blade pointing down the trail; with a bit of wild grapevine he tied back the sapling. Then he ran for his life. The hounds raised their voices as they hit the fresh scent. Rainsford knew now how an animal at bay feels.

He had to stop to get his breath. The baying of the hounds stopped abruptly, and Rainsford's heart stopped too. They must have reached the knife.

He shinned excitedly up a tree and looked back. His pursuers had stopped. But the hope that was in

Rainsford's brain when he climbed died, for he saw in the shallow valley that General Zaroff was still on his feet. But Ivan was not. The knife, driven by the recoil of the springing tree, had not wholly failed.

Rainsford had hardly tumbled to the ground when the pack took up the cry again.

"Nerve, nerve, nerve!" he panted, as he dashed along. A blue gap showed between the trees dead ahead. Ever nearer drew the hounds. Rainsford forced himself on toward that gap. He reached it. It was the shore of the sea. Across a cove he could see the gloomy gray stone of the chateau. Twenty feet below him the sea rumbled and hissed. Rainsford hesitated. He heard the hounds. Then he leaped far out into the sea. . . .

When the general and his pack reached the place by the sea, the Cossack stopped. For some minutes he stood regarding the blue-green expanse of water. He shrugged his shoulders. Then he sat down, took a drink of brandy from a silver flask, lit a cigarette, and hummed a bit from "Madame Butterfly."

General Zaroff had an exceedingly good dinner in his great paneled dining hall that evening. With it he had a bottle of Pol Roger and half a bottle of Chambertin. Two slight annoyances kept him from perfect enjoyment. One was the thought that it would be difficult to replace Ivan; the other was that

his quarry had escaped him; of course the American hadn't played the game—so thought the general as he tasted his after-dinner liqueur. In his library he read, to soothe himself, from the works of Marcus Aurelius. At ten he went up to his bedroom. He was deliciously tired, he said to himself, as he locked himself in. There was a little moonlight, so, before turning on his light, he went to the window and looked down at the courtyard. He could see the great hounds, and he called, "Better luck another time," to them. Then he switched on the light.

A man, who had been hiding in the curtains of the bed, was standing there.

"Rainsford!" screamed the general. "How in God's name did you get here?"

"Swam," said Rainsford. "I found it quicker than walking through the jungle."

The general sucked in his breath and smiled. "I congratulate you," he said. "You have won the game."

Rainsford did not smile. "I am still a beast at bay," he said, in a low, hoarse voice. "Get ready, General Zaroff."

The general made one of his deepest bows. "I see," he said. "Splendid! One of us is to furnish a repast for the hounds. The other will sleep in this very excellent bed. On guard, Rainsford." . . .

He had never slept in a better bed, Rainsford decided.

Haircut

I GOT *another* barber that comes over from Carterville and helps me out Saturdays, but the rest of the time I can get along all right alone. You see for yourself that this ain't no New York City and besides that, the most of the boys works all day and don't have no leisure to drop in here and get themselves prettied up.

You're a newcomer, ain't you? I thought I hadn't seen you round before. I hope you like it good enough to stay. As I say, we ain't no New York City or Chicago, but we have pretty good times. Not as good, though, since Jim Kendall got killed. When he was alive, him and Hod Meyers used to keep this town in an uproar. I bet they was more laughin' done here than any town its size in America.

Jim was comical, and Hod was pretty near a match for him. Since Jim's gone, Hod tries to hold his end up just the same as ever, but it's tough goin' when you ain't got nobody to kind of work with.

They used to be plenty fun in here Saturdays. This place is jam-packed Saturdays, from four o'clock on. Jim and Hod would show up right after their supper, round six o'clock. Jim would set himself down in that big chair, nearest the blue spittoon. Whoever had been settin' in that chair, why they'd get up when Jim come in and give it to him.

You'd of thought it was a reserved seat like they have sometimes in a theayter. Hod would generally always stand or walk up and down, or some Saturdays, of course, he'd be settin' in this chair part of the time, gettin' a haircut.

Well, Jim would set there a w'ile without openin' his mouth only to spit, and then finally he'd say to me, "Whitey,"—my right name, that is, my right first name, is Dick, but everybody round here calls me Whitey—Jim would say, "Whitey, your nose looks like a rosebud tonight. You must of been drinkin' some of your aw de cologne."

So I'd say, "No, Jim, but you look like you'd been drinkin' somethin' of that kind or somethin' worse."

Jim would have to laugh at that, but then he'd speak up and say, "No, I ain't had nothin' to drink, but that ain't sayin' I wouldn't like somethin'. I wouldn't even mind if it was wood alcohol."

Then Hod Meyers would say, "Neither would your wife." That would set everybody to laughin' because Jim and his wife wasn't on very good terms. She'd of divorced him only they wasn't no chance to get alimony and she didn't have no way to take care of herself and the kids. She couldn't never understand Jim. He *was* kind of rough, but a good fella at heart.

Him and Hod had all kinds of sport with Milt Sheppard. I don't suppose you've seen Milt. Well, he's got an Adam's apple that looks more like a mushmelon. So I'd be shavin' Milt and when I'd start to shave down here on his neck, Hod would holler, "Hey, Whitey, wait a minute! Before you cut into it, let's make up a pool and see who can guess closest to the number of seeds."

And Jim would say, "If Milt hadn't of been so hoggish, he'd of ordered a half a cantaloupe instead of a whole one and it might not of stuck in his throat."

All the boys would roar at this and Milt himself would force a smile, though the joke was on him. Jim certainly was a card!

There's his shavin' mug, settin' on the shelf, right next to Charley Vail's. "Charles M. Vail." That's the druggist. He comes in regular for his shave, three times a week. And Jim's is the cup next to Charley's. "James H. Kendall." Jim won't need no shavin' mug no more, but I'll leave it there just the same for old time's sake. Jim certainly was a character!

Years ago, Jim used to travel for a canned goods concern over in Carterville. They sold canned goods. Jim had the whole northern half of the state and was on the road five days out of every week. He'd drop in here Saturdays and tell his experiences for that week. It was rich.

I guess he paid more attention to playin' jokes than makin' sales. Finally the concern let him out and he come right home here and told everybody he'd been fired instead of sayin' he'd resigned like most fellas would of.

It was a Saturday and the shop was full and Jim got up out of that chair and says, "Gentlemen, I got an important announcement to make. I been fired from my job."

Well, they asked him if he was in earnest and he said he was and nobody could think of nothin' to say till Jim finally broke the ice himself. He says, "I been sellin' canned goods and now I'm canned goods myself."

You see, the concern he'd been workin' for was a factory that made canned goods. Over in Carterville. And now Jim said he was canned himself. He was certainly a card!

Jim had a great trick that he used to play w'ile he was travelin'. For instance, he'd be ridin' on a train and they'd come to some little town like, well, like, we'll say, like Benton. Jim would look out the train window and read the signs on the stores.

For instance, they'd be a sign, "Henry Smith, Dry Goods." Well, Jim would write down the name and the name of the town and when he got to wherever he was goin' he'd mail back a postal card to Henry Smith at Benton and not sign no name to it, but he'd write on the card, well, somethin' like "Ask your wife about that book agent that spent the afternoon last week," or "Ask your Missus who kept her from gettin' lonesome the last time you was in Carterville." And he'd sign the card, "A Friend."

Of course, he never knew what really come of none of those jokes, but he could picture what *probably* happened and that was enough.

Jim didn't work very steady after he lost his position with the Carterville people. What he did earn, doin' odd jobs round town, why he spent pretty near all of it on gin and his family might of starved if the stores hadn't of carried them along. Jim's wife tried her hand at dressmakin', but they ain't nobody goin' to get rich makin' dresses in this town.

As I say, she'd of divorced Jim, only she seen that she couldn't support herself and the kids and she was always hopin' that some day Jim would cut out his habits and give her more than two or three dollars a week.

They was a time when she would go to whoever he was workin' for and ask them to give her his wages, but after she done this once or twice, he beat her to it by borrowin' most of his pay in advance. He told it all round town, how he had outfoxed his Missus. He certainly was a caution!

But he wasn't satisfied with just outwittin' her. He was sore the way she had acted, tryin' to grab off his pay. And he made up his mind he'd get even. Well, he waited till Evans's Circus was advertised to come to town. Then he told his wife and two kiddies that he was goin' to take them to the circus. The day of the circus, he told them he would get the tickets and meet them outside the entrance to the tent.

Well, he didn't have no intentions of bein' there or buyin' tickets or nothin'. He got full of gin and laid round Wright's poolroom all day. His wife and kids waited and waited and of course he didn't show up. His wife didn't have a dime with her, or nowhere else, I guess. So she finally had to tell the kids it was all off and they cried like they wasn't never goin' to stop.

Well, it seems, w'ile they was cryin', Doc Stair came along and he asked what was the matter, but Mrs. Kendall was stubborn and wouldn't tell him, but the kids told him and he insisted on takin' them and their mother in to the show. Jim found this out afterwards and it was one reason why he had it in for Doc Stair.

Doc Stair come here about a year and a half ago. He's a mighty handsome young fella and his clothes always look like he has them made to order. He goes to Detroit two or three times a year and w'ile he's there he must have a tailor take his measure and then make him a suit to order. They cost pretty near twice as much, but they fit a whole lot better than if you just bought them in a store.

For a w'ile everybody was wonderin' why a young doctor like Doc Stair should come to a town like this where we already got old Doc Gamble and Doc Foote that's both been here for years and all the practice in town was always divided between the two of them.

Then they was a story got round that Doc Stair's gal had throwed him over, a gal up in the Northern Peninsula somewheres, and the reason he come here was to hide himself away and forget it. He said himself that he thought they wasn't nothin' like general practice in a place like ours to fit a man to be a good all round doctor. And that's why he'd came.

Anyways, it wasn't long before he was makin' enough to live on, though they tell me that he never dunned nobody for what they owed him, and the folks here certainly has got the owin' habit, even in my

business. If I had all that was comin' to me for just shaves alone, I could go to Carterville and put up at the Mercer for a week and see a different picture every night. For instance, they's old George Purdy— but I guess I shouldn't ought to be gossipin'.

Well, last year, our coroner died, died of the flu. Ken Beatty, that was his name. He was the coroner. So they had to choose another man to be coroner in his place and they picked Doc Stair. He laughed at first and said he didn't want it, but they made him take it. It ain't no job that anybody would fight for and what a man makes out of it in a year would just about buy seeds for their garden. Doc's the kind, though, that can't say no to nothin' if you keep at him long enough.

But I was goin' to tell you about a poor boy we got here in town— Paul Dickson. He fell out of a tree when he was about ten years old. Lit on his head and it done somethin' to him and he ain't never been right. No harm in him, but just silly. Jim Kendall used to call him cuckoo; that's a name Jim had for anybody that was off their head, only he called people's head their bean. That was another of his gags, callin' head bean and callin' crazy people cuckoo. Only poor Paul ain't crazy, but just silly.

You can imagine that Jim used to have all kinds of fun with Paul. He'd send him to the White Front Garage for a left-handed monkey wrench. Of course they ain't no such a thing as a left-handed monkey wrench.

And once we had a kind of a fair here and they was a baseball game between the fats and the leans and before the game started Jim called Paul over and sent him way down to Schrader's hardware store to get a key for the pitcher's box.

They wasn't nothing in the way of gags that Jim couldn't think up, when he put his mind to it.

Poor Paul was always kind of suspicious of people, maybe on account of how Jim had kept foolin' him. Paul wouldn't have much to do with anybody only his own mother and Doc Stair and a girl here in town named Julie Gregg. That is, she ain't a girl no more, but pretty near thirty or over.

When Doc first came to town, Paul seemed to feel like here was a real friend and he hung round Doc's office most of the w'ile; the only time he wasn't there was when he'd go home to eat or sleep or when he seen Julie Gregg doin' her shoppin'.

When he looked out Doc's window and seen her, he'd run downstairs and join her and tag along with her to the different stores. The poor boy was crazy about Julie and she always treated him mighty nice and made him feel like he was welcome, though of course it wasn't nothin' but pity on her side.

Doc done all he could to improve Paul's mind and he told me once that he really thought the boy was gettin' better, that they was times

when he was as bright and sensible as anybody else.

But I was goin' to tell you about Julie Gregg. Old Man Gregg was in the lumber business, but got to drinkin' and lost the most of his money and when he died, he didn't leave nothin' but the house and just enough insurance for the girl to skimp along on.

Her mother was a kind of a half invalid and didn't hardly ever leave the house. Julie wanted to sell the place and move somewheres else after the old man died, but the mother said she was born here and would die here. It was tough on Julie, as the young people round this town—well, she's too good for them.

She's been away to school and Chicago and New York and different places and they ain't no subject she can't talk on, where you take the rest of the young folks here and you mention anything to them outside of Gloria Swanson or Tommy Meighan and they think you're delirious. Did you see Gloria in "Wages of Virtue"? You missed somethin'!

Well, Doc Stair hadn't been here more than a week when he come in one day to get shaved and I recognized who he was as he had been pointed out to me, so I told him about my old lady. She's been ailin' for a couple years and either Doc Gamble or Doc Foote, neither one, seemed to be helpin' her. So he said he would come out and see her, but if she was able to get out herself, it would be better to bring her to his office where he could make a completer examination.

So I took her to his office and w'ile I was waitin' for her in the reception room, in come Julie Gregg. When somebody comes in Doc Stair's office, they's a bell that rings in his inside office so he can tell they's somebody to see him.

So he left my old lady inside and come out to the front office and that's the first time him and Julie met and I guess it was what they call love at first sight. But it wasn't fifty-fifty. This young fella was the slickest lookin' fella she'd ever seen in this town and she went wild over him. To him she was just a young lady that wanted to see the doctor.

She'd came on about the same business I had. Her mother had been doctorin' for years with Doc Gamble and Doc Foote and with no results. So she'd heard they was a new doc in town and decided to give him a try. He promised to call and see her mother that same day.

I said a minute ago that it was love at first sight on her part. I'm not only judgin' by how she acted afterwards but how she looked at him that first day in his office. I ain't no mind reader, but it was wrote all over her face that she was gone.

Now Jim Kendall, besides bein' a jokesmith and a pretty good drinker, well, Jim was quite a lady-killer. I guess he run pretty wild durin' the time he was on the road for them Carterville people, and besides that, he'd had a couple little affairs of the heart right here in town. As I say, his wife could of divorced him, only she couldn't.

But Jim was like the majority of men, and women, too, I guess. He wanted what he couldn't get. He wanted Julie Gregg and worked his head off tryin' to land her. Only he'd of said bean instead of head.

Well, Jim's habits and his jokes didn't appeal to Julie and of course he was a married man, so he didn't have no more chance than, well, than a rabbit. That's an expression of Jim's himself. When somebody didn't have no chance to get elected or somethin', Jim would always say they didn't have no more chance than a rabbit.

He didn't make no bones about how he felt. Right in here, more than once, in front of the whole crowd, he said he was stuck on Julie and anybody that could get her for him was welcome to his house and his wife and kids included. But she wouldn't have nothin' to do with him; wouldn't even speak to him on the street. He finally seen he wasn't gettin' nowheres with his usual line so he decided to try the rough stuff. He went right up to her house one evenin' and when she opened the door he forced his way in and grabbed her. But she broke loose and before he could stop her, she run in the next room and locked the door and phoned to Joe Barnes. Joe's the marshal. Jim could hear who she was phonin' to and he beat it before Joe got there.

Joe was an old friend of Julie's pa. Joe went to Jim the next day and told him what would happen if he ever done it again.

I don't know how the news of this little affair leaked out. Chances is that Joe Barnes told his wife and she told somebody else's wife and they told their husband. Anyways, it did leak out and Hod Meyers had the nerve to kid Jim about it, right here in this shop. Jim didn't deny nothin' and kind of laughed it off and said for us all to wait; that lots of people had tried to make a monkey out of him, but he always got even.

Meanw'ile everybody in town was wise to Julie's bein' wild mad over the Doc. I don't suppose she had any idear how her face changed when him and her was together; of course she couldn't of, or she'd kept away from him. And she didn't know that we was all noticin' how many times she made excuses to go up to his office or pass it on the other side of the street and look up in his window to see if he was there. I felt sorry for her and so did most other people.

Hod Meyers kept rubbin' it into Jim about how the Doc had cut him out. Jim didn't pay no attention to the kiddin' and you could see he was plannin' one of his jokes.

One trick Jim had was the knack of changin' his voice. He could make you think he was a girl talk-in' and he could mimic any man's voice. To show you how good he was along this line, I'll tell you the joke he played on me once.

You know, in most towns of any size, when a man is dead and needs a shave, why the barber that shaves him soaks him five dollars for the job; that is, he don't soak *him,* but whoever ordered the shave. I just charge three dollars because personally I don't mind much shavin' a dead person. They lay a whole lot stiller than live customers. The only thing is that you don't feel like talkin' to them and you get kind of lonesome.

Well, about the coldest day we ever had here, two years ago last winter, the phone rung at the house w'ile I was home to dinner and I answered the phone and it was a woman's voice and she said she was Mrs. John Scott and her husband was dead and would I come out and shave him.

Old John had always been a good customer of mine. But they live seven miles out in the country, on the Streeter road. Still I didn't see how I could say no.

So I said I would be there, but would have to come in a jitney and it might cost three or four dollars besides the price of the shave. So she, or the voice, it said that was all right, so I got Frank Abbott to drive me out to the place and when I got there, who should open the door but old John himself! He wasn't no more dead than, well, than a rabbit.

It didn't take no private detective to figure out who had played me this little joke. Nobody could of thought it up but Jim Kendall. He certainly was a card!

I tell you this incident just to show you how he could disguise his voice and make you believe it was somebody else talkin'. I'd of swore it was Mrs. Scott had called me. Anyways, some woman.

Well, Jim waited till he had Doc Stair's voice down pat; then he went after revenge.

He called Julie up on a night when he knew Doc was over in Carterville. She never questioned but what it was Doc's voice. Jim said he must see her that night; he couldn't wait no longer to tell her somethin'. She was all excited and told him to come to the house. But he said he was expectin' an important long distance call and wouldn't she please forget her manners for once and come to his office. He said they couldn't nothin' hurt her and nobody would see her and he just *must* talk to her a little w'ile. Well, poor Julie fell for it.

Doc always keeps a night light in his office, so it looked to Julie like they was somebody there.

Meanw'ile Jim Kendall had went to Wright's poolroom, where they was a whole gang amusin' themselves. The most of them had drank plenty of gin, and they was a rough bunch even when sober. They was always strong for Jim's jokes and when he told them to come with him and see some fun they give up their card games and pool games and followed along.

Doc's office is on the second floor. Right outside his door they's a flight of stairs leadin' to the floor above. Jim and his gang hid in the dark behind these stairs.

Well, Julie come up to Doc's door and rung the bell and they was nothin' doin'. She rung it again and she rung it seven or eight times. Then she tried the door and found it locked. Then Jim made some kind of a noise and she heard it and waited a minute, and then she says, "Is that you, Ralph?" Ralph is Doc's first name.

They was no answer and it must of came to her all of a sudden that she'd been bunked. She pretty near fell downstairs and the whole gang after her. They chased her all the way home, hollerin', "Is that you, Ralph?" and "Oh, Ralphie, dear, is that you?" Jim says he couldn't holler it himself, as he was laughin' too hard.

Poor Julie! She didn't show up here on Main Street for a long, long time afterward.

And of course Jim and his gang told everybody in town, everybody but Doc Stair. They was scared to tell him, and he might of never knowed only for Paul Dickson. The poor cuckoo, as Jim called him, he was here in the shop one night when Jim was still gloatin' yet over what he'd done to Julie. And Paul took in as much of it as he could understand and he run to Doc with the story.

It's a cinch Doc went up in the air and swore he'd make Jim suffer. But it was a kind of a delicate thing, because if it got out that he had beat Jim up, Julie was bound to hear of it and then she'd know that Doc knew and of course knowin' that he knew would make it worse for her than ever. He was goin' to do somethin', but it took a lot of figurin'.

Well, it was a couple of days later when Jim was here in the shop again, and so was the cuckoo. Jim was goin' duckshootin' the next day and had come in lookin' for Hod Meyers to go with him. I happened to know that Hod had went over to Carterville and wouldn't be home till the end of the week. So Jim said he hated to go alone and he guessed he would call it off. Then poor Paul spoke up and said if Jim would take him he would go along. Jim thought a w'ile and then he said, well, he guessed a half-wit was better than nothin'.

I suppose he was plottin' to get Paul out in the boat and play some joke on him, like pushin' him in the water. Anyways, he said Paul could go. He asked him had he ever shot a duck and Paul said no, he'd never even had a gun in his hands. So Jim said he could set in the boat and watch him and if he behaved himself, he might lend him his gun for a couple of shots. They made a date to meet in the mornin' and that's the last I seen of Jim alive.

Next mornin', I hadn't been open more than ten minutes when Doc Stair come in. He looked kind of nervous. He asked me had I seen Paul Dickson. I said no, but I knew where he was, out duck shootin' with Jim Kendall. So Doc says that's what he had heard, and he couldn't understand it because Paul had told him he wouldn't never have no more to do with Jim as long as he lived.

He said Paul had told him about the joke Jim had played on Julie. He said Paul had asked him what he thought of the joke and the Doc had told him that anybody that would do a thing like that ought not to be let live.

I said it had been a kind of a raw thing, but Jim just couldn't resist no kind of a joke, no matter how raw. I said I thought he was all right at heart, but just bubblin' over with mischief. Doc turned and walked out.

At noon he got a phone call from old John Scott. The lake where Jim and Paul had went shootin' is on John's place. Paul had came runnin' up to the house a few minutes before and said they'd been an accident. Jim had shot a few ducks and then give the gun to Paul and told him to try his luck. Paul hadn't never handled a gun and he was nervous. He was shakin' so hard that he couldn't control the gun. He let fire and Jim sunk back in the boat, dead.

Doc Stair, bein' the coroner, jumped in Frank Abbott's flivver and rushed out to Scott's farm. Paul and old John was down on the shore of the lake. Paul had rowed the boat to shore, but they'd left the body in it, waitin' for Doc to come.

Doc examined the body and said they might as well fetch it back to town. They was no use leavin' it there or callin' a jury, as it was a plain case of accidental shootin'.

Personally I wouldn't never leave a person shoot a gun in the same boat I was in unless I was sure they knew somethin' about guns. Jim was a sucker to leave a new beginner have his gun, let alone a half-wit. It probably served Jim right, what he got. But still we miss him round here. He certainly was a card!

Comb it wet or dry?

PAMELA FRANKAU

The Duchess and the Smugs

THERE HAD been two crises already that day before the cook's husband called to assassinate the cook. The stove caught fire in my presence; the postman had fallen off his bicycle at the gate and been bitten by Charlemagne, our sheep dog, whose policy it was to attack people only when they were down.

Whenever there were two crises my stepmother Jeanne said, *"Jamais deux sans trois."* This morning she and Francis (my father) had debated whether the two things happening to the postman could be counted as two separate crises and might therefore be said to have cleared matters up. I thought that they were wasting their time. In our household things went on and on and on happening. It was a hotel, which made the doom worse: it would have been remarkable to have two days without a crisis and even if we did, I doubted whether the rule would apply in reverse, so that we could augur a third. I was very fond of the word augur.

202

I was not very fond of the cook. But when I was sitting on the terrace in the shade working on my Anthology of Hates, and a man with a bristled chin told me in *patois* that he had come to kill her, I thought it just as well for her, though obviously disappointing for her husband, that she was off for the afternoon. He carried a knife that did not look particularly sharp; he smelt of licorice, which meant that he had been drinking Pernod. He stamped up and down, making speeches about his wife and Laurent the waiter, whom he called a *salaud* and many other words new to me and quite difficult to understand.

I said at last, "Look, you can't do it now, because she has gone over to St. Raphael in the bus. But if you wait I will fetch my father." I took the Anthology with me in case he started cutting it up.

I went down the red rock steps that sloped from the garden to the pool. The garden looked the way it always looked, almost as brightly colored as the post cards of it that you could buy at the desk. There was purple bougainvillaea splashing down the white walls of the hotel; there were hydrangeas of the exact shade of pink blotting paper; there were huge silver-gray cacti and green umbrella pines against a sky that was darker blue than the sky in England.

I could not love this garden. Always it seemed to me artificial, spiky with color, not quite true. My idea of a garden was a green lawn and a little apple orchard behind a gray stone house in the Cotswolds. I saw that garden only once a year, in September. I could conjure it by repeating inside my head—

And autumn leaves of blood and gold
That strew a Gloucester lane.

Then the homesickness for the place that was not my home would make a sharp pain under my ribs. I was ashamed to feel so; I could not talk about it; not even to Francis, with whom I could talk about most things.

I came to the top of the steps and saw them lying around the pool, Francis and Jeanne and the two novelists who had come from Antibes for lunch. They were all flat on the yellow mattresses, talking.

I said, "Excuse me for interrupting you, but the cook's husband has come to assassinate the cook."

Francis got up quickly. He looked like Mephistopheles. There were gray streaks in his black hair; all the lines of his face went upward and the pointed mustache followed the lines. His body was dark brown and hairy, except that the scars on his back and legs, where he was burned when the airplane was shot down, did not tan with the sun.

"It's a hot afternoon for an assassination," said the male novelist as they ran up the steps together.

"Perhaps," said Francis, "he can be persuaded to wait until the evening."

"He will have to," I said, "because the cook is in St. Raphael. I told him so."

"Penelope," said my stepmother, sitting up on the yellow mattress, "you had better stay with us."

"But I am working on my book."

"All right, *chérie;* work on it here."

The lady novelist, who had a sparkling, triangular face like a cat, said, "I wish you would read some of it to us. It will take our minds off the current bloodcurdling events."

I begged her to excuse me, adding that I did not anticipate any bloodcurdling events because of the battered look of the knife.

Jeanne said that the cook would have to go in any case, but that her love for Laurent was of a purely spiritual character.

I said, "Laurent is a smoothy, and I do not see how anybody could be in love with him."

"A certain smoothness is not out

of place in a headwaiter," said the lady novelist.

I did not tell her my real reason for disliking Laurent; he made jokes. I hated jokes more than anything. They came first in the Anthology: they occupied whole pages: I had dozens and dozens: it was a loose-leaf book, so that new variations of hates already listed could be inserted at will.

Retiring from the conversation, I went to sit on the flat rock at the far end of the pool. Francis and the male novelist returned very soon. Francis came over to me. I shut the loose-leaf book.

"The cook's husband," he said, "has decided against it."

"I thought he would. I imagine that if you are really going to murder somebody you do not impart the intention to others."

"Don't you want to swim?" said Francis.

"No, thank you. I'm working."

"You couldn't be sociable for half an hour?"

"I would rather not."

"I'll write you down for RCI," he threatened.

RCI was Repulsive Children Incorporated, an imaginary foundation which Francis had invented a year before. It came about because a family consisting mainly of unusually spoiled children stayed at the hotel for two days, and were asked by Francis to leave on the third, although the rooms were booked for a month. According to Francis, RCI did a tremendous

business and there were qualifying examinations wherein the children were tested for noise, bad manners, whining, and brutal conduct. I tried to pretend that I thought this funny.

"Will you please let me work for a quarter of an hour?" I asked him. "After all, I was disturbed by the assassin."

"All right. Fifteen minutes," he said. "After which you qualify."

In fact I was not telling him the truth. I had a rendezvous at this hour every day. At four o'clock precisely I was sure of seeing the people from the next villa. I had watched them for ten days and I knew how Dante felt when he waited for Beatrice to pass him on the Ponte Vecchio. Could one, I asked myself, be in love with four people at once? The answer seemed to be Yes. These people had become a secret passion.

The villa was called La Lézardière; a large, stately pink shape with green shutters; there was a gravel terrace, planted with orange trees and descending in tiers, to a pool that did not sprawl in a circle of red rocks as ours did, but was of smooth gray concrete. At the tip of this pool there was a real diving board. A long gleaming speedboat lay at anchor in the deep water. The stage was set and I waited for the actors.

They had the quality of Vikings; the father and mother were tall, handsome, white-skinned, and fair-haired. The boy and girl followed the pattern. They looked as I should have preferred to look. (I was as dark as Francis, and, according to the never-ceasing stream of personal remarks that seemed to be my lot at this time, I was much too thin. And not pretty. If my eyes were not so large I knew that I should be quite ugly. In Francis' opinion, my face had character. "But this, as Miss Edith Cavell said of patriotism," I told him, "is not enough.")

Oh, to look like the Bradleys; to be the Bradleys, I thought, waiting for the Bradleys. They were fair, august, and enchanted; they wore the halo of being essentially English. They were Dad and Mum and Don and Eva. I spied on them like a huntress, strained my ears for their words, cherished their timetable. It was regular as the clock. They swam before breakfast and again at ten, staying beside the pool all the morning. At a quarter to one the bell would ring from the villa for their lunch. Oh, the beautiful punctuality of those meals! Sometimes we did not eat luncheon until three and although Jeanne told me to go and help myself from the kitchen, this was not the same thing at all.

In the afternoon the Bradleys rested on their terrace in the shade. At four they came back to the pool. They went fishing or water-skiing. They were always doing something. They would go for drives in a magnificent gray car with a white hood that folded back. Sometimes they played a catching game beside the pool; or they did exercises in a row, with the father leading them. They had cameras and butterfly nets and field glasses. They never seemed to lie around and talk, the loathed recreation in which I was expected to join.

I took Don and Eva to be twins; and perhaps a year younger than I. I was just fourteen. To be a twin would, I thought, be a most satisfying destiny. I would even have changed places with the youngest member of the Bradley family, a baby in a white perambulator with a white starched nurse in charge of it. If I could be the baby, I should at least be sure of growing up and becoming a Bradley, in a white shirt and gray shorts.

Their magic linked with the magic of my yearly fortnight in England, when, besides having the gray skies and the green garden, I had acquaintance with other English children not in the least like me: solid, pink-cheeked sorts with ponies; they came over to tea at my aunt's house and it was always more fun in anticipation than in fact, because I seemed to make them shy. And I could never tell them that I yearned for them.

So, in a way, I was content to watch the Bradleys at a distance. I felt that it was hopeless to want to be friends with them; to do the things that they did. I was not only different on the outside, but different on the inside, which was worse. On the front page of the Anthology

I had written: "I was born to trouble as the sparks fly upward," one of the more consoling quotations because it made the matter seem inevitable.

Now it was four o'clock. My reverie of the golden Bradleys became the fact of the golden Bradleys, strolling down to the water. Dad and Don were carrying the water-skis. I should have only a brief sight of them before they took the speed-boat out into the bay. They would skim and turn far off, tantalizing small shapes on the shiny silky sea. Up on the third tier of the terrace, between the orange trees, the neat white nurse was pushing the perambulator. But she was only faintly touched with the romance that haloed the others. I mourned.

Then a most fortunate thing happened. There was a drift of strong current around the rocks and as the speedboat moved out toward the bay, one of the water-skis slipped off astern, and was carried into the pool under the point where I sat. Don dived in after it; I ran down the slope of rock on their side, to shove it off from the edge of the pool.

"Thanks most awfully," he said. He held on to the fringed seaweed and hooked the water-ski under his free arm. Now that he was so close to me I could see that he had freckles; it was a friendly smile and he spoke in the chuffy, English boy's voice that I liked.

"It's rather fun, water-skiing."

"It looks fun. I have never done it."

"Would you like to come out with us?" he jerked his head toward the boat: "Dad's a frightfully good teacher."

I groaned within me, like the king in the Old Testament. Here were the gates of Paradise opening and I must let them shut again, or be written down for RCI.

"Painful as it is to refuse," I said, "my father has acquired visitors and I have sworn to be sociable. The penalty is ostracism." (Ostracism was another word that appealed to me.)

Don, swinging on the seaweed, gave a gurgle of laughter.

"What's funny?" I asked.

"I'm terribly sorry. Wasn't that meant to be funny?"

"Wasn't what meant to be funny?"

"The way you talked."

"No, it's just the way I talk," I said, drooping with sadness.

"I like it awfully," said Don. This was warming to my heart. By now the speedboat was alongside the rock point. I could see the Viking heads; the delectable faces in detail. Mr. Bradley called: "Coming aboard?"

"She can't," said Don. "Her father has visitors; she'll be ostracized." He was still giggling and his voice shook.

"Oh dear, that's too bad," said Mrs. Bradley. "Why don't you ask your father if you can come tomorrow?"

"I will, most certainly," I said, though I knew that I need never ask permission of Jeanne or Francis for anything that I wanted to do.

I felt as though I had been addressed by a goddess. Don gurgled again. He flashed through the water and they pulled him into the boat.

I had to wait for a few minutes alone, hugging my happiness, preparing a kind of vizor to pull down over it when I went back to the group on the yellow mattresses.

"Making friends with the Smugs?" Francis greeted me.

"What an enchanting name," said the lady novelist.

"It isn't their name; it's what they are," said Francis.

I heard my own voice asking thinly: "Why do you call them that?" He shocked me so much that my heart began to beat heavily and I shivered. I tried to conceal this by sitting crouched and hugging my knees. I saw him watching me.

"Well, aren't they?" he said gently. I had given myself away. He had guessed that they meant something to me.

"I don't know. I don't think so. I want to know why you think so."

"Partly from observation," said Francis. "Their gift for organized leisure; their continual instructions to their children; the expressions on their faces. And the one brief conversation that I've conducted with Bradley—he congratulated me on being able to engage in a commercial enterprise on French soil. According to Bradley, you can never trust the French." He imitated the chuffy English voice.

"Isn't 'commercial enterprise' rather an optimistic description of Chez François?" asked the lady novelist, and the male novelist laughed. Francis was still looking at me.

"Why do you like them, Penelope?"

I replied with chilled dignity: "I did not say that I liked them. They invited me to go water-skiing with them tomorrow."

Jeanne said quickly: "That will be fun. You know, Francis, you are becoming too intolerant of your own countrymen, it is enough in these days for you to meet an Englishman for you to dislike him." This was comforting; I could think this and feel better. Nothing, I thought, could make me feel worse than for Francis to attack the Bradleys. It was another proof that my loves, like my hates, must remain secret, and this was loneliness.

II

I awoke next morning full of a wild surmise. I went down early to the pool and watched Francis taking off for Marseilles in his small, ramshackle seaplane. He flew in a circle over the garden as he always did, and when the seaplane's long boots pointed for the west, I saw Don and Eva Bradley standing still on the gravel terrace to watch it. They were coming down to the pool alone. Offering myself to them, I went out to the flat rock. They waved and beckoned and shouted.

"Is that your father flying the seaplane?"

"Yes."

"Does he take you up in it?"

"Sometimes."

"Come and swim with us," Don called.

I ran down the rock slope on their side. I was shy now that we stood together. I saw that Eva was a little taller than Don; that she also was freckled; and that they had oiled their skins against sunburn as the grownups did. Don wore white trunks and Eva a white swimming suit. They laughed when I shook hands with them, and Don made me an elaborate bow after the handshake. Then they laughed again.

"Are you French or English?"

That saddened me. I said, "I am English, but I live here because my stepmother is a Frenchwoman and my father likes the Riviera."

"We know that," said Don quickly. "He was shot down and taken prisoner by the Germans and escaped and fought with the Resistance, didn't he?"

"Yes. That is how he met Jeanne."

"And he's Francis Wells, the poet?"

"Yes."

"And the hotel is quite mad, isn't it?"

"Indubitably," I said. It was another of my favorite words. Eva

doubled up with laughter. "Oh, that's wonderful. I'm *always* going to say indubitably."

"Is it true," Don said, "that guests only get served if your father likes the look of them, and that he charges nothing sometimes, and that all the rooms stay empty for weeks if he wants them to?"

"It is true. It does not seem to me the most intelligent way of running an hotel, but that is none of my business."

"Is he very rich?" asked Eva.

Don said quickly: "Don't, Eva, that's not polite."

"He isn't rich or poor," I said. I could not explain our finances to the Bradleys any more than I could explain them to myself. Sometimes we had money. When we had not, we were never poor in the way that other people were poor. We were "broke" which, as far as I could see, meant being in debt but living as usual and talking about money.

"Do you go to school in England?"

"No," I said, handing over my chief shame. "I am a day boarder at a convent school near Grasse. It is called Notre Dame des Oliviers."

"Do you like it?"

"I find it unobjectionable," I said. It would have been disloyal to Francis and Jeanne to tell these people how little I liked it.

"Do they teach the same things as English schools?"

"Roughly."

"I expect you're awfully clever,"

said Eva, "and top at everything."

How did she know that? Strenuously, I denied it. Heading the class in literature, composition, and English poetry was just one more way of calling attention to myself. It was part of the doom of being noticeable, of not being like Other People. At Les Oliviers, Other People were French girls, strictly brought up, formally religious, cut to a foreign pattern. I did not want to be they, as I wanted to be the Bradleys: I merely envied their uniformity.

God forbid that I should tell the Bradleys about winning a special prize for a sonnet; about being chosen to recite Racine to hordes of parents; about any of it. I defended myself by asking questions in my turn. Eva went to an English boarding school in Sussex; Don would go to his first term at public school this autumn. I had guessed their ages correctly. They were just thirteen. "Home" was Devonshire.

"I would greatly love to live in England," I said.

"I'd far rather live in a hotel on the French Riviera. Lucky Penelope."

"I am not lucky Penelope; I am subject to dooms."

"How heavenly. What sort of dooms?"

"For example, getting an electric shock in science class, and finding a whole nest of mice in my desk," I said. "And being the only person present when a lunatic arrived believing the school to be Paradise."

"Go on. Go on," they said. "It's wonderful. Those aren't dooms, they are adventures."

"Nothing that happens all the time is an adventure," I said. "The hotel is also doomed."

They turned their heads to look up at it; from here, through the pines and the cactus, we could see the red crinkled tiles of its roof, the bougainvillaea, the top of the painted blue sign that announced "Chez François."

"It can't be doomed," Don said. "Don't famous people come here?"

"Oh yes. But famous people are more subject to dooms than ordinary people."

"How?"

"In every way you can imagine. Important telegrams containing money do not arrive. Their wives leave them; they are recalled on matters of state."

"Does Winston Churchill come?"

"Yes."

"And Lord Beaverbrook and Elsa Maxwell and the Duke of Windsor and Somerset Maugham?"

"Yes. Frequently. All their signed photographs are kept in the bar. Would you care to see them?"

Here I encountered the first piece of Bradley dogma. Don and Eva, who were splashing water on each other's hair ("Dad is most particular about our not getting sunstroke") looked doubtful.

"We *would* love to."

"I'm sure it's all right, Eva; because she lives there."

"I don't know. I think we ought to ask first. It is a bar, after all."

Ashamed, I hid from them the fact that I often served in the bar when Laurent was off duty.

"Oh, do let's chance it," said Don.

"I don't believe we ought to."

Mr. and Mrs. Bradley had gone over to Nice and would not return until the afternoon, so a deadlock threatened. The white starched nurse appeared at eleven o'clock with a Thermos flask of cold milk and a plate of buns. I gave birth to a brilliant idea; I told her that my stepmother had invited Don and Eva to lunch with us.

It was a little difficult to convince them after the nurse had gone that Jeanne would be pleased to have them to lunch without an invitation. When I led them up through our garden, they treated it as an adventure, like tiger shooting.

Jeanne welcomed them, as I had foretold, and the lunch was highly successful, although it contained several things, such as *moules,* which the Bradleys were not allowed to eat. We had the terrace to ourselves. Several cars drove up and their owners were told politely that lunch could not be served to them. This delighted Don and Eva. They were even more delighted when Jeanne told them of Francis' ambition, which was to have a notice: "Keep Out; This Means You," printed in seventeen languages. One mystery about the Bradleys was that they seemed to like jokes. They thought that I made jokes. When they laughed at my phrases they

did not laugh as the grownups did, but in the manner of an appreciative audience receiving a comedian. Eva would hold her stomach and cry: "Oh *stop!* It hurts to giggle like this; it really hurts."

I took them on a tour of the hotel. The salon was furnished with some good Empire pieces. The bedrooms were not like hotel bedrooms, but more like rooms in clean French farmhouses, with pale walls and dark wood and chintz. All the rooms had balconies where the guests could eat their breakfast. There were no guests.

"And Dad says people *clamor* to stay here in the season," Don said, straddled in the last doorway.

"Yes, they do. Probably some will be allowed in at the end of the week," I explained, "but the Duchess is arriving from Venice at any moment and Francis always waits for her to choose which room she wants, before he lets any. She is changeable."

Eva said, "I can't get over you calling your father Francis. Who is the Duchess?"

"The Duchessa di Terracini. She is half Italian and half American."

"Is she very beautiful?"

"Very far from it. She is seventy and she looks like a figure out of a waxworks. She was celebrated for her lovers but now she only loves roulette." I did not wish to be uncharitable about the Duchess, whose visit was to be dreaded, and these were the nicest things that I could make myself say. The only thing in her favor was that she had been a friend of my mother, who was American and utterly beautiful and whom I did not remember.

"*Lovers?*" Eva said, looking half pleased and half horrified. Don flushed and looked at his feet. I had learned from talks at school that reactions to a mention of the facts of life could be like this. I knew also that Francis despised the expression, "the facts of life," because, he said, it sounded as though all the other things that happened in life were figments of the imagination.

"A great many people loved the Duchess desperately," I said. "She was engaged to an Austrian Emperor; he gave her emeralds, but somebody shot him."

"Oh well, then, she's practically history, isn't she?" Eva said, looking relieved.

III

I might have known that the end of the day would bring doom. It came hard upon the exquisite pleasure of my time in the speedboat with the Bradleys. This was even better than I had planned it in anticipation, a rare gift. I thought that the occasion must be under the patronage of a benign saint or what the Duchess would call a favorable aura; the only worry was Mrs. Bradley's worry about my having no dry clothes to put on after swimming; but with typical Bradley organization there were an extra white shirt

and gray shorts in the boat. Dressed thus I felt like a third twin.

The sea changed color; the sea began to be white and the rocks a darker red.

"Would you like to come back and have supper with us, Penelope?"

I replied, "I can imagine nothing that I would like more."

"She *does* say wonderful things, doesn't she?" said Eva. I was drunk by now on Bradley admiration and almost reconciled to personal remarks.

"Penelope speaks very nice English," said Mrs. Bradley.

"Will you ask your stepmother then?" she added as we tied up the boat. I was about to say this was unnecessary when Don gave my ribs a portentous nudge; he said quickly, "Eva and I will walk you up there." It was obvious that the hotel exercised as much fascination for them as they for me.

When the three of us set off across the rocks Mr. Bradley called, "Seven o'clock sharp, now!" and Eva made a grimace. She said, "Wouldn't it be nice not to have to be punctual for anything?"

"I never have to be," I said, "except at school, and I think that I prefer it to having no timetable at all."

"Oh, my goodness! Why?"

"I like days to have a shape," I said.

"Can you just stay out to supper when you want to? Always? Without telling them?"

"Oh, yes."

"What would happen if you stayed away a whole night?"

I said that I had never tried. And now we went into the bar because Don said that he wanted to see the photographs again. Laurent was there; straw-colored and supercilious in his white coat. He began to make his jokes: *"Mesdames, monsieur, bon soir. What may I serve you? A Pernod? A champagne cocktail?"* He flashed along the shelves, reading out the name of each drink, muttering under his breath, *"Mais non; c'est terrible; we have nothing that pleases our distinguished visitors."* I saw that the Bradleys were enchanted with him.

We walked all round the gallery of photographs and were lingering beside Winston Churchill when the worst thing happened. I heard it coming. One could always hear the Duchess coming. She made peals of laughter that sounded like opera; the words came fast and high between the peals.

And here she was, escorted by Francis. She cried, "Ah my love, my love," and I was swept into a complicated, painful embrace, scratched by her jewelry, crushed against her stays, and choked with her scent before I got a chance to see her in perspective. When I did, I saw that there were changes since last year and that these were for the worse. Her hair, which had been dyed black, was now dyed bright red. Her powder was whiter and thicker than ever; her eyelids were dark

blue; she had new false eyelashes of great length that made her look like a Jersey cow.

She wore a dress of dark blue chiffon, sewn all over with sequin stars, and long red gloves with her rings on the outside; she tilted back on her heels, small and bony, gesticulating with the gloves.

"Beautiful — beautiful — beautiful!" was one of her slogans. She said it now; she could not conceivably mean me; she just meant everything. The Bradleys had become awed and limp all over. When I introduced them they shook hands jerkily, snatching their hands away at once. Francis took from Laurent the bottle of champagne that had been on ice awaiting the Duchess; he carried it to her favorite table, the corner table beside the window. She placed upon the table a sequin bag of size, a long chiffon scarf, and a small jeweled box that held *bonbons au miel,* my least favorite sweets, reminding me of scented glue.

Francis uncorked the champagne.

"But glasses for all of us," the Duchess said. "A glass for each." The Bradleys said, "No thank you very much," so quickly that they made it sound like one syllable and I imitated them.

"But how good for you," cried the Duchess. "The vitalizing, the magnificent, the harmless grape. All children should take a little to combat the lassitude and depressions of growth. My mother used to give me a glass every morning after my fencing lesson. *Et toi,* Penelope? More than once last year you have taken your *petit verre* with me."

"Oh, didn't you know? Penelope is on the water wagon," said Francis, and the Duchess again laughed like opera. She cried, *"Santé, santé!"* raising her glass to each of us. Francis helped himself to a Pernod and perched on the bar, swinging his legs. The Bradleys and I stood in a straight, uncomfortable row.

"Of youth," said the Duchess, "I recall three things. The sensation of time seeming endless, as though one were swimming against a current; the insipid insincerity of one's teachers; and bad dreams, chiefly about giants."

Sometimes she expected an answer to statements of this character; at other times she went on talking: I had known her to continue without a break for fifteen minutes.

"I used to dream about giants," said Eva.

"How old are you, Miss?"

"Thirteen."

"At fifteen the dreams become passionate," said the Duchess, sounding lugubrious about it.

"What do you dream about now?" asked Don, who had not removed his eyes from her since she came.

"Packing; missing airplanes; losing my clothes," said the Duchess. "Worry—worry—worry; but one is never bored in a dream, which is more than can be said for real life. Give me your hand," she snapped at Eva. She pored over it a mo-

ment, and then said briskly, "You are going to marry very young and have three children; an honest life; always be careful in automobiles." Don's hand was already stretched out and waiting. She gave him two wives, a successful business career, and an accident "involving a horse between the ages of twenty and twenty-three."

"That is tolerably old for a horse," Francis interrupted.

"Sh-h," said the Duchess, "perhaps while steeplechasing; it is not serious." She blew me a little kiss: "Penelope I already know. She is as clear to me as a book written by an angel. Let me see if there is any change," she commanded, a medical note in her voice: "Beautiful—beautiful—beautiful! Genius and fame and passion, are all here."

"Any dough?" asked Francis.

"I beg your pardon," said the Duchess, who knew perfectly well what dough meant, but who always refused to recognize American slang.

"I refer to cash," said Francis looking his most Mephisophelean: "My ambition for Penelope is that she acquire a rich husband, so that she may subsidize Papa in his tottering old age."

"Like so many creative artists, you have the soul of a fishmonger," said the Duchess. She was still holding my hand; she planted a champagne-wet kiss on the palm before she let it go. "I have ordered our dinner, Penelope. It is to be the *écrevisses au gratin* that you like, with small *goûters* of caviar to begin with and *fraises des bois* in kirsch afterward."

I had been anticipating this hurdle; she always insisted that I dine with her on her first evening, before she went to the Casino at nine o'clock.

"I am very sorry, Duchessa; you must excuse me. I am having supper with Don and Eva." I saw Francis raise one eyebrow at me. "I really didn't know you were coming tonight," I pleaded.

"No, that is true," said the Duchess, "but I am very disappointed. I have come to regard it as a regular tryst." She put her head on one side. "Why do you not all three stay and dine with me? We will make it a *partie carrée*. It could be managed, Francis? Beautiful—beautiful—beautiful! There. That is settled."

"I'm most awfully sorry; we'd love to," Eva said. "But we couldn't possibly. Supper's at seven and Mum's expecting us."

"Thank you very much, though," said Don, who was still staring at her. "Could we do it another time?"

"But of course! Tomorrow; what could be better? Except tonight," said the Duchess. "I was looking to Penelope to bring me good luck. Do you remember last year, how I took you to dine at the Carlton and won a fortune afterward?"

"And lost it on the following afternoon," said Francis. The Duchess said an incomprehensible Italian word that sounded like a snake hissing. She took a little ivory hand

out of her bag and pointed it at him.

"I thought one never could win at roulette," said Don. "According to my father, the game is rigged in favor of the Casino."

"Ask your father why there are no taxes in Monaco," said the Duchess. "In a game of this mathematic there is no need for the Casino to cheat. The majority loses naturally, not artificially. And tell him further that all European Casinos are of the highest order of probity, with the possible exception of Estoril and Budapest. Do you know the game?"

When the Bradleys said that they did not, she took from her bag one of the cards that had upon it a replica of the wheel and the cloth. She embarked upon a roulette lesson. The Bradleys were fascinated and of course we were late for supper. Francis delayed me further, holding me back to speak to me on the terrace: "Do you have to have supper with the Smugs?"

"Please don't call them that. Yes, I do."

"It would be reasonable, I should think, to send a message saying that an old friend of the family had arrived unexpectedly."

Of course it would have been reasonable; Mrs. Bradley had expected me to ask permission. But nothing would have made me stay.

"I'm extremely sorry, Francis; I can't do it."

"You should know how much it means to her. She has ordered your favorite dinner. All right," he said,

"I see that it is useless to appeal to your better nature. Tonight you qualify for RCI." He went back to the bar, calling, "The verdict can always be withdrawn if the candidate shows compensating behavior."

"Didn't you want to stay and dine with the Duchess?" asked Don, as we raced through the twilit garden.

"I did not. She embarrasses me greatly."

"I thought she was terrific. I do hope Mum and Dad will let us have dinner with her tomorrow."

"But *don't* say it's *écrevisses,* Don, whatever you do. There's always a row about shell fish," Eva reminded him.

"I wouldn't be such an ass," Don said. "And the only thing that would give it away would be if you were ill afterward."

"Why should it be me?"

"Because it usually is," said Don.

I awoke with a sense of doom. I lay under my mosquito curtain, playing the scenes of last evening through in my mind. A slight chill upon the Viking parents, due to our being late; smiles pressed down over crossness, because of the visitor. Don and Eva pouring forth a miscellany of information about the Duchess and the signed photographs; myself making mental notes, a devoted sociologist studying a favorite tribe: grace before supper; no garlic in anything; copies of *Punch* and the English newspapers; silver napkin rings; apple pie.

The secret that I found in the Cotswold house was here, I told myself; the house in Devonshire took shape; on the walls there were photographs of it; a stream ran through the garden; they rode their ponies on Dartmoor; they had two wire-haired terriers called Snip and Snap. I collected more evidence of Bradley organization: an expedition tomorrow to the Saracen village near Brignoles; a Current-Affairs Quiz that was given to the family by their father once a month.

"No," I said to myself, brooding under my mosquito net, "nothing went wrong until after the apple pie." That was when Eva had said, "The Duchess told all our fortunes." The lines spoken were still in my head:

Don saying, "Penelope's was an absolute fizzer; the Duchess says she will have genius, fame, and passion." Mr. Bradley's Viking profile becoming stony; Mrs. Bradley's smooth white forehead puckering a little as she asked me gently, "Who is this wonderful lady?"

Myself replying, "The Duchessa de Terracini," and Mrs. Bradley remarking that this was a beautiful name. But Mr. Bradley's stony face growing stonier and his officer-to-men voice saying, "Have we all finished?"; then rising so that we rose too and pushed in our chairs and bowed our heads while he said grace.

After that there was a spirited game of Monopoly. "But the atmosphere," I said to myself, "went on being peculiar." I had waited for Don and Eva to comment on it when they walked me home, but they were in a rollicking mood and appeared to have noticed nothing.

"Indubitably there is a doom," I thought while I put on my swimming suit, "and since I shall not see them until this evening because of the Saracen village, I shall not know what it is."

As I crossed the terrace, the Duchess popped her head out of the corner window above me; she leaned like a little gargoyle above the bougainvillaea; she wore a lace veil fastened under her chin with a large diamond.

"Good morning, Duchessa. Did you win?"

"I lost consistently, and your friends cannot come to dine tonight, as you may know; so disappointing, though the note itself is courteous." She dropped it into my hands. It was written by Mrs. Bradley; fat, curly handwriting on paper headed.

CROSSWAYS

CHAGFORD

DEVON

It thanked the Duchess and regretted that owing to the expedition, Don and Eva would not be able to accept her kind invitation to supper.

I knew that the Bradleys would be back by six.

IV

I spent most of the day alone working on the Anthology. I had found quite a new Hate, which was headed "Characters." People called the Duchess a character and this was said of others who came here. I made a brief description of each and included some of their sayings and habits.

There was the usual paragraph about the Duchess in the *Continental Daily Mail;* it referred to her gambling and her emeralds and her *joie-de-vivre. Joie-de-vivre* seemed to be a worthy subject for Hate and I entered it on a separate page, as a subsection of Jokes.

At half-past-four, to my surprise, I looked up from my rock writing desk and saw the Bradleys'' car sweeping in from the road. Presently Eva came running down the tiers of terrace alone. When she saw me she waved, put her finger to her lips, and signaled to me to stay where I was. She came scrambling up.

"I'm so glad to see you. There's a row. I can't stay long. Don has been sent to bed."

"Oh, dear. I was conscious of an unfavorable aura," I said. "What happened?"

Eva looked miserable. "It isn't anything against you, of course. They like you terribly. Mum says you have beautiful manners. When Don and I said we wanted you to come and stop a few days with us at Crossways in September, it went down quite *well*. Would you like to," she asked, gazing at me, "or would it be awfully boring?"

I was momentarily deflected from the doom and the row. "I cannot imagine anything that would give me greater pleasure," I said. She wriggled her eyebrows, as usual, at my phrases.

"That isn't just being polite?"

"I swear by yonder hornèd moon it isn't."

"But of course it may not happen now," she said in melancholy, "although it wasn't *your* fault. After all you didn't make us meet the Duchess on purpose."

"Was the row about the Duchess?"

"Mm—m."

"Because of her telling your fortunes and teaching you to play roulette? I did have my doubts, I admit."

"Apparently they were quite cross about that, but of course they couldn't say so in front of you. Daddy had *heard* of the Duchess, anyway. And they cracked down on the dinner party and sent a note. And Don kept on asking why until he made Daddy furious; and there seems to have been something in the *Continental Mail,* which we are not allowed to read."

"Here it is," I said helpfully. She glanced upward over her shoulder. I said, "Have no fear. We are invisible from the villa at this angle."

She raised her head from the pa-per and her eyes shone; she said, "Isn't it wonderful?" I had thought it a pedestrian little paragraph, but I hid my views.

"Mummy said that the Duchess wasn't at all the sort of person she liked us to mix with, and that no lady would sit in a bar drinking champagne when there were children present, and that we shouldn't have gone into the bar again anyway. And Don lost his temper and was quite rude. So that we came home early instead of having tea out; and Dad said that Don had spoiled the day and asked him to apologize. And Don said a word that we aren't allowed to use and now he's gone to bed. Which is awful for him because he's too big to be sent to bed. And I'll have to go back. I'm terribly sorry."

"So am I," I said. "Please tell your mother that I deplore the Duchess deeply, and that I always have."

As soon as I had spoken, I became leaden inside myself with remorse. It was true that I deplored the Duchess because she was possessive, overpowering, and embarrassing, but I did not disapprove of her in the way that the Bradleys did. I was making a desperate effort to salvage the thing that mattered most to me.

In other words, I was assuming a virtue though I had it not, and while Shakespeare seemed to approve of this practice, I was certain that it was wrong. (And I went on with it. I added that Francis would not have dreamed of bringing the Duchess into the bar if he had known that we were there. This was an outrageous lie. Francis would have brought the Duchess into the bar if the Archbishop of Canterbury were there—admittedly an unlikely contingency.)

When Eva said that this might improve matters and might also make it easier for Don to apologize, because he had stuck up for the Duchess, I felt lower than the worms.

Which is why I quarreled with Francis. And knew that was why. I had discovered that if one were feeling guilty one's instinct was to put the blame on somebody else as soon as possible.

Francis called to me from the bar door as I came up onto the terrace. I had been freed from RCI on the grounds of having replaced Laurent before lunch at short notice. He grinned at me. "Be an angel and take these cigarettes to Violetta's room, will you, please? I swear that woman smokes two at a time."

"I am sorry," I said. "I have no wish to run errands for the Duchess just now."

Francis, as usual, was reasonable. "How has she offended you?" he asked.

I told him about the Bradleys, about the possible invitation to Devonshire; I said that, thanks to the Duchess cutting such a pretty figure in the bar, not to mention the *Continental Mail*, my future was

being seriously jeopardized. I saw Francis' eyebrows twitching.

He said, "Penelope, you are a thundering ass. These people are tedious *petits bourgeois,* and there is no reason to put on their act just because you happen to like their children. And I see no cause to protect anybody, whether aged seven or seventy, from the sight of Violetta drinking champagne."

"Mrs. Bradley said that no lady would behave in such a way."

"Tell Mrs. Bradley with my love and a kiss that if she were a tenth as much of a lady as Violetta she would have cause for pride. And I am not at all sure," he said, "that I like the idea of your staying with them in Devonshire."

This was, as the French said, the *comble.*

"Do you mean that you wouldn't let me go?" I asked, feeling as though I had been struck by lightning.

"I did not say that. I said I wasn't sure that I liked the idea."

"My God, why not?"

"Do not imagine when you say, 'My God,' " said Francis, "that you add strength to your protest. You merely add violence."

He could always make me feel a fool when he wanted to. And I could see that he was angry; less with me than with the Bradleys. He said, "I don't think much of the Smugs, darling, as you know. And I think less after this. Violetta is a very remarkable old girl, and if they knew what she went through in Rome when the Germans were there, some of that heroism might penetrate even their thick heads. Run along with those cigarettes now, will you please?"

I was trembling with rage; the worst kind of rage, hating me as well as everything else. I took the cigarettes with what I hoped was a dignified gesture, and went.

The Duchess was lying on the chaise longue under her window; she was swathed like a mummy in yards of cyclamen chiffon trimmed with marabou. She appeared to be reading three books at once: a novel by Ignazio Silone, Brewer's *Dictionary of Phrase and Fable,* and a *Handbook of Carpentry for Beginners.*

The room, the best of the rooms, having two balconies, had become unrecognizable. It worried me with its rampaging disorder. Three wardrobe trunks crowded it: many dresses, scarves, and pairs of small pointed shoes had escaped from the wardrobe trunks. The Duchess always brought with her large unexplained pieces of material; squares of velvet, crepe de Chine, and damask, which she spread over the furniture. The writing table had been made to look like a table in a museum; she had put upon it a black crucifix and two iron candlesticks, a group of ivory figures, and a velvet book with metal clasps.

Despite the heat of the afternoon the windows were shut; the room smelled of smoke and scent.

"Beautiful — beautiful — beautiful!" said the Duchess, holding out her hands for the cigarettes. "There are the *bonbons au miel* on the bedside table. Help yourself liberally, and sit down and talk to me."

"No, thank you very much. If you will excuse me, Duchessa, I have to do some work now."

"I will not excuse you, darling. Sit down here. Do you know why I will not excuse you?"

I shook my head.

"Because I can see that you are unhappy, frustrated, and restless." She joined her fingertips and stared at me over the top of them. "Some of it I can guess," she said, "and some of I should dearly like to know. Your mother would have known."

I was silent; she was hypnotic when she spoke of my mother, but I could not make myself ask her questions.

"Genius is not a comfortable possession. What do you want to do most in the world, Penelope?"

The truthful reply would have been, "To be like other people. To live in England; with an ordinary father and mother who do not keep a hotel. To stop having dooms; never to be told that I am a genius, and to have people of my own age to play with so that I need not spend my life listening to grownups."

I said, "I don't know."

The Duchess sighed and beat a tattoo with her little feet inside the marabou; they looked like clockwork feet.

"You are, beyond doubt, crying for the moon. Everybody at your age cries for the moon. But if you will not tell me which moon, I cannot be of assistance. What is the book that you are writing?"

"It is an Anthology of Hates," I said, and was much surprised that I had told her because I had not told anybody.

"Oho," said the Duchess. "Have you enough Hates to make an anthology?"

I nodded.

"Is freedom one of your hates?"

I frowned; I did not want to discuss the book with her at all and I could not understand her question. She was smiling in a maddening way that implied more knowledge of me than I myself had.

"Freedom is the most important thing that there is. You have more freedom than the average child knows. One day you will learn to value this and be grateful for it. I will tell you why." Her voice had taken on the sing-song, lecturing note that preceded a fifteen-minute monologue. I stared at the figures on the writing table. She had let her cigarette lie burning in the ash tray, and a small spiral of smoke went up like incense before the crucifix; there was this, there was the hot scented room and the sound of her voice: "It is necessary to imprison children to a certain degree, for their discipline and their protection. In schools, they are largely hidden away from life, like bees in a hive.

This means that they learn a measure of pleasant untruth; a scale of simple inadequate values that resemble the true values in life only as much as a plain colored poster of the Riviera resembles the actual coastline.

"When they emerge from the kindly-seeming prisons, they meet the world of true dimensions and true values. These are unexpectedly painful and irregular. Reality is always irregular and generally painful. To be unprepared for its shocks and to receive the shocks upon a foundation of innocence is the process of growing up. In your case, Penelope, you will be spared many of those pains. Not only do you have now a wealth of freedom which you cannot value because you have not experienced the opposite, but you are also endowing yourself with a future freedom; freedom from fear and shock and shyness which make the transition from youth to maturity more uncomfortable than any other period of existence. Francis is bringing you up through the looking-glass, back-to-front. You are learning what the adult learns, and walking through these lessons toward the light-heartedness that is usually to be found in childhood but lost later. I wonder how long it will take you to find that out." She sat up on her elbows and stared at me again. "Do you know what I think will happen to your Anthology of Hates when you do find it out? You will read it through and find that these are not Hates any more."

By this last remark she had annoyed me profoundly, and now she clapped her hands and cried, "If young people were only allowed to gamble! It takes the mind off every anxiety. If I could take you to the Casino with me tonight, Penelope! Wouldn't that be splendid? Disguised as a young lady of fashion!" She sprang off the chaise longue, snatched the square of velvet from the bed and flung it over my shoulders. Its weight almost bore me to the ground; it was heavy as a tent and it smelled musty. "Look at yourself in the mirror!" cried the Duchess. "Beautiful—beautiful—beautiful! A Principessa!" She scuttled past me. "We will place this silver girdle here." She lashed it so tightly that it hurt my stomach; I was stifled; it felt like being dressed in a carpet. "Take this fan and these gloves." They were long white kid gloves, as hard as biscuits; she forced my fingers in and cajoled the gloves up my arms as far as the shoulders.

"The little amethyst circlet for your head."

She caught some single hairs as she adjusted it and put one finger in my eye. Sweat was trickling all over me.

"Now you have a very distinct resemblance to your mother," said the Duchess, standing before me and regarding me with her head on one side.

"This is the forecast of your womanhood. Will you please go downstairs at once and show yourself to Jeanne?"

I said that I would rather not. She was peevishly disappointed. I struggled out of the ridiculous costume; hot, dispirited, no fonder of myself than before, I got away.

v

My bedroom was on the ground floor, with a window that opened onto the far end of the terrace. It was late, but I was still awake and heard Francis and Jeanne talking outside. I did not mean to listen, but their voices were clear and when I heard the name "Bradley" I could not help listening.

"I agree with you," Jeanne said, "that it is all an outrageous fuss. But these Bradleys mean a great deal to Penelope."

"Wish I knew why," said Francis. "They represent the worst and dullest aspect of English 'county'; a breed that may soon become extinct and no loss, either."

"They are the kind of friends that she has never had; English children of her own age."

Their footsteps ceased directly outside my window. I heard Francis sigh. *"Ought* we to send her to school in England, do you think?"

"Perhaps next year."

"That will be too late, beloved."

I had heard him call Jeanne "beloved" before, but tonight the word touched my heart, perhaps because I was already unhappy; it made me want to cry. "She will be fifteen."

Francis said. "First she'll kill herself trying to fit into the pattern and if she succeeds in the task, we shall never see her again. God knows what we'll get but it won't be Penelope."

"She will change in any case, whether she stays or goes, darling; they always do."

"Perhaps I've done a poor job with her from the beginning," Francis said: he spoke my mother's name. And then I was so sure I must listen no more, that I covered my ears with my hands. When I took them away Jeanne was saying, "You are always sad when your back is hurting you. Come to bed. Tomorrow I'll invite the Bradley children for lunch again; on Thursday when Violetta's in Monte Carlo."

"Why should we suck up to the Smugs?" Francis grumbled, and Jeanne replied, "Only because of Penelope, *tu le sais*," and they walked away down the terrace.

I wept because they destroyed my defenses; my conscience still troubled me for the speeches of humbug that I had made to Eva, for quarreling with Francis, and for being uncivil to the Duchess. It was a weary load. If the Bradleys accepted the invitation to lunch, it would seem that God was not intending to punish me for it, but exactly the reverse, and that was a bewildering state of affairs.

By morning, however, God's plan became clear. Jeanne brought me my breakfast on the terrace. She

sat with me while I ate it. I thought, as I had thought before, that she looked very young; more an elder sister than a stepmother, with her short, flying dark hair, the blue eyes in the brown face, the long slim brown legs. She smoked a *caporal* cigarette.

I could hardly wait for her to tell me whether she had healed the breach with the Bradleys. But I dared not ask. Their talk on the terrace had been too intimate for me to admit that I had heard it. She said, "Penelope, the situation with your friends at La Lézardière has become a little complex."

My heart beat downward heavily and I did not want to eat any more.

"I thought that it would give you pleasure if I asked them to lunch and would perhaps clear up any misunderstanding. But I have been talking to Mrs. Bradley and apparently she would prefer them not to visit the hotel."

I did not know whether I was blushing for the hotel, for my own disappointment, or for the Bradleys; I was only aware of the blush, flaming all over my skin, most uncomfortably.

"Mrs. Bradley was friendly and polite, you must not think otherwise. She wants you to swim with them as much as you like; she said that she hoped you would go out in the speedboat again. But her exact phrase was, 'We feel that the hotel surroundings are just a little too grown-up for Don and Eva.'"

I was silent.

"So, I thought that I would tell you. And ask you not to be unhappy about it. People are entitled to their views, you know, even when one does not oneself agree with them."

"Thank you, Jeanne: I am not at all unhappy," I said, wishing that my voice would not shake. "And if the Bradleys will not come to me, I am certainly not going to them." And I rose from the table. She came after me, but when she saw that I was near to tears she gave me a pat on the back and left me alone.

This was the point at which I discovered that hate did not cast out love, but that it was, on the contrary, possible to hate and love at the same time. I could not turn off my infatuation for the Bradleys, much as I longed to do so. They were still the desirable Vikings. The stately pink villa above the orange trees, the gray rocks where the diving board jutted and the speedboat lay at anchor, remained the site of romance, the target of forlorn hopes. It hurt me to shake my head and retire from the flat rock when Don and Eva beckoned me. They seemed to understand quickly enough, more quickly than their parents did. Mr. Bradley still called, "Coming aboard?" and Mrs. Bradley waved to me elaborately on every possible occasion. The children turned their heads away. For two days I saw them all like figures set behind a glass screen; only the echo of their voices reached me; I gave

up haunting the beach and worked in a corner of the garden; the regularity of their timetable made it easy to avoid the sight of them. I told myself that they were loathsome, that they were the Smugs, that Don and Eva were both candidates for RCI. I even considered including them in the Anthology of Hates, but I found it too difficult. Now they had indeed become the moon that the Duchess told me I cried for. I cherished dreams of saving Don's life or Eva's at great risk to myself, and being humbly thanked and praised by their parents. Then I hoped that they would all die in a fire, or better still that I would die and they would come to my funeral.

In these two days I found myself looking at my home differently; seeing it in Bradley perspective. I had been plagued by the crises and irregularities but never ashamed of them. Was I ashamed now? I could not be sure; the feeling was one of extra detachment and perception; I was more than ever aware of the garden's bright colors, of the garlic smells from the kitchen, of the dusky coolness in the bar; every time that I walked through the salon I looked at it with startled visitors' eyes; Bradleys' eyes:

"It's pretty, of course; it's like a little room in a museum, but it isn't the sort of place where one wants to *sit.*" The terrace with the blue and white umbrellas above the tables, the stone jars on the balustrade, the lizards flickering along the wall, seemed as temporary as the deck of a ship on a short voyage. I felt as though I were staying here, not living here. And there was no consolation in my own room with my own books because here the saddest thoughts came and they seemed to hang in the room waiting for me, as palpable as the tented mosquito net above the bed.

I found that I was seeing Francis, Jeanne, and the Duchess through a grotesque lens; they were at once complete strangers and people whom I knew intimately. I could place them in a Bradley context, thinking, "That is Francis Wells, the poet, the poet who keeps the mad hotel. He always seems to wear the same red shirt. He looks like Mephistopheles when he laughs. And that is his wife, his *second* wife; younger than he is; very gay always, isn't she? What very *short* shorts. And there goes the Duchessa di Terracini, rather a terrible old lady who gambles at the Casino and drinks champagne; doesn't she look ridiculous in all that make-up and chiffon?" And then I would be talking to them in my own voice and with my own thoughts and feeling like a traitor.

I knew that they were sorry for me; that Francis above all approved my defiant refusal. I was aware of their hands held back from consoling gestures, to spare me too much overt sympathy. Even the Duchess did not speak to me of the Bradleys.

For once I welcomed the crises **as** diversion. And these two days

naturally were not free from crisis; a British ambassador and his wife found themselves *en panne* at our gates. All the entrails of their car fell out upon the road and we were obliged to give them rooms for the night.

This would not of itself have been other than a mechanical crisis, because the ambassador and Francis were old friends. Unfortunately the ambassador and the press baron from Cap d'Ail, who was dining with the Duchess, were old enemies. So a fierce political fight was waged in the bar, with both elderly gentlemen calling each other poltroon, and they would have fought a duel had not the electric current failed and the hotel been plunged in darkness till morning. (My only grief was that Don and Eva had missed it. All roads led to the Bradleys.)

On the third morning, which was Thursday, doom accelerated. I woke to find Francis standing beside my bed.

"Sorry, darling; trouble," he said. "A telephone call just came through from Aix; Jeanne's mother is very ill and I'm going to drive her over there now. Can you take care of you for today?"

He never asked me such questions: this was like a secret signal saying, "I know you are miserable and I am sorry."

"But of course. Please don't worry."

"There are no guests, thank God. Violetta's going over to Monte Carlo; Laurent will be in charge to-night. You might see that he locks up, if I'm not back."

"I will do that."

"But don't let him lock Violetta out, for Heaven's sake."

"I will see that he does not. Can I help Jeanne or do anything for you?"

"No, my love. We are off now. I'll telephone you later." He ducked under the mosquito curtain to kiss me.

"You must pray rather than worry," the Duchess said to me, standing on the doorstep. For her expedition to Monte Carlo, she wore a coat and skirt of white shantung, a bottle-green frilly blouse, and the usual chiffon scarf. She was topped by a bottle-green tricorn hat with a green veil descending from it. "Death is a part of life," she added, pulling on her white gloves.

I could feel little emotion for my stepgrandmother who lived in seclusion near Aix-en-Province, but I was sorry for Jeanne.

"The best thing that you could do, Penelope," said the Duchess, grasping her parasol like a spear, "would be to come over with me to Monte Carlo. We will lunch delightfully on the balcony of the Hotel de Paris; then you shall eat ices while I am at the tables; then a little stroll and a little glass and we could dine on the port at Ville-franche and drive home under the moon. The moon is at the full to-night and I look forward to it. *Viens, chérie, ça te changera les*

idées," she added, holding out her hand.

I thanked her very much and said that I would rather stay here.

When she was placed inside the high purple Isotta-Fraschini, I thought that she and her old hooky chauffeur looked like a Punch-and-Judy show. The car was box-shaped with a fringed canopy under the roof and they swayed as it moved off. I waved good-by.

The first part of the day seemed endless. I sat in the garden on a stone bench under the largest of the umbrella pines. That way I had my back to La Lézardière. I could hear their voices and that was all. When the bell rang for their lunch, I went down to the pool and swam. I swam for longer than usual; then I climbed to the flat rock and lay in the sun. I was almost asleep when I heard Eva's voice. "Penelope!"

She was halfway up the rock; she said, "Look; we are so miserable we've written you this note. I have to go back and rest now." She was like a vision out of the long past; the freckles, the sunburn, and the wet hair. I watched her scuttle down and she turned to wave to me from the lowest tier of the terrace. I gave her a half-wave and opened the note.

It said:

Dear Penelope,
Please don't be cross with us. Mum and Dad are going out to supper to-

night. Don't you think that you could come? They have asked us to ask you.
Always your friends,
Don and Eva.

I wrote my reply at the *écritoire* in the salon. I wrote:

Much as I appreciate the invitation, I am unable to accept it. Owing to severe illness in the family my father and stepmother have left for Aix. I feel it necessary to stay here and keep an eye on things.
Penelope.

To run no risk of meeting them, I went into the bar and asked Laurent if he would be so kind as to leave this note at La Lézardière.

Laurent was in one of his moods; he replied sarcastically that it gave him great pleasure to run errands and do favors for young ladies who had not the energy to perform these for themselves. I echoed the former cook's husband, the assassin, and said, *"Salaud,"* but not until he was gone.

After I had answered the note, I alternated between wishing that I had accepted and wishing that I had given them more truthful reasons for my refusal.

Later, I sought comfort by writing to my aunt in England; I sat there conjuring the fortnight as it would be and putting in the letter long descriptions of the things that I wanted to see and do again. It helped. I had covered twelve pages when the telephone rang.

Francis' voice spoke over a bad line: "Hello, Child of Confusion. Everything all right?"

"Yes, indeed. Nothing is happening at all. What is the news?"

"Better," he said, "but Jeanne will have to stay. I may be very late getting back. See that Laurent gives you the cold lobster. Jeanne sends her love."

Nothing would have induced me to ask Laurent for my dinner, but I was perfectly capable of getting it myself and the reference to cold lobster had made me hungry. No reason why I should not eat my dinner at six o'clock. I was on my way to the kitchen by way of the terrace when I heard a voice calling me:

"Penelope!"

I turned, feeling that horrible all-over blush begin. Mrs. Bradley stood at the doorway from the salon onto the terrace. She looked golden and statuesque in a white dress with a scarlet belt. The sight of her was painful. It seemed as though I had forgotten how lovely she was.

"May I talk to you a moment, my dear?"

"Please do," I said, growing hotter and hotter.

"Shall we sit here?" She took a chair beneath one of the blue and white umbrellas. She motioned to me to take the other chair. I said, "Thank you, but I prefer to stand."

She smiled at me. I could feel in my heart the alarming collision of love and hate and now I could see her in two contexts; as a separate symbol, the enemy; as a beloved haunting of my own mind, the

Mrs. Bradley of the first days, whom I had made my private possession. Her arms and hands were beautifully shaped, pale brown now against the white of her dress.

"Can't we be friends, Penelope? I think we can, you know, if we try. Don and Eva are so sad and it all seems such a pity."

I said, "But, Mrs. Bradley, you made it happen."

"No, dear. That is what I want to put right. When I talked to your stepmother, I made it quite clear that we all hoped to see much more of you."

"But," I said, "that Don and Eva couldn't come here. As though it were an awful place."

She put her hand on mine; she gave a soft low laugh. "Penelope, how foolish of you. Of course it isn't an awful place. You have just imagined our thinking that, you silly child."

"Did I imagine what you said about the Duchess?"

Still she smiled and kept her hand on mine. "I expect that what I said about the Duchess was quite a little exaggerated to you by Eva and Don. That was an uncomfortable day for all of us. We don't often quarrel in our family; I don't suppose that you do, either. Quarrels are upsetting to everybody and nobody likes them."

"Certainly," I said, "I don't like them."

"Let's try to end this one, Penelope."

Did she guess how badly I wanted to end it? I could not tell.

"Supposing," she said, "that you let me put my point of view to you, as one grown-up person to another. You are very grown-up for your age, you know."

"I do know, and I deplore it."

She gave another little low laugh. "Well, I shouldn't go on deploring it if I were you. Think what a dull world it would be if we were all made alike."

I winced inside at the cliché because Francis had taught me to wince at clichés. But I pretended that she had not said it. She went on: "Listen, dear. Just because you are so grown-up and this place is your home, you have a very different life from the life that Don and Eva have. I'm not saying that one sort of life is right and the other wrong. They just happen to be different. Now, my husband and I have to judge what is good for Don and Eva, don't we? You'll agree? Just as your father and stepmother have to judge what is good for you."

"Yes. I agree to that." It sounded reasonable; the persuasion of her manner was beginning to work.

"Well, we think that they aren't quite grown-up enough yet to understand and appreciate all the things that you understand and appreciate. That's all. It's as though you had a stronger digestion and could eat foods that might upset them. Do you see?"

When I was still silent, she added, "I think you should. Your stepmother saw perfectly."

"I suppose I see."

"Do try."

In fact I was trying hard; but the struggle was different from the struggle that she imagined. I felt as though I were being pulled over the line in a tug of war. Inside me there was a voice saying, "No, no. This is wrong. Nothing that she says can make it right. It is not a matter of seeing her point of view; you *can* see it; she has sold it to you. But you mustn't surrender." Oddly, the voice seemed to be the voice of the Duchess. I felt as though the Duchess were inside me, arguing.

I looked into the lovely, smiling face. "Do try," Mrs. Bradley repeated. "And do please come and have supper with the children tonight. Let's start all over again; shall we?"

When she held out both hands to me, she had won. I found myself in her arms and she was kissing my hair. I heard her say, "Poor little girl."

v

Only the smallest shadow stayed in my heart and I forgot it for long minutes. We talked our heads off. It was like meeting them again after years. I found myself quoting in my head: "And among the grass shall find the golden dice wherewith we played of yore." They still loved me; they still laughed at everything I said. When I ended the description of the ambassador fighting the press baron and the failure of the electric lights, they were sobbing in separate corners of the sofa.

"Go on; go on. What did the Duchess do?"

"I think she enjoyed it mightily. She had an electric torch in her bag and she flashed it over them both like a searchlight."

"You do have the loveliest time," said Eva.

"Where is the Duchess tonight?" asked Don.

"In fact I think I heard her car come back about ten minutes ago." I began to describe the car and the chauffeur.

"*Older* than the Duchess? He can't be. I'd love to see them bouncing away under the fringe. Let's go out and look."

"Too late," I said. "At night he takes the car to the garage in Théoule."

"Hark, though," Don said. "There's a car now." He ran to the window; but I knew that it wasn't the Isotta-Fraschini. It was the putt-putt noise of Laurent's little Peugeot.

"How exactly like Laurent," I said. "As soon as the Duchess gets home, he goes out for the evening. And Francis has left him in charge."

It occurred to me now that I should go back. I reminded myself that Charlemagne was an effective watchdog. But I was not comfortable about it.

"D'you mean you ought to go and put the Duchess to bed? Undo her stays; help her off with her wig?"

"It isn't a wig; it's her own hair, and she requires no help. But I do think I should go back. The telephone may ring."

"Well then, the Duchess will answer it."

"She will not. She claims that she has never answered a telephone in her life. She regards them as an intrusion upon privacy."

"Isn't there anybody else in the hotel?"

"No."

"Oh you *can't* go yet," said Eva. I sat on a little longer. Then I knew that it was no good. "I shall have remorse if I don't," I said, "and that is the worst thing."

"All right, then. We'll go with you."

"Oh, Don—" said Eva.

"Mum and Dad won't be back yet awhile," said Don, "and we'll only stay ten minutes."

"They'll be furious."

"We won't tell them."

Eva looked at me. I said, "I cannot decide for you. I only know I must go."

"Of course if you want to stay behind," Don said to Eva.

"Of course I don't. What shall we say to Nanny?"

"We can say we went down to the beach."

We crept out, silent in the spirit of adventure. The moon had risen, the full moon, promised by the Duchess, enormous and silver and

sad; its light made a splendid path over the sea; the palms and the orange trees, the rock shapes on the water, were all sharp and black.

"Here we go on Tom Tiddler's ground," Eva sang. We took the short cut, scrambling through the oleander hedge instead of going round by the gate, I could hear Don panting with excitement beside me. Almost, their mood could persuade me that the hotel was an enchanted place. We came onto the terrace and darted into the empty bar; Laurent had turned off the lights; I turned them up for the Bradleys to look at the photographs.

"What'll we drink?" said Don facetiously, hopping onto a stool.

"Champagne," said Eva.

"If the Duchess was still awake, she'd give us some champagne."

"You wouldn't drink it," said Eva.

"I would."

"You wouldn't."

"I jolly well would."

"She's probably in the salon," I said. "She never goes to bed early."

I put out the lights again and led them to the salon by way of the terrace. The salon lights were lit. We looked through the windows.

"There she is," said Don. "She's lying on the sofa."

They bounded in ahead of me. I heard Don say, "Good evening, Duchessa," and Eva echoed it. There was no reply from the Duchess. With the Bradleys, I stood still staring at her. She was propped on the Empire sofa; her red head had fallen sideways on the stiff satin cushion. Her little pointed shoes and thin ankles stuck out from the hem of her shantung skirt and the skirt, which was of great width, drooped down over the edge of the sofa to the floor. On the table beside her she had placed the green tricorn hat, the green scarf, and her green velvet bag. A bottle of champagne stood in an ice pail; the glass had fallen to the floor; since one of her arms dangled limply, I thought that she must have dropped the glass as she went off to sleep.

"Please wake up, Duchessa; we want some champagne," said Don.

He took a step forward and peered into her face, which was turned away from us.

"She looks sort of horrid," he said; "I think she's ill."

For no reason that I could understand I felt that it was impertinent of him to be leaning there so close to her. When he turned back to us, I saw that his face was pale; the freckles were standing out distinctly on the bridge of his nose.

"She is ill, I'm sure," he said. "She's unconscious." He looked at the bottle of champagne. "She must be—" He stopped. I saw that he thought that the Duchess was intoxicated and that he could not bring himself to say so.

"Let's go," Eva said in a thin scared voice. She grabbed Don's hand. "Come on, Penelope. Quick."

"But of course I'm not coming." They halted. "You can't stay

here," Don said. Eva was shivering. There was no sound nor movement from the figure on the sofa. I said, "Certainly I can stay here. What else can I do? If she is ill, I must look after her."

I saw them straining against their own panic. Suddenly they seemed like puppies, very young indeed.

"But *we* can't stay here," Eva said. "Oh, please, Penelope, come with us."

"No indeed. But you go," I said. "It's what you want to do, isn't it?"

"It's what we ought to do," Eva stammered through chattering teeth. Don looked a little more doubtful. "Look here, Penelope, you needn't stay with her. When they—they get like that, they sleep it off."

Now I was angry with him. "Please go at once," I said. "This is my affair. And I know what you mean and it isn't true." I found that I had clapped my hands to shoo them off; they went; I heard the panic rush of their feet on the terrace. I was alone with the Duchess.

Now that they were gone, I had no hesitation in approaching her. I said softly, "Hello, Duchessa. It's only me," and I bent above her as Don had done. I saw what he had seen; the shrunken look of the white face with the false eyelashes. Indeed she looked shrunken all over, like a very old doll.

I lowered my head until my ear

touched the green frilled chiffon at her breast. I listened for the beat of her heart. When I could not hear it, I lifted the little pointed hand and felt the wrist. There was no pulse here that I could find.

I despised myself because I began to shiver as Eva Bradley had shivered. My fingers would not stay still; it was difficult to unfasten the clasp of the green velvet bag. I thought that there would be a pocket mirror inside and that I must hold this to her lips. Searching for the mirror I found other treasures; the ivory hand that she had aimed at Francis, a cut-glass smelling-bottle, some colored plaques from the Casino, a chain holding a watch, and a cluster of seals.

The mirror, when I found it, was in a folding morocco case with visiting cards in the pocket on the other side. I said, "Excuse me, please, Duchessa," as I held it in front of her face. I held it there a long time; when I took it away the bright surface was unclouded. I knew that the Duchess was dead.

A profound curiosity took away my fear. I had never seen a person lying dead before. It was so strange to think of someone I knew well, as having stopped. But the more I stared at her, the less she looked as though she had stopped; rather, she had gone. This was not the Duchess lying here; it was a little old doll, a toy thing of which the Duchess had now no need. Where, I wondered, had she gone? What had happened to all the things that she

remembered, the fencing lessons, and the child's dreams, and the Emperor? What happened, I wondered, to the memories that you carried around in your head? Did they go on with your soul or would a soul not want them? What did a soul want? Did the Duchess' soul like roulette? Theology had never been my strongest subject and I found myself baffled by the rush of abstract questions flowing through my mind.

Then I became aware of her in relation to me. It was impossible to believe that I would not talk to her again. I was suddenly deeply sorry that I had not dined with her on the first evening, that I had not gone down in the fancy-dress to show myself to Jeanne. She had asked me to do this; she had asked me to come to Monte Carlo with her. *"Viens, chérie, ça te changera les idées."* Always she had been kind. I had not. I had never been nice to her because she embarrassed me and now I should never have another chance to be nice to her.

Automatically I began to perform small meaningless services. I covered her face with the green scarf, drawing it round her head so that it made a dignified veil. I fetched a rug and laid it across her feet; I did not want to see the little shoes. I carried the untouched champagne back to the bar. I lifted her tricorn hat, her bag and gloves off the table; I took them up to her room. It was more difficult to be in her room, with the bed turned down and the night clothes laid there, than it was to be in the salon with her body. I put the hat, bag, and gloves down on the nearest chair and I was running out when I saw the crucifix on the table. I thought that she might be pleased to have this near her ("Although," I said to myself, "she isn't there any more, one still goes on behaving as if she is") and I carried it down; I set it on the table beside her. There seemed to be too many lights here now. I turned off all but one lamp; this room became a suitable place for her to lie in state, the elegant little shell of a room with the Empire furnishings. I pulled a high-backed chair from the wall, set it at the foot of the sofa, and sat down to watch with her.

Outside the windows the moonlight lay in the garden. I heard her saying, "The moon is at the full tonight. I look forward to it." I heard her saying, "Naturally, you cry for the moon." I heard her saying, "Death is a part of life," as she pulled on her white gloves.

At intervals I was afraid again; the fear came and went like intermittent seasickness. I did not know what brought it. She was so small and still and gone that I could not fear her. But I felt as though I were waiting for a dreadful thing to walk upon the terrace, and the only poem that would stay in my head was one that had always frightened me a little, "The Lykewake Dirge":

This ae nighte, this ae nighte,
Everye nighte and alle,
Fire and sleet and candlelyte,
And Christe receive thy saule.

It made shivers down my back. I would have liked to fetch Charlemagne from his kennel, but I had heard that dogs howled in the presence of the dead and this I did not want.

Sitting there so stiffly I became terribly tired: "But it is a vigil," I said to myself, "and it is all that I can do for her." It was not much. It was no true atonement for having failed her in kindness; it could not remit my having betrayed her to the Bradleys. It seemed hours since I had thought of the Bradleys. Now I wondered whether the parents had returned, and with the question there came incredulity that Don and Eva should not have come back. They had simply run off and left me, because they were afraid. The memory of their scared faces made them small and silly in my mind. Beside it, I uncovered the memory of my talk with Mrs. Bradley: the talk that had left a shadow. I admitted the shadow now: it was the note of patronage at the end of all the spellbinding. She had called me "poor little girl."

"You never called me poor little girl," I said in my thoughts to the Duchess. She had called me fortunate and a genius. She had spoken to me of the world, of freedom and maturity. That was truly grown-up conversation. In comparison the echo of Mrs. Bradley saying, "As one grown-up person to another," sounded fraudulent. Some of the magic had left the Bradleys tonight.

I was so tired. I did not mean to sleep, because this was vigil. But I found my head falling forward and the moonlight kept vanishing and the Duchess' voice was quite loud in my ears. "Of death," she said, "I remember three things; being tired, being quiet, and being gone. That's how it is, Penelope." She seemed to think that I could not hear her. She went on calling, "Penelope! Penelope!"

I sat up with a start. Somebody was in fact calling "Penelope": a man's voice from the terrace. I climbed down stiffly from the chair. "Who's that?" I asked, my voice sounding cracked and dry. Mr. Bradley stood against the moonlight.

"Are you there, child? Yes, you are. Come along out of this at once." He looked large and golden and worried; he seized my hand; then he saw the Duchess on the sofa.

"Lord," he said. "She's still out, is she?" He started again. "Did you cover her up like that?"

"Yes. Please talk quietly," I said. "She is dead."

He dropped my hand, lifted the scarf a little way from her face, and put it back. I saw him looking at the crucifix.

"I put it there. I thought that she would like it. I am watching by her," I said.

He looked pale, ruffled, not the

way, I thought, that grown-up people should look. "I'm terribly sorry," he said in a subdued voice. "Terribly sorry. Young Don came along to our room, said he couldn't sleep for knowing you were over here with her. Of course he didn't think—"

"I know what he thought, Mr. Bradley," I said coldly. "Don and Eva are only babies really. Thank you for coming, just the same."

He said, in his officer-to-men voice, "Out of here now. There's a good girl."

"I beg your pardon?"

"You're coming to our house. I'll telephone the doctor from there." He took my hand again; I pulled it free.

"I'll stay with her, please. You telephone the doctor."

He looked down at me, amazed, almost smiling. He dropped his voice again. "No, no, no, Penelope. You mustn't stay."

I said, "I must."

"No, you mustn't. You can't do her any good."

"It is a vigil."

"That's just morbid and foolish. You're coming over to our house now."

"I am not."

"Yes, you are," he said, and he picked me up in his arms. To struggle in the presence of the Duchess would have been unseemly. I remained tractable, staying in his arms until he had carried me onto the terrace. He began to put me down and at once I twisted free.

"I'm not coming with you. I'm staying with her. She is my friend and she is not your friend. You were rude about her, and stupid," I said to him.

He grabbed me again and I fought: he imprisoned me with my arms to my sides. For the moment he did not try to lift me. He simply held me there.

"Listen, Penelope, don't be hysterical. I'm doing what's best for you. That's all. You can't possibly sit up all night alone with the poor old lady; it's nearly one o'clock now."

"I shall stay with her till dawn; and she is not a poor old lady, just because she is dead. That is a ridiculous cliché."

I was aware of his face close to mine, the stony, regular features, the blue eyes and clipped mustache in the moonlight. The face seemed to struggle for speech. Then it said, "I don't want insolence any more than I want hysteria. You just pipe down and come along. This is no place for you."

"It is my home," I said.

He shook me gently. "Have some sense, will you? I wouldn't let my kids do what you're doing and I won't let you do it."

"Your children," I said, "wouldn't want to do it anyway; they are, in vulgar parlance, a couple of sissies."

At this he lifted me off my feet again and I struck at his face. I had the absurd idea that the Duchess had come to stand in the doorway

and was cheering me on. And at this moment there came the miracle. The noise of the car sweeping in from the road was not the little noise of Laurent's car, but the roaring powerful engine that meant that Francis had come home.

The headlights swung yellow upon the moonlit garden. Still aloft in Mr. Bradley's clutch I said, "That is my father, who will be able to handle the situation with dignity."

He set me down as Francis braked the car and jumped out.

"That you, Bradley?" said Francis. "What, precisely, are you doing?"

Mr. Bradley said, "I am trying to make your daughter behave in a sensible manner. I'm very glad to see you."

Francis came up the steps onto the terrace. He sounded so weary that I knew his back hurt him: "Why should it be your concern to make my daughter behave in any manner whatsoever?"

"Really, Wells, you'll have to know the story. There's been a tragedy here tonight, I'm afraid. Just doing what I could to help."

"I will tell him," I said. I was grateful for Francis' arm holding me; my legs had begun to feel as though they were made of spaghetti.

"You let me do the talking, young woman," said Mr. Bradley.

"If you don't mind, I'd prefer to hear it from Penelope," said Francis.

I told him. I told him slowly, leaving out none of it; there seemed less and less breath in my lungs as I continued. "And Mr. Bradley called it morbid and foolish and removed me by force," I ended.

"Very silly of you, Bradley," said Francis.

"Damn it, look at the state she's in!"

"Part of which might be due to your methods of persuasion, don't you think? All right, Penelope, easy now." I could not stop shivering.

"Leaving her alone like that in a place like this. You ought to be ashamed of yourself," Mr. Bradley boomed.

"Quiet, please," said Francis in his most icy voice.

"Damned if I'll be quiet. It's a disgrace and I don't want any part of it."

"Nobody," I said, "asked you to take any part in it, Mr. Bradley."

"Hush," said Francis. "Mr. Bradley meant to be kind and you must be grateful."

"I am not in the least."

"Fine manners you teach her," said Mr. Bradley.

"Quiet, please," said Francis again. "Penelope has perfect manners, mitigated at the moment by perfect integrity and a certain amount of overstrain." Looking up at him, I could see the neat Mephistophelean profile, the delicate shape of his head. I loved him more than I had ever loved him. Mr. Bradley, large and blowing like a bull, was outside this picture, nothing to do with either of us.

Suddenly he looked as though he realized this. He said: "I don't want my wife or my kids mixed up in it either."

"Mixed up in what, precisely?" Francis asked.

I said, "It is possible that he is referring to the inquest. Or do you mean mixed up with me? Because if you do, no problem should arise. After tonight I have not the slightest wish to be mixed up with them or you."

It would have been more effective had I been able to stop shivering; I was also feeling rather sick, never a help when attempting to make dignified speeches.

Mr. Bradley faded away in the moonlight.

Francis said gently, "Did you mean it? It is easy to say those things in anger."

"I think I meant it. Was the vigil, in your opinion, the right thing to do?"

"It was. I am very pleased with you."

I said, "But I am not sure that I can continue with it for a moment. I feel funny."

Francis took me into the bar; he poured out a glass of brandy and a glass of water, making me drink them in alternate swallows.

"Of course," he said gloomily, "it may make you sick. In which event the last state will be worse than the first."

But it did not; it made me warm.

"They can't *help* being the Smugs, can they?" I said suddenly, and then for the first time I wanted to cry.

"They're all right," said Francis. "They are merely lacking in imagination."

I managed to say, "Sorry," and no more. I knew that he disliked me to cry. This time he said, watching me, "On some occasions it is better to weep."

I put my head down on the table and sobbed, "If only she could come back; I would be nice."

Francis said, "You gave her great pleasure always."

"Oh, not enough."

"Nobody can give anybody enough."

"Not ever?"

"No, not ever. But one must go on trying."

"And doesn't one ever value people until they are gone?"

"Rarely," said Francis.

I went on weeping; I saw how little I had valued him; how little I had valued anything that was mine. Presently he said, "Do you think that you can cry quite comfortably by yourself for a few minutes because I must telephone the doctor?"

Though I said, "Yes, indeed," I stopped crying immediately. As I sat waiting for him, I was saying good-by, to my first dead, to a love that was ended, and to my dream of being like other people.

The next day I tore the Anthology of Hates into pieces and cast the pieces into the sea. I did not read through the pages first, so certain was I that I had done with hating.

Part 3

STORIES TO THINK ABOUT

Part 3

Paul's Case

It was Paul's afternoon to appear before the faculty of the Pittsburgh High School to account for his various misdemeanors. He had been suspended a week ago, and his father had called at the Principal's office and confessed his perplexity about his son. Paul entered the faculty room suave and smiling. His clothes were a trifle outgrown, and the tan velvet on the collar of his open overcoat was frayed and worn; but for all that there was something of the dandy about him, and he wore an opal pin in his neatly knotted black four-in-hand, and a red carnation in his buttonhole. This latter adornment the faculty somehow felt was not properly significant of the contrite spirit befitting a boy under the ban of suspension.

Paul was tall for his age and very thin, with high, cramped shoulders and a narrow chest. His eyes were remarkable for a certain hysterical brilliancy, and he continually used them in a conscious, theatrical sort of way, peculiarly offensive in a boy. The pupils were abnormally large, as though he were addicted to belladonna, but there was a glassy glitter about them which that drug does not produce.

When questioned by the Principal as to why he was there, Paul stated, politely enough, that he wanted to come back to school. This was a lie, but Paul was quite accustomed to lying; found it, indeed, indispensable for overcoming friction. His teachers were asked to state their respective charges against him, which they did with such a rancor and aggrievedness as evinced that this was not a usual case. Disorder and impertinence were among the offenses named, yet each of his instructors felt that it was scarcely possible to put into words the real cause of the trouble, which lay in a sort of hysterically defiant manner of the boy's; in the contempt which they all knew he felt for them, and which he seemingly made not the least effort to

239

conceal. Once, when he had been making a synopsis of a paragraph at the blackboard, his English teacher had stepped to his side and attempted to guide his hand. Paul had started back with a shudder and thrust his hands violently behind him. The astonished woman could scarcely have been more hurt and embarrassed had he struck at her. The insult was so involuntary and definitely personal as to be unforgettable. In one way and another, he had made all his teachers, men and women alike, conscious of the same feeling of physical aversion. In one class he habitually sat with his hand shading his eyes; in another he always looked out of the window during the recitation; in another he made a running commentary on the lecture, with humorous intent.

His teachers felt this afternoon that his whole attitude was symbolized by his shrug and his flippantly red carnation flower, and they fell upon him without mercy, his English teacher leading the pack. He stood through it smiling, his pale lips parted over his white teeth. (His lips were continually twitching, and he had a habit of raising his eyebrows that was contemptuous and irritating to the last degree.) Older boys than Paul had broken down and shed tears under the ordeal, but his set smile did not once desert him, and his only sign of discomfort was the nervous trembling of the fingers that toyed with the buttons of his overcoat, and an occasional jerking of the other hand which held his hat. Paul was always smiling, always glancing about him, seeming to feel that people might be watching him and trying to detect something. This conscious expression, since it was as far as possible from boyish mirthfulness, was usually attributed to insolence or "smartness."

As the inquisition proceeded, one of his instructors repeated an impertinent remark of the boy's, and the Principal asked him whether he thought that a courteous speech to make to a woman. Paul shrugged his shoulder slightly and his eyebrows twitched.

"I don't know," he replied. "I didn't mean to be polite or impolite, either. I guess it's a sort of way I have, of saying things regardless."

The Principal asked him whether he didn't think that a way it would be well to get rid of. Paul grinned and said he guessed so. When he was told that he could go, he bowed gracefully and went out. His bow was like a repetition of the scandalous red carnation.

His teachers were in despair, and his drawing master voiced the feeling of them all when he declared there was something about the boy which none of them understood. He added: "I don't really believe that smile of his comes altogether from insolence; there's something sort of haunted about it. The boy is not strong, for one thing. There is something wrong about the fellow."

The drawing master had come to

realize that, in looking at Paul, one saw only his white teeth and the forced animation of his eyes. One warm afternoon the boy had gone to sleep at his drawing board, and his master had noted with amazement what a white, blue-veined face it was; drawn and wrinkled like an old man's about the eyes, the lips twitching even in his sleep.

His teachers left the building dissatisfied and unhappy; humiliated to have felt so vindictive toward a mere boy, to have uttered this feeling in cutting terms, and to have set each other on, as it were, in the gruesome game of intemperate reproach. One of them remembered having seen a miserable street cat set at bay by a ring of tormentors.

As for Paul, he ran down the hill whistling the Soldiers' Chorus from *Faust,* looking wildly behind him now and then to see whether some of his teachers were not there to witness his light-heartedness. As it was now late in the afternoon and Paul was on duty that evening as usher at Carnegie Hall, he decided that he would not go home to supper.

When he reached the concert hall the doors were not yet open. It was chilly outside, and he decided to go up into the picture gallery—always deserted at this hour—where there were some of Raffelli's gay studies of Paris streets and an airy blue Venetian scene or two that always exhilarated him. He was delighted to find no one in the gallery but the old guard, who sat in the corner, a newspaper on his knee, a black patch over one eye and the other closed. Paul possessed himself of the place and walked confidently up and down, whistling under his breath. After a while he sat down before a blue Rico and lost himself. When he bethought him to look at his watch, it was after seven o'clock, and he rose with a start and ran downstairs, making a face at Augustus Cæsar, peering out from the cast-room, and an evil gesture at the Venus of Milo as he passed her on the stairway.

When Paul reached the ushers' dressing-room half a dozen boys were there already, and he began excitedly to tumble into his uniform. It was one of the few that at all approached fitting, and Paul thought it very becoming—though he knew the tight, straight coat accentuated his narrow chest, about which he was exceedingly sensitive. He was always excited while he dressed, twangling all over to the tuning of the strings and the preliminary flourishes of the horns in the music-room; but tonight he seemed quite beside himself, and he teased and plagued the boys until, telling him that he was crazy, they put him down on the floor and sat on him.

Somewhat calmed by his suppression, Paul dashed out to the front of the house to seat the early comers. He was a model usher. Gracious and smiling he ran up and down the aisles. Nothing was too much trouble for him; he carried messages and brought programs as though it were his greatest pleasure in life, and all the people in his section thought him a charming boy, feeling that he remembered and admired them. As the house filled, he grew more and more vivacious and animated, and the color came to his cheeks and lips. It was very much as though this were a great reception and Paul were the host. Just as the musicians came out to take their places, his English teacher arrived with checks for the seats which a prominent manufacturer had taken for the season. She betrayed some embarrassment when she handed Paul the tickets, and a hauteur which subsequently made her feel very foolish. Paul was startled for a moment, and had the feeling of wanting to put her out; what business had she here among all these fine people and gay colors? He looked her over and decided that she was not appropriately dressed and must be a fool to sit downstairs in such togs. The tickets had probably been sent her out of kindness, he reflected, as he put down a seat for her, and she had about as much right to sit there as he had.

When the symphony began Paul sank into one of the rear seats with a long sigh of relief, and lost himself as he had done before the Rico. It was not that symphonies, as such, meant anything in particular to Paul, but the first sigh of the instruments seemed to free some hilarious spirit within him; something that struggled there like the Genius in the bottle found by the Arab fisherman. He felt a sudden zest of life; the lights danced before his eyes and the concert hall blazed into unimaginable splendor. When the soprano soloist came on, Paul forgot even the nastiness of his teacher's being there, and gave himself up to the peculiar intoxication such personages always had for him. The soloist chanced to be a German woman, by no means in her first youth, and the mother of many children; but she wore a satin gown and a tiara, and she had that indefinable air of achievement, that world-shine upon her, which always blinded Paul to any possible defects.

After a concert was over, Paul was often irritable and wretched until he got to sleep—and tonight he was even more than usually restless. He had the feeling of not being able to let down; of its being impossible to give up this delicious excitement which was the only thing that could be called living at all. During the last number he withdrew and, after hastily changing his clothes in the dressing room, slipped out to the side door where the singer's carriage stood. Here he began pacing rapidly up and down the walk, waiting to see her come out.

Over yonder the Schenley, in its vacant stretch, loomed big and square through the fine rain, the windows of its twelve stories glowing like those of a lighted cardboard house under a Christmas tree. All the actors and singers of any importance stayed there when they were in the city, and a number of the big manufacturers of the place lived there in the winter. Paul had often hung about the hotel, watching the people go in and out, longing to enter and leave schoolmasters and dull care behind him forever.

At last the singer came out, accompanied by the conductor, who helped her into her carriage and closed the door with a cordial *auf Wiedersehen*—which set Paul to wondering whether she were not an old sweetheart of his. Paul followed the carriage over to the hotel, walking so rapidly as not to be far from the entrance when the singer alighted and disappeared behind the swinging glass doors which were opened by a Negro in a tall hat and a long coat. In the moment that the door was ajar, it seemed to Paul that he, too, entered. He seemed to feel himself go after her up the steps, into the warm, lighted building, into an exotic, a tropical world of shiny, glistening surfaces and basking ease. He reflected upon the mysterious dishes that were brought into the dining room, the green bottles in buckets of ice, as he had seen them in the supper party pictures of the Sunday supplement. A quick gust of wind brought the rain down with sudden vehemence, and Paul was startled to find that he was still outside in the slush of the gravel driveway; that his boots were letting in the water and his scanty overcoat was clinging wet about him; that the lights in front of the concert hall were out, and that the rain was driving in sheets between him and the orange glow of the windows above him. There it was, what he wanted—tangibly before him, like the fairy world of a Christmas pantomime; as the rain beat in his face, Paul wondered whether he were destined always to shiver in the black night outside, looking up at it.

He turned and walked reluctantly toward the car tracks. The end had to come some time; his father in his nightclothes at the top of the stairs, explanations that did not explain, hastily improvised fictions that were forever tripping him up, his upstairs room and its horrible yellow wallpaper, the creaking bureau with the greasy plush collarbox, and over his painted wooden bed the pictures of George Washington and John Calvin, and the framed motto, "Feed My Lambs," which had been worked in red worsted by his mother, whom Paul could not remember.

Half an hour later, Paul alighted from the Negley Avenue car and went slowly down one of the side streets off the main thoroughfare. It was a highly respectable street, where all the houses were exactly alike, and where businessmen of moderate means begot and reared large families of children, all of whom went to Sabbath-school and learned the shorter catechism, and were interested in arithmetic; all of whom were as exactly alike as their homes, and of a piece with the monotony in which they lived. Paul never went up Cordelia Street without a shudder of loathing. His home was next the house of the Cumberland minister. He approached it tonight with the nerveless sense of defeat, the hopeless feeling of sinking back forever into ugliness and commonness that he had always had when he came home. The moment he turned into Cordelia Street he felt the waters close above his head. After each of these orgies of living, he experienced all the physical depression which follows a debauch; the loathing of respectable beds, of common food, of a house permeated by kitchen odors; a shuddering repulsion for the flavorless, colorless mass of everyday existence; a morbid desire for cool things and soft lights and fresh flowers.

The nearer he approached the house, the more absolutely unequal Paul felt to the sight of it all; his ugly sleeping chamber; the cold bathroom with the grimy zinc tub, the cracked mirror, the dripping spigots; his father, at the top of the stairs, his hairy legs sticking out from his nightshirt, his feet thrust into carpet slippers. He was so much later than usual that there would certainly be inquiries and reproaches. Paul stopped short before the door. He felt that he could not be accosted by his father to-

night; that he could not toss again on that miserable bed. He would not go in. He would tell his father that he had no car fare, and it was raining so hard he had gone home with one of the boys and stayed all night.

Meanwhile, he was wet and cold. He went around to the back of the house and tried one of the basement windows, found it open, raised it cautiously, and scrambled down the cellar wall to the floor. There he stood, holding his breath, terrified by the noise he had made; but the floor above him was silent, and there was no creak on the stairs. He found a soapbox, and carried it over to the soft ring of light that streamed from the furnace door, and sat down. He was horribly afraid of rats, so he did not try to sleep, but sat looking distrustfully at the dark, still terrified lest he might have awakened his father. In such reactions, after one of the experiences which made days and nights out of the dreary blanks of the calendar, when his senses were deadened, Paul's head was always singularly clear. Suppose his father had heard him getting in at the window and had come down and shot him for a burglar? Then, again, suppose his father had come down, pistol in hand, and he had cried out in time to save himself, and his father had been horrified to think how nearly he had killed him? Then, again, suppose a day should come when his father would remember that night, and wish there had been no warning cry to stay his hand? With this last supposition Paul entertained himself until daybreak.

The following Sunday was fine; the sodden November chill was broken by the last flash of autumnal summer. In the morning Paul had to go to church and Sabbath-school, as always. On seasonable Sunday afternoons the burghers of Cordelia Street usually sat out on their front "stoops," and talked to their neighbors on the next stoop, or called to those across the street in neighborly fashion. The men sat placidly on gay cushions placed upon the steps that led down to the sidewalk, while the women, in their Sunday "waists," sat in rockers on the cramped porches, pretending to be greatly at their ease. The children played in the streets; there were so many of them that the place resembled the recreation grounds of a kindergarten. The men on the steps—all in their shirt sleeves, their vests unbuttoned—sat with their legs well apart, their stomachs comfortably protruding, and talked of the prices of things, or told anecdotes of the sagacity of their various chiefs and overlords. They occasionally looked over the multitude of squabbling children, listened affectionately to their high-pitched, nasal voices, smiling to see their own proclivities reproduced in their offspring, and interspersed their legends of the iron kings with remarks about their sons' progress at school, their grades in arithmetic,

and the amounts they had saved in their toy banks. On this last Sunday of November, Paul sat all the afternoon on the lowest step of his "stoop," staring into the street, while his sisters, in their rockers, were talking to the minister's daughters next door about how many shirtwaists they had made in the last week, and how many waffles someone had eaten at the last church supper. When the weather was warm, and his father was in a particularly jovial frame of mind, the girls made lemonade, which was always brought out in a red-glass pitcher, ornamented with forget-me-nots in blue enamel. This the girls thought very fine, and the neighbors joked about the suspicious color of the pitcher.

Today Paul's father, on the top step, was talking to a young man who shifted a restless baby from knee to knee. He happened to be the young man who was daily held up to Paul as a model, and after whom it was his father's dearest hope that he would pattern. This young man was of a ruddy complexion, with a compressed, red mouth, and faded near-sighted eyes, over which he wore thick spectacles, with gold bows that curved about his ears. He was clerk to one of the magnates of a great steel corporation, and was looked upon in Cordelia Street as a young man with a future. There was a story that, some five years ago—he was now barely twenty-six—he had been a trifle "dissipated," but in order to curb his appetites and save the loss of time and strength that a sowing of wild oats might have entailed, he had taken his chief's advice, oft reiterated to his employees, and at twenty-one had married the first woman whom he could persuade to share his fortunes. She happened to be an angular school mistress, much older than he, who also wore thick glasses, and who had now borne him four children, all near-sighted, like herself.

The young man was relating how his chief, now cruising in the Mediterranean, kept in touch with all the details of the business, arranging his office hours on his yacht just as though he were at home, and "knocking off work enough to keep two stenographers busy." His father told, in turn, the plan his corporation was considering, of putting in an electric railway plant at Cairo. Paul snapped his teeth; he had an awful apprehension that they might spoil it all before he got there. Yet he rather liked to hear these legends of the iron kings, that were told and retold on Sundays and holidays; these stories of palaces in Venice, yachts on the Mediterranean, and high play at Monte Carlo appealed to his fancy, and he was interested in the triumphs of cash boys who had become famous, though he had no mind for the cash-boy stage.

After supper was over, and he had helped to dry the dishes, Paul nervously asked his father whether he could go to George's to get some help in his geometry, and still more nervously asked for car fare. This latter request he had to repeat, as his father, on principle, did not like to hear requests for money, whether much or little. He asked Paul whether he could not go to some boy who lived nearer, and told him that he ought not to leave his school work until Sunday; but he gave him the dime. He was not a poor man, but he had a worthy ambition to come up in the world. His only reason for allowing Paul to usher was that he thought a boy ought to be earning a little.

Paul bounded upstairs, scrubbed the greasy odor of the dishwater from his hands with the ill-smelling soap he hated, and then shook over his fingers a few drops of violet water from the bottle he kept hidden in his drawer. He left the house with his geometry conspicuously under his arm, and the moment he got out of Cordelia Street and boarded a downtown car, he shook off the lethargy of two deadening days, and began to live again.

The leading juvenile of the permanent stock company which played at one of the downtown theaters was an acquaintance of Paul's, and the boy had been invited to drop in at the Sunday night rehearsals whenever he could. For more than a year Paul had spent every available moment loitering about Charley Edwards' dressing-room. He had won a place among Edwards' following not only because the young actor, who could not afford to employ a dresser, often found him useful, but because he recognized in Paul something akin to what churchmen termed "vocation."

It was at the theater and at Carnegie Hall that Paul really lived; the rest was but a sleep and a forgetting. This was Paul's fairy tale, and it had for him all the allurement of a secret love. The moment he inhaled the gassy, painty, dusty odor behind the scenes, he breathed like a prisoner set free, and felt within him the possibility of doing or saying splendid, brilliant things. The moment the cracked orchestra beat out the overture from *Martha,* or jerked at the serenade from *Rigoletto,* all stupid and ugly things slid from him, and his senses were deliciously, yet delicately fired.

Perhaps it was because, in Paul's world, the natural nearly always wore the guise of ugliness, that a certain element of artificiality seemed to him necessary in beauty. Perhaps it was because his experience of life elsewhere was so full of Sabbath-school picnics, petty economies, wholesome advice as to how to succeed in life, and the unescapable odors of cooking, that he found this existence so alluring, these smartly-clad men and women so attractive, that he was so moved by these starry apple orchards that bloomed perennially under the limelight.

It would be difficult to put it strongly enough how convincingly the stage entrance of that theater was for Paul the actual portal of Romance. Certainly none of the company ever suspected it, least of all Charley Edwards. It was very like the old stories that used to float about London of fabulously rich Jews, who had subterranean halls, with palms, and fountains, and soft lamps and richly apparelled women who never saw the disenchanting light of London day. So, in the midst of that smoke-palled city, enamored of figures and grimy toil, Paul had his secret temple, his wishing-carpet, his bit of blue-and-white Mediterranean shore bathed in perpetual sunshine.

Several of Paul's teachers had a theory that his imagination had been perverted by garish fiction; but the truth was, he scarcely ever read at all. The books at home were not such as would either tempt or corrupt a youthful mind, and as for reading the novels that some of his friends urged upon him—well, he got what he wanted much more quickly from music; any sort of music, from an orchestra to a barrel organ. He needed only the spark, the indescribable thrill that made his imagination master of his senses, and he could make plots and pictures enough of his own. It was equally true that he was not stage-struck—not, at any rate, in the usual acceptation of that expression. He had no desire to become an actor, any more than he had to become a musician. He felt no necessity to do any of these things; what he wanted was to see, to be in the atmosphere, float on the wave of it, to be carried out, blue league after blue league, away from everything.

After a night behind the scenes, Paul found the schoolroom more than ever repulsive; the bare floors and naked walls; the prosy men who never wore frock coats, or violets in their buttonholes; the women with their dull gowns, shrill voices, and pitiful seriousness about prepositions that govern the dative. He could not bear to have the other pupils think, for a moment, that he took these people seriously; he must convey to them that he considered it all trivial, and was there only by way of a joke, anyway. He had autograph pictures of all the members of the stock company, which he showed his classmates, telling them the most incredible stories of his familiarity with these people, of his acquaintance with the soloists who came to Carnegie Hall, his suppers with them and the flowers he sent them. When these stories lost their effect, and his audience grew listless, he would bid all the boys goodby, announcing that he was going to travel for a while; going to Naples, to California, to Egypt. Then, next Monday, he would slip back, conscious and nervously smiling; his sister was ill, and he would have to defer his voyage until spring.

Matters went steadily worse with Paul at school. In the itch to let his instructors know how heartily he despised them, and how thoroughly he was appreciated elsewhere, he

mentioned once or twice that he had no time to fool with theorems; adding—with a twitch of the eyebrows and a touch of that nervous bravado which so perplexed them—that he was helping the people down at the stock company; they were old friends of his.

The upshot of the matter was that the Principal went to Paul's father, and Paul was taken out of school and put to work. The manager at Carnegie Hall was told to get another usher in his stead; the doorkeeper at the theater was warned not to admit him to the house; and Charley Edwards remorsefully promised the boy's father not to see him again.

The members of the stock company were vastly amused when some of Paul's stories reached them —especially the women. They were hard-working women, most of them supporting indolent husbands or brothers, and they laughed rather bitterly at having stirred the boy to such fervid and florid inventions. They agreed with the faculty and with his father, that Paul's was a bad case.

The east-bound train was plowing through a January snowstorm; the dull dawn was beginning to show gray when the engine whistled a mile out of Newark. Paul started up from the seat where he had lain curled in uneasy slumber, rubbed the breath-misted window glass with his hand, and peered out. The snow was whirling in curling eddies above the white bottom lands, and the drifts lay already deep in the fields and along the fences, while here and there the long dead grass and dried weed stalks protruded black above it. Lights shone from the scattered houses, and a gang of laborers who stood beside the track waved their lanterns.

Paul had slept very little, and he felt grimy and uncomfortable. He had made the all-night journey in a day coach because he was afraid if he took a Pullman he might be seen by some Pittsburgh business-man who had noticed him in Denny & Carson's office. When the whistle woke him, he clutched quickly at his breast pocket, glancing about him with an uncertain smile. But the little, clay-bespattered Italians were still sleeping, the slatternly women across the aisle were in open-mouthed oblivion, and even the crumby, crying babies were for the nonce stilled. Paul settled back to struggle with his impatience as best he could.

When he arrived at the Jersey City station, he hurried through his breakfast, manifestly ill at ease and keeping a sharp eye about him. After he reached the Twenty-third Street station, he consulted a cabman, and had himself driven to a men's furnishing establishment which was just opening for the day. He spent upward of two hours there, buying with endless recon-sidering and great care. His new street suit he put on in the fitting room; the frock coat and dress clothes he had bundled into the cab with his new shirts. Then he drove to a hatter's and a shoe house. His next errand was at Tiffany's, where he selected silver-mounted brushes and a scarf pin. He would not wait to have his silver marked, he said. Lastly, he stopped at a trunk shop on Broadway, and had his purchases packed into various traveling bags.

It was a little after one o'clock when he drove up to the Waldorf, and, after settling with the cabman, went into the office. He registered from Washington; said his mother and father had been abroad, and that he had come down to await the arrival of their steamer. He told his story plausibly and had no trouble, since he offered to pay for them in advance, in engaging his rooms; a sleeping room, sitting room, and bath.

Not once, but a hundred times Paul had planned this entry into New York. He had gone over every detail of it with Charley Edwards, and in his scrapbook at home there were pages of description about New York hotels, cut from the Sunday papers.

When he was shown to his sitting room on the eighth floor, he saw at a glance that everything was as it should be; there was but one detail in his mental picture that the place did not realize, so he rang for the bell boy and sent him down for flowers. He moved about nervously until the boy returned, putting away his new linen and fingering it delightedly as he did so. When the flowers came, he put them hastily into water, and then tumbled into a hot bath. Presently he came out of his white bathroom, resplendent in his new silk underwear, and playing with the tassels of his red robe. The snow was whirling so fiercely outside his windows that he could scarcely see across the street; but within, the air was deliciously soft and fragrant. He put the violets and jonquils on the tabouret beside the couch, and threw himself down with a long sigh, covering himself with a Roman blanket. He was thoroughly tired; he had been in such haste, he had stood up to such a strain, covered so much ground in the last twenty-four hours, that he wanted to think how it had all come about. Lulled by the sound of the wind, the warm air, and the cool fragrance of the flowers, he sank into deep, drowsy retrospection.

It had been wonderfully simple; when they had shut him out of the theater and concert hall, when they had taken away his bone, the whole thing was virtually determined. The rest was a mere matter of opportunity. The only thing that at all surprised him was his own courage—for he realized well enough that he had always been tormented by fear, a sort of apprehensive dread that, of late years, as the meshes of the lies he had told closed about him, had been pulling

the muscles of his body tighter and tighter. Until now, he could not remember a time when he had not been dreading something. Even when he was a little boy, it was always there—behind him, or before, or on either side. There had always been the shadowed corner, the dark place into which he dared not look, but from which something seemed always to be watching him—and Paul had done things that were not pretty to watch, he knew.

But now he had a curious sense of relief, as though he had at last thrown down the gauntlet to the thing in the corner.

Yet it was but a day since he had been sulking in the traces; but yesterday afternoon that he had been sent to the bank with Denny & Carson's deposit, as usual—but this time he was instructed to leave the book to be balanced. There was above two thousand dollars in checks, and nearly a thousand in the bank notes which he had taken from the book and quietly transferred to his pocket. At the bank he had made out a new deposit slip. His nerves had been steady enough to permit of his returning to the office, where he had finished his work and asked for a full day's holiday tomorrow, Saturday, giving a perfectly reasonable pretext. The bank book, he knew, would not be returned before Monday or Tuesday, and his father would be out of town for the next week. From the time he slipped the bank notes into his pocket until he boarded the night train for New York, he had not known a moment's hesitation.

How astonishingly easy it had all been; here he was, the thing done; and this time there would be no awakening, no figure at the top of the stairs. He watched the snowflakes whirling by his window until he fell asleep.

When he awoke, it was four o'clock in the afternoon. He bounded up with a start; one of his precious days gone already! He spent nearly an hour in dressing, watching every stage of his toilet carefully in the mirror. Everything was quite perfect; he was exactly the kind of boy he had always wanted to be.

When he went downstairs, Paul took a carriage and drove up Fifth Avenue toward the Park. The snow had somewhat abated; carriages and tradesmen's wagons were hurrying soundlessly to and fro in the winter twilight; boys in woolen mufflers were shoveling off the doorsteps; the avenue stages made fine spots of color against the white street. Here and there on the corners whole flower gardens blooming behind glass windows, against which the snowflakes stuck and melted; violets, roses, carnations, lilies of the valley—somehow vastly more lovely and alluring that they blossomed thus unnaturally in the snow. The Park itself was a wonderful stage winter-piece.

When he returned, the pause of the twilight had ceased, and the tune of the streets had changed. The snow was falling faster, lights streamed from the hotels that reared their many stories fearlessly up into the storm, defying the raging Atlantic winds. A long, black stream of carriages poured down the avenue, intersected here and there by other streams, tending horizontally. There were a score of cabs about the entrance of his hotel, and his driver had to wait. Boys in livery were running in and out of the awning stretched across the sidewalk, up and down the red velvet carpet laid from the door to the street. Above, about, within it all, was the rumble and roar, the hurry and toss of thousands of human beings as hot for pleasure as himself, and on every side of him towered the glaring affirmation of the omnipotence of wealth.

The boy set his teeth and drew his shoulders together in a spasm of realization; the plot of all dramas, the text of all romances, the nerve-stuff of all sensations was whirling about him like the snowflakes. He burnt like a faggot in a tempest.

When Paul came down to dinner, the music of the orchestra floated up the elevator shaft to greet him. As he stepped into the thronged corridor, he sank back into one of the chairs against the wall to get his breath. The lights, the chatter, the perfumes, the bewildering medley of color—he had, for a moment, the feeling of not being able to stand it. But only for a moment; these were his own people, he told himself. He went slowly about the corridors, through the writing rooms, smoking rooms, reception rooms, as though he were exploring the chambers of an enchanted palace, built and peopled for him alone.

When he reached the dining room he sat down at a table near a window. The flowers, the white linen, the many-colored wine glasses, the gay toilettes of the women, the low popping of corks, the undulating repetitions of the "Blue Danube" from the orchestra, all flooded Paul's dream with bewildering radiance. When the roseate tinge of his champagne was added ––that cold, precious, bubbling stuff that creamed and foamed in his glass––Paul wondered that there were honest men in the world at all. This was what all the world was fighting for, he reflected; this was what all the struggle was about. He doubted the reality of his past. Had he ever known a place called Cordelia Street, a place where fagged-looking businessmen boarded the early car? Mere rivets in a machine they seemed to Paul––sickening men, with combings of children's hair always hanging to their coats, and the smell of cooking in their clothes. Cordelia Street––ah, that belonged to another time and country! Had he not always been thus, had he not sat here night after night, from as far back as he could remember, looking pensively over just such shimmering textures, and slowly twirling the stem of a glass like this one between his thumb and middle finger? He rather thought he had.

He was not in the least abashed or lonely. He had no especial desire to meet or to know any of these people; all he demanded was the right to look on and conjecture, to watch the pageant. The mere stage properties were all he contended for. Nor was he lonely later in the evening, in his loge at the opera. He was entirely rid of his nervous misgivings, of his forced aggressiveness, of the imperative desire to show himself different from his surroundings. He felt now that his surroundings explained him. Nobody questioned the purple; he had only to wear it passively. He had only to glance down at his dress coat to reassure himself that here it would be impossible for anyone to humiliate him.

He found it hard to leave his beautiful sitting room to go to bed that night, and sat long watching the raging storm from his turret window. When he went to sleep, it was with the lights turned on in his bedroom; partly because of his old timidity, and partly so that, if he should wake in the night, there would be no wretched moment of doubt, no horrible suspicion of yellow wallpaper, or of Washington and Calvin above his bed.

On Sunday morning the city was practically snowbound. Paul breakfasted late, and in the afternoon he fell in with a wild San Francisco boy, a freshman at Yale, who said he had run down for a "little flyer" over Sunday. The young man offered to show Paul the night side of the town, and the two boys went off together after dinner, not returning to the hotel until seven o'clock the next morning. They had started out in the confiding warmth of a champagne friendship, but their parting in the elevator was singularly cool. The freshman pulled himself together to make his train, and Paul went to bed. He awoke at two o'clock in the afternoon, very thirsty and dizzy, and rang for ice water, coffee, and the Pittsburgh papers.

On the part of the hotel management, Paul excited no suspicion. There was this to be said for him, that he wore his spoils with dignity and in no way made himself conspicuous. His chief greediness lay in his ears and eyes, and his excesses were not offensive ones. His dearest pleasures were the gray winter twilights in his sitting room; his quiet enjoyment of his flowers, his clothes, his wide divan, his cigarette, and his sense of power. He could not remember a time when he had felt so at peace with himself. The mere release from the necessity of petty lying, lying every day and every day, restored his self-respect. He had never lied for pleasure, even at school; but to make himself noticed and admired, to assert his difference from other Cordelia Street boys; and he felt a good deal

more manly, more honest, even, now that he had no need for boastful pretensions, now that he could, as his actor friends used to say, "dress the part." It was characteristic that remorse did not occur to him. His golden days went by without a shadow, and he made each as perfect as he could.

On the eighth day after his arrival in New York, he found the whole affair exploited in the Pittsburgh papers, exploited with a wealth of detail which indicated that local news of a sensational nature was at a low ebb. The firm of Denny & Carson announced that the boy's father had refunded the full amount of his theft, and that they had no intention of prosecuting. The Cumberland minister had been interviewed, and expressed his hope of yet reclaiming the motherless lad, and Paul's Sabbath-school teacher declared that she would spare no effort to that end. The rumor had reached Pittsburgh that the boy had been seen in a New York hotel, and his father had gone East to find him and bring him home.

Paul had just come in to dress for dinner; he sank into a chair, weak in the knees, and clasped his head in his hands. It was to be worse than jail, even; the tepid waters of Cordelia Street were to close over him finally and forever. The gray monotony stretched before him in hopeless, unrelieved years; Sabbath-school, Young People's Meeting, the yellow-papered room, the damp dish towels; it all rushed back upon him with sickening vividness. He had the old feeling that the orchestra had suddenly stopped, the sinking sensation that the play was over. The sweat broke out on his face, and he sprang to his feet, looked about him with his white, conscious smile, and winked at himself in the mirror. With something of the childish belief in miracles with which he had so often gone to class, all his lessons unlearned, Paul dressed and dashed whistling down the corridor to the elevator.

He had no sooner entered the dining room and caught the measure of the music, than his remembrance was lightened by his old elastic power of claiming the moment, mounting with it, and finding it all sufficient. The glare and glitter about him, the mere scenic accessories had again, and for the last time, their old potency. He would show himself that he was game, he would finish the thing splendidly. He doubted, more than ever, the existence of Cordelia Street, and for the first time he drank his wine recklessly. Was he not, after all, one of these fortunate beings? Was he not still himself, and in his own place? He drummed a nervous accompaniment to the music and looked about him, telling himself over and over that it had paid.

He reflected drowsily, to the swell of the violin and the chill sweetness of his wine, that he might

have done it more wisely. He might have caught an outbound steamer and been well out of their clutches before now. But the other side of the world had seemed too far away and too uncertain then; he could not have waited for it; his need had been too sharp. If he had to choose over again, he would do the same thing tomorrow. He looked affectionately about the dining room, now gilded with a soft mist. Ah, it had paid indeed!

Paul was awakened next morning by a painful throbbing in his head and feet. He had thrown himself across the bed without undressing, and had slept with his shoes on. His limbs and hands were lead heavy, and his tongue and throat were parched. There came upon him one of those fateful attacks of clear-headedness that never occurred except when he was physically exhausted and his nerves hung loose. He lay still and closed his eyes and let the tide of realities wash over him.

His father was in New York; "stopping at some joint or other," he told himself. The memory of successive summers on the front stoop fell upon him like a weight of black water. He had not a hundred dollars left; and he knew now, more than ever, that money was everything, the wall that stood between all he loathed and all he wanted. The thing was winding itself up; he had thought of that on his first glorious day in New York, and had even provided a way to snap the thread. It lay on his dressing table now; he had got it out last night when he came blindly up from dinner—but the shiny metal hurt his eyes, and he disliked the look of it, anyway.

He rose and moved about with a painful effort, succumbing now and again to attacks of nausea. It was the old depression exaggerated; all the world had become Cordelia Street. Yet somehow he was not afraid of anything, was absolutely calm; perhaps because he had looked into the dark corner at last, and knew. It was bad enough, what he saw there; but somehow not so bad as his long fear of it had been. He saw everything clearly now. He had a feeling that he had made the best of it, that he had lived the sort of life he was meant to live, and for half an hour he sat staring at the revolver point. But he told himself that was not the way, so he went downstairs and took a cab to the ferry.

When Paul arrived at Newark, he got off the train and took another cab, directing the driver to follow the Pennsylvania tracks out of the town. The snow lay heavy on the roadways and had drifted deep in the open fields. Only here and there the dead grass or dried weed stalks projected, singularly black, above it. Once well into the country, Paul dismissed the carriage and walked, floundering along the tracks, his mind a medley of irrelevant things. He seemed to hold in his brain an actual picture of every-thing he had seen that morning. He remembered every feature of both his drivers, the toothless old woman from whom he had bought the red flowers in his coat, the agent from whom he had got his ticket, and all of his fellow passengers on the ferry. His mind, unable to cope with vital matters near at hand, worked feverishly and deftly at sorting and grouping these images. They made for him a part of the ugliness of the world, of the ache in his head, and the bitter burning on his tongue. He stooped and put a handful of snow into his mouth as he walked, but that, too, seemed hot. When he reached a little hillside, where the tracks ran through a cut some twenty feet below him, he stopped and sat down.

The carnations in his coat were drooping with the cold, he noticed; all their red glory over. It occurred to him that all the flowers he had seen in the show windows that first night must have gone the same way, long before this. It was only one splendid breath they had, in spite of their brave mockery at the winter outside the glass. It was a losing game in the end, it seemed, this revolt against the homilies by which the world is run. Paul took one of the blossoms carefully from his coat and scooped a little hole in the snow, where he covered it up. Then he dozed a while, from his weak condition, seeming insensible to the cold.

The sound of an approaching

train woke him, and he started to his feet, remembering only his resolution, and afraid lest he should be too late. He stood watching the approaching locomotive, his teeth chattering, his lips drawn away from them in a frightened smile; once or twice he glanced nervously sidewise, as though he were being watched. When the right moment came, he jumped. As he fell, the folly of his haste occurred to him with merciless clearness, the vastness of what he had left undone.

There flashed through his brain, clearer than ever before, the blue of Adriatic water, the yellow of Algerian sands.

He felt something strike his chest —his body was being thrown swiftly through the air, on and on, immeasurably far and fast, while his limbs gently relaxed. Then, because the picture-making mechanism was crushed, the disturbing visions flashed into black, and Paul dropped back into the immense design of things.

Richard Cory

EDWIN ARLINGTON ROBINSON

Whenever Richard Cory went down town,
*   We people on the pavement looked at him:*
He was a gentleman from sole to crown,
*   Clean favored, and imperially slim.*

And he was always quietly arrayed,
*   And he was always human when he talked;*
But still he fluttered pulses when he said,
*   "Good-morning," and he glittered when he walked.*

And he was rich—yes, richer than a king—
*   And admirably schooled in every grace:*
In fine, we thought that he was everything
*   To make us wish that we were in his place.*

So on we worked, and waited for the light,
*   And went without the meat, and cursed the bread;*
And Richard Cory, one calm summer night,
*   Went home and put a bullet through his head.*

Barn Burning

THE STORE in which the Justice of the Peace's court was sitting smelled of cheese. The boy, crouched on his nail keg at the back of the crowded room, knew he smelled cheese, and more: from where he sat he could see the ranked shelves close-packed with the solid, squat, dynamic shapes of tin cans whose labels his stomach read, not from the lettering which meant nothing to his mind but from the scarlet devils and the silver curve of fish—this, the cheese which he knew he smelled and the hermetic meat which his intestines believed he smelled coming in intermittent gusts momentary and brief between the other constant one, the smell and sense just a little of fear because mostly of despair and grief, the old fierce pull of blood. He could not see the table where the Justice sat and before which his father and his father's enemy (*our enemy* he thought in that despair; *ourn! mine and hisn both! He's my father!*) stood, but he could hear them, the two of them that is, be-

cause his father had said no word yet:

"But what proof have you, Mr. Harris?"

"I told you. The hog got into my corn. I caught it up and sent it back to him. He had no fence that would hold it. I told him so, warned him. The next time I put the hog in my pen. When he came to get it I gave him enough wire to patch up his pen. The next time I put the hog up and kept it. I rode down to his house and saw the wire I gave him still rolled on to the spool in his yard. I told him he could have the hog when he paid me a dollar pound fee. That evening a Negro came with the dollar and got the hog. He was a strange Negro. He said, 'He say to tell you wood and hay kin burn.' I said, 'What?' 'That whut he say to tell you,' the Negro said. 'Wood and hay kin burn.' That night my barn burned. I got the stock out but I lost the barn."

"Where is the Negro? Have you got him?"

"He was a strange Negro, I tell

257

you. I don't know what became of him."

"But that's not proof. Don't you see that's not proof?"

"Get that boy up here. He knows." For a moment the boy thought too that the man meant his older brother until Harris said, "Not him. The little one. The boy," and, crouching, small for his age, small and wiry like his father, in patched and faded jeans even too small for him, with straight, uncombed, brown hair and eyes gray and wild as storm scud, he saw the men between himself and the table part and become a lane of grim faces, at the end of which he saw the Justice, a shabby, collarless, graying man in spectacles, beckoning him. He felt no floor under his bare feet; he seemed to walk beneath the palpable weight of the grim turning faces. His father, stiff in his black Sunday coat donned not for the trial but for the moving, did not even look at him. *He aims for me to lie,* he thought, again with that frantic grief and despair. *And I will have to do hit.*

"What's your name, boy?" the Justice said.

"Colonel Sartoris Snopes," the boy whispered.

"Hey?" the Justice said. "Talk louder. Colonel Sartoris? I reckon anybody named for Colonel Sartoris in this country can't help but tell the truth, can they?" The boy said nothing. *Enemy! Enemy!* he thought; for a moment he could not even see, could not see that the Jus-

tice's face was kindly nor discern that his voice was troubled when he spoke to the man named Harris: "Do you want me to question this boy?" But he could hear, and during those subsequent long seconds while there was absolutely no sound in the crowded little room save that of quiet and intent breathing it was as if he had swung outward at the end of a grape vine, over a ravine, and at the top of the swing had been caught in a prolonged instant of mesmerized gravity, weightless in time.

"No!" Harris said violently, explosively. "Damnation! Send him out of here!" Now time, the fluid world, rushed beneath him again, the voices coming to him again through the smell of cheese and sealed meat, the fear and despair and the old grief of blood:

"This case is closed. I can't find against you, Snopes, but I can give you advice. Leave this country and don't come back to it."

His father spoke for the first time, his voice cold and harsh, level, without emphasis: "I aim to. I don't figure to stay in a country among people who . . ." he said something unprintable and vile, addressed to no one.

"That'll do," the Justice said. "Take your wagon and get out of this country before dark. Case dismissed."

His father turned, and he followed the stiff black coat, the wiry figure walking a little stiffly from where a Confederate provost's man's musket ball had taken him in the heel on a stolen horse thirty years ago, followed the two backs now, since his older brother had appeared from somewhere in the crowd, no taller than the father but thicker, chewing tobacco steadily, between the two lines of grim-faced men and out of the store and across the worn gallery and down the sagging steps and among the dogs and half-grown boys in the mild May dust, where as he passed a voice hissed:

"Barn burner!"

Again he could not see, whirling; there was a face in a red haze, moonlike, bigger than the full moon, the owner of it half again his size, he leaping in the red haze toward the face, feeling no blow, feeling no shock when his head struck the earth, scrabbling up and leaping again, feeling no blow this time either and tasting no blood, scrabbling up to see the other boy in full flight and himself already leaping into pursuit as his father's hand jerked him back, the harsh, cold voice speaking above him: "Go get in the wagon."

It stood in a grove of locusts and mulberries across the road. His two hulking sisters in their Sunday dresses and his mother and her sister in calico and sunbonnets were already in it, sitting on and among the sorry residue of the dozen and more movings which even the boy could remember—the battered stove, the broken beds and chairs, the clock inlaid with mother-of-

pearl, which would not run, stopped at some fourteen minutes past two o'clock of a dead and forgotten day and time, which had been his mother's dowry. She was crying, though when she saw him she drew her sleeve across her face and began to descend from the wagon. "Get back," the father said.

"He's hurt. I got to get some water and wash his . . ."

"Get back in the wagon," his father said. He got in too, over the tail-gate. His father mounted to the seat where the older brother already sat and struck the gaunt mules two savage blows with the peeled willow, but without heat. It was not even sadistic; it was exactly that same quality which in later years would cause his descendants to overrun the engine before putting a motor car into motion, striking and reining back in the same movement. The wagon went on, the store with its quiet crowd of grimly watching men dropped behind; a curve in the road hid it. *Forever* he thought. *Maybe he's done satisfied now, now that he has* . . . stopping himself, not to say it aloud even to himself. His mother's hand touched his shoulder.

"Does hit hurt?" she said.

"Naw," he said. "Hit don't hurt. Lemme be."

"Can't you wipe some of the blood off before hit dries?"

"I'll wash tonight," he said. "Lemme be, I tell you."

The wagon went on. He did not know where they were going. None of them ever did or ever asked, because it was always somewhere, always a house of sorts waiting for them a day or two days or even three days away. Likely his father had already arranged to make a crop on another farm before he . . . Again he had to stop himself. He (the father) always did. There was something about his wolflike independence and even courage when the advantage was at least neutral which impressed strangers, as if they got from his latent ravening ferocity not so much a sense of dependability as a feeling that his ferocious conviction in the rightness of his own actions would be of advantage to all whose interest lay with his.

That night they camped, in a grove of oaks and beeches where a spring ran. The nights were still cool and they had a fire against it, of a rail lifted from a near-by fence and cut into lengths—a small fire, neat, niggard almost, a shrewd fire; such fires were his father's habit and custom always, even in freezing weather. Older, the boy might have remarked this and wondered why not a big one; why should not a man who had not only seen the waste and extravagance of war, but who had in his blood an inherent voracious prodigality with material not his own, have burned everything in sight? Then he might have gone a step farther and thought that that was the reason: that niggard blaze was the living fruit of nights passed during those four years in the woods hiding from all men, blue or gray, with his strings of horses (captured horses, he called them). And older still, he might have divined the true reason: that the element of fire spoke to some deep mainspring of his father's being, as the element of steel or of powder spoke to other men, as the one weapon for the preservation of integrity, else breath were not worth the breathing, and hence to be regarded with respect and used with discretion.

But he did not think this now and he had seen those same niggard blazes all his life. He merely ate his supper beside it and was already half asleep over his iron plate when his father called him, and once more he followed the stiff back, the stiff and ruthless limp, up the slope and on to the starlit road where, turning, he could see his father against the stars but without face or depth—a shape black, flat, and bloodless as though cut from tin in the iron folds of the frockcoat which had not been made for him, the voice harsh like tin and without heat like tin:

"You were fixing to tell them. You would have told him." He didn't answer. His father struck him with the flat of his hand on the side of the head, hard but without heat, exactly as he had struck the two mules at the store, exactly as he would strike either of them with any stick in order to kill a horse fly, his voice still without fear or anger: "You're getting to be a man. You got to learn. You got to learn to stick to your own blood or you ain't going to have any blood to stick to you. Do you think either of them, any man there this morning, would? Don't you know all they wanted was a chance to get at me because they knew I had them beat? Eh?" Later, twenty years later, he was to tell himself, "If I had said they wanted only truth, justice, he would have hit me again." But now he said nothing. He was not crying. He just stood there. "Answer me," his father said.

"Yes," he whispered. His father turned.

"Get on to bed. We'll be there tomorrow."

Tomorrow they were there. In the early afternoon the wagon stopped before a paintless two-room house identical almost with the dozen others it had stopped before even in the boy's ten years, and again, as on the other dozen occasions, his mother and aunt got down and began to unload the wagon, although his two sisters and his father and brother had not moved.

"Likely hit ain't fitten for hawgs," one of the sisters said.

"Nevertheless, fit it will and you'll hog it and like it," his father said. "Get out of them chairs and help your Ma unload."

The two sisters got down, big, bovine, in a flutter of cheap ribbons; one of them drew from the jumbled wagon bed a battered lantern, the other a worn broom. His father handed the reins to the older son and began to climb stiffly over the wheel. "When they get unloaded, take the team to the barn and feed them." Then he said, and at first the boy thought he was still speaking to his brother: "Come with me."

"Me?" he said.

"Yes," his father said. "You."

"Abner," his mother said. His father paused and looked back—the harsh level stare beneath the shaggy, graying, irascible brows.

"I reckon I'll have a word with the man that aims to begin tomorrow owning me body and soul for the next eight months."

They went back up the road. A week ago—or before last night, that is—he would have asked where they were going, but not now. His father had struck him before last night but never before had he paused afterward to explain why; it was as if the blow and the following calm, outrageous voice still rang, repercussed, divulging nothing to him save the terrible handicap of being young, the light weight of his few years, just heavy enough to prevent his soaring free of the world as it seemed to be ordered but not heavy enough to keep him footed solid in it, to resist it and try to change the course of its events.

Presently he could see the grove of oaks and cedars and the other flowering trees and shrubs where the house would be, though not the house yet. They walked beside a fence massed with honeysuckle and Cherokee roses and came to a gate swinging open between two brick pillars, and now, beyond a sweep of drive, he saw the house for the first time and at that instant he forgot his father and the terror and despair both, and even when he remembered his father again (who had not stopped) the terror and despair did not return. Because, for all the twelve movings, they had sojourned until now in a poor country, a land of small farms and fields and houses, and he had never seen a house like this before. *Hit's big as a courthouse* he thought quietly, with a surge of peace and joy whose reason he could not have thought into words, being too young for that: *They are safe from him. People whose lives are a part of this peace and dignity are beyond his touch, he no more to them than a buzzing wasp: capable of stinging for a little moment but that's all; the spell of this peace and dignity rendering even the barns and stable and cribs which belong to it impervious to the puny flames he might contrive . . .* this, the peace and joy, ebbing for an instant as he looked again at the stiff black back, the stiff and implacable limp of the figure which was not dwarfed by the house, for the reason that it had never looked big anywhere and which now, against the serene columned backdrop, had more than ever that impervious quality of something cut ruthlessly from tin, depthless, as though, sidewise to the sun, it would cast no shadow. Watching him, the boy remarked the abso-

lutely undeviating course which his father held and saw the stiff foot come squarely down in a pile of fresh droppings where a horse had stood in the drive and which his father could have avoided by a simple change of stride. But it ebbed only for a moment, though he could not have thought this into words either, walking on in the spell of the house, which he could even want but without envy, without sorrow, certainly never with that ravening and jealous rage which unknown to him walked in the ironlike black coat before him: *Maybe he will feel it too. Maybe it will even change him now from what maybe he couldn't help but be.*

They crossed the portico. Now he could hear his father's stiff foot as it came down on the boards with clocklike finality, a sound out of all proportion to the displacement of the body it bore and which was not dwarfed either by the white door before it, as though it had attained to a sort of vicious and ravening minimum not to be dwarfed by anything—the flat, wide, black hat, the formal coat of broadcloth which had once been black but which had now that friction-glazed greenish cast of the bodies of old house flies, the lifted sleeve which was too large, the lifted hand like a curled claw. The door opened so promptly that the boy knew the Negro must have been watching them all the time, an old man with neat grizzled hair, in a linen jacket, who stood barring the door with his body, saying, "Wipe yo foots, white man, fo you come in here. Major ain't home nohow."

"Get out of my way," his father said, without heat too, flinging the door back and the Negro also and entering, his hat still on his head. And now the boy saw the prints of the stiff foot on the doorjamb and saw them appear on the pale rug behind the machinelike deliberation of the foot which seemed to bear (or transmit) twice the weight which the body compassed. The Negro was shouting "Miss Lula! Miss Lula!" somewhere behind them, then the boy, deluged as though by a warm wave by a suave turn of carpeted stair and a pendant glitter of chandeliers and a mute gleam of gold frames, heard the swift feet and saw her too, a lady—perhaps he had never seen her like before either —in a gray, smooth gown with lace at the throat and an apron tied at the waist and the sleeves turned back, wiping cake or biscuit dough from her hands with a towel as she came up the hall, looking not at his father at all but at the tracks on the blond rug with an expression of incredulous amazement.

"I tried," the Negro cried. "I tole him to . . ."

"Will you please go away?" she said in a shaking voice. "Major de Spain is not at home. Will you please go away?"

His father had not spoken again. He did not speak again. He did not even look at her. He just stood stiff in the center of the rug, in his hat,

the shaggy iron-gray brows twitching slightly above the pebble-colored eyes as he appeared to examine the house with brief deliberation. Then with the same deliberation he turned; the boy watched him pivot on the good leg and saw the stiff foot drag round the arc of the turning, leaving a final long and fading smear. His father never looked at it, he never once looked down at the rug. The Negro held the door. It closed behind them, upon the hysteric and indistinguishable woman-wail. His father stopped at the top of the steps and scraped his boot clean on the edge of it. At the gate he stopped again. He stood for a moment, planted stiffly on the stiff foot, looking back at the house. "Pretty and white, ain't it?" he said. "That's sweat. Negro sweat. Maybe it ain't white enough yet to suit him. Maybe he wants to mix some white sweat with it."

Two hours later the boy was chopping wood behind the house within which his mother and aunt and the two sisters (the mother and aunt, not the two girls, he knew that; even at this distance and muffled by walls the flat loud voices of the two girls emanated an incorrigible idle inertia) were setting up the stove to prepare a meal, when he heard the hooves and saw the linen-clad man on a fine sorrel mare, whom he recognized even before he saw the rolled rug in front of the Negro youth following on a fat bay carriage horse—a suffused, angry face vanishing, still at full gallop, beyond the corner of the house where his father and brother were sitting in the two tilted chairs; and a moment later, almost before he could have put the ax down, he heard the hooves again and watched the sorrel mare go back out of the yard, already galloping again. Then his father began to shout one of the sisters' names, who presently emerged backward from the kitchen door dragging the rolled rug along the ground by one end while the other sister walked behind it.

"If you ain't going to tote, go on and set up the wash pot," the first said.

"You, Sarty!" the second shouted. "Set up the wash pot!" His father appeared at the door, framed against that shabbiness, as he had been against that other bland perfection, impervious to either, the mother's anxious face at his shoulder.

"Go on," the father said. "Pick it up." The two sisters stooped, broad, lethargic; stooping, they presented an incredible expanse of pale cloth and a flutter of tawdry ribbons.

"If I thought enough of a rug to have to git hit all the way from France I wouldn't keep hit where folks coming in would have to tromp on hit," the first said. They raised the rug.

"Abner," the mother said. "Let me do it."

"You go back and git dinner," his father said. "I'll tend to this."

From the woodpile through the rest of the afternoon the boy watched them, the rug spread flat in the dust beside the bubbling wash pot, the two sisters stooping over it with that profound and lethargic reluctance, while the father stood over them in turn, implacable and grim, driving them though never raising his voice again. He could smell the harsh homemade lye they were using; he saw his mother come to the door once and look toward them with an expression not anxious now but very like despair; he saw his father turn, and he fell to with the ax and saw from the corner of his eye his father raise from the ground a flattish fragment of field stone and examine it and return to the pot, and this time his mother actually spoke: "Abner. Abner. Please don't. Please, Abner."

Then he was done too. It was dusk; the whippoorwills had already begun. He could smell coffee from the room where they would presently eat the cold food remaining from the mid-afternoon meal, though when he entered the house he realized they were having coffee again probably because there was a fire on the hearth, before which the rug now lay spread over the backs of the two chairs. The tracks of his father's foot were gone. Where they had been were now long, water-cloudy scoriations resembling the sporadic course of a Lilliputian mowing machine.

It still hung there while they ate the cold food and then went to bed, scattered without order or claim up and down the two rooms, his mother in one bed, where his father would later lie, the older brother in the other, himself, the aunt, and the two sisters on pallets on the floor. But his father was not in bed yet. The last thing the boy remembered was the depthless, harsh silhouette of the hat and coat bending over the rug and it seemed to him that he had not even closed his eyes when the silhouette was standing over him, the fire almost dead behind it, the stiff foot prodding him awake. "Catch up the mule," his father said.

When he returned with the mule his father was standing in the black door, the rolled rug over his shoulder. "Ain't you going to ride?" he said.

"No. Give me your foot."

He bent his knee into his father's hand, the wiry, surprising power flowed smoothly, rising, he rising with it, on to the mule's bare back (they had owned a saddle once; the boy could remember it though not when or where) and with the same effortlessness his father swung the rug up in front of him. Now in the starlight they retraced the afternoon's path, up the dusty road rife with honeysuckle, through the gate and up the black tunnel of the drive to the lightless house, where he sat on the mule and felt the rough warp of the rug drag across his thighs and vanish.

"Don't you want me to help?" he whispered. His father did not answer and now he heard again that stiff foot striking the hollow portico

with that wooden and clocklike deliberation, that outrageous overstatement of the weight it carried. The rug, hunched, not flung (the boy could tell that even in the darkness) from his father's shoulder struck the angle of wall and floor with a sound unbelievably loud, thunderous, then the foot again, unhurried and enormous; a light came on in the house and the boy sat, tense, breathing steadily and quietly and just a little fast, though the foot itself did not increase its beat at all, descending the steps now; now the boy could see him.

"Don't you want to ride now?" he whispered. "We kin both ride now," the light within the house altering now, flaring up and sinking. *He's coming down the stairs now,* he thought. He had already ridden the mule up beside the horse block; presently his father was up behind him and he doubled the reins over and slashed the mule across the neck, but before the animal could begin to trot the hard, thin arm came round him, the hard, knotted hand jerking the mule back to a walk.

In the first red rays of the sun they were in the lot, putting plow gear on the mules. This time the sorrel mare was in the lot before he heard it at all, the rider collarless and even bareheaded, trembling, speaking in a shaking voice as the woman in the house had done, his father merely looking up once before stooping again to the hame he was buckling, so that the man on the mare spoke to his stooping back:

"You must realize you have ruined that rug. Wasn't there anybody here, any of your women . . ." he ceased, shaking, the boy watching him, the older brother leaning now in the stable door, chewing, blinking slowly and steadily at nothing apparently. "It cost a hundred dollars. But you never had a hundred dollars. You never will. So I'm going to charge you twenty bushels of corn against your crop. I'll add it in your contract and when you come to the commissary you can sign it. That won't keep Mrs. de Spain quiet but maybe it will teach you to wipe your feet off before you enter her house again."

Then he was gone. The boy looked at his father, who still had not spoken or even looked up again, who was now adjusting the loggerhead in the hame.

"Pap," he said. His father looked at him—the inscrutable face, the shaggy brows beneath which the gray eyes glinted coldly. Suddenly the boy went toward him, fast, stopping as suddenly. "You done the best you could!" he cried. "If he wanted hit done different why didn't he wait and tell you how? He won't git no twenty bushels! He won't git none! We'll gether hit and hide hit! I kin watch . . ."

"Did you put the cutter back in that straight stock like I told you?"

"No, sir," he said.

"Then go do it."

That was Wednesday. During the rest of that week he worked steadily, at what was within his scope and some which was beyond it, with an industry that did not need to be driven nor even commanded twice; he had this from his mother, with the difference that some at least of what he did he liked to do, such as splitting wood with the half-size ax which his mother and aunt had earned, or saved money somehow, to present him with at Christmas. In company with the two older women (and on one afternoon, even one of the sisters), he built pens for the shoat and the cow which were a part of his father's contract with the landlord, and one afternoon, his father being absent, gone somewhere on one of the mules, he went to the field.

They were running a middle buster now, his brother holding the plow straight while he handled the reins, and walking beside the straining mule, the rich black soil shearing cool and damp against his bare ankles, he thought *Maybe this is the end of it. Maybe even that twenty bushels that seems hard to have to pay for just a rug will be a cheap price for him to stop forever and always from being what he used to be;* thinking, dreaming now, so that his brother had to speak sharply to him to mind the mule: *Maybe he even won't collect the twenty bushels. Maybe it will all add up and balance and vanish—corn, rug, fire; the terror and grief, the being pulled two ways like between two teams of horses—gone, done with for ever and ever.*

Then it was Saturday; he looked up from beneath the mule he was harnessing and saw his father in the black coat and hat. "Not that," his father said. "The wagon gear." And then, two hours later, sitting in the wagon bed behind his father and brother on the seat, the wagon accomplished a final curve, and he saw the weathered paintless store with its tattered tobacco- and patent-medicine posters and the tethered wagons and saddle animals below the gallery. He mounted the gnawed steps behind his father and brother, and there again was the lane of quiet, watching faces for the three of them to walk through. He saw the man in spectacles sitting at the plank table and he did not need to be told this was a Justice of the Peace; he sent one glare of fierce, exultant, partisan defiance at the man in collar and cravat now, whom he had seen but twice before in his life, and that on a galloping horse, who now wore on his face an expression not of rage but of amazed unbelief which the boy could not have known was at the incredible circumstance of being sued by one of his own tenants, and came and stood against his father and cried at the Justice: "He ain't done it! He ain't burnt . . ."

"Go back to the wagon," his father said.

"Burnt?" the Justice said. "Do I understand this rug was burned too?"

"Does anybody here claim it

was?" his father said. "Go back to the wagon." But he did not, he merely retreated to the rear of the room, crowded as that other had been, but not to sit down this time, instead, to stand pressing among the motionless bodies, listening to the voices:

"And you claim twenty bushels of corn is too high for the damage you did to the rug?"

"He brought the rug to me and said he wanted the tracks washed out of it. I washed the tracks out and took the rug back to him."

"But you didn't carry the rug back to him in the same condition it was in before you made the tracks on it."

His father did not answer, and now for perhaps half a minute there was no sound at all save that of breathing, the faint, steady suspiration of complete and intent listening.

"You decline to answer that, Mr. Snopes?" Again his father did not answer. "I'm going to find against you, Mr. Snopes. I'm going to find that you were responsible for the injury to Major de Spain's rug and hold you liable for it. But twenty bushels of corn seems a little high for a man in your circumstances to have to pay. Major de Spain claims it cost a hundred dollars. October corn will be worth about fifty cents. I figure that if Major de Spain can stand a ninety-five dollar loss on something he paid cash for, you can stand a five-dollar loss you haven't earned yet.

I hold you in damages to Major de Spain to the amount of ten bushels of corn over and above your contract with him, to be paid to him out of your crop at gathering time. Court adjourned."

It had taken no time hardly, the morning was but half begun. He thought they would return home and perhaps back to the field, since they were late, far behind all other farmers. But instead his father passed on behind the wagon, merely indicating with his hand for the older brother to follow with it, and crossed the road toward the blacksmith shop opposite, pressing on after his father, overtaking him, speaking, whispering up at the harsh, calm face beneath the weathered hat: "He won't git no ten bushels neither. He won't git one. We'll . . ." until his father glanced for an instant down at him, the face absolutely calm, the grizzled eyebrows tangled above the cold eyes, the voice almost pleasant, almost gentle:

"You think so? Well, we'll wait till October anyway."

The matter of the wagon—the setting of a spoke or two and the tightening of the tires—did not take long either, the business of the tires accomplished by driving the wagon into the spring branch behind the shop and letting it stand there, the mules nuzzling into the water from time to time, and the boy on the seat with the idle reins, looking up the slope and through the sooty tunnel of the shed where the slow hammer rang and where his father sat on an upended cypress bolt, easily, either talking or listening, still sitting there when the boy brought the dripping wagon up out of the branch and halted it before the door.

"Take them on to the shade and hitch," his father said. He did so and returned. His father and the smith and a third man squatting on his heels inside the door were talking, about crops and animals; the boy, squatting too in the ammoniac dust and hoof-parings and scales of rust, heard his father tell a long and unhurried story out of the time before the birth of the older brother even when he had been a professional horsetrader. And then his father came up beside him where he stood before a tattered last year's circus poster on the other side of the store, gazing rapt and quiet at the scarlet horses, the incredible poisings and convolutions of tulle and tights and the painted leers of comedians, and said, "It's time to eat."

But not at home. Squatting beside his brother against the front wall, he watched his father emerge from the store and produce from a paper sack a segment of cheese and divide it carefully and deliberately into three with his pocket knife and produce crackers from the same sack. They all three squatted on the gallery and ate, slowly, without talking; then in the store again, they drank from a tin dipper tepid water smelling of the cedar bucket and of living beech trees. And still they did not go home. It was a horse lot this time, a tall rail fence upon and along which men stood and sat and out of which one by one horses were led, to be walked and trotted and then cantered back and forth along the road while the slow swapping and buying went on and the sun began to slant westward, they—the three of them—watching and listening, the older brother with his muddy eyes and his steady, inevitable tobacco, the father commenting now and then on certain of the animals, to no one in particular.

It was after sundown when they reached home. They ate supper by lamplight, then, sitting on the doorstep, the boy watched the night fully accomplish, listening to the whippoorwills and the frogs, when he heard his mother's voice: "Abner! No! No! Oh, God. Oh, God. Abner!" and he rose, whirled, and saw the altered light through the door where a candle stub now burned in a bottle neck on the table and his father, still in the hat and coat, at once formal and burlesque as though dressed carefully for some shabby and ceremonial violence, emptying the reservoir of the lamp back into the five-gallon kerosene can from which it had been filled, while the mother tugged at his arm until he shifted the lamp to the other hand and flung her back, not savagely or viciously, just hard, into the wall, her hands flung out against the wall for balance, her mouth open and in her face the same quality of hopeless despair as

had been in her voice. Then his father saw him standing in the door.

"Go to the barn and get that can of oil we were oiling the wagon with," he said. The boy did not move. Then he could speak.

"What . . ." he cried. "What are you . . ."

"Go get that oil," his father said. "Go."

Then he was moving, running, outside the house, toward the stable: this the old habit, the old blood which he had not been permitted to choose for himself, which had been bequeathed him willy nilly and which had run for so long (and who knew where, battening on what of outrage and savagery and lust) before it came to him. *I could keep on,* he thought. *I could run on and on and never look back, never need to see his face again. Only I can't. I can't,* the rusted can in his hand now, the liquid sploshing in it as he ran back to the house and into it, into the sound of his mother's weeping in the next room, and handed the can to his father.

"Ain't you going to even send a Negro?" he cried. "At least you sent a Negro before!"

This time his father didn't strike him. The hand came even faster than the blow had, the same hand which had set the can on the table with almost excruciating care flashing from the can toward him too quick for him to follow it, gripping him by the back of his shirt and on to tiptoe before he had seen it quit the can, the face stooping at him in breathless and frozen ferocity, the cold, dead voice speaking over him to the older brother who leaned against the table, chewing with that steady, curious, sidewise motion of cows:

"Empty the can into the big one and go on. I'll catch up with you."

"Better tie him up to the bed-post," the brother said.

"Do like I told you," the father said. Then the boy was moving, his bunched shirt and the hard, bony hand between his shoulder-blades, his toes just touching the floor, across the room and into the other one, past the sisters sitting in the two chairs over the cold hearth, and to where his mother and aunt sat side by side on the bed, the aunt's arms about his mother's shoulders.

"Hold him," the father said. The aunt made a startled movement. "Not you," the father said. "Lennie. Take hold of him. I want to see you do it." His mother took him by the wrist. "You'll hold him better than that. If he gets loose don't you know what he is going to do? He will go up yonder." He jerked his head toward the road. "Maybe I'd better tie him."

"I'll hold him," his mother whispered.

"See you do then." Then his father was gone, the stiff foot heavy and measured upon the boards, ceasing at last.

Then he begun to struggle. His mother caught him in both arms, he jerking and wrenching at them.

He would be stronger in the end, he knew that. But he had no time to wait for it. "Lemme go!" he cried. "I don't want to have to hit you!"

"Let him go!" the aunt said. "If he don't go, before God, I am going up there myself!"

"Don't you see I can't?" his mother cried. "Sarty! Sarty! No! No! Help me, Lizzie!"

Then he was free. His aunt grasped at him but it was too late. He whirled, running, his mother stumbled forward on to her knees behind him, crying to the nearer sister: "Catch him, Net! Catch him!" But that was too late too, the sister (the sisters were twins, born at the same time, yet either of them now gave the impression of being, encompassing as much living meat and volume and weight as any other two of the family) not yet having begun to rise from the chair, her head, face, alone merely turned, presenting to him in the flying instant an astonishing expanse of young female features untroubled by any surprise even, wearing only an expression of bovine interest. Then he was out of the room, out of the house, in the mild dust of the starlit road and the heavy rifeness of honeysuckle, the pale ribbon unspooling with terrific slowness under his running feet, reaching the gate at last and turning in, running, his heart and lungs drumming, on up the drive toward the lighted house, the lighted door. He did not knock, he burst in, sobbing for breath, incapable for the moment of speech; he saw the astonished face of the Negro in the linen jacket without knowing when the Negro had appeared.

"De Spain!" he cried, panted. "Where's . . ." then he saw the white man too emerging from a white door down the hall. "Barn!" he cried. "Barn!"

"What?" the white man said. "Barn?"

"Yes!" the boy cried. "Barn!"

"Catch him!" the white man shouted.

But it was too late this time too. The Negro grasped his shirt, but the entire sleeve, rotten with washing, carried away, and he was out that door too and in the drive again, and had actually never ceased to run even while he was screaming into the white man's face.

Behind him the white man was shouting, "My horse! Fetch my horse!" and he thought for an instant of cutting across the park and climbing the fence into the road, but he did not know the park nor how high the vine-massed fence might be and he dared not risk it. So he ran on down the drive, blood and breath roaring; presently he was in the road again though he could not see it. He could not hear either: the galloping mare was almost upon him before he heard her, and even then he held his course, as if the very urgency of his wild grief and need must in a moment more find him wings, waiting until the ultimate instant to hurl himself aside and into the weed-choked roadside ditch as the horse thundered past and on, for an instant in furious silhouette against the stars, the tranquil early summer night sky which, even before the shape of the horse and rider vanished, stained abruptly and violently upward: a long, swirling roar incredible and soundless, blotting the stars, and he springing up and into the road again, running again, knowing it was too late yet still running even after he heard the shot and, an instant later, two shots, pausing now without knowing he had ceased to run, crying "Pap! Pap!", running again before he knew he had begun to run, stumbling, tripping over something and scrabbling up again without ceasing to run, looking backward over his shoulder at the glare as he got up, running on among the invisible trees, panting, sobbing, "Father! Father!"

At midnight he was sitting on the crest of a hill. He did not know it was midnight and he did not know how far he had come. But there was no glare behind him now and he sat now, his back toward what he had called home for four days anyhow, his face toward the dark woods which he would enter when breath was strong again, small, shaking steadily in the chill darkness, hugging himself into the remainder of his thin, rotten shirt, the grief and despair now no longer terror and fear but just grief and despair. *Father. My father,* he thought. "He was brave!" he cried suddenly, aloud but not loud, no more than a whisper: "He was! He was in the war! He was in Colonel Sartoris' cav'ry!" not knowing that his father had gone to that war a private in the fine old European sense, wearing no uniform, admitting the authority of and giving fidelity to no man or army or flag, going to war as Malbrouck himself did: for booty—it meant nothing and less than nothing to him if it were enemy booty or his own.

The slow constellations wheeled on. It would be dawn and then sunup after a while and he would be hungry. But that would be tomorrow and now he was only cold, and and walking would cure that. His breathing was easier now and he decided to get up and go on, and then he found that he had been asleep because he knew it was almost dawn, the night almost over. He could tell that from the whippoorwills. They were everywhere now among the dark trees below him, constant and inflectioned and ceaseless, so that, as the instant for giving over to the day birds drew nearer and nearer, there was no interval at all between them. He got up. He was a little stiff, but walking would cure that too as it would the cold, and soon there would be the sun. He went on down the hill, toward the dark woods within which the liquid silver voices of the birds called unceasing—the rapid and urgent beating of the urgent and choiring heart of the late spring night. He did not look back.

My First Two Women

I HAVE BEEN trying to remember when and where I saw my father's second wife for the first time. I must have seen her frequently, without singling her out or being aware of her, at many of those houses, full of friends, where my father and I were guests in the summer of 1928. My father had many friends, and it seems to me (I was not more than four years old at the time) that, at week ends at least, we were made much of at a whole roster of houses, from tiny shacks, which young couples had "fixed up" for themselves, to semi-mansions, where we had two guest rooms and a bathroom all to ourselves. Whether we sat under a peach tree on painted homemade chairs at a shack, or around the swimming pool on cane chaises longues at a mansion, the atmosphere of those Saturdays and Sundays was the same: the glasses of warm beer, full of sun, into which I sometimes stuck a finger; the light and color of a Johannesburg summer, with thousands of midges, grasshoppers, and other weightless leaping atoms exploding softly over your face as you lay down on the grass; the laughter and voices of the men and women, as comforting and pleasant as the drunken buzz of the great bluebottles that fell sated from rotting fruit, or bees that hung a moment over your head, on their way to and fro between elaborate flowering rockeries. She must have been there often—one of the women who would help me into the spotted rubber Loch Ness monster that kept me afloat, or bring me a lemonade with a colored straw to drink it through—so often that I ceased to see her.

During the months of that summer, I lived at one or another of those friends' houses, along with the children of the house; sometimes my father stayed there with me, and sometimes he did not. But even if he was not actually living in the same place with me, he was in and out every day, and the whole period has in my mind the blurring change and excitement of a prolonged holiday—children to play with, a series of affectionate women who arranged treats, settled fights, and gave me presents. The whereabouts of my mother were vague to me and not particularly troubling. It seems to me that I believed her not to be back yet from her visit to my grandmother in Kenya, and yet I have the recollection of once speaking to her on the telephone, as if she were in Johannesburg after all. I remember saying, "When are you coming back?" and then not waiting for her to answer but going on, "Guess what I've got in my hand?" (It was a frog, which had just been discovered to have completed its metamorphosis from a tadpole in a tin basin full of stones and water.)

The previous winter, when my mother had gone to Kenya, my father and I had lived in our house, my parents' own house, alone. This was not unusual; I am aware that I had been alone with him, in the care of servants, time and again before that. In fact, any conception I have in my mind of my mother and father and me living together as a family includes her rather as a presence—rooms that were hers, books and trinkets belonging to her, the mute testimony of her grand piano —rather than a flesh-and-blood actuality. Even if she *was* there she did little or nothing of an intimate nature for me; I do not connect her with meal or bath times. So it came about, I suppose, that I scarcely un-

derstood, that summer, that there was a real upheaval and change over my head. My father and I were never to go back to that house together. In fact, we both had left it for good; even though I, before the decision was to be made final for me, was to return for a few weeks, it was not to the *same house,* in any but the brick-and-mortar sense, and my position in it and the regrouping of its attention in relation to me were so overwhelmingly changed that they wiped out, in a blaze of self-importance and glory, the dim near babyhood that had gone before.

For, suddenly, in a beautiful autumn month (it must have been March) I found myself back in our house with my mother. The willows around the lawn were fountains spouting pale yellow leaves on the grass that was kept green all year round. I slept with my mother, in her bed. Surely I had not done so before. When I said to her, "Mummy, didn't I used to sleep in the nursery before you went to Kenya?" she said, "Darling, I really have no idea where your Daddy put you to sleep while I was away."

She had short, shiny black hair cut across her forehead in a fringe. She took me to the barber and had my hair, my black hair, cut in a fringe. (Daddy used to brush my hair back, first dipping the brush in water. "Water dries out the hair," she said.) We would get out of her car together, at the houses of friends, and she would walk with me slowly up the path toward them, hand in hand. We looked exactly alike, they all said, exactly alike; it was incredible that a small boy could look so much the image of his mother.

My mother would put me up on the long stool beside her while she played the piano; I had never been so close to a piano while it was being played, and sometimes the loud parts of the music swelled through my head frighteningly, like the feeling once when I slipped through my Loch Ness monster and went under in a swimming pool. Then I got used to the sensation and found it exciting, and I would say to her, "Play loudly, Mummy. Make it boom." Sometimes she would stop playing suddenly and whirl around and hold me tight, looking out over my head at the guests who had been listening. I would hear the last reverberation die away in the great rosewood shape behind us while silence held in the room.

My mother walked up and down a room when she talked, and she talked a great deal, to people who seemed to have no chance to answer her, but were there to listen. Once, in the bathroom, I threw a wet toy and it hit my African nanny on the mouth, and when she smacked my behind and I yelled, my mother rushed in and raged at her, yelling as loudly as I did. My mother was beautiful when she was angry, for she was one of those women who cry with anger, and her eyes glistened and her natural pal-lor was stained bright with rising blood.

She took me to a circus. She took me to a native mineworkers' "war" dance. She came home from town with a pile of educational toys and sat over me, watching, while I hesitated, caught her long, black, urging eye, brilliant as the eye of an animal that can see in the dark, and then, with a kind of hypnotized instinct born of the desire to please, fitted the right shape on the right peg.

There were still a few leaves, like droplets not yet shaken off, on the twigs of the willows when my clothes and toys were packed up again and my father came to fetch me away.

This time I went to the sea, with the family of three little boys and their mother, with whom I had stayed before. I had a wonderful time, and when I came back, it was to a new house that I had never seen. In it were my father and his second wife.

I was not surprised to see this woman, and, as I have said, she was not a stranger to me. I liked her, and, made gregarious by the life of the past year, asked, "How much days can Deb stay with us?"

"For always," said my father.

"Doesn't she ever have to go home?"

"This is her home, and yours, and Daddy's."

"Why?"

"Because she is married to me now, Nick. She is my wife, and husbands and wives love each other and live together in the same house."

There was a pause, and when I spoke again, what I said must have been very different from what they expected. They did not know that while I was on holiday at the sea I had been taken, one rainy afternoon, along with the older children, to the cinema. There I had seen, in all the rose and crystalline blur of Technicolor, a man and woman dance out beneath the chandeliers of a ballroom. When I had asked what they were doing, I was told that this was a wedding—the man and the woman had just been married.

"Do you mean like this?" I asked my father and my stepmother, taking my father's hand, bending my knees, and shaping out my arms in a jiglike posture. I hopped around solemnly, dragging him with me.

"Dancing?" guessed my father, mystified and affectionate, appealing to his wife.

"Oh, that's wonderful!" she cried in sudden delight. "Bless his formal heart! A real wedding!"

There followed a confusion of hugging, all around. I was aware only that in some way I had pleased them.

I was now nearly five years old and due to begin going to school. My stepmother took me to town with her, and together we bought the supplies for my birthday party, and my school uniform, and a satchel with a fancy lock—soon to be stained as greasy as an old fish-and-chip wrapping with the print of successive school lunches—and the elaborate equipment of pencil sharpeners, erasers, and rulers indispensable to the child who has not yet learned to write. Deb understood what a birthday party for a five-year-old boy should be like. She had ideas of her own, and could sway a wavering torment of indecision between candleholders in the guise of soldiers or elephants, imparting to the waverer a comforting sense of the rightness of the final choice, but she also knew when to efface her own preferences entirely and let me enjoy my own choice for my own unexplained reasons. In fact, she was so good at the calm management of the practical details of my small life that I suppose I quickly assumed this stability as my right, and took it altogether for granted, as children, in their fierce unconscious instinct for personal salvation, take all those rights which, if withheld from them, they cannot consciously remark, but whose lack they exhibit and revenge with equal unconscious ferocity. Of course Deb bought neat and comfortable clothes for me, found the books I would best like to hear her read from, took me with her on visits that would be interesting to me, but left me at home to play when she was going where there would be nothing to amuse me; she always had, hadn't she, right from the first day?

The children at school wanted to know why I called my mother "Deb." When I said that she was not my mother, they insisted that she must be. "Are you my mother now, Deb?" I asked her.

"No," she said. "You know that you have your own mother."

"They say you must be, because you live with Daddy and me."

"I'm your second mother," she said, looking to see if that would do.

"Like my godmother?"

"That's right."

I dashed off to play; it was perfectly satisfactory.

There came a stage when school, the preparation for which had been so enjoyable, palled. I suppose there must have been some incident there, some small failure which embarrassed or shamed me. I do not remember. But I know that, suddenly, I didn't want to go to school. Deb was gentle but insistent. I remember my own long, sullen silence one day, after a wrangle of "Why's" from me and firm explanations from her. At last I said, "When I'm at my mother's I stay home all the time."

My stepmother was squatting on her heels in front of a low cupboard, and her eyes opened up toward me like the eyes of those sleeping dolls which girl children alternately lower and raise by inclining the doll's body, but her voice was the same as usual. "If you lived with your mother now, you would go to school just as you do here," she said.

I stood right in front of her. She looked up at me again, and I said, "No, I wouldn't." I waited. Then I said, "She lets me do what I like." I waited again. "I can even play her piano. She's got a big piano. As big as this room."

My stepmother went on slowly putting back into the cupboard the gramophone records she had been sorting and cleaning. Standing over her, I could see the top of her head, an unfamiliar aspect of a grownup. It was then, I think, that I began to see her for the first time, not as one of the succession of pretty ladies who petted and cared for me, but as Deb, as someone connected in wordless depths with my father and me, as my father and I and, yes, my mother were connected. Someone who had entered, irrevocably, the atavistic tension of that cunning battle for love and supremacy that exists between children and parents sometimes even beyond the grave, when one protagonist is dead and mourned, and lives on in the fierce dissatisfaction of the other's memory.

She was a fair woman, this Deb, this woman beloved of my father; on all faces there is some feature, some plane that catches the light in characteristic prominence of that face, and on her face, at that moment and always, it was her long golden eyebrows, shining. They were bleached from much swimming, but her dull, curly hair, always protected from sun and water by a cap, hung colorless and nowhere smooth enough to shine. The face was broad and brown across strong cheekbones, and she had a big, orange-painted mouth, the beautiful underlip of which supported the upper as calmly as a carved pediment. Her eyes, moving from record to cupboard, lowered under my presence, were green or blue, depending upon what color she wore. She was the sort of fair woman who would never be called a blonde.

Deb. I knew what it smelled like in that pink freckled neck. I knew the stiff and ugly ears that she kept hidden under that hair, and that sometimes, when she was hot and lifted her hair off her neck a moment for coolness, were suddenly discovered.

I shall never forget the feeling I had as I stood there over her. If I search my adult experience as a man to approximate it, I can only say that now it seems to me that physically it was rather like the effect of the first drink you take after a long wet day of some strenuous exercise —rowing or hunting. It was a feeling of power that came like an inflow of physical strength. I was only five years old but power is something of which I am convinced there is no innocence this side of the womb, and I knew what it was, all right; I understood, without a name for it, what I had. And with it came all the weapons—that

bright, clinical set that I didn't need to have explained to me, as my father had had to explain to me the uses of the set of carpenter's tools I had been given for my birthday. My hand would go out unfalteringly for these drills and probes, and the unremembered pain of where they had been used on me would guide me to their application.

"Deb," I said, "why didn't Daddy marry my mother?"

"He did," she said. "Once he was married to her. But they were not happy with each other. Not like Daddy and me—and you. Not happy together like us." She did not ask me if I remembered this, but her voice suggested the question, in spite of her.

Daddy. My mother. My mother was simply a word I was using at that moment. I could not see her in my head. She was a mouth moving, singing; for a second she sat at the piano, smiled at me, one of her swift, startling smiles that was like someone jumping out of concealment and saying "Boo!" Inside me, it gave me a fright. If my dog had been there, I would have pulled back his ears, hard, to hear him yelp. There was Deb, squatting in front of me. I said, "My mother's got a piano as big as this house. I want to go and stay with her."

Deb got up from the floor. "Soon," she said. "You'll go on a visit soon, I'm sure. Let's see if tea's ready." We did not take each other's hand, but walked out onto the porch side by side, with a space between us.

It was after that day that I began to be conscious of the relationship between my father and Deb. This was not the way he and those others —the pretty, helpful friends who were the mothers of my friends— had behaved toward each other. I watched with unbiased interest as I would have watched a bird bringing his mate tidbits where she balanced on our paling fence, when my father ate an apple bite-and-bite-about with this woman, or, passing her chair at breakfast, after he had kissed me good-by in the morning, paused to press his cheek silently, and with closed eyes, against hers. Sometimes, in the evenings, both she and I sat on his lap at once.

There were no images in my memory to which to match these. They were married, Deb and my father. This behavior was marriage. Deb herself had told me that marriage once had existed between my father and my mother. One day I came home from a visit to my mother and remarked, conversationally, in the bedroom Deb and my father shared, "My mother's got a bed just like yours, Deb, and that's where Daddy and she used to sleep when he lived there, didn't you, Daddy?"

It was Sunday, and my father still lay in bed, reading the paper, though Deb's place was empty and she was gathering her clothes together before she went off to the bathroom. He said, "No, son. Don't you remember? Mine was the room with the little balcony."

"Oh, yes," I said. "Of course, I know." All at once I remembered the smell of that rather dark, high room, a smell of shirts fresh from the iron, of the two leather golf bags in the corner, and some chemical with which the carpet had been cleaned. All this—the smell of my father—had disappeared under the warmer, relaxing, and polleny scents of the room he now shared with a woman, where peach-colored dust from her powder settled along his hairbrushes, and the stockings she peeled off retained the limp, collapsed semblance of her legs, like the newly shed skin of a snake I had come upon in the bush when I was on holiday at the sea.

I think there must have been something strongly attractive to me in the ease of this feminine intimacy to which my father and I found ourselves admitted with such naturalness. Yet because it was unfamiliar, the very seductiveness of its comfort seemed, against the confusion of my short life, a kind of disloyalty, to which I was party and of which I was guilty. Disloyalty— to what? Guilty—of what?

I was too young for motives; I could only let them bubble up, manifest in queer little words and actions. I know that that Sunday morning I said stoutly, as if I were explaining some special system of living, "There we each had our *own* rooms. Everybody slept in their own room."

Before the end of the first year of the marriage that power that had come to me like a set of magical weapons, the day when my stepmother knelt before me at the record cupboard, became absolute. It crushed upon my little-boy's head the vainglory and triumph of the tyrant, crown or thorn. I was to wear it as my own for the rest of my childhood.

I was cuddling Deb, secure in her arms one day, when I said, out of some gentle honey of warmth that I felt peacefully within me, "I'm going to call you Mummy because I love you best." I am sure that she knew that the statement was not quite so stunning and meaningful as it sounds now, out of the context of childhood. Quite often, she had heard me say of an animal or a new friend, "You know whom I love. I love only Eddie." (Or "Sam," or "Chris.") Sometimes the vehement preference was expressed not out of real feeling for the friend or animal in question, but out of pique toward some other child or animal. At other times it was merely an unreasonable welling up of well-being that had to find an object. But I had never before said this particular thing to her. She shook back her hair fumblingly and held her face away from mine to look at me; she was awkward with joy. I looked up into the stare of her eyes—grownup eyes that fell before mine—and in me, like milk soured by a flash of lightning, the sweet secretion of affection became insipid in the fearful, amazed thrill of victim turned victor.

That was our story, really, for many years. My father and Deb were deeply in love and theirs was a serene marriage. The three of us lived together in amity; it was a place of warmth for a child to grow in. I visited my mother at regular, if widely spaced, intervals. I went to her for short periods at Christmas, birthdays, and during holidays. Thus along with her, with that elegant black head and those hard wrists volatile with all the wonderful bracelets she had picked up all over the world, went excitement and occasion, treats and parties, people who exclaimed over me, and the abolishment of that guillotine of joys, bedtime. Sometimes the tide of grown-up activities would pass on over my head and leave me stranded and abandoned on a corner of somebody's sofa, rubbing my eyes against the glare of forgotten lights. It did not matter; the next day, or the day after that, I was sure to be delivered back to Deb and my father and the comfort of my child's pace.

Thus it was, too, that along with home and Deb and my father went everyday life, the greater part of life, with time for boredom, for transgressions and punishments. When I visited my mother for a week end or a day, I was on my best behavior, befitting a treat or an occasion; I was never with her long enough to need chastisement. So when, at home, I was naughty and my father or Deb had to punish me, I would inflame myself against them with the firm belief that my mother would never punish me. At these times of resentment and injury, I would see her clearly and positively, flaming in the light of a Christmas tree or the fiery ring of candles on a birthday cake, my champion against a world that would not bend entirely to my own will. In the same way, for the first few days after my return from a visit to her, everything about the way she lived and the things about her were lit up by the occasion with which my visit had coincided; her flat (when I was seven or eight she moved into a luxurious penthouse in a block overlooking a country club) was like the glowing cardboard interior of the king's castle, carried away in my mind from a pantomime matinee. "There's a swimming pool right on top of the building, on the roof garden," I would tell Deb. "I swim there every morning. Once I swam at night. My mother lets me. The lift doesn't go up to the top—you have to walk the last flight of stairs from the twelfth floor." "My mother's got a car with an overhead drive. Do you know what that is, Deb? It means you don't have to change the gears with your hands." "I wish we had a swimming pool here. I don't like this old house without even a swimming pool."

Deb always answered me quietly and evenly. Never, even when I was very young, did she try to point out rival attractions at home. But in time, when I grew older and was perhaps eleven or twelve, I struggled against something that went more than quiet—went dead —in her during these one-sided conversations. I felt not that she was not listening, but that she was listless, without interest in what I said. And then I did not know at whom the resentment I suddenly felt was directed, whether at my mother— that glossy-haired kingfisher flashing in and out of my life—for having a roof-garden swimming pool and a car without gears, or at Deb, for her lack of attention and negative reaction to my relation of these wonders. This reaction of hers was all the more irking, and in some vague, apprehensive way dismaying, when one remembered the way she watched and listened to me sometimes, with that look in her eyes that wanted something from me, wondered, hesitated, hopeful— that look I had known how to conjure up ever since the first day when I suggested I would call her my mother, and that, in perverse, irresistible use of the same power, I had also known how never to allow to come to articulacy, to emotional fulfillment, between us. The business of my calling her mother, for instance; it had come up several times again, while I was small. But she, in the silence that followed, had never managed anything more than, once, an almost unintelligibly murmured "If you like." And I, once the impulsive, casually pronounced sentence had exploded and left its peculiar after-silence, had dropped my avowal as I left a toy, here or there, for someone else to pick up in house or garden. I never did call her mother; in time, I think I should have been surprised to hear that there had ever been any question that she should be anything else but "Deb."

I was strongly attached to her, and when, at twelve or thirteen, I entered adolescence and boarding school at the same time, there was in fact a calm friendship between us, unusual between a woman and a boy walking the knife edge dividing small-boy scorn of the feminine from awakening sex interest. I suppose, if she had been truly in the position of a mother, this relationship would not have been possible. Her position must have been curiously like that of the woman who, failing to secure as a lover the man with whom she has fallen in love, is offered instead his respect and his confidences.

I was fifteen when I asked the question that had taken a thousand different forms—doubts, anxieties, and revenges—all through my life but had never formulated itself directly. The truth was, I had never known what that question *was*— only felt it, in all my blood and bones, fumbled toward it under the kisses of people who loved me,

asked it with my seeking of my father's hands, the warmth of Deb's lap, the approval of my form master's eye, the smiles of my friends. Now it came to me matter-of-factly, in words.

I was home from school for the week end, and there had been guests at lunch. They had discussed the divorce of a common friend and the wrangle over the custody of the children of the marriage. One of the guests was a lawyer, and he had gone into the legal niceties in some detail. After the guests had gone, my father went off for his nap and Deb and I dragged our favorite canvas chairs out onto the lawn. As I settled mine at a comfortable angle, I asked her, curiously, "Deb, how was it that my mother didn't get me? The custody of me, I mean."

She thought for a moment, and I thought she must be trying how best to present some legal technicality in a way that both she and I would understand.

"I mean, their divorce was an arranged thing, wasn't it—one of those things arranged to look like desertion that Derrick spoke about? Why didn't my mother get me?" The lawyer had explained that where parents contested the custody, unless there was some strong factor to suggest that the mother was unsuitable to rear a child, a young child was usually awarded to her care.

Then quite suddenly Deb spoke. Her face was red and she looked strange, and she spoke so fast that what she said was almost blurted. "She gave you up."

Her face and tone so astonished me that the impact of what she had said missed its mark. I stared at her, questioning.

She met my gaze stiffly, with a kind of jerky bravado, intense, looking through me.

"How do you mean?"

"Voluntarily. She gave you over to your father."

The pressure in her face died slowly down; her hands moved, as if released, on the chair arms. "I should never have told you," she said flatly. "I'd promised myself I never should."

"You mean she didn't want me?"

"We don't know what her reasons were, Nick. We can't know them."

"Didn't try to get me?"

There was a long silence. "We made up our minds. We decided it was best. We decided we would try and make your relationship with her as normal as possible. Never say anything against her. I promised myself I wouldn't try—for myself. I often wanted to tell you—oh, lots of things. I wanted to punish you for what I withheld for your sake. I wanted to hurt you; I suppose I forgot you were a child. . . . Well, what does it matter anyway? It's all worked itself out, long ago. Only I shouldn't have told you now. It's

pointless." She smiled at me, as at a friend who can be counted on to understand a confession. "It didn't even give me any pleasure."

My stepmother talked about this whole situation in which we had all lived as if it were something remembered from the past, instead of a living situation out of the continuity of which I was then, at that moment, beginning my life as a man. All worked itself out, long ago. Perhaps it had. Yes, she was right. All worked itself out, without me. Above and about me, over my head, saving me the risk and the opportunity of my own volition.

My mother? That black-haired, handsome woman become rather fleshy, who, I discovered while I sat, an awkward visitor among her admiring friends (I had inherited her love of music), sang off-key.

But it was not toward her that I felt anger, regret, and a terrible, mournful anguish of loss, which brought up from somewhere in my tall, coarse, half-man's, half-child's body what I was alarmed to recognize as the racking turmoil that precedes tears.

"We're really good friends, aren't we?" said my stepmother lovingly, with quiet conviction.

It was true: that was what we were—all we were.

I have never forgiven her for it.

Molly Morgan

MOLLY MORGAN got off the train in Salinas and waited three quarters of an hour for the bus. The big automobile was empty except for the driver and Molly.

"I've never been to the Pastures of Heaven, you know," she said. "Is it far from the main road?"

"About three miles," said the driver.

"Will there be a car to take me into the valley?"

"No, not unless you're met."

"But how do people get in there?"

The driver ran over the flattened body of a jack rabbit with apparent satisfaction. "I only hit 'em when they're dead," he apologized. "In the dark, when they get caught in the lights, I try to miss 'em."

"Yes, but how am I going to get into the Pastures of Heaven?"

" I dunno. Walk, I guess. Most people walk if they ain't met."

When he set her down at the entrance to the dirt side road, Molly Morgan grimly picked up her suitcase and marched toward the draw

in the hills. An old Ford truck squeaked up beside her.

"Goin' into the valley, ma'am?"

"Oh—yes, yes, I am."

"Well, get in, then. Needn't be scared. I'm Pat Humbert. I got a place in the Pastures."

Molly surveyed the grimy man and acknowledged his introduction. "I'm the new school teacher. I mean, I think I am. Do you know where Mr. Whiteside lives?"

"Sure, I go right by there. He's clerk of the board. I'm on the school board myself, you know. We wondered what you'd look like." Then he grew embarrassed at what he had said, and flushed under his coating of dirt. "Course I mean what you'd *be* like. Last teacher we had gave a good deal of trouble. She was all right, but she was sick —I mean, sick and nervous. Finally quit because she was sick."

Molly picked at the fingertips of her gloves. "My letter says I'm to call on Mr. Whiteside. Is he all right? I don't mean that. I mean— is he—what kind of a man is he?"

"Oh, you'll get along with him all right. He's a fine old man. Born in that house he lives in. Been to college, too. He's a good man. Been clerk of the board for over twenty years."

When he put her down in front of the big old house of John Whiteside, she was really frightened. "Now it's coming," she said to herself. "But there's nothing to be afraid of. He can't do anything to me." Molly was only nineteen. She felt that this moment of interview for her first job was a tremendous inch in her whole existence.

The walk up to the door did not reassure her, for the path lay between tight little flower beds hedged in with clipped box, seemingly planted with the admonition, "Now grow and multiply, but don't grow too high, nor multiply too greatly, and above all things, keep out of this path!" There was a hand on those flowers, a guiding and a correcting hand. The large white house was very dignified. Venetian blinds of yellow wood were tilted down to keep out the noon sun. Halfway up the path she came in sight of the entrance. There was a veranda as broad and warm and welcoming as an embrace. Through her mind flew the thought, "Surely you can tell the hospitality of a house by its entrance. Suppose it had a little door and no porch." But in spite of the welcoming of the wide steps and the big doorway, her timidities clung to her when she rang the bell. The big door

opened, and a large, comfortable woman stood smiling at Molly.

"I hope you're not selling something," said Mrs. Whiteside. "I never want to buy anything, and I always do, and then I'm mad."

Molly laughed. She felt suddenly very happy. Until that moment she hadn't known how frightened she really was. "Oh, no," she cried. "I'm the new school teacher. My letter says I'm to interview Mr. Whiteside. Can I see him?"

"Well, it's noon, and he's just finishing his dinner. Did you have dinner?"

"Oh, of course. I mean, no."

Mrs. Whiteside chuckled and stood aside for her to enter. "Well, I'm glad you're sure." She led Molly into a large dining room, lined with mahogany, glass-fronted dish closets. The square table was littered with the dishes of a meal. "Why, John must have finished and gone. Sit down, young woman. I'll bring back the roast."

"Oh, no. Really, thank you, no. I'll just talk to Mr. Whiteside and then go along."

"Sit down. You'll need nourishment to face John."

"Is—is he very stern, with new teachers, I mean?"

"Well," said Mrs. Whiteside. "That depends. If they haven't had their dinner, he's a regular bear. He shouts at them. But when they've just got up from the table, he's only just fierce."

Molly laughed happily. "You have children," she said. "Oh,

you've raised lots of children—and you like them."

Mrs. Whiteside scowled. "One child raised me. Raised me right through the roof. It was too hard on me. He's out raising cows now, poor devil. I don't think I raised him very high."

When Molly had finished eating, Mrs. Whiteside threw open a side door and called, "John, here's someone to see you." She pushed Molly through the doorway into a room that was a kind of a library, for big bookcases were loaded with thick, old comfortable books, all filigreed in gold. And it was a kind of a sitting room. There was a fireplace of brick with a mantel of little red tile bricks and the most extraordinary vases on the mantel. Hung on a nail over the mantel, slung really, like a rifle on a shoulder strap, was a huge meerschaum pipe in the Jaegar fashion. Big leather chairs with leather tassels hanging to them, stood about the fireplace, all of them patent rocking chairs with the kind of springs that chant when you rock them. And lastly, the room was a kind of an office, for there was an old-fashioned roll-top desk, and behind it sat John Whiteside. When he looked up, Molly saw that he had at once the kindest and the sternest eyes she had ever seen, and the whitest hair, too. Real blue-white, silky hair, a great duster of it.

"I am Mary Morgan," she began formally.

"Oh, yes, Miss Morgan, I've been

expecting you. Won't you sit down?"

She sat in one of the big rockers, and the springs cried with sweet pain. "I love these chairs," she said. "We used to have one when I was a little girl." Then she felt silly. "I've come to interview you about this position. My letter said to do that."

"Don't be so tense, Miss Morgan. I've interviewed every teacher we've had for years. And," he said, smiling, "I still don't know how to go about it."

"Oh—I'm glad, Mr. Whiteside. I never asked for a job before. I was really afraid of it."

"Well, Miss Mary Morgan, as near as I can figure, the purpose of this interview is to give me a little knowledge of your past and of the kind of person you are. I'm supposed to know something about you when you've finished. And now that you know my purpose, I suppose you'll be self-conscious and anxious to give a good impression. Maybe if you just tell me a little about yourself, everything'll be all right. Just a few words about the kind of girl you are, and where you came from."

Molly nodded quickly. "Yes, I'll try to do that, Mr. Whiteside," and she dropped her mind back into the past.

There was the old, squalid, unpainted house with its wide back porch and the round washtubs leaning against the rail. High in the great willow tree her two brothers, Joe and Tom, crashed about crying.

"Now I'm an eagle." "I'm a parrot." "Now I'm an old chicken. Watch me!"

The screen door on the back porch opened, and their mother leaned tiredly out. Her hair would not lie smoothly no matter how much she combed it. Thick strings of it hung down beside her face. Her eyes were always a little red, and her hands and wrists painfully cracked. "Tom, Joe," she called. "You'll get hurt up there. Don't worry me so, boys! Don't you love your mother at all?" The voices in the tree were hushed. The shrieking spirits of the eagle and the old chicken were drenched in self-reproach. Molly sat in the dust, wrapping a rag around a stick and doing her best to imagine it a tall lady in a dress. "Molly, come in and stay with your mother. I'm so tired today."

Molly stood up the stick in the deep dust. "You, miss," she whispered fiercely. "You'll get whipped on your bare bottom when I come back." Then she obediently went into the house.

Her mother sat in a straight chair in the kitchen. "Draw up, Molly. Just sit with me for a little while. Love me, Molly! Love your mother a little bit. You are mother's good little girl, aren't you?" Molly squirmed on her chair. "Don't you love your mother, Molly?"

The little girl was very miserable. She knew her mother would cry in a moment, and then she would be compelled to stroke the stringy hair. Both she and her brothers knew they should love their mother. She did everything for them, everything. They were ashamed that they hated to be near her, but they couldn't help it. When she called to them and they were not in sight, they pretended not to hear, and crept away, talking in whispers.

"Well, to begin with, we were very poor," Molly said to John Whiteside. "I guess we were really poverty-stricken. I had two brothers a little older than I. My father was a traveling salesman, but even so, my mother had to work. She worked terribly hard for us."

About once in every six months a great event occurred. In the morning the mother crept silently out of the bedroom. Her hair was brushed as smoothly as it could be; her eyes sparkled, and she looked happy and almost pretty. She whispered, "Quiet, children! Your father's home."

Molly and her brothers sneaked out of the house, but even in the yard they talked in excited whispers. The news traveled quickly about the neighborhood. Soon the yard was filled with whispering children. "They say their father's home." "Is your father really home?" "Where's he been this time?" By noon there were a dozen children in the yard, standing in expectant little groups, cautioning one another to be quiet.

About noon the screen door on the porch sprang open and

whacked against the wall. Their father leaped out. "Hi," he yelled. "Hi, kids!" Molly and her brothers flung themselves upon him and hugged his legs, while he plucked them off and hurled them into the air like kittens.

Mrs. Morgan fluttered about, clucking with excitement. "Children, children. Don't muss your father's clothes."

The neighbor children threw handsprings and wrestled and shrieked with joy. It was better than any holiday.

"Wait till you see," their father cried. "Wait till you see what I brought you. It's a secret now." And when the hysteria had quieted a little he carried his suitcase out on the porch and opened it. There were presents such as no one had ever seen, mechanical toys unknown before—tin bugs that crawled, dancing wooden Negroes, and astounding steam shovels that worked in sand. There were superb glass marbles with bears and dogs right in their centers. He had something for everyone, several things for everyone. It was all the great holidays packed into one.

Usually it was midafternoon before the children became calm enough not to shriek occasionally. But eventually George Morgan sat on the steps, and they all gathered about while he told his adventures. This time he had been to Mexico while there was a revolution. Again he had gone to Honolulu, had seen the volcano and had himself ridden

on a surfboard. Always there were cities and people, strange people; always adventures and a hundred funny incidents, funnier than anything they had ever heard. It couldn't all be told at one time. After school they had to gather to hear more and more. Throughout the world George Morgan tramped, collecting glorious adventures.

"As far as my home life went," Miss Morgan said, "I guess I almost didn't have any father. He was able to get home very seldom from his business trips."

John Whiteside nodded gravely. Molly's hands rustled in her lap and her eyes were dim.

One time he brought a dumpy, woolly puppy in a box, and it wet on the floor immediately.

"What kind of a dog is it?" Tom asked in his most sophisticated manner.

Their father laughed loudly. He was so young! He looked twenty years younger than their mother. "It's a dollar and a half dog," he explained. "You get an awful lot of kinds of dog for a dollar and a half. It's like this. . . . Suppose you go into a candy store and say, 'I want a nickel's worth of peppermints and gumdrops and licorice and raspberry chews.' Well, I went in and said, 'Give me a dollar and a half's worth of mixed dog.' That's the kind it is. It's Molly's dog, and she has to name it."

"I'm going to name it George," said Molly.

Her father bowed strangely to

her, and said, "Thank you Molly."
They all noticed that he wasn't
laughing at her, either.

Molly got up very early the next
morning and took George about
the yard to show him the secrets.
She opened the hoard where two
pennies and a gold policeman's button were buried. She hooked his
little front paws over the back fence
so he could look down the street at
the schoolhouse. Lastly she climbed
into the willow tree, carrying
George under one arm. Tom came
out of the house and sauntered under the tree. "Look out you don't
drop him," Tom called, and just at
that moment the puppy squirmed
out of her arms and fell. He landed
on the hard ground with a disgusting little thump. One leg bent out
at a crazy angle, and the puppy
screamed long, horrible screams,
with sobs between breaths. Molly
scrambled out of the tree, dull and
stunned by the accident. Tom was
standing over the puppy, his face
white and twisted with pain, and
George, the puppy, screamed on
and on.

"We can't let him," Tom cried.
"We can't let him." He ran to the
woodpile and brought back a hatchet. Molly was too stupefied to look
away, but Tom closed his eyes and
struck. The screams stopped suddenly. Tom threw the hatchet from
him and leaped over the back fence.
Molly saw him running away as
though he were being chased.

At that moment Joe and her father came out of the back door. Mol-

ly remembered how haggard and
thin and gray her father's face was
when he looked at the puppy. It was
something in her father's face that
started Molly to crying. "I dropped
him out of the tree, and he hurt
himself, and Tom hit him, and then
Tom ran away." Her voice sounded
sulky. Her father hugged Molly's
head against his hip.

"Poor Tom!" he said. "Molly,
you must remember never to say
anything to Tom about it, and
never to look at him as though you
remembered." He threw a gunny
sack over the puppy. "We must
have a funeral," he said. "Did I
ever tell you about the Chinese
funeral I went to, about the colored
paper they throw in the air, and the
little fat roast pigs on the grave?"
Joe edged in closer, and even Molly's eyes took on a gleam of interest. "Well, it was this way. . . ."

Molly looked up at John Whiteside and saw that he seemed to be
studying a piece of paper on his
desk. "When I was twelve years
old, my father was killed in an
accident," she said.

The great visits usually lasted
about two weeks. Always there
came an afternoon when George
Morgan walked out into the town
and did not come back until late at
night. The mother made the children go to bed early, but they could
hear him come home, stumbling a
little against the furniture, and they
could hear his voice through the
wall. These were the only times
when his voice was sad and dis-

couraged. *Lying with held breaths, in their beds, the children knew what that meant. In the morning he would be gone, and their hearts would be gone with him.*

They had endless discussions about what he was doing. Their father was a glad Argonaut, a silver knight. Virtue and Courage and Beauty—he wore a coat of them. "Sometime," *the boys said,* "sometime when we're big, we'll go with him and see all those things."

"I'll go, too," *Molly insisted.*

"Oh, you're a girl. You couldn't go, you know."

"But he'd let me go, you know he would. Sometime he'll take me with him. You see if he doesn't."

When he was gone their mother grew plaintive again, and her eyes reddened. Querulously she demanded their love, as though it were a package they could put in her hand.

One time their father went away, and he never came back. He had never sent any money, nor had he ever written to them, but this time he just disappeared for good. For two years they waited, and then their mother said he must be dead. The children shuddered at the thought, but they refused to believe it, because no one so beautiful and fine as their father could be dead. Some place in the world he was having adventures. There was some good reason why he couldn't come back to them. Some day when the reason was gone, he would come: Some morning he would be there

with finer presents and better stories than ever before. But their mother said he must have had an accident. He must be dead. Their mother was distracted. She read those advertisements which offered to help her make money at home. The children made paper flowers and shamefacedly tried to sell them. The boys tried to develop magazine routes, and the whole family nearly starved. Finally when they couldn't stand it any longer, the boys ran away and joined the navy. After that Molly saw them as seldom as she had seen her father, and they were so changed, so hard and boisterous, that she didn't even care, for her brothers were strangers to her.

"I went through high school, and then I went to San José and entered Teachers' College. I worked for my board and room at the home of Mrs. Allen Morit. Before I finished school my mother died, so I guess I'm a kind of an orphan, you see."

"I'm sorry," John Whiteside murmured gently.

Molly flushed. "That wasn't a bid for sympathy, Mr. Whiteside. You said you wanted to know about me. Everyone has to be an orphan some time."

"Yes," he agreed. "I'm an orphan too, I guess."

Molly worked for her board and room. She did the work of a full-time servant, only she received no pay. Money for clothes had to be accumulated by working in a store during summer vacation. Mrs.

Morit trained her girls. "I can take a green girl, not worth a cent," she often said, "and when that girl's worked for me six months, she can get fifty dollars a month. Lots of women know it, and they just snap up my girls. This is the first school-girl I've tried, but even she shows a lot of improvement. She reads too much though. I always say a serv-ant should be asleep by ten o'clock, or else she can't do her work right."

Mrs. Morit's method was one of constant criticism and nagging, car-ried on in a just, firm tone. "Now, Molly, I don't want to find fault, but if you don't wipe the silver drier than that, it'll have streaks."— "The butter knife goes this way, Molly. Then you can put the tum-bler here."

"I always give a reason for every-thing," she told her friends.

In the evening, after the dishes were washed, Molly sat on her bed and studied, and when the light was off, she lay on her bed and thought of her father. It was ridicu-lous to do it, she knew. It was a waste of time. Her father came up to the door, wearing a cutaway coat, and striped trousers and a top hat. He carried a huge bouquet of red roses in his hand. "I couldn't come before, Molly. Get on your coat quickly. First we're going down to get that evening dress in the window of Prussia's, but we'll have to hurry. I have tickets for the train to New York tonight. Hurry up, Molly! Don't stand there gawp-

ing." It was silly. Her father was dead. No, she didn't really believe he was dead. Somewhere in the world he lived beautifully, and sometime he would come back.

Molly told one of her friends at school, "I don't really believe it, you see, but I don't disbelieve it. If I ever knew he was dead, why it would be awful. I don't know what I'd do then. I don't want to think about knowing he's dead."

When her mother died, she felt little besides shame. Her mother had wanted so much to be loved and she hadn't known how to draw love. Her importunities had both-ered the children and driven them away.

"Well, that's about all," Molly finished. "I got my diploma, and then I was sent down here."

"It was about the easiest inter-view I ever had," John Whiteside said.

"Do you think I'll get the posi-tion, then?"

The old man gave a quick, twin-kly glance at the big meerschaum hanging over the mantel.

"That's his friend," Molly thought. "He has secrets with that pipe."

"Yes, I think you'll get the job. I think you have it already. Now, Miss Morgan, where are you going to live? You must find board and room some place."

Before she knew she was going to say it, she had blurted, "I want to live here."

John Whiteside opened his eyes

in astonishment. "But we never take boarders, Miss Morgan."

"Oh, I'm sorry I said that. I just liked it so much here, you see."

He called, "Willa," and when his wife stood in the half-open door, "This young lady wants to board with us. She's the new teacher."

Mrs. Whiteside frowned. "Couldn't think of it. We never take boarders. She's too pretty to be around that fool of a Bill. What would happen to those cows of his? It'd be a lot of trouble. You can sleep in the third bedroom upstairs," she said to Molly. "It doesn't catch much sun anyway."

Life changed its face. All of a sudden Molly found she was a queen. From the first day the children of the school adored her, for she understood them, and what was more, she let them understand her. It took her some time to realize that she had become an important person. If two men got to arguing at the store about a point of history or literature or mathematics, and the argument deadlocked, it ended up, "Take it to the teacher! If she doesn't know, she'll find it." Molly was very proud to be able to decide such questions. At parties she had to help with the decorations and to plan refreshments.

"I think we'll put pine boughs around everywhere. They're pretty, and they smell so good. They smell like a party." She was supposed to know everything and to help with everything, and she loved it.

At the Whiteside home she slaved in the kitchen under the mutterings of Willa. At the end of six months, Mrs. Whiteside grumbled to her husband, "Now if Bill only had any sense. But then," she continued, "if *she* has any sense—" and there she left it.

At night Molly wrote letters to the few friends she had made in Teachers' College, letters full of little stories about her neighbors, and full of joy. She must attend every party because of the social prestige of her position. On Saturdays she ran about the hills and brought back ferns and wild flowers to plant about the house.

Bill Whiteside took one look at Molly and scuttled back to his cows. It was a long time before he found the courage to talk to her very much. He was a big, simple young man who had neither his father's balance nor his mother's humor. Eventually, however, he trailed after Molly and looked after her from distances.

One evening, with a kind of feeling of thanksgiving for her happiness, Molly told Bill about her father. They were sitting in canvas chairs on the wide veranda, waiting for the moon. She told him about the visits, and then about the disappearance. "Do you see what I have, Bill?" she cried. "My lovely father is some place. He's mine. You think he's living, don't you, Bill?"

"Might be," said Bill. "From what you say, he was a kind of an irresponsible cuss, though. Excuse me, Molly. Still, if he's alive, it's funny he never wrote."

Molly felt cold. It was just the kind of reasoning she had successfully avoided for so long. "Of course," she said stiffly, "I know that. I have to do some work now, Bill."

High up on a hill that edged the valley of the Pastures of Heaven, there was an old cabin which commanded a view of the whole country and of all the roads in the vicinity. It was said that the bandit Vasquez had built the cabin and lived in it for a year while the posses went crashing through the country looking for him. It was a landmark. All the people of the valley had been to see it at one time or another. Nearly everyone asked Molly whether she had been there yet. "No," she said, "but I will go up some day. I'll go some Saturday. I know where the trail to it is." One morning she dressed in her new hiking boots and corduroy skirt. Bill sidled up and offered to accompany her. "No," she said. "You have work to do. I can't take you away from it."

"Work be hanged!" said Bill.

"Well, I'd rather go alone. I don't want to hurt your feelings, but I just want to go alone, Bill." She was sorry not to let him accompany her, but his remark about her father had frightened her. "I want to have an adventure," she said to herself. "If Bill comes along, it won't be an adventure at all. It'll just be a trip." It took her an hour

and a half to climb up the steep trail under the oaks. The leaves on the ground were as slippery as glass, and the sun was hot. The good smell of ferns and dank moss and yerba buena filled the air. When Molly came at last to the ridge crest, she was damp and winded. The cabin stood in a small clearing in the brush, a little square wooden room with no windows. Its doorless entrance was a black shadow. The place was quiet, the kind of humming quiet that flies and bees and crickets make. The whole hillside sang softly in the sun. Molly approached on tiptoe. Her heart was beating violently.

"Now I'm having an adventure," she whispered. "Now I'm right in the middle of an adventure at Vasquez' cabin." She peered in at the doorway and saw a lizard scuttle out of sight. A cobweb fell across her forehead and seemed to try to restrain her. There was nothing at all in the cabin, nothing but the dirt floor and the rotting wooden walls, and the dry, deserted smell of the earth that has long been covered from the sun. Molly was filled with excitement. "At night he sat in there. Sometimes when he heard noises like men creeping up on him, he went out of the door like the ghost of a shadow, and just melted into the darkness." She looked down on the valley of the Pastures of Heaven. The orchards lay in dark green squares; the grain was yellow, and the hills behind, a light brown washed with lavender. Among the farms the roads twisted and curled, avoiding a field, looping around a huge tree, half circling a hill flank. Over the whole valley was stretched a veil of heat shimmer. "Unreal," Molly whispered, "fantastic. It's a story, a real story, and I'm having an adventure." A breeze rose out of the valley like the sigh of a sleeper, and then subsided.

"In the daytime that young Vasquez looked down on the valley just as I'm looking. He stood right here, and looked at the roads down there. He wore a purple vest braided with gold, and the trousers on his slim legs widened at the bottom like the mouths of trumpets. His spur rowels were wrapped with silk ribbons to keep them from clinking. Sometimes he saw the posses riding by on the road below. Lucky for him the men bent over their horses' necks, and didn't look up at the hilltops. Vasquez laughed, but he was afraid, too. Sometimes he sang. His songs were soft and sad because he knew he couldn't live very long."

Molly sat down on the slope and rested her chin in her cupped hands. Young Vasquez was standing beside her, and Vasquez had her father's gay face, his shining eyes as he came on the porch shouting, "Hi, kids!" This was the kind of adventure her father had. Molly shook herself and stood up. "Now I want to go back to the first time and think it all over again."

In the late afternoon Mrs. White-side sent Bill out to look for Molly. "She might have turned an ankle, you know." But Molly emerged from the trail just as Bill approached it from the road.

"We were beginning to wonder if you'd got lost," he said. "Did you go up to the cabin?"

"Yes."

"Funny old box, isn't it? Just an old woodshed. There are a dozen just like it down here. You'd be surprised, though, how many people go up there to look at it. The funny part is, nobody's sure Vasquez was ever there."

"Oh, I think he must have been there."

"What makes you think that?"

"I don't know."

Bill became serious. "Everybody thinks Vasquez was a kind of a hero, when really he was just a thief. He started in stealing sheep and horses and ended up robbing stages. He had to kill a few people to do it. It seems to me, Molly, we ought to teach people to hate robbers, not worship them."

"Of course, Bill," she said wearily. "You're perfectly right. Would you mind not talking for a little while, Bill? I guess I'm a little tired, and nervous, too."

The year wheeled around. Pussywillows had their kittens, and wild flowers covered the hills. Molly found herself wanted and needed in the valley. She even attended school board meetings. There had been a time when those secret and august conferences were held behind closed doors, a mystery and a terror to everyone. Now that Molly was asked to step into John Whiteside's sitting room, she found that the board discussed crops, told stories, and circulated mild gossip.

Bert Munroe had been elected early in the fall, and by the springtime he was the most energetic member. He it was who planned dances at the schoolhouse, who insisted upon having plays and picnics. He even offered prizes for the best report cards in the school. The board was coming to rely pretty much on Bert Munroe.

One evening Molly came down late from her room. As always, when the board was meeting, Mrs. Whiteside sat in the dining room. "I don't think I'll go in to the meeting," Molly said. "Let them have one time to themselves. Sometimes I feel that they would tell other kinds of stories if I weren't there."

"You go on in, Molly! They can't hold a board meeting without you. They're so used to you, they'd be lost. Besides, I'm not at all sure I want them to tell those other stories."

Obediently Molly knocked on the door and went into the sitting room. Bert Munroe paused politely in the story he was narrating. "I was just telling about my new farm hand, Miss Morgan. I'll start over again, 'cause it's kind of funny. You see, I needed a hay hand, and I picked this fellow up under the Salinas River bridge. He was pretty drunk, but he wanted a job. Now

I've got him, I find he isn't worth a cent as a hand, but I can't get rid of him. That son of a gun has been every place. You ought to hear him tell about the places he's been. My kids wouldn't let me get rid of him if I wanted to. Why, he can take the littlest thing he's seen and make a fine story out of it. My kids just sit around with their ears spread, listening to him. Well, about twice a month he walks into Salinas and goes on a bust. He's one of those dirty, periodic drunks. The Salinas cops always call me up when they find him in a gutter, and I have to drive in to get him. And you know, when he comes out of it, he's always got some kind of present in his pocket for my kid Manny. There's nothing you can do with a man like that. He disarms you. I don't get a dollar's worth of work a month out of him."

Molly felt a sick dread rising in her. The men were laughing at the story. "You're too soft, Bert. You can't afford to keep an entertainer on the place. I'd sure get rid of him quick."

Molly stood up. She was dreadfully afraid someone would ask the man's name. "I'm not feeling very well tonight," she said. "If you gentlemen will excuse me, I think I'll go to bed." The men stood up while she left the room. In her bed she buried her head in the pillow. "It's crazy," she said to herself. "There isn't a chance in the world. I'm forgetting all about it right now." But she found to her dismay that she was crying.

The next few weeks were agonizing to Molly. She was reluctant to leave the house. Walking to and from school she watched the road ahead of her. "If I see any kind of a stranger I'll run away. But that's foolish. I'm being a fool." Only in her own room did she feel safe. Her terror was making her lose color, was taking the glint out of her eyes.

"Molly, you ought to go to bed," Mrs. Whiteside insisted. "Don't be a little idiot. Do I have to smack you the way I do Bill to make you go to bed?" But Molly would not go to bed. She thought too many things when she was in bed.

The next time the board met, Bert Munroe did not appear. Molly felt reassured and almost happy at his absence.

"You're feeling better, aren't you, Miss Morgan?"

"Oh, yes. It was only a little thing, a kind of a cold. If I'd gone to bed I might have been really sick."

The meeting was an hour gone before Bert Munroe came in. "Sorry to be late," he apologized. "The same old thing happened. My so-called hay hand was asleep in the street in Salinas. What a mess! He's out in the car sleeping it off now. I'll have to hose the car out tomorrow."

Molly's throat closed with terror. For a second she thought she was going to faint. "Excuse me, I must go," she cried, and ran out of the

room. She walked into the dark hallway and steadied herself against the wall. Then slowly and automatically she marched out of the front door and down the steps. The night was filled with whispers. Out in the road she could see the black mass that was Bert Munroe's car. She was surprised at the way her footsteps plodded down the path of their own volition. "Now I'm killing myself," she said. "Now I'm throwing everything away. I wonder why." The gate was under her hand, and her hand flexed to open it. Then a tiny breeze sprang up and brought to her nose the sharp foulness of vomit. She heard a blubbering, drunken snore. Instantly something whirled in her head. Molly spun around and ran frantically back to the house. In her room she locked the door and sat stiffly down, panting with the effort of her run. It seemed hours before she heard the men go out of the house, calling their good nights. Then Bert's motor started, and the sound of it died away down the road. Now that she was ready to go she felt paralyzed.

John Whiteside was writing at his desk when Molly entered the sitting room. He looked up questioningly at her. "You aren't well, Miss Morgan. You need a doctor."

She planted herself woodenly beside the desk. "Could you get a substitute teacher for me?" she asked.

"Of course I could. You pile right into bed and I'll call a doctor."

"It isn't that, Mr. Whiteside. I want to go away tonight."

"What are you talking about? You aren't well."

"I told you my father was dead. I don't know whether he's dead or not. I'm afraid—I want to go away tonight."

He stared intently at her. "Tell me what you mean," he said softly.

"If I should see that drunken man of Mr. Munroe's—" she paused, suddenly terrified at what she was about to say.

John Whiteside nodded very slowly.

"No," she cried. "I don't think that. I'm sure I don't."

"I'd like to do something, Molly."

"I don't want to go, I love it here —but I'm afraid. It's so important to me."

John Whiteside stood up and came close to her and put his arm about her shoulders. "I don't think I understand, quite," he said. "I don't think I want to understand. That isn't necessary." He seemed to be talking to himself. "It wouldn't be quite courteous—to understand."

"Once I'm away I'll be able not to believe it," Molly whimpered.

He gave her shoulders one quick squeeze with his encircling arm. "You run upstairs and pack your things, Molly," he said. "I'll get out the car and drive you right in to Salinas now."

The Rocking-Horse Winner

THERE WAS a woman who was beautiful, who started with all the advantages, yet she had no luck. She married for love, and the love turned to dust. She had bonny children, yet she felt they had been thrust upon her, and she could not love them. They looked at her coldly, as if they were finding fault with her. And hurriedly she felt she must cover up some fault in herself. Yet what it was that she must cover up she never knew. Nevertheless, when her children were present, she always felt the center of her heart go hard. This troubled her, and in her manner she was all the more gentle and anxious for her children, as if she loved them very much. Only she herself knew that at the center of her heart was a hard little place that could not feel love, no, not for anybody. Everybody else said of her: "She is such a good mother. She adores her children." Only she herself, and her children themselves, knew it was not so. They read it in each other's eyes.

There were a boy and two little girls. They lived in a pleasant house, with a garden, and they had discreet servants, and felt themselves superior to anyone in the neighborhood.

Although they lived in style, they felt always an anxiety in the house. There was never enough money. The mother had a small income, and the father had a small income, but not nearly enough for the social position which they had to keep up. The father went in to town to some office. But though he had good prospects, these prospects never materialized. There was always the grinding sense of the shortage of money, though the style was always kept up.

At last the mother said: "I will see if I can't make something." But she did not know where to begin. She racked her brains, and tried this thing and the other, but could not find anything successful. The failure made deep lines come into her

208

face. Her children were growing up; they would have to go to school. There must be more money, there must be more money. The father, who was always very handsome and expensive in his tastes, seemed as if he never *would* be able to do anything worth doing. And the mother, who had a great belief in herself, did not succeed any better, and her tastes were just as expensive.

And so the house came to be haunted by the unspoken phrase: *There must be more money! There must be more money!* The children could hear it all the time, though nobody said it aloud. They heard it at Christmas, when the expensive and splendid toys filled the nursery. Behind the shining modern rocking horse, behind the smart doll's-house, a voice would start whispering: "There *must* be more money! There *must* be more money!" And the children would stop playing, to listen for a moment. They would look into each other's eyes, to see if they had all heard. And each one saw in the eyes of the other two that they too had heard. "There *must* be more money! There *must* be more money!"

It came whispering from the springs of the still-swaying rocking horse, and even the horse, bending his wooden, champing head, heard it. The big doll, sitting so pink and smirking in her new pram, could hear it quite plainly, and seemed to be smirking all the more self-conseiously because of it. The foolish

puppy, too, that took the place of the teddy bear, he was looking so extraordinarily foolish for no other reason but that he heard the secret whisper all over the house: "There *must* be more money!"

Yet nobody ever said it aloud. The whisper was everywhere, and therefore no one spoke it. Just as no one ever says: "We are breathing!" in spite of the fact that breath is coming and going all the time.

"Mother," said the boy Paul one day, "why don't we keep a car of our own? Why do we always use uncle's, or else a taxi?"

"Because we're the poor members of the family," said the mother.

"But why *are* we, mother?"

"Well—I suppose," she said slowly and bitterly, "it's because your father has no luck."

The boy was silent for some time.

"Is luck money, mother?" he asked rather timidly.

"No, Paul. Not quite. It's what causes you to have money."

"Oh!" said Paul vaguely. "I thought when Uncle Oscar said *filthy lucker,* it meant money."

"*Filthy lucre* does mean money," said the mother. "But it's lucre, not luck."

"Oh!" said the boy. "Then what *is* luck, mother?"

"It's what causes you to have money. If you're lucky you have money. That's why it's better to be born lucky than rich. If you're rich, you may lose your money. But if you're lucky, you will always get more money."

"Oh, will you? And is father not lucky?"

"Very unlucky, I should say," she said bitterly.

The boy watched her with unsure eyes.

"Why?" he asked.

"I don't know. Nobody ever knows why one person is lucky and another unlucky."

"Don't they? Nobody at all? Does *nobody* know?"

"Perhaps God. But He never tells."

"He ought to, then. And aren't you lucky either, mother?"

"I can't be, if I married an unlucky husband."

"But by yourself, aren't you?"

"I used to think I was, before I married. Now I think I am very unlucky indeed."

"Why?"

"Well—never mind! Perhaps I'm not really," she said.

The child looked at her, to see if she meant it. But he saw, by the lines of her mouth, that she was only trying to hide something from him.

"Well, anyhow," he said stoutly, "I'm a lucky person."

"Why?" said his mother, with a sudden laugh.

He stared at her. He didn't even know why he had said it.

"God told me," he asserted, brazening it out.

"I hope He did, dear!" she said, again with a laugh, but rather bitter.

"He did, mother!"

"Excellent!" said the mother, using one of her husband's exclamations.

The boy saw she did not believe him; or, rather, that she paid no attention to his assertion. This angered him somewhat, and made him want to compel her attention.

He went off by himself, vaguely, in a childish way, seeking for the clue to "luck." Absorbed, taking no heed of other people, he went about with a sort of stealth, seeking inwardly for luck. He wanted luck, he wanted it, he wanted it. When the two girls were playing dolls in the nursery, he would sit on his big rocking horse, charging madly into space, with a frenzy that made the little girls peer at him uneasily. Wildly the horse careered, the waving dark hair of the boy tossed, his eyes had a strange glare in them. The little girls dared not speak to him.

When he had ridden to the end of his mad little journey, he climbed down and stood in front of his rocking horse, staring fixedly into its lowered face. Its red mouth was slightly open, its big eye was wide and glassy-bright.

"Now!" he would silently command the snorting steed. "Now, take me to where there is luck! Now take me!"

And he would slash the horse on the neck with the little whip he had asked Uncle Oscar for. He *knew* the horse could take him to where there was luck, if only he forced it. So he would mount again, and start on his furious ride, hoping at last to get there. He knew he could get there.

"You'll break your horse, Paul!" said the nurse.

"He's always riding like that! I wish he'd leave off!" said his elder sister Joan.

But he only glared down on them in silence. Nurse gave him up. She could make nothing of him. Anyhow he was growing beyond her.

One day his mother and his Uncle Oscar came in when he was on one of his furious rides. He did not speak to them.

"Hallo, you young jockey! Riding a winner?" said his uncle.

"Aren't you growing too big for a rocking horse? You're not a very little boy any longer, you know," said his mother.

But Paul only gave a blue glare from his big, rather close-set eyes. He would speak to nobody when he was in full tilt. His mother watched him with an anxious expression on her face.

At last he suddenly stopped forcing his horse into the mechanical gallop, and slid down.

"Well, I got there!" he announced fiercely, his blue eyes still flaring, and his sturdy long legs straddling apart.

"Where did you get to?" asked his mother.

"Where I wanted to go," he flared back at her.

"That's right, son!" said Uncle Oscar. "Don't you stop till you get there. What's the horse's name?"

"He doesn't have a name," said the boy.

"Gets on without all right?" asked the uncle.

"Well, he has different names. He was called Sansovino last week."

"Sansovino, eh? Won the Ascot. How did you know his name?"

"He always talks about horse races with Bassett," said Joan.

The uncle was delighted to find that his small nephew was posted with all the racing news. Bassett, the young gardener, who had been wounded in the left foot in the war and had got his present job through Oscar Cresswell, whose batman he had been, was a perfect blade of the "turf." He lived in the racing events, and the small boy lived with him.

Oscar Cresswell got it all from Bassett.

"Master Paul comes and asks me, so I can't do more than tell him, sir," said Bassett, his face terribly serious, as if he were speaking of religious matters.

"And does he ever put anything on a horse he fancies?"

"Well—I don't want to give him away—he's a young sport, a fine sport, sir. Would you mind asking him himself? He sort of takes a pleasure in it, and perhaps he'd feel I was giving him away, sir, if you don't mind."

Bassett was serious as a church.

The uncle went back to his nephew and took him off for a ride in the car.

"Say, Paul, old man, do you ever

put anything on a horse?" the uncle asked.

The boy watched the handsome man closely.

"Why, do you think I oughtn't to?" he parried.

"Not a bit of it! I thought perhaps you might give me a tip for the Lincoln."

The car sped on into the country, going down to Uncle Oscar's place in Hampshire.

"Honor bright?" said the nephew.

"Honor bright, son!" said the uncle.

"Well, then, Daffodil."

"Daffodil! I doubt it, sonny. What about Mirza?"

"I only know the winner," said the boy. "That's Daffodil."

"Daffodil, eh?"

There was a pause. Daffodil was an obscure horse comparatively.

"Uncle!"

"Yes, son?"

"You won't let it go any further, will you? I promised Bassett."

"Bassett be damned, old man! What's he got to do with it?"

"We're partners. We've been partners from the first. Uncle, he lent me my first five shillings, which I lost. I promised him, honor bright, it was only between me and him; only you gave me that ten-shilling note I started winning with, so I thought you were lucky. You won't let it go any further, will you?"

The boy gazed at his uncle from those big, hot, blue eyes, set rather close together. The uncle stirred and laughed uneasily.

"Right you are, son! I'll keep your tip private. Daffodil, eh? How much are you putting on him?"

"All except twenty pounds," said the boy. "I keep that in reserve."

The uncle thought it a good joke

"You keep twenty pounds in reserve, do you, you young romancer? What are you betting, then?"

"I'm betting three hundred," said the boy gravely. "But it's between you and me, Uncle Oscar! Honor bright?"

The uncle burst into a roar of laughter.

"It's between you and me all right, you young Nat Gould," he said, laughing. "But where's your three hundred?"

"Bassett keeps it for me. We're partners."

"You are, are you! And what is Bassett putting on Daffodil?"

"He won't go quite as high as I do, I expect. Perhaps he'll go a hundred and fifty."

"What, pennies?" laughed the uncle.

"Pounds," said the child, with a surprised look at his uncle. "Bassett keeps a bigger reserve than I do."

Between wonder and amusement Uncle Oscar was silent. He pursued the matter no further, but he determined to take his nephew with him to the Lincoln races.

"Now, son," he said, "I'm putting twenty on Mirza, and I'll put five for you on any horse you fancy. What's your pick?"

"Daffodil, uncle."

"No, not the fiver on Daffodil!"

"I should if it was my own fiver," said the child.

"Good! Good! Right you are! A fiver for me and a fiver for you on Daffodil."

The child had never been to a race-meeting before, and his eyes were blue fire. He pursed his mouth tight, and watched. A Frenchman just in front had put his money on Lancelot. Wild with excitement, he flayed his arms up and down, yelling *"Lancelot! Lancelot!"* in his French accent.

Daffodil came in first, Lancelot second, Mirza third. The child, flushed and with eyes blazing, was curiously serene. His uncle brought him four five-pound notes, four to one.

"What am I to do with these?" he cried, waving them before the boy's eyes.

"I suppose we'll talk to Bassett," said the boy. "I expect I have fifteen hundred now; and twenty in reserve; and this twenty."

His uncle studied him for some moments.

"Look here, son!" he said. "You're not serious about Bassett and that fifteen hundred, are you?"

"Yes, I am. But it's between you and me, uncle. Honor bright!"

"Honor bright all right, son! But I must talk to Bassett."

"If you'd like to be a partner, uncle, with Bassett and me, we could all be partners. Only, you'd

have to promise, honor bright, uncle, not to let it go beyond us three. Bassett and I are lucky, and you must be lucky, because it was your ten shillings I started winning with. . . ."

Uncle Oscar took both Bassett and Paul into Richmond Park for an afternoon, and there they talked.

"It's like this, you see, sir," Bassett said. "Master Paul would get me talking about racing events, spinning yarns, you know, sir. And he was always keen on knowing if I'd made or if I'd lost. It's about a year since, now, that I put five shilling on Blush of Dawn for him—and we lost. Then the luck turned, with that ten shillings he had from you, that we put on Singhalese. And since that time, it's been pretty steady, all things considering. What do you say, Master Paul?"

"We're all right when we're sure," said Paul. "It's when we're not quite sure that we go down."

"Oh, but we're careful then," said Bassett.

"But when are you *sure?*" smiled Uncle Oscar.

"It's Master Paul, sir," said Bassett, in a secret, religious voice. "It's as if he had it from heaven. Like Daffodil, now, for the Lincoln. That was as sure as eggs."

"Did you put anything on Daffodil?" asked Oscar Cresswell.

"Yes, sir. I made my bit."

"And my nephew?"

Bassett was obstinately silent, looking at Paul.

"I made twelve hundred, didn't

I, Bassett? I told uncle I was putting three hundred on Daffodil."

"That's right," said Bassett, nodding.

"But where's the money?" asked the uncle.

"I keep it safe locked up, sir. Master Paul he can have it any minute he likes to ask for it."

"What, fifteen hundred pounds?"

"And twenty! And *forty,* that is, with the twenty he made on the course."

"It's amazing!" said the uncle.

"If Master Paul offers you to be partners, sir, I would, if I were you; if you'll excuse me," said Bassett.

Oscar Cresswell thought about it.

"I'll see the money," he said.

They drove home again, and sure enough, Bassett came round to the garden-house with fifteen hundred pounds in notes. The twenty pounds reserve was left with Joe Glee, in the Turf Commission deposit.

"You see, it's all right, uncle, when I'm *sure!* Then we go strong, for all we're worth. Don't we, Bassett?"

"We do that, Master Paul."

"And when are you sure?" said the uncle, laughing.

"Oh, well, sometimes I'm *absolutely* sure, like about Daffodil," said the boy; "and sometimes I have an idea; and sometimes I haven't even an idea, have I, Bassett? Then we're careful, because we mostly go down."

"You do, do you! And when you're sure, like about Daffodil, what makes you sure, sonny?"

"Oh, well, I don't know," said the boy uneasily. "I'm sure, you know, uncle; that's all."

"It's as if he had it from heaven, sir," Bassett reiterated.

"I should say so!" said the uncle.

But he became a partner. And when the Leger was coming on, Paul was "sure" about Lively Spark, which was a quite inconsiderable horse. The boy insisted on putting a thousand on the horse, Bassett went for five hundred, and Oscar Cresswell two hundred. Lively Spark came in first, and the betting had been ten to one against him. Paul had made ten thousand.

"You see," he said, "I was absolutely sure of him."

Even Oscar Cresswell had cleared two thousand.

"Look here, son," he said, "this sort of thing makes me nervous."

"It needn't, uncle! Perhaps I shan't be sure again for a long time."

"But what are you going to do with your money?" asked the uncle.

"Of course," said the boy, "I started it for mother. She said she had no luck, because father is unlucky, so I thought if *I* was lucky, it might stop whispering."

"What might stop whispering?"

"Our house. I *hate* our house for whispering."

"What does it whisper?"

"Why—why"—the boy fidgeted—"why, I don't know. But it's always short of money, you know, uncle."

"I know it, son, I know it."

"You know people send mother writs, don't you, uncle?"

"I'm afraid I do," said the uncle.

"And then the house whispers, like people laughing at you behind your back. It's awful, that is! I thought if I was lucky . . ."

"You might stop it," added the uncle.

The boy watched him with big blue eyes, that had an uncanny cold fire in them, and he said never a word.

"Well, then!" said the uncle. "What are we doing?"

"I shouldn't like mother to know I was lucky," said the boy.

"Why not, son?"

"She'd stop me."

"I don't think she would."

"Oh!"—and the boy writhed in an odd way—"I *don't* want her to know, uncle."

"All right, son! We'll manage it without her knowing."

They managed it very easily. Paul, at the other's suggestion, handed over five thousand pounds to his uncle, who deposited it with the family lawyer, who was then to inform Paul's mother that a relative had put five thousand pounds into his hands, which sum was to be paid out a thousand pounds at a time, on the mother's birthday, for the next five years.

"So she'll have a birthday present of a thousand pounds for five successive years," said Uncle Oscar. "I hope it won't make it all the harder for her later."

Paul's mother had her birthday in November. The house had been "whispering" worse than ever lately, and, even in spite of his luck, Paul could not bear up against it. He was very anxious to see the effect of the birthday letter, telling his mother about the thousand pounds.

When there were no visitors, Paul now took his meals with his parents, as he was beyond the nursery control. His mother went into town nearly every day. She had discovered that she had an odd knack of sketching furs and dress materials, so she worked secretly in the studio of a friend who was the chief "artist" for the leading drapers. She drew the figures of ladies in furs and ladies in silk and sequins for the newspaper advertisements. This young woman artist earned several thousand pounds a year, but Paul's mother only made several hundreds, and she was again dissatisfied. She so wanted to be first in something, and she did not succeed, even in making sketches for drapery advertisements.

She was down to breakfast on the morning of her birthday. Paul watched her face as she read her letters. He knew the lawyer's letter. As his mother read it, her face hardened and became more expressionless. Then a cold, determined look came on her mouth. She hid the letter under the pile of others, and said not a word about it.

"Didn't you have anything nice in the post for your birthday, mother?" said Paul.

"Quite moderately nice," she said, her voice cold and absent.

She went away to town without saying more.

But in the afternoon Uncle Oscar appeared. He said Paul's mother had had a long interview with the lawyer, asking if the whole five thousand could not be advanced at once, as she was in debt.

"What do you think, uncle?" said the boy.

"I leave it to you, son."

"Oh, let her have it, then! We can get some more with the other," said the boy.

"A bird in the hand is worth two in the bush, laddie!" said Uncle Oscar.

"But I'm sure to *know* for the Grand National; or the Lincolnshire; or else the Derby. I'm sure to know for *one* of them," said Paul.

So Uncle Oscar signed the agreement, and Paul's mother touched the whole five thousand. Then something very curious happened. The voices in the house suddenly went mad, like a chorus of frogs on a spring evening. There were certain new furnishings, and Paul had a tutor. He was *really* going to Eton, his father's school, in the following autumn. There were flowers in the winter, and a blossoming of the luxury Paul's mother had been used to do. And yet the voices in the house, behind the sprays of mimosa and almond blossom, and from under the piles of iridescent cushions, simply trilled and screamed in a sort of ecstasy: "There

must be more money! Oh-h-h; there *must* be more money. Oh, now, now-w! Now-w-w—there *must* be more money!—more than ever! More than ever!"

It frightened Paul terribly. He studied away at his Latin and Greek with his tutors. But his intense hours were spent with Bassett. The Grand National had gone by: he had not "known," and had lost a hundred pounds. Summer was at hand. He was in agony for the Lincoln. But even for the Lincoln he didn't "know," and he lost fifty pounds. He became wild-eyed and strange, as if something were going to explode in him.

"Let it alone, son! Don't you bother about it!" urged Uncle Oscar. But it was as if the boy couldn't really hear what his uncle was saying.

"I've got to know for the Derby! I've got to know for the Derby!" the child reiterated, his big blue eyes blazing with a sort of madness.

His mother noticed how over-wrought he was.

"You'd better go to the seaside. Wouldn't you like to go now to the seaside, instead of waiting? I think you'd better," she said, looking down at him anxiously, her heart curiously heavy because of him.

But the child lifted his uncanny blue eyes.

"I couldn't possibly go before the Derby, mother!" he said. "I couldn't possibly!"

"Why not?" she said, her voice becoming heavy when she was opposed. "Why not? You can still go from the seaside to see the Derby with your Uncle Oscar, if that's what you wish. No need for you to wait here. Besides, I think you care too much about these races. It's a bad sign. My family has been a gambling family, and you won't know till you grow up how much damage it has done. But it has done damage. I shall have to send Bassett away, and ask Uncle Oscar not to talk racing to you, unless you promis to be reasonable about it; go away to the seaside and forget it. You're all nerves!"

"I'll do what you like, mother, so long as you don't send me away till after the Derby," the boy said.

"Send you away from where? Just from this house?"

"Yes," he said, gazing at her.

"Why, you curious child, what makes you care about this house so much, suddenly? I never knew you loved it."

He gazed at her without speaking. He had a secret within a secret, something he had not divulged, even to Bassett or to his Uncle Oscar.

But his mother, after standing undecided and a little bit sullen for some moments, said:

"Very well, then! Don't go to the seaside till after the Derby, if you don't wish it. But promise me you won't let your nerves go to pieces. Promise you won't think so much about horse racing and *events,* as you call them!"

"Oh, no," said the boy casually.

"I won't think much about them, mother. You needn't worry. I wouldn't worry, mother, if I were you."

"If you were me and I were you," said his mother, "I wonder what we *should* do!"

"But you know you needn't worry, mother, don't you?" the boy repeated.

"I should be awfully glad to know it," she said wearily.

"Oh, well, you *can,* you know. I mean, you *ought* to know you needn't worry," he insisted.

"Ought I? Then I'll see about it," she said.

Paul's secret of secrets was his wooden horse, that which had no name. Since he was emancipated from a nurse and a nursery-governess, he had had his rocking horse removed to his own bedroom at the top of the house.

"Surely, you're too big for a rocking horse!" his mother had remonstrated.

"Well, you see, mother, till I can have a *real* horse, I like to have *some* sort of animal about," had been his quaint answer.

"Do you feel he keeps you company?" she laughed.

"Oh, yes! He's very good, he always keeps me company, when I'm there," said Paul.

So the horse, rather shabby, stood in an arrested prance in the boy's bedroom.

The Derby was drawing near, and the boy grew more and more tense. He hardly heard what was spoken to him, he was very frail, and his eyes were really uncanny. His mother had sudden strange seizures of uneasiness about him. Sometimes, for half an hour, she would feel a sudden anxiety about him that was almost anguish. She wanted to rush to him at once, and know he was safe.

Two nights before the Derby, she was at a big party in town, when one of her rushes of anxiety about her boy, her first-born, gripped her heart till she could hardly speak. She fought with the feeling, might and main, for she believed in common sense. But it was too strong. She had to leave the dance and go downstairs to telephone to the country. The children's nursery-governess was terribly surprised and startled at being rung up in the night.

"Are the children all right, Miss Wilmot?"

"Oh, yes, they are quite all right."

"Master Paul? Is he all right?"

"He went to bed as right as a trivet. Shall I run up and look at him?"

"No," said Paul's mother reluctantly. "No! Don't trouble. It's all right. Don't sit up. We shall be home fairly soon." She did not want her son's privacy intruded upon.

"Very good," said the governess.

It was about one o'clock when Paul's mother and father drove up to their house. All was still. Paul's mother went to her room and slipped off her white fur cloak. She had told her maid not to wait up for her. She heard her husband downstairs, mixing a whisky-and-soda.

And then, because of the strange anxiety at her heart, she stole upstairs to her son's room. Noiselessly she went along the upper corridor. Was there a faint noise? What was it?

She stood, with arrested muscles, outside his door, listening. There was a strange, heavy, and yet not loud noise. Her heart stood still. It was a soundless noise, yet rushing and powerful. Something huge, in violent, hushed motion. What was it? What in God's name was it? She ought to know. She felt that she knew the noise. She knew what it was.

Yet she could not place it. She couldn't say what it was. And on and on it went, like a madness.

Softly, frozen with anxiety and fear, she turned the door handle.

The room was dark. Yet in the space near the window, she heard and saw something plunging to and fro. She gazed in fear and amazement.

Then suddenly she switched on the light, and saw her son, in his green pajamas, madly surging on the rocking horse. The blaze of light suddenly lit him up, as he urged the wooden horse, and lit her up, as she stood, blonde, in her dress of pale green and crystal, in the doorway.

"Paul!" she cried. "Whatever are you doing?"

"It's Malabar!" he screamed, in a

powerful, strange voice. "It's Malabar!"

His eyes blazed at her for one strange and senseless second, as he ceased urging his wooden horse. Then he fell with a crash to the ground, and she, all her tormented motherhood flooding upon her, rushed to gather him up.

But he was unconscious, and unconscious he remained, with some brain fever. He talked and tossed, and his mother sat stonily by his side.

"Malabar! It's Malabar! Bassett, Bassett, I *know*! It's Malabar!"

So the child cried, trying to get up and urge the rocking horse that gave him his inspiration.

"What does he mean by Malabar?" asked the heart-frozen mother.

"I don't know," said the father stonily.

"What does he mean by Malabar?" she asked her brother Oscar.

"It's one of the horses running for the Derby," was the answer.

And, in spite of himself, Oscar Cresswell spoke to Bassett, and himself put a thousand on Malabar: at fourteen to one.

The third day of the illness was critical: they were waiting for a change. The boy, with his rather long, curly hair, was tossing ceaselessly on the pillow. He neither slept nor regained consciousness, and his eyes were like blue stones. His mother sat, feeling her heart had gone, turned actually into a stone.

In the evening, Oscar Cresswell did not come, but Bassett sent a message, saying could he come up for one moment, just one moment? Paul's mother was very angry at the intrusion, but on second thought she agreed. The boy was the same. Perhaps Bassett might bring him to consciousness.

The gardener, a shortish fellow with a little brown mustache, and sharp little brown eyes, tip-toed into the room, touched his imaginary cap to Paul's mother, and stole to the bedside, staring with glittering, smallish eyes, at the tossing, dying child.

"Master Paul!" he whispered. "Master Paul! Malabar came in first all right, a clean win. I did as you told me. You've made over seventy thousand pounds, you have; you've got over eighty thousand. Malabar came in all right, Master Paul."

"Malabar! Malabar! Did I say Malabar, mother? Did I say Malabar? Do you think I'm lucky, mother? I knew Malabar, didn't I? Over eighty thousand pounds! I call that lucky, don't you, mother? Over eighty thousand pounds! I knew, didn't I know I knew? Malabar came in all right. If I ride my horse till I'm sure, then I tell you, Bassett, you can go as high as you like. Did you go for all you were worth, Bassett?"

"I went a thousand on it, Master Paul."

"I never told you, mother, that if I can ride my horse, and *get there,* then I'm absolutely sure—oh, absolutely! Mother, did I ever tell you? I *am* lucky!"

"No, you never did," said the mother.

But the boy died in the night.

And even as he lay dead, his mother heard her brother's voice saying to her: "My God, Hester, you're eighty-odd thousand to the good, and a poor devil of a son to the bad. But, poor devil, poor devil, he's best gone out of a life where he rides his rocking horse to find a winner."

Piano

D. H. LAWRENCE

Softly, in the dusk, a woman is singing to me;
Taking me back down the vista of years, till I see
A child sitting under the piano, in the boom of the tingling strings
And pressing the small, poised feet of the mother who smiles as she sings.

In spite of myself, the insidious mastery of song
Betrays me back, till the heart of me weeps to belong
To the old Sunday evenings at home, with the winter outside
And hymns in the cozy parlor, the tinkling piano our guide.

So now it is vain for the singer to burst into clamor
With the great black piano appassionato. The glamour
Of the childish days is upon me, my manhood is cast
Down in a flood of remembrance, I weep like a child for the past.

Bernice Bobs Her Hair

AFTER DARK on Saturday night one could stand on the first tee of the golf course and see the country-club windows as a yellow expanse over a very black and wavy ocean. The waves of this ocean, so to speak, were the heads of many curious caddies, a few of the more ingenious chauffeurs, the golf professional's deaf sister—and there were usually several stray, diffident waves who might have rolled inside had they so desired. This was the gallery.

The balcony was inside. It consisted of the circle of wicker chairs that lined the wall of the combination clubroom and ballroom. At these Saturday night dances it was largely feminine; a great babble of middle-aged ladies with sharp eyes and icy hearts behind lorgnettes and large bosoms. The main function of the balcony was critical. It occasionally showed grudging admiration, but never approval, for it is well known among ladies over thirty-five that when the younger set dance in the summertime it is with the very worst intentions in the world, and if they are not bombarded with stony eyes stray couples will dance weird barbaric interludes in the corners, and the more popular, more dangerous girls will sometimes be kissed in the parked limousines of unsuspecting dowagers.

But, after all, this critical circle is not close enough to the stage to see the actors' faces and catch the subtler byplay. It can only frown and lean, ask questions and make satisfactory deductions from its set of postulates, such as the one which states that every young man with a large income leads the life of a hunted partridge. It never really appreciates the drama of the shifting, semicruel world of adolescence. No; boxes, orchestra-circle, principals, and chorus are represented by the medley of faces and voices that sway to the plaintive African rhythm of Dyer's dance orchestra.

From sixteen-year-old Otis Ormonde, who has two more years at Hill School, to G. Reece Stoddard, over whose bureau at home hangs a Harvard law diploma; from little Madeleine Hogue, whose hair still feels strange and uncomfortable on top of her head, to Bessie MacRae, who has been the life of the party a little too long—more than ten years —the medley is not only the center of the stage but contains the only people capable of getting an unobstructed view of it.

With a flourish and a bang the music stops. The couples exchange artificial, effortless smiles, facetiously repeat *"la-de-da-da* dum-*dum,"* and then the clatter of young feminine voices soars over the burst of clapping.

A few disappointed stags caught in midfloor as they had been about to cut in subsided listlessly back to the walls, because this was not like the riotous Christmas dances—these summer hops were considered just pleasantly warm and exciting, where even the younger marrieds rose and performed ancient waltzes and terrifying fox trots to the tolerant amusement of their younger brothers and sisters.

Warren McIntyre, who casually attended Yale, being one of the unfortunate stags, felt in his dinnercoat pocket for a cigarette and strolled out onto the wide, semidark veranda, where couples were scattered at tables, filling the lantern-hung night with vague words and hazy laughter. He nodded here and there at the less absorbed and

as he passed each couple some half-forgotten fragment of a story played in his mind, for it was not a large city and every one was Who's Who to every one else's past. There, for example, were Jim Strain and Ethel Demorest, who had been privately engaged for three years. Every one knew that as soon as Jim managed to hold a job for more than two months she would marry him. Yet how bored they both looked, and how wearily Ethel regarded Jim sometimes, as if she wondered why she had trained the vines of her affection on such a wind-shaken poplar.

Warren was nineteen and rather pitying with those of his friends who hadn't gone East to college. But, like most boys, he bragged tremendously about the girls of his city when he was away from it. There was Genevieve Ormonde, who regularly made the rounds of dances, house parties, and football games at Princeton, Yale, Williams, and Cornell; there was black-eyed Roberta Dillon, who was quite as famous to her own generation as Hiram Johnson or Ty Cobb; and, of course, there was Marjorie Harvey, who besides having a fairylike face and a dazzling, bewildering tongue was already justly celebrated for having turned five cart-wheels in succession during the past pump-and-slipper dance at New Haven.

Warren, who had grown up across the street from Marjorie, had long been "crazy about her." Sometimes she seemed to reciprocate his feeling with a faint gratitude, but she had tried him by her infallible test and informed him gravely that she did not love him. Her test was that when she was away from him she forgot him and had affairs with other boys. Warren found this discouraging, especially as Marjorie had been making little trips all summer, and for the first two or three days after each arrival home he saw great heaps of mail on the Harveys' hall table addressed to her in various masculine handwritings. To make matters worse, all during the month of August she had been visited by her cousin Bernice from Eau Claire, and it seemed impossible to see her alone. It was always necessary to hunt round and find someone to take care of Bernice. As August waned this was becoming more and more difficult.

Much as Warren worshiped Marjorie, he had to admit that Cousin Bernice was sorta hopeless. She was pretty, with dark hair and high color, but she was no fun on a party. Every Saturday night he danced a long arduous duty dance with her to please Marjorie, but he had never been anything but bored in her company.

"Warren"—a soft voice at his elbow broke in upon his thoughts, and he turned to see Marjorie, flushed and radiant as usual. She laid a hand on his shoulder and a glow settled almost imperceptibly over him.

"Warren," she whispered, "do something for me—dance with Ber-nice. She's been stuck with little Otis Ormonde for almost an hour."

Warren's glow faded.

"Why—sure," he answered half-heartedly.

"You don't mind, do you? I'll see that you don't get stuck."

" 'Sall right."

Marjorie smiled—that smile that was thanks enough.

"You're an angel, and I'm obliged loads."

With a sigh the angel glanced round the veranda, but Bernice and Otis were not in sight. He wandered back inside, and there in front of the women's dressing room he found Otis in the center of a group of young men who were convulsed with laughter. Otis was brandishing a piece of timber he had picked up, and discoursing volubly.

"She's gone in to fix her hair," he announced wildly. "I'm waiting to dance another hour with her."

Their laughter was renewed.

"Why don't some of you cut in?" cried Otis resentfully. "She likes more variety."

"Why, Otis," suggested a friend, "you've just barely got used to her."

"Why the two-by-four, Otis?" inquired Warren, smiling.

"The two-by-four? Oh, this? This is a club. When she comes out I'll hit her on the head and knock her in again."

Warren collapsed on a settee and howled with glee.

"Never mind, Otis," he articulated finally. "I'm relieving you this time."

Otis simulated a sudden fainting attack and handed the stick to Warren.

"If you need it, old man," he said hoarsely.

No matter how beautiful or brilliant a girl may be, the reputation of not being frequently cut in on makes her position at a dance unfortunate. Perhaps boys prefer her company to that of the butterflies with whom they dance a dozen times an evening, but youth in this jazz-nourished generation is temperamentally restless, and the idea of fox-trotting more than one full fox trot with the same girl is distasteful, not to say odious. When it comes to several dances and the intermissions between, she can be quite sure that a young man, once relieved, will never tread on her wayward toes again.

Warren danced the next full dance with Bernice, and finally, thankful for the intermission, he led her to a table on the veranda. There was a moment's silence while she did unimpressive things with her fan.

"It's hotter here than in Eau Claire," she said.

Warren stifled a sigh and nodded. It might be for all he knew or cared. He wondered idly whether she was a poor conversationalist because she got no attention or got no attention because she was a poor conversationalist.

"You going to be here much longer?" he asked, and then turned rather red. She might suspect his reasons for asking.

"Another week," she answered, and stared at him as if to lunge at his next remark when it left his lips.

Warren fidgeted. Then with a sudden charitable impulse he decided to try part of his line on her. He turned and looked at her eyes.

"You've got an awfully kissable mouth," he began quietly.

This was a remark that he sometimes made to girls at college proms when they were talking in just such half dark as this. Bernice distinctly jumped. She turned an ungraceful red and became clumsy with her fan. No one had ever made such a remark to her before.

"Fresh!"—the word had slipped out before she realized it, and she bit her lip. Too late she decided to be amused, and offered him a flustered smile.

Warren was annoyed. Though not accustomed to have that remark taken seriously, still it usually provoked a laugh or a paragraph of sentimental banter. And he hated to be called fresh, except in a joking way. His charitable impulse died and he switched the topic.

"Jim Strain and Ethel Demorest sitting out as usual," he commented.

This was more in Bernice's line, but a faint regret mingled with her relief as the subject changed. Men did not talk to her about kissable mouths, but she knew that they talked in some such way to other girls.

"Oh, yes," she said, and laughed. "I hear they've been mooning round for years without a red penny. Isn't it silly?"

Warren's disgust increased. Jim Strain was a close friend of his brother's, and anyway he considered it bad form to sneer at people for not having money. But Bernice had had no intention of sneering. She was merely nervous.

II

When Marjorie and Bernice reached home at half after midnight they said good night at the top of the stairs. Though cousins, they were not intimates. As a matter of fact Marjorie had no female intimates—she considered girls stupid. Bernice on the contrary all through this parent-arranged visit had rather longed to exchange those confidences flavored with giggles and tears that she considered an indispensable factor in all feminine intercourse. But in this respect she found Marjorie rather cold; felt somehow the same difficulty in talking to her that she had in talking to men. Marjorie never giggled, was never frightened, seldom embarrassed, and in fact had very few of the qualities which Bernice considered appropriately and blessedly feminine.

As Bernice busied herself with toothbrush and paste this night she wondered for the hundredth time why she never had any attention when she was away from home. That her family were the wealthiest in Eau Claire; that her mother entertained tremendously, gave little dinners for her daughter before all dances and bought her a car of her own to drive round in, never occurred to her as factors in her hometown social success. Like most girls she had been brought up on the warm milk prepared by Annie Fellows Johnston and on novels in which the female was beloved because of certain mysterious womanly qualities, always mentioned but never displayed.

Bernice felt a vague pain that she was not at present engaged in being popular. She did not know that had it not been for Marjorie's campaigning she would have danced the entire evening with one man; but she knew that even in Eau Claire other girls with less position and less pulchritude were given a much bigger rush. She attributed this to something subtly unscrupulous in those girls. It had never worried her, and if it had her mother would have assured her that the other girls cheapened themselves and that men really respected girls like Bernice.

She turned out the light in her bathroom, and on an impulse decided to go in and chat for a moment with her Aunt Josephine, whose light was still on. Her soft slippers bore her noiselessly down the carpeted hall, but hearing voices inside she stopped near the partly opened door. Then she caught her own name, and without any definite intention of eavesdropping lingered—and the thread of the conversation going on inside pierced her consciousness sharply as if it had been drawn through with a needle.

"She's absolutely hopeless!" It was Marjorie's voice. "Oh, I know what you're going to say! So many people have told you how pretty and sweet she is, and how she can cook! What of it? She has a bum time. Men don't like her."

"What's a little cheap popularity?"

Mrs. Harvey sounded annoyed.

"It's everything when you're eighteen," said Marjorie emphatically. "I've done my best. I've been polite and I've made men dance with her, but they just won't stand being bored. When I think of that gorgeous coloring wasted on such a ninny, and think what Martha Carey could do with it—oh!"

"There's no courtesy these days."

Mrs. Harvey's voice implied that modern situations were too much for her. When she was a girl all young ladies who belonged to nice families had glorious times.

"Well," said Marjorie, "no girl can permanently bolster up a lame-duck visitor, because these days it's every girl for herself. I've even tried to drop her hints about clothes and things, and she's been furious—given me the funniest looks. She's sensitive enough to know she's not getting away with much, but I'll bet she consoles herself by thinking that she's very virtuous and that I'm too gay and fickle and will come to a bad end. All unpopular

girls think that way. Sour grapes! Sarah Hopkins refers to Genevieve and Roberta and me as gardenia girls! I'll bet she'd give ten years of her life and her European education to be a gardenia girl and have three or four men in love with her and be cut in on every few feet at dances."

"It seems to me," interrupted Mrs. Harvey rather wearily, "that you ought to be able to do something for Bernice. I know she's not very vivacious."

Marjorie groaned.

"Vivacious! Good grief! I've never heard her say anything to a boy except that it's hot or the floor's crowded or that she's going to school in New York next year. Sometimes she asks them what kind of car they have and tells them the kind she has. Thrilling!"

There was a short silence, and then Mrs. Harvey took up her refrain:

"All I know is that other girls not half so sweet and attractive get partners. Martha Carey, for instance, is stout and loud, and her mother is distinctly common. Roberta Dillon is so thin this year that she looks as though Arizona were the place for her. She's dancing herself to death."

"But, mother," objected Marjorie impatiently, "Martha is cheerful and awfully witty and an awfully slick girl, and Roberta's a marvelous dancer. She's been popular for ages!"

Mrs. Harvey yawned.

"I think it's that crazy Indian blood in Bernice," continued Marjorie. "Maybe she's a reversion to type. Indian women all just sat round and never said anything."

"Go to bed, you silly child," laughed Mrs. Harvey. "I wouldn't have told you that if I'd thought you were going to remember it. And I think most of your ideas are perfectly idiotic," she finished sleepily.

There was another silence, while Marjorie considered whether or not convincing her mother was worth the trouble. People over forty can seldom be permanently convinced of anything. At eighteen our convictions are hills from which we look; at forty-five they are caves in which we hide.

Having decided this, Marjorie said good night. When she came out into the hall it was quite empty.

III

While Marjorie was breakfasting late next day Bernice came into the room with a rather formal good morning, sat down opposite, stared intently over, and slightly moistened her lips.

"What's on your mind?" inquired Marjorie, rather puzzled.

Bernice paused before she threw her hand grenade.

"I heard what you said about me to your mother last night."

Marjorie was startled, but she showed only a faintly heightened color and her voice was quite even when she spoke.

"Where were you?"

"In the hall. I didn't mean to listen—at first."

After an involuntary look of contempt Marjorie dropped her eyes and became very interested in balancing a stray corn flake on her finger.

"I guess I'd better go back to Eau Claire—if I'm such a nuisance." Bernice's lower lip was trembling violently and she continued on a wavering note: "I've tried to be nice, and—and I've been first neglected and then insulted. No one ever visited me and got such treatment."

Marjorie was silent.

"But I'm in the way, I see. I'm a drag on you. Your friends don't like me." She paused, and then remembered another one of her grievances. "Of course I was furious last week when you tried to hint to me that that dress was unbecoming. Don't you think I know how to dress myself?"

"No," murmured Marjorie less than half-aloud.

"What?"

"I didn't hint anything," said Marjorie succinctly. "I said, as I remember, that it was better to wear a becoming dress three times straight than to alternate it with two frights."

"Do you think that was a very nice thing to say?"

"I wasn't trying to be nice." Then after a pause: "When do you want to go?"

Bernice drew in her breath sharply.

"Oh!" It was a little half-cry. Marjorie looked up in surprise.

"Didn't you say you were going?"

"Yes, but—"

"Oh, you were only bluffing!"

They stared at each other across the breakfast table for a moment. Misty waves were passing before Bernice's eyes, while Marjorie's face wore that rather hard expression that she used when slightly intoxicated undergraduates were making love to her.

"So you were bluffing," she repeated as if it were what she might have expected.

Bernice admitted it by bursting into tears. Marjorie's eyes showed boredom.

"You're my cousin," sobbed Bernice. "I'm v-v-visiting you. I was to stay a month, and if I go home my mother will know and she'll wah-wonder—"

Marjorie waited until the shower of broken words collapsed into little sniffles.

"I'll give you my month's allowance," she said coldly, "and you can spend this last week anywhere you want. There's a very nice hotel—"

Bernice's sobs rose to a flute note, and rising of a sudden she fled from the room.

An hour later, while Marjorie was in the library absorbed in composing one of those non-committal, marvelously elusive letters that only a young girl can write, Bernice reappeared, very red-eyed and consciously calm. She cast no glance at Marjorie but took a book at random from the shelf and sat down as if to read. Marjorie seemed absorbed in her letter and continued writing. When the clock showed noon Bernice closed her book with a snap.

"I suppose I'd better get my railroad ticket."

This was not the beginning of the speech she had rehearsed upstairs, but as Marjorie was not getting her cues—wasn't urging her to be reasonable; it's all a mistake—it was the best opening she could muster.

"Just wait till I finish this letter," said Marjorie without looking round. "I want to get it off in the next mail."

After another minute, during which her pen scratched busily, she turned round and relaxed with an air of "at your service." Again Bernice had to speak.

"Do you want me to go home?"

"Well," said Marjorie, considering, "I suppose if you're not having a good time you'd better go. No use being miserable."

"Don't you think common kindness—"

"Oh, please don't quote *Little Women!*" cried Marjorie impatiently. "That's out of style."

"You think so?"

"Heavens, yes! What modern girl could live like those inane females?"

"They were the models for our mothers."

Marjorie laughed.

"Yes, they were—not! Besides,

our mothers were all very well in their way, but they know very little about their daughters' problems."

Bernice drew herself up.

"Please don't talk about my mother."

Marjorie laughed.

"I don't think I mentioned her."

Bernice felt that she was being led away from her subject.

"Do you think you've treated me very well?"

"I've done my best. You're rather hard material to work with."

The lids of Bernice's eyes reddened.

"I think you're hard and selfish, and you haven't a feminine quality in you."

"Oh, my Lord!" cried Marjorie in desperation. "You little nut! Girls like you are responsible for all the tiresome colorless marriages; all those ghastly inefficiencies that pass as feminine qualities. What a blow it must be when a man with imagination marries the beautiful bundle of clothes that he's been building ideals round, and finds that she's just a weak, whining, cowardly mass of affectations!"

Bernice's mouth had slipped half open.

"The womanly woman!" continued Marjorie. "Her whole early life is occupied in whining criticisms of girls like me who really do have a good time."

Bernice's jaw descended farther as Marjorie's voice rose.

"There's some excuse for an ugly girl whining. If I'd been irretrieva-

bly ugly I'd never have forgiven my parents for bringing me into the world. But you're starting life without any handicap—" Marjorie's little fist clinched. "If you expect me to weep with you you'll be disappointed. Go or stay, just as you like." And picking up her letters she left the room.

Bernice claimed a headache and failed to appear at luncheon. They had a matinee date for the afternoon, but the headache persisting, Marjorie made explanations to a not very downcast boy. But when she returned late in the afternoon she found Bernice with a strangely set face waiting for her in her bedroom.

"I've decided," began Bernice without preliminaries, "that maybe you're right about things—possibly not. But if you'll tell me why your friends aren't—aren't interested in me I'll see if I can do what you want me to."

Marjorie was at the mirror shaking down her hair.

"Do you mean it?"

"Yes."

"Without reservations? Will you do exactly what I say?"

"Well, I—"

"Well nothing! Will you do exactly as I say?"

"If they're sensible things."

"They're not! You're no case for sensible things."

"Are you going to make—to recommend—"

"Yes, everything. If I tell you to take boxing lessons you'll have to do it. Write home and tell your mother you're going to stay another two weeks."

"If you'll tell me—"

"All right—I'll just give you a few examples now. First, you have no ease of manner. Why? Because you're never sure about your personal appearance. When a girl feels that she's perfectly groomed and dressed she can forget that part of her. That's charm. The more parts of yourself you can afford to forget the more charm you have."

"Don't I look all right?"

"No; for instance, you never take care of your eyebrows. They're black and lustrous, but by leaving them straggly they're a blemish. They'd be beautiful if you'd take care of them in one-tenth the time you take doing nothing. You're going to brush them so that they'll grow straight."

Bernice raised the brows in question.

"Do you mean to say that men notice eyebrows?"

"Yes—subconsciously. And when you go home you ought to have your teeth straightened a little. It's almost imperceptible, still—"

"But I thought," interrupted Bernice in bewilderment, "that you despised little dainty feminine things like that."

"I hate dainty minds," answered Marjorie. "But a girl has to be dainty in person. If she looks like a million dollars she can talk about Russia, ping-pong, or the League of Nations and get away with it."

"What else?"

"Oh, I'm just beginning! There s your dancing."

"Don't I dance all right?"

"No, you don't—you lean on a man; yes, you do—ever so slightly. I noticed it when we were dancing together yesterday. And you dance standing up straight instead of bending over a little. Probably some old lady on the side line once told you that you looked so dignified that way. But except with a very small girl it's much harder on the man, and he's the one that counts."

"Go on." Bernice's brain was reeling.

"Well, you've got to learn to be nice to men who are sad birds. You look as if you'd been insulted whenever you're thrown with any except the most popular boys. Why, Bernice, I'm cut in on every few feet—and who does most of it? Why, those very sad birds. No girl can afford to neglect them. They're the big part of any crowd. Young boys too shy to talk are the very best conversational practice. Clumsy boys are the best dancing practice. If you can follow them and yet look graceful you can follow a baby tank across a barb-wire skyscraper."

Bernice sighed profoundly, but Marjorie was not through.

"If you go to a dance and really amuse, say, three sad birds that dance with you; if you talk so well to them that they forget they're stuck with you, you've done something. They'll come back next time, and gradually so many sad birds will dance with you that the attractive boys will see there's no danger of being stuck—then they'll dance with you."

"Yes," agreed Bernice faintly. "I think I begin to see."

"And finally," concluded Marjorie, "poise and charm will just come. You'll wake up some morning knowing you've attained it, and men will know it too."

Bernice rose.

"It's been awfully kind of you—but nobody's ever talked to me like this before, and I feel sort of startled."

Marjorie made no answer but gazed pensively at her own image in the mirror.

"You're a peach to help me," continued Bernice.

Still Marjorie did not answer, and Bernice thought she had seemed too grateful.

"I know you don't like sentiment," she said timidly.

Marjorie turned to her quickly.

"Oh, I wasn't thinking about that. I was considering whether we hadn't better bob your hair."

Bernice collapsed backward upon the bed.

IV

On the following Wednesday evening there was a dinner-dance at the country club. When the guests strolled in, Bernice found her place card with a slight feeling of irritation. Though at her right sat G. Reece Stoddard, a most desirable and distinguished young bachelor,

the all-important left held only Charley Paulson. Charley lacked height, beauty, and social shrewdness, and in her new enlightenment Bernice decided that his only qualification to be her partner was that he had never been stuck with her. But this feeling of irritation left with the last of the soup plates, and Marjorie's specific instruction came to her. Swallowing her pride she turned to Charley Paulson and plunged.

"Do you think I ought to bob my hair, Mr. Charley Paulson?"

Charley looked up in surprise.

"Why?"

"Because I'm considering it. It's such a sure and easy way of attracting attention."

Charley smiled pleasantly. He could not know this had been rehearsed. He replied that he didn't know much about bobbed hair. But Bernice was there to tell him.

"I want to be a society vampire, you see," she announced coolly, and went on to inform him that bobbed hair was the necessary prelude. She added that she wanted to ask his advice, because she had heard he was so critical about girls.

Charley, who knew as much about the psychology of women as he did of the mental states of Buddhist contemplatives, felt vaguely flattered.

"So I've decided," she continued, her voice rising slightly, "that early next week I'm going down to the Sevier Hotel barbershop, sit in the first chair, and get my hair bobbed."

She faltered, noticing that the people near her had paused in their conversation and were listening; but after a confused second Marjorie's coaching told, and she finished her paragraph to the vicinity at large. "Of course I'm charging admission, but if you'll all come down and encourage me I'll issue passes for the inside seats."

There was a ripple of appreciative laughter, and under cover of it G. Reece Stoddard leaned over quickly and said close to her ear: "I'll take a box right now."

She met his eyes and smiled as if he had said something surpassingly brilliant.

"Do you believe in bobbed hair?" asked G. Reece in the same undertone.

"I think it's unmoral," affirmed Bernice gravely. "But, of course, you've either got to amuse people or feed 'em or shock 'em." Marjorie had culled this from Oscar Wilde. It was greeted with a ripple of laughter from the men and a series of quick, intent looks from the girls. And then as though she had said nothing of wit or moment Bernice turned again to Charley and spoke confidentially in his ear.

"I want to ask you your opinion of several people. I imagine you're a wonderful judge of character."

Charley thrilled faintly—paid her a subtle compliment by overturning her water.

Two hours later, while Warren McIntyre was standing passively in the stag line abstracted watching the dancers and wondering whither and with whom Marjorie had disappeared, an unrelated perception began to creep slowly upon him—a perception that Bernice, cousin to Marjorie, had been cut in on several times in the past five minutes. He closed his eyes, opened them, and looked again. Several minutes back she had been dancing with a visiting boy, a matter easily accounted for; a visiting boy would know no better. But now she was dancing with someone else, and there was Charley Paulson headed for her with enthusiastic determination in his eye. Funny—Charley seldom danced with more than three girls an evening.

Warren was distinctly surprised when—the exchange having been effected—the man relieved proved to be none other than G. Reece Stoddard himself. And G. Reece seemed not at all jubilant at being relieved. Next time Bernice danced near, Warren regarded her intently. Yes, she was pretty, distinctly pretty; and tonight her face seemed really vivacious. She had that look that no woman, however histrionically proficient, can successfully counterfeit—she looked as if she were having a good time. He liked the way she had her hair arranged, wondered if it was brilliantine that made it glisten so. And that dress was becoming—a dark red that set off her shadowy eyes and high coloring. He remembered that he had thought her pretty when she first came to town, before he had realized that she was dull. Too bad she was dull—dull girls unbearable —certainly pretty though.

His thoughts zigzagged back to Marjorie. This disappearance would be like other disappearances. When she reappeared he would demand where she had been—would be told emphatically that it was none of his business. What a pity she was so sure of him! She basked in the knowledge that no other girl in town interested him; she defied him to fall in love with Genevieve or Roberta.

Warren sighed. The way to Marjorie's affections was a labyrinth indeed. He looked up. Bernice was again dancing with the visiting boy. Half unconsciously he took a step out from the stag line in her direction, and hesitated. Then he said to himself that it was charity. He walked toward her—collided suddenly with G. Reece Stoddard.

"Pardon me," said Warren.

But G. Reece had not stopped to apologize. He had again cut in on Bernice.

That night at one o'clock Marjorie, with one hand on the electric-light switch in the hall, turned to take a last look at Bernice's sparkling eyes.

"So it worked?"

"Oh, Marjorie, yes!" cried Bernice.

"I saw you were having a gay time."

"I did! The only trouble was that about midnight I ran short of talk. I had to repeat myself—with different men of course. I hope they won't compare notes."

"Men don't," said Marjorie, yawning, "and it wouldn't matter if they did—they'd think you were even trickier."

She snapped out the light, and as they started up the stairs Bernice grasped the banister thankfully. For the first time in her life she had been danced tired.

"You see," said Marjorie at the top of the stairs, "one man sees another man cut in and he thinks there must be something there. Well, we'll fix up some new stuff tomorrow. Good night."

"Good night."

As Bernice took down her hair she passed the evening before her in review. She had followed instructions exactly. Even when Charley Paulson cut in for the eighth time she had simulated delight and had apparently been both interested and flattered. She had not talked about the weather or Eau Claire or automobiles or her school, but had confined her conversation to me, you, and us.

But a few minutes before she fell asleep a rebellious thought was churning drowsily in her brain—after all, it was she who had done it. Marjorie, to be sure, had given her her conversation, but then Marjorie got much of her conversation out of things she read. Bernice had bought the red dress, though she had never valued it highly before

Marjorie dug it out of her trunk—and her own voice had said the words, her own lips had smiled, her own feet had danced. Marjorie nice girl—vain, though—nice evening—nice boys—like Warren—Warren—Warren—what's-his-name—Warren—

She fell asleep.

v

To Bernice the next week was a revelation. With the feeling that people really enjoyed looking at her and listening to her came the foundation of self-confidence. Of course there were numerous mistakes at first. She did not know, for instance, that Draycott Deyo was studying for the ministry; she was unaware that he had cut in on her because he thought she was a quiet, reserved girl. Had she known these things she would not have treated him to the line which began "Hello, Shell Shock!" and continued with the bathtub story—"It takes a frightful lot of energy to fix my hair in the summer—there's so much of it—so I always fix it first and powder my face and put on my hat; then I get into the bathtub, and dress afterward. Don't you think that's the best plan?"

Though Draycott Deyo was in the throes of difficulties concerning baptisms by immersion and might possibly have seen a connection, it must be admitted that he did not. He considered feminine bathing an immoral subject, and gave her

some of his ideas on the depravity of modern society.

But to offset that unfortunate occurrence Bernice had several signal successes to her credit. Little Otis Ormonde pleaded off from a trip East and elected instead to follow her with a puppylike devotion, to the amusement of his crowd and to the irritation of G. Reece Stoddard, several of whose afternoon calls Otis completely ruined by the disgusting tenderness of the glances he bent on Bernice. He even told her the story of the two-by-four and the dressing room to show her how frightfully mistaken he and every one else had been in their first judgment of her. Bernice laughed off that incident with a slight sinking sensation.

Of all Bernice's conversation perhaps the best known and most universally approved was the line about the bobbing of her hair.

"Oh, Bernice, when you goin' to get the hair bobbed?"

"Day after tomorrow maybe," she would reply, laughing. "Will you come and see me? Because I'm counting on you, you know."

"Will we? You know! But you better hurry up."

Bernice, whose tonsorial intentions were strictly dishonorable, would laugh again.

"Pretty soon now. You'd be surprised."

But perhaps the most significant symbol of her success was the gray car of the hypercritical Warren McIntyre, parked daily in front of the

Harvey house. At first the parlor-maid was distinctly startled when he asked for Bernice instead of Marjorie; after a week of it she told the cook that Miss Bernice had gotta holda Miss Marjorie's best fella.

And Miss Bernice had. Perhaps it began with Warren's desire to rouse jealousy in Marjorie; perhaps it was the familiar though unrecognized strain of Marjorie in Bernice's conversation; perhaps it was both of these and something of sincere attraction besides. But somehow the collective mind of the younger set knew within a week that Marjorie's most reliable beau had made an amazing face-about and was giving an indisputable rush to Marjorie's guest. The question of the moment was how Marjorie would take it. Warren called Bernice on the 'phone twice a day, sent her notes, and they were frequently seen together in his roadster, obviously engrossed in one of these tense, significant conversations as to whether or not he was sincere.

Marjorie on being twitted only laughed. She said she was mighty glad that Warren had at last found someone who appreciated him. So the younger set laughed, too, and guessed that Marjorie didn't care and let it go at that.

One afternoon when there were only three days left of her visit Bernice was waiting in the hall for Warren, with whom she was going to a bridge party. She was in rather

a blissful mood, and when Marjorie—also bound for the party—appeared beside her and began casually to adjust her hat in the mirror, Bernice was utterly unprepared for anything in the nature of a clash. Marjorie did her work very coldly and succinctly in three sentences.

"You may as well get Warren out of your head," she said coldly.

"What?" Bernice was utterly astounded.

"You may as well stop making a fool of yourself over Warren McIntyre. He doesn't care a snap of his fingers about you."

For a tense moment they regarded each other—Marjorie scornful, aloof; Bernice astounded, half-angry, half-afraid. Then two cars drove up in front of the house and there was a riotous honking. Both of them gasped faintly, turned, and side by side hurried out.

All through the bridge party Bernice strove in vain to master a rising uneasiness. She had offended Marjorie, the sphinx of sphinxes. With the most wholesome and innocent intentions in the world she had stolen Marjorie's property. She felt suddenly and horribly guilty. After the bridge game, when they sat in an informal circle and the conversation became general, the storm gradually broke. Little Otis Ormonde inadvertently precipitated it.

"When you going back to kindergarten, Otis?" someone had asked.

"Me? Day Bernice gets her hair bobbed."

"Then your education's over," said Marjorie quickly. "That's only a bluff of hers. I should think you'd have realized."

"That a fact?" demanded Otis, giving Bernice a reproachful glance.

Bernice's ears burned as she tried to think up an effectual comeback. In the face of this direct attack her imagination was paralyzed.

"There's a lot of bluffs in the world," continued Marjorie quite pleasantly. "I should think you'd be young enough to know that, Otis."

"Well," said Otis, "maybe so. But gee! With a line like Bernice's—"

"Really?" yawned Marjorie. "What's her latest bon mot?"

No one seemed to know. In fact, Bernice, having trifled with her muse's beau, had said nothing memorable of late.

"Was that really all a line?" asked Roberta curiously.

Bernice hesitated. She felt that wit in some form was demanded of her, but under her cousin's suddenly frigid eyes she was completely incapacitated.

"I don't know," she stalled.

"Splush!" said Marjorie. "Admit it!"

Bernice saw that Warren's eyes had left a ukulele he had been tinkering with and were fixed on her questioningly.

"Oh, I don't know!" she repeated steadily. Her cheeks were glowing.

"Splush!" remarked Marjorie again.

"Come through, Bernice," urged Otis. "Tell her where to get off."

Bernice looked round again—she seemed unable to get away from Warren's eyes.

"I like bobbed hair," she said hurriedly, as if he had asked her a question, "and I intend to bob mine."

"When?" demanded Marjorie.

"Any time."

"No time like the present," suggested Roberta.

Otis jumped to his feet.

"Good stuff!" he cried. "We'll have a summer bobbing party. Sevier Hotel barbershop, I think you said."

In an instant all were on their feet. Bernice's heart throbbed violently.

"What?" she gasped.

Out of the group came Marjorie's voice, very clear and contemptuous.

"Don't worry—she'll back out!"

"Come on, Bernice!" cried Otis, starting toward the door.

Four eyes—Warren's and Marjorie's—stared at her, challenged her, defied her. For another second she wavered wildly.

"All right," she said swiftly, "I don't care if I do."

An eternity of minutes later, riding downtown through the late afternoon beside Warren, the others following in Roberta's car close behind, Bernice had all the sensations of Marie Antoinette bound for the guillotine in a tumbrel.

Vaguely she wondered why she did not cry out that it was all a mistake. It was all she could do to keep from clutching her hair with both hands to protect it from the suddenly hostile world. Yet she did neither. Even the thought of her mother was no deterrent now. This was the test supreme of her sportsmanship; her right to walk unchallenged in the starry heaven of popular girls.

Warren was moodily silent, and when they came to the hotel he drew up at the curb and nodded to Bernice to precede him out. Roberta's car emptied a laughing crowd into the shop, which presented two bold plate-glass windows to the street.

Bernice stood on the curb and looked at the sign, Sevier Barbershop. It was a guillotine indeed, and the hangman was the first barber, who, attired in a white coat and smoking a cigarette, leaned nonchalantly against the first chair. He must have heard of her; he must have been waiting all week, smoking eternal cigarettes beside that portentous, too-often-mentioned first chair. Would they blindfold her? No, but they would tie a white cloth round her neck lest any of her blood—nonsense—hair—should get on her clothes.

"All right, Bernice," said Warren quickly.

With her chin in the air she crossed the sidewalk, pushed open the swinging screen door, and giving not a glance to the uproarious, riotous row that occupied the waiting bench, went up to the first barber.

"I want you to bob my hair."

The first barber's mouth slid somewhat open. His cigarette dropped to the floor.

"Huh?"

"My hair—bob it!"

Refusing further preliminaries, Bernice took her seat on high. A man in the chair next to her turned on his side and gave her a glance, half lather, half amazement. One barber started and spoiled little Willy Schuneman's monthly haircut. Mr. O'Reilly in the last chair grunted and swore musically in ancient Gaelic as a razor bit into his cheek. Two bootblacks became wide-eyed and rushed for her feet. No, Bernice didn't care for a shine.

Outside a passer-by stopped and stared; a couple joined him; half a dozen small boys' noses sprang into life, flattened against the glass; and snatches of conversation borne on the summer breeze drifted in through the screen door.

"Lookada long hair on a kid!"

"Where'd yuh get 'at stuff? 'At's a bearded lady he just finished shavin'."

But Bernice saw nothing, heard nothing. Her only living sense told her that this man in the white coat had removed one tortoise-shell comb and then another; that his fingers were fumbling clumsily with unfamiliar hairpins; that this hair, this wonderful hair of hers, was going—she would never again feel its long voluptuous pull as it hung in a dark-brown glory down her back. For a second she was near breaking down, and then the picture before her swam mechanically into her vision—Marjorie's mouth curling in a faint ironic smile as if to say:

"Give up and get down! You tried to buck me and I called your bluff. You see you haven't got a prayer."

And some last energy rose up in Bernice, for she clinched her hands under the white cloth, and there was a curious narrowing of her eyes that Marjorie remarked on to someone long afterward.

Twenty minutes later the barber swung her round to face the mirror, and she flinched at the full extent of the damage that had been wrought. Her hair was not curly, and now it lay in lank lifeless blocks on both sides of her suddenly pale face. It was ugly as sin—she had known it would be ugly as sin. Her face's chief charm had been a Madonna-like simplicity. Now that was gone and she was—well, frightfully mediocre—not stagey; only ridiculous, like a Greenwich Villager who had left her spectacles at home.

As she climbed down from the chair she tried to smile—failed miserably. She saw two of the girls exchange glances; noticed Marjorie's mouth curved in attenuated mockery—and that Warren's eyes were suddenly very cold.

"You see"—her words fell into

an awkward pause—"I've done it."

"Yes, you've—done it," admitted Warren.

"Do you like it?"

There was a half-hearted "Sure" from two or three voices, another awkward pause, and then Marjorie turned swiftly and with serpentlike intensity to Warren.

"Would you mind running me down to the cleaners?" she asked. "I've simply got to get a dress there before supper. Roberta's driving right home and she can take the others."

Warren stared abstractedly at some infinite speck out the window. Then for an instant his eyes rested coldly on Bernice before they turned to Marjorie.

"Be glad to," he said slowly.

VI

Bernice did not fully realize the outrageous trap that had been set for her until she met her aunt's amazed glance just before dinner.

"Why, Bernice!"

"I've bobbed it, Aunt Josephine."

"Why, child!"

"Do you like it?"

"Why, Ber-nice!"

"I suppose I've shocked you."

"No, but what'll Mrs. Deyo think tomorrow night? Bernice, you should have waited until after the Deyos' dance—you should have waited if you wanted to do that."

"It was sudden, Aunt Josephine. Anyway, why does it matter to

Mrs. Deyo particularly?"

"Why, child," cried Mrs. Harvey, "in her paper on 'The Foibles of the Younger Generation' that she read at the last meeting of the Thursday Club she devoted fifteen minutes to bobbed hair. It's her pet abomination. And the dance is for you and Marjorie!"

"I'm sorry."

"Oh, Bernice, what'll your mother say? She'll think I let you do it."

"I'm sorry."

Dinner was an agony. She had made a hasty attempt with a curling iron, and burned her finger and much hair. She could see that her aunt was both worried and grieved, and her uncle kept saying, "Well, I'll be darned!" over and over in a hurt and faintly hostile tone. And Marjorie sat very quietly, intrenched behind a faint smile, a faintly mocking smile.

Somehow she got through the evening. Three boys called; Marjorie disappeared with one of them, and Bernice made a listless unsuccessful attempt to entertain the two others—sighed thankfully as she climbed the stairs to her room at half past ten. What a day!

When she had undressed for the night the door opened and Marjorie came in.

"Bernice," she said, "I'm awfully sorry about the Deyo dance. I'll give you my word of honor I'd forgotten all about it."

" 'Sall right," said Bernice shortly. Standing before the mirror she passed her comb slowly through her short hair.

"I'll take you downtown tomorrow," continued Marjorie, "and the hairdresser'll fix it so you'll look slick. I didn't imagine you'd go through with it. I'm really mighty sorry."

"Oh, 'sall right!"

"Still it's your last night, so I suppose it won't matter much."

Then Bernice winced as Marjorie tossed her own hair over her shoulders and began to twist it slowly into two long blonde braids until in her cream-colored negligee she looked like a delicate painting of some Saxon princess. Fascinated, Bernice watched the braids grow. Heavy and luxurious they were, moving under the supple fingers like restive snakes—and to Bernice remained this relic and the curling iron and a tomorrow full of eyes. She could see G. Reece Stoddard, who liked her, assuming his Harvard manner and telling his dinner partner that Bernice shouldn't have been allowed to go to the movies so much; she could see Draycott Deyo exchanging glances with his mother and then being conscientiously charitable to her. But then perhaps by tomorrow Mrs. Deyo would have heard the news; would send round an icy little note requesting that she fail to appear—and behind her back they would all laugh and know that Marjorie had made a fool of her; that her chance at beauty had been sacrified to the jealous whim of a selfish girl. She sat down suddenly before the mirror, biting the inside of her cheek.

"I like it," she said with an effort. "I think it'll be becoming."

Marjorie smiled.

"It looks all right. For heaven's sake, don't let it worry you!"

"I won't."

"Good night, Bernice."

But as the door closed something snapped within Bernice. She sprang dynamically to her feet, clinching her hands, then swiftly and noiselessly crossed over to her bed and from underneath it dragged out her suitcase. Into it she tossed toilet articles and a change of clothing. Then she turned to her trunk and quickly dumped in two drawerfuls of lingerie and summer dresses. She moved quietly, but with deadly efficiency, and in three-quarters of an hour her trunk was locked and strapped and she was fully dressed in a becoming new traveling suit that Marjorie had helped her pick out.

Sitting down at her desk she wrote a short note to Mrs. Harvey, in which she briefly outlined her reasons for going. She sealed it, addressed it, and laid it on her pillow. She glanced at her watch. The train left at one, and she knew that if she walked down to the Marborough Hotel two blocks away she could easily get a taxicab.

Suddenly she drew in her breath sharply and an expression flashed into her eyes that a practiced character reader might have connected vaguely with the set look she had worn in the barber's chair—somehow a development of it. It was quite a new look for Bernice—and it carried consequences.

She went stealthily to the bureau, picked up an article that lay there, and turning out all the lights stood quietly until her eyes became accustomed to the darkness. Softly she pushed open the door to Marjorie's room. She heard the quiet, even breathing of an untroubled conscience asleep.

She was by the bedside now, very deliberate and calm. She acted swiftly. Bending over she found one of the braids of Marjorie's hair, followed it up with her hand to the point nearest the head, and then holding it a little slack so that the sleeper would feel no pull, she reached down with the shears and severed it. With the pigtail in her hand she held her breath. Marjorie had muttered something in her sleep. Bernice deftly amputated the other braid, paused for an instant, and then flitted swiftly and silently back to her own room.

Downstairs she opened the big front door, closed it carefully behind her, and feeling oddly happy and exuberant stepped off the porch into the moonlight, swinging her heavy grip like a shopping bag. After a minute's brisk walk she discovered that her left hand still held the two blonde braids. She laughed unexpectedly—had to shut her mouth hard to keep from emitting an absolute peal. She was passing

Warren's house now, and on the impulse she set down her baggage, and swinging the braids like pieces of rope flung them at the wooden porch, where they landed with a slight thud. She laughed again, no longer restraining herself.

"Huh!" she giggled wildly. "Scalp the selfish thing!"

Then picking up her suitcase she set off at a half-run down the moonlit street.

An Epitaph

WALTER DE LA MARE

Here lies a most beautiful lady,
Light of step and heart was she;
I think she was the most beautiful lady
That ever was in the West Country.

But beauty vanishes; beauty passes;
However rare—rare it be;
And when I crumble, who will remember
This lady of the West Country?

The Answer

"Fifteen minutes!" . . . The loudspeakers blared on the flight deck, boomed below, and murmured on the bridge where the brass was assembling. The length of the carrier was great. Consonants from distant horns came belatedly to every ear, and metal fabric set up echoes besides. So the phrase stuttered through the ship and over the sea. Fifteen minutes to the bomb test.

Major General Marcus Scott walked to the cable railing around the deck and looked at the very blue morning. The ship's engines had stopped and she lay still, aimed west toward the target island like an arrow in a drawn bow.

Men passing saluted. The general returned the salutes, bringing a weathered hand to a lofty forehead, to straight, coal-black hair above gray eyes and the hawk nose of an Indian.

His thoughts veered to the weather. The far surface of the Pacific was lavender; the near-by water

seen deeper, a lucent violet. White clouds passed gradually—clouds much of a size and shape—with cobalt avenues between. The general, to whom the sky was more familiar than the sea, marveled at that mechanized appearance. It was as if some cosmic weather engine—east, and below the Equator—puffed clouds from Brobdingnagian stacks and sent them rolling over the earth, as regular and even-spaced as the white snorts of a climbing locomotive.

He put away the image. Such fantasy belonged in another era, when he had been a young man at West Point, a brilliant young man, more literary than military, a young man fascinated by the "soldier poets" of the first World War. The second, which he had helped to command in the air, produced no romanticists. Here a third war was in the making, perhaps, a third that might put an end to poetry forever.

"Ten minutes! All personnel complete checks, take assigned stations for test!"

General Scott went across the iron deck on scissoring legs that seemed to hurry the tall man without themselves hurrying. Sailors had finished stringing the temporary cables which, should a freak buffet from the H-bomb reach the area, would prevent them from being tossed overboard. They were gathering, now, to watch. Marc Scott entered the carrier's island and hastened to the bridge on turning steps of metal, not using the shined brass rail.

Admiral Stanforth was there—anvil shoulders, marble hair, feldspar complexion. Pouring coffee for Senator Blaine with a good-host chuckle and that tiger look in the corners of his eyes. "Morning, Marc! Get any sleep at all?" He gave the general no time to answer. "This is General Scott, gentlemen. In charge of today's drop. Commands base on Sangre Islands. Senator Blaine—"

The senator had the trappings of office: the *embonpoint* and shrewd eyes, the pince-nez on a ribbon, the hat with the wide brim that meant a Western or Southern senator. He had the William Jennings Bryan voice. But these were for his constituents.

The man who used the voice said genuinely, "General, I'm honored. Your record in the Eighth Air Force is one we're almost too proud of to mention in front of you."

"Thank you, sir."

"You know Doctor Trumbul?"

Trumbul was thin and thirty, an all-brown scholar whose brown eyes were so vivid the rest seemed but a background for his eyes. His hand clasped Scott's. "All too well! I flew with Marc Scott when we dropped Thermonuclear Number Eleven—on a parachute!"

There was some laughter; they knew about that near-disastrous test.

"How's everybody at Los Alamos?" the general asked.

The physicist shrugged. "Same. They'll feel better later today—if this one comes up to expectations."

The admiral was introducing again. "Doctor Antheim, General. Antheim's from MIT. He's also the best amateur magician I ever saw perform. Too bad you came aboard so late last night."

Antheim was as quietly composed as a family physician—a big man in a gray suit.

"Five minutes!" the loudspeaker proclaimed.

You could see the lonely open ocean, the sky, the cumulus clouds. But the target island—five miles long and jungle-painted—lay over the horizon. An island created by volcanic cataclysm millions of years ago and destined this day to vanish in a man-patented calamity. Somewhere a hundred thousand feet above, Scott's own ship, a B-III, was moving at more than seven hundred miles an hour, closing on an imaginary point from which, along an imaginary line, a big bomb would curve earthward, never to hit, but utterly to devastate. You could not see his B-111 and you would probably not even see the high, far-off tornadoes of smoke when, the bomb away, she let go with her rockets to hurtle off even faster from the expanding sphere of blast.

"Personally," Antheim, the MIT scientist, was saying to General Larsen, "it's my feeling that whether or not your cocker is a fawning type depends on your attitude as a dog owner. I agree, all cockers have Saint Bernard appetites. Nevertheless, I'm sold on spaniels. In all the field trials last autumn—"

Talking about dogs. Well, why not? Random talk was the best antidote for tension, for the electrically counted minutes that stretched unbearably because of their measurement. Scott had a dog—his kids had one, rather: Pompey, the mutt, whose field trials took place in the yards and playgrounds of Baltimore, Maryland, in the vicinity of Millbrook Road. He wondered what would be happening at home —where Ellen would be—he calculated time belts, the hour-wide, orange-peel-shaped sections into which man had carved his planet. Be evening on Millbrook Road—

John Farrier arrived—Farrier, of the great Farrier Corporation. His pale blue eyes looked out over the ship's flat deck toward the west, the target. But he was saying to somebody, in his crisp yet not uncourteous voice, "I consider myself something of a connoisseur in the matter of honey. We have our own apiary at Hobe Sound. Did you ever taste antidesma honey? Or the honey gathered from palmetto flowers?"

"Two minutes!"

The count-down was the hardest part of a weapons test. What went before was work—sheer work, detailed, exhausting. But what came after had excitements, real and potential, like hazardous exploring, the general thought; you never knew precisely what would ensue. Not precisely.

Tension, Scott repeated to himself. And he thought, *Why do I feel sad? Is it prescience of failure? Will we finally manage to produce a dud?*

Fatigue, he answered himself. Setting up this one had been a colossal chore. They called it Bugaboo—Operation Bugaboo in Test Series Avalanche. Suddenly he wished Bugaboo wouldn't go off.

"One minute! All goggles in place! Exposed personnel without goggles, sit down, turn backs toward west, cover eyes with hands!"

Before he blacked out the world, he took a last look at the sky, the sea—and the sailors, wheeling, sitting, covering their eyes. Then he put on the goggles. The obsidian lenses brought absolute dark. From habit, he cut his eyes back and forth to make certain there was no leak of light—light that could damage the retina.

"Ten seconds!"

The ship drew a last deep breath

and held it. In an incredibly long silence, the general mused on thousands upon thousands of other men in other ships, ashore and in the air, who now were also holding back breathing.

"Five!"

An imbecile notion flickered in the general's brain and expired: He could leap up and cry "Stop!" He still could. A word from Stanforth. A button pressed. The whole she-bang would chute on down, unexploded. And umpteen million dollars' worth of taxpayers' money would be wasted by that solitary syllable of his.

"Four!"

Still, the general thought, his lips smiling, his heart frozen, why should they—or anybody—*be doing this?*

"Three seconds . . . two . . . one . . . zero!"

Slowly, the sky blew up.

On the horizon, a supersun grabbed up degrees of diameter and rose degrees. The sea, ship, praying sailors became as plain as they had been bare-eyed in full sun, then plainer still. Eyes, looking through the inky glass, saw the universe stark white. A hundred-times-sun-sized sun mottled itself with lesser whiteness, bulked up, became the perfect sphere, ascending hideously and setting forth on the Pacific a molten track from ship to livid self. Tumors of light more brilliant than the sun sprang up on the mathematical sphere; yet these, less blazing than the fireball, appeared as

blacknesses.

The thing swelled and swelled and rose; nonetheless, instant miles of upthrust were diminished by the expansion. Abruptly, it exploded around itself a white lewd ring, a halo.

For a time there was no air beneath it, only the rays and neutrons in vacuum. The atmosphere beyond —incandescent, compressed harder than steel—moved toward the spectators. No sound.

The fireball burned within itself and around itself, burnt the sea away—a hole in it—and a hole in the planet. It melted part way, lop-sided, threw out a cubic mile of fire this way—a scarlet asteroid, that.

To greet the birthing of a new, brief star, the regimental sky hung a bunting on every cloud. The mushroom formed quietly, immensely, and in haste; it towered, spread, and the incandescent air hurtled at the watchers on the circumferences. In the mushroom new fire burst forth, cubic miles of phosphorpale flame. The general heard Antheim sigh. That would be the "igniter effect," the new thing, to set fire, infinitely, in the wake of the fire blown out by the miles-out blast. A hellish bit of physics.

Again, again, again the thorium-lithium pulse! Each time—had it been other than jungle and sea; had it been a city, Baltimore—the urban tinder, and the people, would have hair-fired in the debris.

The mushroom climbed on its stalk, the ten-mile circle of what had been part of earth. It split the atmospheric layers and reached for the purple dark, that the flying general knew, where the real sun was also unbearably bright.

Mouths agape, goggles now dangling, the men on the bridge of the *Ticonderoga* could look naked-eyed at the sky's exploded rainbows and seething prismatics.

"Stand by for the blast wave!"

It came like the shadow of eclipse. The carrier shuddered. Men sagged, spun on their bottoms. The general felt the familiar compression, a thousand boxing gloves, padded but hitting squarely every part of his body at once.

Then Antheim and Trumbul were shaking hands.

"Congratulations! That ought to be—about it!"

It for what? The enemy? A city? Humanity?

"Magnificent," said Senator Blaine. He added, "We seem O.K."

"Good thing too," a voice laughed. "A dozen of the best sets of brains in America, right in this one spot."

The general thought about that. Two of the world's leading nuclear physicists, the ablest member of the Joint Chiefs of Staff, a senator wise for all his vaudeville appearance, an unbelievably versatile industrialist, the Navy's best tactician. Good brains. But what an occupation for human brains!

Unobtrusively he moved to the iron stairs—the "ladder." Let the good brains and the sightseers gape at the kaleidoscope aloft. He hurried to his assigned office.

An hour later he had received the important reports.

His B-111 was back on the field, "hot," but not dangerous; damaged, but not severely; the crew in good shape. Celebrating, Major Stokely had bothered to add.

Two drones lost; three more landed in unapproachable condition. One photo recon plane had been hit by a flying chunk of something eighteen miles from ground zero and eight minutes—if the time was right—after the blast. Something that had been thrown mighty high or somehow remained aloft a long while. Wing damage and radioactivity; but, again, no personnel injured.

Phones rang. Messengers came—sailors—quick, quiet, polite. The *Ticonderoga* was moving, moving swiftly, in toward the place where nothing was, in under the colored bomb clouds.

He had a sensation that something was missing, that more was to be done, that news awaited—which he attributed again to tiredness. Tiredness: what a general was supposed never to feel—and the burden that settled on every pair of starred shoulders. He sighed and picked up the book he had read in empty spaces of the preceding night: Thoreau's *Walden Pond*.

Why had he taken Thoreau on this trip? He knew the answer. To be as far as possible, in one way, from the torrent of technology in mid-Pacific; to be as close as possible to a proper view of Atomic-Age Man, in a different way. But now he closed the book as if it had blank pages. After all, Thoreau couldn't take straight Nature, himself; a couple of years beside his pond and he went back to town and lived in Emerson's backyard. For the general that was an aggrieved and aggrieving thought.

Lieutenant Tobey hurried in from the next office. "Something special on TLS. Shall I switch it?"

His nerves tightened. He had expected "something special" on his most restricted wire, without a reason for the expectation. He picked up the instrument when the light went red. "Scott here."

"Rawson. Point L 15."

"Right." That would be instrument site near the mission school on Tempest Island.

"Matter of Import Z." Which meant an emergency.

"I see." General Scott felt almost relieved. Something was wrong; to know even that was better than to have a merely mystifying sense of wrongness.

Rawson—Major Dudley Rawson, the general's cleverest Intelligence officer, simply said, "Import Z, and, I'd say, General, the Z Grade."

"Can't clarify?"

"No, sir."

General Scott marveled for a moment at the tone of Rawson's voice: it was high and the syllables shook. He said, "Right, Raw. Be over." He leaned back in his chair and spoke to the lieutenant, "Would you get me Captain Elverson? I'd like a whirlybird ride."

The helicopter deposited the general in the center of the playing field where the natives at the mission school learned American games. Rawson and two others were waiting. The general gave the customary grateful good-by to his naval escort; then waited for the racket of the departing helicopter to diminish.

He observed that Major Rawson, a lieutenant he did not know, and a technical sergeant were soaked with perspiration. But that scarcely surprised him; the sun was now high and the island steamed formidably.

Rawson said, "I put it through Banjo, direct to you, sir. Took the liberty. There's been a casualty."

"Lord!" The general shook his head. "Who?"

"I'd rather show you, sir." The major's eyes traveled to the road that led from the field, through banyan trees, toward the mission. Corrugated-metal roofs sparkled behind the trees, and on the road in the shade a jeep waited.

The general started for the vehicle. "Just give me what particulars you can—"

"I'd rather you saw—it—for yourself."

General Scott climbed into the car, sat, looked closely at the major.

He'd seen funk, seen panic. This was that—and more. The three men sweated like horses, yet they were pallid. They shook—and made no pretense of hiding or controlling it. A "casualty"—and they were soldiers! No casualty could—

"You said 'it,'" the general said. "Just what—"

"For the love of God, don't ask me to explain! It's just behind the mission buildings." Major Rawson tapped the sergeant's shoulder, "Can you drive O.K., Sam?"

The man jerked his head and started the motor. The jeep moved.

The general had impressions of buildings, or brown boys working in a banana grove, and native girls flapping along in such clothes as missionaries consider moral. Then they entered a colonnade of tree trunks which upheld the jungle canopy.

He was afraid in some new way. He must not show it. He concentrated on seeming not to concentrate.

The jeep stopped. Panting slightly, Rawson stepped out, pushed aside the fronds of a large fern tree and hurried along a leafy tunnel. "Little glade up here. That's where the casualty dropped."

"Who found—it?"

"The missionary's youngest boy. Kid named Ted. His dad too. The padre—or whatever the Devoted Brethren call 'em."

The glade appeared—a clear pool of water bordered by terrestrial orchids. A man lay in their way, face down, his clerical collar unbuttoned, his arms extended, hands clasped, breath issuing in hoarse groans.

From maps, memoranda, somewhere, the general remembered the man's name. "You mean Reverend Simms is the victim?" he asked in amazement.

"No," said Rawson; "up ahead." He led the general around the bole of a jacaranda tree. "There."

For a speechless minute the general stood still. On the ground, almost at his feet, in the full sunshine, lay the casualty.

"Agnostic," the general had been called by many; "mystic," by more; "natural philosopher," by devoted chaplains who had served with him. But he was not a man of orthodox religion.

What lay on the fringe of purple flowers was recognizable. He could not, would not, identify it aloud.

Behind him, the major, the lieutenant, and the sergeant were waiting shakily for him to name it. Near them, prostrate on the earth, was the missionary—who had already named it and commenced to worship.

It was motionless. The beautiful human face slept in death; the alabastrine body was relaxed in death; the unimaginable eyes were closed and the immense white wings were folded. It was an angel.

The general could bring himself to say, in a soft voice, only, "It looks like one."

The three faces behind him were distracted. "It's an angel," Rawson said in a frantic tone. "And everything we've done, and thought, and believed is nuts! Science is nuts! Who knows, now, what the next move will be?"

The sergeant had knelt and was crossing himself. A babble of repentance issued from his lips—as if he were at confessional. Seeing the general's eyes on him, he interrupted himself to murmur, "I was brought up Catholic." Then, turning back to the figure, with the utmost fright, he crossed himself and went on in a compulsive listing of his sad misdemeanors.

The lieutenant, a buck-toothed young man, was now laughing in a morbid way. A way that was the sure prelude to hysteria.

"Shut up!" the general said; then strode to the figure among the flowers and reached down for its pulse.

At that, Reverend Simms made a sound near to a scream and leaped to his feet. His garments were stained with the black humus in which he had lain; his clerical collar flapped loosely at his neck.

"Don't you even touch it! Heretic! You are not fit to be here! You —and your martial kind—your scientists! Do you not see what you have done? Your last infernal bomb has shot down Gabriel, angel of the Lord! This is the end of the world!" His voice tore his throat. "And you are responsible! You are the destroyers!"

The general could not say but that every word the missionary had spoken was true. The beautiful being might indeed be Gabriel. Cer-

tainly it was an unearthly creature. The general felt a tendency, if not to panic, at least to take seriously the idea that he was now dreaming or had gone mad. Human hysteria, however, was a known field, and one with which he was equipped to deal.

He spoke sharply, authoritatively, somehow keeping his thoughts a few syllables ahead of his ringing voice, "Reverend Simms, I am a soldier in charge here. If your surmise is correct, God will be my judge. But you have not examined this pathetic victim. That is neither human nor Christian. Suppose it is only hurt, and needs medical attention? What sort of Samaritans would we be, then, to let it perish here in the heat? You may also be mistaken, and that would be a greater cruelty. Suppose it is not what you so logically assume? Suppose it merely happens to be a creature like ourselves, from some real but different planet—thrown, say, from its space-voyaging vehicle by the violence of the morning test?"

The thought, rushing into the general's mind from nowhere, encouraged him. He was at that time willing to concede the likelihood that he stood in the presence of a miracle—and a miracle of the most horrifying sort, since the angel was seemingly dead. But to deal with men, with their minds, and even his own thought process, he needed a less appalling possibility to set alongside apparent fact. If he were to accept the miracle, he would be obliged first to alter his own deep and hard-won faith, along with its corollaries—and that would mean a change in the general's very personality. It would take pain, and time. Meanwhile there were men to deal with—men in mortal frenzy.

The missionary heard him vaguely, caught the suggestion that the general might doubt the being on the ground to be Gabriel, and burst into grotesque, astounding laughter. He rushed from the glade.

After his antic departure, the general said grimly, "That man has about lost his mind! A stupid way to behave, if what he believes is the case!" Then, in drill-sergeant tones, he barked, "Sergeant! Take a leg. . . . Lieutenant, the other. . . . Rawson, help me here."

He took gentle hold. The flesh, if it was flesh, felt cool, but not yet cold. When he lifted, the shoulder turned easily; it was less heavy than he had expected. The other men, slowly, dubiously, took stations and drew nerving breaths.

"See to it, men," the general ordered—as if it were mere routine and likely to be overlooked by second-rate soldiers—"that those wings don't drag on the ground! Let's go!"

He could observe and think a little more analytically as they carried the being toward the jeep. The single garment worn by the angel was snow-white and exquisitely pleated. The back and shoulder muscles were obviously of great

power, and constructed to beat the great wings. They were, he gathered, operational wings, not vestigial. Perhaps the creature came from a small planet where gravity was so slight that these wings sufficed for flying about. That was at least thinkable.

A different theory which he entertained briefly—because he was a soldier—seemed impossible on close scrutiny. The creature they carried from the glade was not a fake—not some biological device of the enemy fabricated to startle the Free World. What they were carrying could not have been man-made, unless the Reds had moved centuries ahead of everyone else in the science of biology. This was no hybrid. The angel had lived, grown, moved its wings, and been of one substance.

It filled the back seat of the jeep. The general said, "I'll drive. . . . Lieutenant . . . Sergeant, meet me at the field. . . . Raw, you get HQ again on a Z line and have them send a helicopter. Two extra passengers for the trip out, tell them. Have General Budford fly in now, if possible. Give no information except that these suggestions are from me."

"Yes, sir."

"Then black out all communications from this island."

"Yes, sir."

"If the Devoted Brethren Mission won't shut its radio off, see that it stops working."

The major nodded, waited a moment, and walked down the jungle track in haunted obedience.

"I'll drive it," the general repeated.

He felt long and carefully for a pulse. Nothing. The body was growing rigid. He started the jeep. Once he glanced back at his incredible companion. The face was perfectly serene; the lurching of the vehicle, for all his care in driving, had parted the lips.

He reached the shade at the edge of the playing field where the jeep had first been parked. He cut the motor. The school compound had been empty of persons when he passed this time. There had been no one on the road; not even any children. Presently the mission bell began to toll slowly. Reverend Simms, he thought, would be holding services. That probably explained the absence of people, the hush in the heat of midday, the jade quietude.

He pulled out a cigarette, hesitated to smoke it. He wondered if there were any further steps which he should take. For his own sake, he again carefully examined the angel, and he was certain afterward only that it was like nothing earthly, that it could be an angel and that it had died, without any external trace of the cause. Concussion, doubtless.

He went over his rationalizations. If men with wings like this did exist on some small, remote planet; if any of them had visited Earth in rocket ships in antiquity, it would explain a great deal about what he had thitherto called "superstitious" beliefs. Fiery chariots, old prophets being taken to heaven by angels, and much else.

If the Russians had "made" it and dropped it to confuse the Free World, then it was all over; they were already too far ahead scientifically.

He lighted the cigarette. Deep in the banyans, behind the screens of thick, aerial roots and oval leaves, a twig snapped. His head swung fearfully. He half expected another form—winged, clothed in light—to step forth and demand the body of its fallen colleague.

A boy emerged—a boy of about nine, sun-tanned, big-eyed, and muscular in the stringy way of boys. He wore only a T-shirt and shorts; both bore marks of his green progress through the jungle.

"You have it," he said. Not accusatively. Not even very emotionally. "Where's father?"

"Are you—"

"I'm Ted Simms." The brown gaze was suddenly excited. "And you're a general!"

The man nodded. "General Scott." He smiled. "You've seen"—he moved his head gently toward the rear seat—"my passenger before?"

"I saw him fall. I was there, getting Aunt Cora a bunch of flowers."

The general remained casual, in tone of voice, "Tell me about it."

"Can I sit in the jeep? I never rode in one yet."

"Sure."

The boy climbed in, looked intently at the angel, and sat beside the general. He sighed. "Sure is handsome, an angel," said the boy. "I was just up there at the spring, picking flowers, because Aunt Cora likes flowers quite a lot, and she was mad because I didn't do my arithmetic well. We had seen the old test shot, earlier, and we're sick and tired of them, anyhow! They scare the natives and make them go back to their old, heathen customs. Well, I heard this whizzing up in the air, and down it came, wings out, trying to fly, but only spiraling, sort of. Like a bird with an arrow through it. You've seen that kind of wobbly flying?"

"Yes."

"It came down. It stood there a second and then it sat."

"Sat?" The general's lips felt dry. He licked them. "Did it—see you?"

"See me? I was right beside it."

The boy hesitated and the general was on the dubious verge of prodding when the larklike voice continued, "It sat there crying for a while."

"Crying!"

"Of course. The H-bomb must of hurt it something awful. It was crying. You could hear it sobbing and trying to get its breath even before it touched the ground. It cried, and then it looked at me and

it stopped crying and it smiled. It had a real wonderful smile when it smiled."

The boy paused. He had begun to look with fascination at the dashboard instruments.

"Then what?" the general murmured.

"Can I switch on the lights?" He responded eagerly to the nod and talked as he switched the lights, tried the horn. "Then not much. It smiled and I didn't know what to do. I never saw an angel before. Father says he knows people who have, though. So I said 'Hello,' and it said 'Hello,' and it said, after a minute or so, 'I was a little too late,' and tears got in its eyes again and it leaned back and kind of tucked in its wings and, after a while, it died."

"You mean the—angel—spoke to you—in English?"

"Don't they know all languages?" the boy asked, smiling.

"I couldn't say," the general replied. "I suppose they do."

He framed another question, and heard a sharp "Look out!" There was a thwack in the foliage. Feet ran. A man grunted. He threw himself in front of the boy.

Reverend Simms had crept from the banyan, carrying a shotgun, intent, undoubtedly, on preventing the removal of the unearthly being from his island. The lieutenant and sergeant, rounding a turn in the road, had seen him, thrown a stone to divert him, and rushed him. There was almost no scuffle.

The general jumped down from the jeep, took the gun, looked into the missionary's eyes and saw no sanity there—just fury and bafflement.

"You've had a terrible shock, Dominie," he said, putting the gun in the front of the jeep. "We all have. But this is a thing for the whole world, if it's what you believe it to be. Not just for here and now and you. We shall have to take it away and ascertain—"

"Ye of little faith!" the missionary intoned.

The general pitied the man and suddenly envied him; it was comforting to be so sure about anything.

Comforting. But was such comfort valid or was it specious? He looked toward the jeep. Who could doubt now?

He could. It was his way of being—to doubt at first. It was also his duty, as he saw duty.

Rawson, looking old and deathly ill, came down the cart track in the green shadows. But he had regained something of his manner. "All set, Marc. No word will leave here. Plane's on the way; General Budford's flying in himself. Old Bloodshed said it better be Z priority." The major eyed the white, folded wings. "I judge he'll be satisfied."

General Scott grinned slightly. "Have a cigarette, Raw." He sat beside the praying missionary with some hope of trying to bring the man's mind from dread and ecstasy back to the human problems —the awesome, unpredictable human enigmas—which would be involved by this "casualty."

One thing was sure. The people who had felt for years that man didn't yet know enough to experiment with the elemental forces of Nature were going to feel entirely justified when this story rocked the planet.

If, the general thought on with a sudden, icy feeling, it wasn't labeled Top Secret and concealed forever.

That could be. The possibility appalled him. He looked up angrily at the hot sky. No bomb effects were visible here; only the clouds' cyclorama toiling across the blue firmament. Plenty of Top Secrets up there still, he thought.

The President of the United States was awakened after a conference. When they told him, he reached for his dressing gown, started to get up, and then sat on the edge of his bed. "Say that again."

They said it again.

The President's white hair was awry, his eyes had the sleep-hung look of a man in need of more rest. His brain, however, came wide awake.

"Let me have that in the right sequence. The Bugaboo test brought down, on Tempest Island, above Salandra Strait, an angel—or something that looked human and had wings, anyhow. Who's outside and who brought that over?"

His aide, Smith, said, "Weatherby, Colton, and Dwane."

The Secretary of State. The chairman of the Joint Chiefs of Staff. The chairman of the Atomic Energy Commission.

"Sure of communications? Could be a terrific propaganda gag. The Reds could monkey with our wave lengths—" The President gestured, put on the dressing gown.

"Quadruple-checked. Budford talked on the scrambler. Also Marc Scott, who made the first investigation of the—er—casualty." Smith's peaceful, professorish face was composed, still, but his eyes were wrong.

"Good men."

"None better. Admiral Stanforth sent independent verification. Green, of AEC, reported in on Navy and Air Force channels. Captain Wilmot, ranking Navy chaplain out there, swore it was a genuine angel. It must be—something, Mr. President! Something all right!"

"Where is it now?"

"On the way, naturally. Scott put it aboard a B-111. Due in here by three o'clock. Coffee waiting in the office."

"I'll go out, Clem. Get the rest of the Cabinet up and here. The rest of the JCS. Get Ames at CIA. This thing has got to stay absolutely restricted till we know more."

"Of course."

"Scott with it?"

"Budford."   Smith   smiled.

"Ranked Scott. Some mission, huh? An angel. Imagine!"

"All my life I've been a God-fearing man," the President replied. "But I can't imagine. We'll wait till it's here." He started toward the door where other men waited tensely. He paused. "Whatever it is, it's the end to—what has been, these last fifteen years. And that's a good thing." The President smiled.

It was, perhaps, the longest morning in the history of the capital. Arrangements had been made for the transportation of the cargo secretly but swiftly from the airfield to the White House. A secret but celebrated group of men had been chosen to examine the cargo. They kept flying in to Washington and arriving in limousines all morning. But they did not know why they had been summoned. Reporters could not reach a single Cabinet member. No one available at State or the Pentagon, at AEC or CIA could give any information at all. So there were merely conjectures, which led to rumors:

Something had gone wrong with an H-bomb.

The President had been assassinated.

Russia had sent an ultimatum.

Hitler had reappeared.

Toward the end of that morning, a call came which the President took in person. About thirty men watched his face, and all of them became afraid.

When he hung up he said un-steadily, "Gentlemen, the B-111 flying it in is overdue at San Francisco and presumed down at sea. All agencies have commenced a search. I have asked, meantime, that those officers and scientists who saw, examined, or had any contact with the —strange being be flown here immediately. Unless they find the plane and recover what it carried, that's all we can do."

"The whole business," Dwane said, after a long silence, "could be a hoax. If the entire work party engaged in Test Series Avalanche formed a conspiracy—"

"Why should they?" asked Weatherby.

"Because, Mr. Secretary," Dwane answered, "a good many people on this globe think mankind has carried this atomic-weapons business too far."

General Colton smiled. "I can see a few frightened men conspiring against the world and their own government, with some half-baked idealistic motive. But not a fleet and an army. Not, for that matter, Stanforth or Scott. Not Scott. Not a hoax."

"They'll report here tonight, gentlemen, in any case." The President walked to a window and looked out at the spring green of a lawn and the budding trees above. "We'll know then what they learned, at least. Luncheon?"

On the evening of the third day afterward, Marc Scott greeted the President formally in his office. At the President's suggestion they went out together, in the warm April twilight, to a low-walled terrace.

"The reason I asked you to come to the White House again," the President began, "was to talk to you entirely alone. I gathered, not from your words, but from your manner at recent meetings, General, that you had some feelings about this matter."

"Feelings, Mr. President?" He had feelings. But would the statesman understand or regard them as naïve, as childish?

The President chuckled and ran his fingers through his thick white hair in a hesitant way that suggested he was uncertain of himself. "I have a fearful decision to make." He sighed and was silent for several seconds as he watched the toy silhouettes of three jet planes move across the lemon-yellow sky. "There are several courses I can take. I can order complete silence about the whole affair. Perhaps a hundred people know. If I put it on a Top Secret basis, rumors may creep out. But they could be scotched. The world would then be deprived of any real knowledge of your—angel.

"Next, I could take up the matter with the other heads of state. The friendly ones." He paused and then nodded his head unsurely. "Yes. Even the Russians. And the satellite governments. With heaven knows what useful effect! Finally, I could simply announce to the world that you and a handful of others found the body of what appears to have been an angel, and that it was irretrievably lost while being flown to Washington."

Since the President stopped with those words, Marc said, "Yes, sir."

"Three equally poor possibilities. If it was an angel—a divine messenger—and our test destroyed it, I have, I feel, no moral right whatever to keep the world from knowing. Irrespective of any consequences."

"The consequences!" Marc Scott murmured.

"You can imagine them!" The President uncrossed his legs, stretched, felt for a cigarette, took a light from the general. "Tremendous, incalculable, dangerous consequences! All truly and decently religious people would be given a tremendous surge of hope, along with an equal despair over the angel's death and the subsequent loss of the—body. Fanatics would literally go mad. The news could produce panic, civil unrest, bloodshed. And we have nothing to show. No proof. Nothing tangible. The enemy could use the whole story for propaganda in a thousand evil ways. Being atheistic, they would proclaim it an American madness— what you will. Even clergymen, among themselves, are utterly unagreed, when they are told the situation."

"I can imagine."

The President smiled a little and went on, "I called half a dozen leaders to Washington. Cardinal Thrace. Bishop Neuermann. Father Bolder. Reverend Matthews. Every solitary man had a different reaction. When they became assured that I meant precisely what I said, they began a theological battle"— the President chuckled ruefully at the memory—"that went on until they left, and looked good for a thousand years. Whole denominations would split! Most of the clergy, however, agreed on one point: it was not an angel."

The general was startled. "Not an angel? Then, what—"

"Because it died. Because it was killed or destroyed. Angels, General, are immortal. They are not human flesh and blood. No. I think you can say that, by and large, the churches would never assent to the idea that the being you saw was Gabriel or any other angel."

"I hadn't thought of that."

"I had," the President replied. "You are not, General, among the orthodox believers, I take it."

"No, Mr. President."

"So I judged. Well, let me get to my reason for asking you to confer privately with me. The churchmen debated hotly—to use the politest possible phrase—over the subject. But the scientists—whom I also consulted"—he drew a breath and swallowed, like a man whose memory of hard-controlled temper is still painful—"the scientists were at scandalous loggerheads. Two of them actually came to blows! I've heard every theory you can conceive of, and a lot I couldn't. Every idea from the one that you, General, and all the rest of you out in the Pacific, were victims of mass hypnosis and the whole thing's an illusion, to a hundred versions of the 'little men from outer space' angle. In the meeting day before yesterday, however, I noticed you were rather quiet and reserved about expressing any opinion. I've since looked up your record. It's magnificent." The President hesitated.

Marc said nothing.

"You're a brave, brilliant, level-headed, sensitive person, and a man's man. Your record makes a great deal too plain for you to deny out of modesty. You are an exceptional man. In short, you're the very sort of person I'd pick to look into a mere report of an incident of that sort. So what I want—why I asked you here—is your impression. Your feelings. Your reactions at the time. Your reflections since. Your man-to-man, down-to-earth, open-hearted emotions about it all—and not more theory, whether theological or allegedly scientific! Do you see?"

The appeal was forceful. Marc felt as if he were all the members of some audiences the President had swayed—all of them in one person, one American citizen—now asked —now all but commanded—to bare his soul. He felt the great, inner power of the President and understood why the people of the nation had chosen him for office.

"I'll tell you," he answered quietly. "For what it's worth. I'm afraid that it is mighty little." He pondered a moment. "First, when I

suddenly saw it, I was shocked. Not frightened, Mr. President—though the rest were. Just—startled. When I really looked at the—casualty, I thought, first of all, that it was beautiful. I thought it had, in its dead face, great intelligence and other qualities."

The President rested his hand on the uniformed knee. "That's it, man! The 'other qualities'! What were they?"

Marc exhaled unevenly. "This is risky. It's all—remembered impression. I thought it looked kind. Noble too. Almost, but not exactly, sweet. I thought it had tremendous courage. The kind that—well, I thought of it as roaring through space and danger and unimagined risks to get here. Daring H-bombs. And I thought, Mr. President, one more thing: I thought it had determination—as if there was a gigantic feel about it of—mission."

There was a long silence. Then the President said in a low voice, "That all, Marc?"

"Yes. Yes, sir."

"So I thought." He stood up suddenly, not a man of reflection and unresolved responsibility, but an executive with work ahead. "Mission! We don't know what it was. If only there was something tangible!" He held out his hand and gripped the general with great strength. "I needed that word to decide. We'll wait. Keep it absolutely restricted. There might be another. The message to us, from them, whoever they are, might come in some different way or by more of these messengers! After all, I cannot represent them to the world—expose this incredible incident—without knowing what the mission was. But to know there was a mission—" He sighed and went on firmly, "When I finally get to bed tonight, I'll sleep, Marc, as I haven't slept since I took office!"

"It's only my guess," the general responded. "I haven't any evidence to explain those feelings."

"You've said enough for me! Thank you, General." Then, to Marc Scott's honor and embarrassment, the President drew himself straight, executed a salute, held it a moment, turned from the terrace, and marched alone into the White House.

During the months-long, single day of Northern Siberia's summertime, on a night that had no darkness, a fireball burst suddenly above the arctic rim. As it rose, it turned the tundra blood-red. For a radius of miles the permafrost was hammered down and a vast, charred basin was formed. In the adjacent polar seas ice melted. A mushroom cloud broke through the atmospheric layers with a speed and to a height that would have perplexed, if not horrified, the Free World's nuclear physicists.

In due course, counters the world around would begin to click and the information would be whispered about that the Russians were ahead in the H-bomb field. That

information would be thereupon restricted so that the American public would never learn the truth.

In Siberia the next morning awed Soviet technicians—and the most detached nuclear physicists have been awed, even stupefied, by their creations—measured the effects of their new bomb carefully: area of absolute incineration, area of absolute destruction by blast, putative scope of fire storm, radius of penetrative radiation, kinds and concentrations of radioactive fallout, half-lives, dispersion of same, kilos of pressure per square centimeter. Then, on maps of the United States of America, these technicians superimposed tinted circles of colored plastics, so that a glance would show exactly what such a bomb would destroy of Buffalo and environs, St. Paul, Seattle, Dallas, as well as New York, Chicago, Philadelphia, Los Angeles, and so on—the better targets. These maps, indicating the imaginary annihilation of millions, were identical with certain American maps, save for the fact that the latter bore such city names as Moscow, Leningrad, Stalingrad, Vladivostok, Ordzhonikidze, Dnepropetrovsk, and the like.

It was while the technicians were correlating their bomb data—and the sky over the test base was still lava—that coded word came in to the commanding officer of the base concerning a "casualty." The casualty had been found in dying condition by a peasant who had been ordered to evacuate his sod hut in that region weeks before. After the casualty, he had been summarily shot for disobedience.

The general went to the scene forthwith—and returned a silent, shaken man. Using communication channels intended only for war emergency, he got in touch with Moscow. The premier was not in his offices in the new, forty-six-story skyscraper; but his aides were persuaded to disturb him at one of his suburban villas. They were reluctant; he had retired to the country with Lamenula, the Communist Italian actress.

The premier listened to the faint, agitated news from Siberia and said, "The garrison must be drunk."

"I assure you, Comrade—"

"Put Vorshiv on."

Vorshiv said, uneasily, the same thing. Yes, he had seen it. . . . Yes, it had wings. . . . No, it could not be an enemy trick. . . . No, there were no interplanetary vehicles about; nothing on the radar in the nature of an unidentified flying object. . . . Certainly, they had been meticulous in the sky watch; this had been a new type of bomb, incorporating a new principle, and it would never have done to let an enemy reconnaissance plane observe the effects.

"I will come," said the premier.

He ordered a new Khalov-239 prepared for the flight. He was very angry. Lamenula had been coy—and the premier had enjoyed the novelty of that, until the call from Siberia had interrupted. Now he would have to make a long, uncomfortable journey in a jet—which always frightened him a little—and he would be obliged to postpone the furthering of his friendship with the talented, beautiful, honey-haired young Italian.

Night came to the Siberian flatlands and the sky clouded so that there was a semblance of darkness. A frigid wind swept from the Pole, freezing the vast area of mud created by the H-bomb. In the morning the premier came in at the base airfield, twelve jets streaming in the icy atmosphere, forward rockets blasting to brake the race of the great ship over the hard-packed terrain. It stopped only a few score rods short of the place where the "inadequate workers" lay buried—the more than ten thousand slaves who had died to make the field.

Curiously enough, it was an Amercan jeep which took the premier out to the scrubby patch of firs. The angel lay untouched, but covered with a tarpaulin and prodigiously guarded round about by men and war machines.

"Take it off."

He stood a long time, simply looking, his silent generals and aides beside him.

Not a tall man, this Soviet premier, but broad, overweight, bearlike in fur clothing—a man with a Mongol face and eyes as dark, as inexpressive and unfeeling as prunes. A man whose face was always shiny, as if he exuded minutely a thin oil. A man highly educated by the standards of his land: a man ruthless by any standard in history.

What went through his head as he regarded the dazzling figure, he would not afterward have catalogued. Not in its entirety. He was afraid, of course. He was always afraid. But he had achieved that level of awareness which acknowledges, and uses, fear. In the angel he saw immediately a possible finish to the dreams of Engels, Marx, the rest. He saw a potential end of Communism, and even of the human race. This milk-white cadaver, this impossible reality, this beauty Praxiteles could never have achieved even symbolically, could mean—anything.

Aloud, he said—his first remark—"Michelangelo would have appreciated this."

Some of the men around him, scared, breathing steam in the gray, purgatorial morning, smiled or chuckled at their chief's erudition and self-possession. Others agreed solemnly: Michelangelo—whoever he was or had been—would have appreciated this incredible carcass.

He then went up and kicked the foot of the angel with his own felted boot. It alarmed him to do so, but he felt, as premier, the duty. First, the noble comment; next, the boot.

He was aware of the fact that the men around him kept glancing from the frozen angel up toward the barely discernible gray clouds. They were wondering, of course, if

it could be God-sent. Sounds came to him—bells of churches, litanies recited, chants—Gregorian music in Caucasian bass. To his nostrils came the smell of incense. He thought, as atheists must: What if they were right?

Against that thought he ranged another speedily enough; it was his custom. He wrenched the ears and eyes of his mind from the church pageantry of recollected boyhood, in the Czar's time, to other parts of his expanding domain. He made himself hear temple bells, watch sacred elephants parade, behold the imbecile sacrifices and rituals of the heathen. They, too, were believers, and they had no angels. Angels, he therefore reasoned, were myths.

It occurred to him—it had already been suggested to him by General Mornsk, of Intelligence—that some such being as this, come on a brief visit from an unknown small planet, had given rise to the whole notion of angels. He chuckled.

Vorshiv had the temerity to ask, "You have formed an opinion, Comrade?"

The premier stared at the stringy, leathern man with his watery eyes and his record: eighteen million unworthy citizens "subdued." "Certainly." He looked once more at the casualty. "Autopsy it. Then destroy the remains."

"No," a voice murmured.

The premier whirled about. "Who said that?"

It was a young man, the youngest general, one born after 1917, one who had seen no world but the Soviet. Now, pale with horror and shame, the young man said, "I merely thought, sir, to preserve this for study."

"I detected sentiment. Credulity. Superstition. Your protest was a whimper."

The young officer showed a further brief flicker of dissent. "Perhaps—this being cannot be destroyed by our means."

The premier nodded at the body, and his thin, long lips became longer, thinner. A smile, perhaps. "Is not our second test planned for the very near future?"

"Tomorrow," Mornsk said. "But we are prepared to postpone it if you think the situation—"

"Postpone it?" The premier smiled. "On the contrary. Follow plans. Autopsy this animal. Attach what remains to the bomb. That should destroy it effectively." He glanced icily at the young general, made a daub at a salute, and tramped over the ice-crisped tundra toward the jeeps.

On the way back to the base, Mornsk, of Intelligence, decided to mention his theory. Mornsk turned in his front seat. "One thing, Comrade. Our American information is not, as you know, what it was. However, we had word this spring of what the British call a 'flap.' Many sudden, very secret conferences. Rumors. We never were able to determine the cause—and the brief state of near-panic among the leadership

has abated. Could it be—the 'flap' followed one of their tests—that they, too, had a 'casualty'?"

"It could be," the premier replied. "What of it?"

"Nothing. I merely would have thought, Comrade, that they would have announced it to the world."

The thin lips drew thinner again. "They are afraid. They would, today, keep secret a thousand things that, yesterday, they would have told one another freely. Freedom. Where is it now? We are driving it into limbo—their kind. To limbo." He shut his prune eyes, opened them, turned to the officer on his left. "Gromov, I hope the food's good here. I'm famished."

An old Russian proverb ran through his mind: "Where hangs the smoke of hate burns a fiercer fire called fear."

The trick, he reflected, was to keep that fire of fear alive, but to know at the same time it might consume you also. Then the trick was to make the fear invisible in the smokes of hatred. Having accomplished that, you would own men's souls and your power would be absolute, so long as you never allowed men to see how their hate was but fear, and so long as you, afraid, knowing it, hence more shrewd and cautious than the rest, did not become a corpse at the hands of the hating fearful.

There, in a nutshell, was the recipe for dictatorship. Over the proletariat. Over the godly believers. Over the heathen. Over all men, even those who imagined they were free and yet could be made to hate:

Frighten; then furnish the whipping boys. Then seize. Like governing children.

If more of these angels showed up, he reflected, it would simply be necessary to pretend they were demons, Lucifers, outer-space men bent on assassinating humanity. So simple.

The slate-hued buildings of the base rose over the tundra. From the frigid outdoors he entered rooms heated to a tropical temperature by the nearby reactors. There, too, the Soviets had somewhat surpassed the free peoples.

His secretary, Maximov, had thoughtfully forwarded Lamenula, to temper the hardships of the premier's Siberian hegira. He was amused, even somewhat stirred, to learn the young lady had objected to the trip, had fought, was even now in a state of alternate hysteria and coma—or simulated coma. A little Communist discipline was evidently needed, and being applied; and he would take pleasure in administering the finishing touches.

Late that night he woke up with a feeling of uneasiness. A feeling, he decided, of fear. The room was quiet, the guards were in place, nothing menaced him in the immediate moment.

What frightened him was the angel. Church music, which he had remembered, but refused to listen to in his mind, now came back to

him. It did not cause him to believe that the visitor had given a new validity to an Old Testament. It had already caused him to speculate that what he, and a billion others, had thitherto regarded as pure myth might actually be founded on scientific fact.

What therefore frightened the premier, as he lay on the great bed in the huge, gaudily decorated bedchamber, was an intuition of ignorance. Neither he nor his physicists, he nor his political philosophers—nor any men in the world that still, ludicrously, blindly, referred to itself as "free"—really knew anything fundamental about the universe. Nobody really knew, and could demonstrate scientifically, the "why" of time and space and energy—or matter. The angel—the very beautiful angel that had lain on the cold tundra—might possibly mean and be something that not he nor any living man, skeptic or believer, could even comprehend.

That idea wakened him thoroughly. Here was a brand-new dimension of the unknown to be faced. He sat up, switched on the light and put a cigarette in his thin mouth.

How, he asked, could this fear of the unknown be translated into a hatred of something known, and so employed to enhance power? His power. That was, invariably, the formulation; once made, it generally supplied its own answer.

You could not, however, set the people in the Soviets and the people in the rest of the world to hating angels. Not when, especially, their reality—or real counterpart—could never be exhibited and had become a military secret.

Mornsk's theory bemused him. Had the Americans also shot one down with an H-bomb? If so, they'd followed a procedure like his own, apparently. Saying nothing. Examining the victim, doubtless.

He realized he should go to sleep. He was to be roused early for the test of the next super-H-bomb, but he kept ruminating, as he smoked, on the people of the United States. *Whom,* he reflected, *we shall destroy in millions* in —— The number of months and days remaining before the blitz of the U.S.A. was so immense a secret that he did not let himself reckon it exactly. *Whom we shall slaughter in sudden millions, soon.*

But suppose something intervened? Angels?

He smiled again. Even if such creatures had visited the earth once before, it was long ago. They might be here again now. They would presumably go away again, for millenniums. Ample time to plant the Red flag everywhere in the world.

Still, he could not know, and not to know was alarming.

There was a phone beside his bed. He could astound telephone operators halfway around the world, and yet, doubtless, in ten minutes, fifteen—perhaps an hour—he could converse with the President of the United States.

"Seen any angels, Mr. President? . . . What do you make of it? . . . Perhaps we aren't as knowing as we imagine. . . . Possibly we should meet and talk things over—postpone any—plans we might have for the near future? At least, until this matter of invading angels is settled."

It wouldn't be that simple or that quick, but it might be done. And it might be that that was the only possible way to save the Soviet, because it might be the one way left to save man and his planet.

He thought about the abandonment of the Communist philosophy, the scrapping of decades of horror and sacrifice, the relaxing of the steely discipline; he thought of the dreams of world domination gone glimmering—of "freedom" being equated with Communism. There welled in him the avalanche of hatred which was his essence and the essence of his world. He ground out his cigarette and tried to sleep. . . .

In the morning, after the test shot —which was also very successful and, the premier thought, frightening—he requested the report on the autopsy of the casualty. He had to ask repeatedly, since it became clear that none of the near-by persons—generals, commissars, aides, technicians—wanted to answer. He commanded Mornsk.

The general sweated in the cold air, under a sky again clear and as palely blue as turquoise. "We have no report, Comrade. The autopsy was undertaken last night by Smidz. An ideal man, we felt—the great biologist, who happened to be here, working on radiation effects on pigs. He labored alone all night, and then—your orders, Comrade—the—remains were fixed to the bomb." Mornsk's glance at the towering mushroom disposed of that matter. "It was then discovered that Smidz made no notes of whatever he learned."

"Get Smidz."

"This morning early, Comrade, he killed himself."

General Scott did not return to the Pacific until nearly Christmastime. He had hoped not to go back at all, particularly since he had spent the autumn with his family in Baltimore, commuting weekdays to the Pentagon. In December, however, he received secret information of still another series of springtime nuclear-weapons tests and.orders to fly again to the Sangre Islands, where he would prepare another of the group for total sacrifice. The death of islands was becoming commonplace to the weaponeers. In the unfinished span of his own military career, a suitable target had grown from a square of canvas stretched over a wooden frame to a building, and then to a city block, next a city's heart, and now, an island the size of Manhattan. This, moreover, was not holed, wrecked, or merely set afire, but wiped off the earth's face, its roots burned away deep

into the sea, its substance thrown, poisonous, across the skies.

He went reluctantly, but as a soldier must, aware that by now he had the broadest experience—among general officers—for the task at hand.

Work went ahead with no more than the usual quota of "bugs"—or what his orderly would have called "snafus." It was a matter of "multiple snafu," however, which finally led the general to order a light plane to fly him to Tempest Island. There had arisen an argument with the natives about property rights; there was some trouble with the placements of instruments; a problem about electric power had come up; and a continuing report of bad chow was being turned in from the island mess hall. Time for a high-echelon look-see.

As he flew in, General Scott noticed the changes which he had helped to devise. The mission playing field had been bulldozed big enough to accommodate fair-sized cargo planes on two X-angled strips. Here and there the green rug of jungle had been macheted open to contain new measuring devices of the scientists. The harbor had been deepened; dredged-up coral made a mole against the purple Pacific as well as the foundation for a sizable pier. Otherwise, Tempest was the same.

Hs mind, naturally, returned to his previous trip and to what had been found on the island. The general had observed a growing tendency, even in Admiral Stanforth and Rawson, now a colonel, to recall the angel more as a figure of a dream than as reality. Just before the landing gear came down he looked for, and saw, the very glade in which the angel had fallen. Its clear spring was an emerald eye and the Bletias were in violet bloom all around.

Then he was on the ground, busy with other officers, busy with the plans and problems of a great nation, scared, arming, ready these days for war at the notice of a moment or at no notice whatever. Even here, thousands upon thousands of miles from the nervous target areas of civilization, the fear and the desperate urgency of man had rolled up, parting the jungle and erecting grim engines associated with ruin.

He was on his way to the headquarters tent when he noticed, and recognized, the young boy.

Teddy Simms, he thought, was about ten now, the age of his own son. But Teddy looked older than ten, and very sad.

The general stepped away from his accompanying officers. "You go on," he said. "I'll soon catch up. This is an old friend of mine." He waved then. "Hi, Ted! Why you all dressed up? Remember me?"

The youngster stopped and did recognize the general, with a look of anxiousness. He nodded and glanced down at his clothes. "I'm gonna leave! Tonight. It'll be"—his face brightened slightly—"my very first airplane ride!"

"That's swell!" The general had been puzzled by signs of apprehension in the boy. "How's your father? And your aunt? Cora, wasn't it?"

"She's O.K. But father—" His lip shook.

Marc Scott no longer smiled. "Your father—"

The boy answered stonily, "Went nuts."

"After—" the general asked, knew the answer, and was unsurprised by the boy's increased anxiousness.

"I'm not allowed to say. I'd go to prison forever."

A jeepful of soldiers passed. The general moved to the boy's side and said, "With me, you are, Ted. Because I know all about it, too. I'm—I'm mighty sorry your father—is ill. Maybe he'll recover, though."

"The board doesn't think so. They're giving up the mission. That's why I'm going away. To school, Stateside. Father"—he fell in step with the general, leaping slightly with each stride—"Father never got any better—after that old day you were here."

"What say, we go back where—it happened? I'd like to see it once more, Ted."

"No." Teddy amended it, "No, sir. I'm not even allowed to talk about it. I don't ever go there!"

"It's too bad. I thought it was the most beautiful thing that ever happened to me in my life."

The boy stared at the man incredulously. "You did? Father thought it was the worst thing ever happened."

"I felt as if you, Ted—and I— all of us—were seeing something completely wonderful!"

The boy's face showed an agreement which changed, slowly, to a pitiable emotion—regret, or fear, perhaps shame. It was the general's intuition which bridged the moment: Teddy knew more than he had ever said about the angel; he had lied originally or omitted something.

"What is it, son?" The general's tone was fatherly.

Eyes darted toward the jungle, back to the general and rested measuringly, then hopelessly. It was as if the youngster had considered aloud running away and had decided his adversary was too powerful to evade.

He stood silent a moment longer; then said almost incoherently, "I never meant to keep it! But it is gold! And we were always so mighty poor! I thought, for a while, if Father sold it— But he couldn't even think of things like selling gold books. He had lost his reason."

If the general's heart surged, if his mind was stunned, he did not show it. "Gold books?" His eyes forgave in advance.

"Just one book, but heavy." The dismal boy looked at the ground. "I didn't steal it, really! That angel —dropped it."

The general's effort was tremendous. Not in battle had composure cost him as dear. "You—read it?"

"Huh!" the boy said. "It was in all kinds of other languages. 'Wisdom,' that angel said it was. 'Gathered from our whole galaxy —for Earth.' Did you ever know—" His voice intensified with the question, as if by asking it he might divert attention from his guilt. "Did you know there are other people on other planets of other suns, all around? Maybe Vega, or the North Star, or Rigel, or more likely old Sirius? That angel mentioned a few names. I forget which."

"No. I didn't realize it. And, you say, this book had a message for the people on Earth, written in all languages. Not English, though?"

"I didn't see any English. I saw— like Japanese and Arabian—and a lot of kinds of alphabets you never heard of—some just dots."

"And you—threw it away?" He asked it easily too.

"Naw. You couldn't do that! It's gold—at least, it looks like gold. All metal pages. It's got hinges, kind of, for every page. I guess it's fireproof and even space-proof, at the least. I didn't throw it away. I hid it under an old rock. Come on. I'll show you."

They returned to the glade. The book lay beneath a flat stone. There had been another the general was never to know about—a book buried beneath a sod hut in Siberia by a peasant who also had intended to sell it, for he, too, had been poor.

But the other book, identical, along with the hovel above it, had been reduced to fractions of its atoms by a certain test weapon which had destroyed the body of its bearer.

This one the general picked up with shaking hands, opened and gazed upon with ashen face.

The hot sun of noon illumined the violet orchids around his tailored legs. The boy stood looking up at him, awaiting judgment, accustomed to harshness; and about them was the black and white filigree of tropical forest. With inexpressible amazement, Marc searched page after page of inscriptions in languages unknown, unsuspected until then. It became apparent that there was one message only, very short, said again and again and again, but he did not know what it was until, toward the last pages, he found the tongues of Earth.

A sound was made by the man as he read them—a sound that began with murmurous despair and ended, as comprehension entered his brain, with a note of exultation. For the message of icy space and flaring stars was this: "Love one another."

Fire and Ice

ROBERT FROST

Some say the world will end in fire,
Some say in ice.
From what I've tasted of desire
I hold with those who favor fire.
But if it had to perish twice,
I think I know enough of hate
To say that for destruction ice
Is also great
And would suffice.

THOMAS MANN

Mario and the Magician

THE ATMOSPHERE of Torre di Venere remains unpleasant in the memory. From the first moment the air of the place made us uneasy, we felt irritable, on edge; then at the end came the shocking business of Cipolla, that dreadful being who seemed to incorporate, in so fateful and so humanly impressive a way, all the peculiar evilness of the situation as a whole. Looking back, we had the feeling that the horrible end of the affair had been preordained and lay in the nature of things; that the children had to be present at it was an added impropriety, due to the false colors in which the weird creature presented himself. Luckily for them, they did not know where the comedy left off and the tragedy began; and we let them remain in their happy belief that the whole thing had been a play up till the end.

Torre di Venere lies some fifteen kilometers from Portoclemente, one of the most popular summer resorts on the Tyrrhenian Sea. Porto-

clemente is urban and elegant and full to overflowing for months on end. Its gay and busy main street of shops and hotels runs down to a wide sandy beach covered with tents and pennanted sand castles and sunburnt humanity, where at all times a lively social bustle reigns, and much noise. But this same spacious and inviting fine-sanded beach, this same border of pine grove and near, presiding mountains, continues all the way along the coast. No wonder then that some competition of a quiet kind should have sprung up further on. Torre di Venere—the tower that gave the town its name is gone long since, one looks for it in vain —is an offshoot of the larger resort, and for some years remained an idyll for the few, a refuge for more unworldly spirits. But the usual history of such places repeated itself: peace has had to retire further along the coast, to Marina Petriera and dear knows where else. We all know how the world at once seeks

358

peace and puts her to flight—rushing upon her in the fond idea that they two will wed, and where she is, there it can be at home. It will even set up its Vanity Fair in a spot and be capable of thinking that peace is still by its side. Thus Torre —though its atmosphere so far is more modest and contemplative than that of Portoclemente—has been quite taken up, by both Italians and foreigners. It is no longer the thing to go to Portoclemente— though still so much the thing that it is as noisy and crowded as ever. One goes next door, so to speak; to Torre. So much more refined, even, and cheaper to boot. And the attractiveness of these qualities persists, though the qualities themselves long ago ceased to be evident. Torre has got a Grand Hotel. Numerous pensions have sprung up, some modest, some pretentious. The people who own or rent the villas and pinetas overlooking the sea no longer have it all their own way on the beach. In July and August it looks just like the beach at Portoclemente: it swarms with a screaming, squabbling, merrymaking crowd, and the sun, blazing down like mad, peels the skin off their necks. Garish little flat-bottomed boats rock on the glittering blue, manned by children, whose mothers hover afar and fill the air with anxious cries of Nino! and Sandro! and Bice! and Maria! Peddlers step across the legs of recumbent sunbathers, selling flowers and corals, oysters, lemonade, and *cornetti al burro,* and crying their wares in the breathy, full-throated southern voice.

Such was the scene that greeted our arrival in Torre: pleasant enough, but after all, we thought, we had come too soon. It was the middle of August, the Italian season was still at its height, scarcely the moment for strangers to learn to love the special charms of the place. What an afternoon crowd in the cafés on the front! For instance, in the Esquisito, where we sometimes sat and were served by Mario, that very Mario of whom I shall have presently to tell. It is well-nigh impossible to find a table; and the various orchestras contend together in the midst of one's conversation with bewildering effect. Of course, it is in the afternoon that people come over from Portoclemente. The excursion is a favorite one for the restless denizens of that pleasure resort, and a Fiat motor-bus plies to and fro, coating inch-thick with dust the oleander and laurel hedges along the highroad—a notable if repulsive sight.

Yes, decidedly one should go to Torre in September, when the great public has left. Or else in May, before the water is warm enough to tempt the Southerner to bathe. Even in the before and after seasons Torre is not empty, but life is less national and more subdued. English, French, and German prevail under the tent awnings and in the pension dining rooms; whereas in August—in the Grand Hotel, at least, where, in default of private addresses, we had engaged rooms—the stranger finds the field so occupied by Florentine and Roman society that he feels quite isolated and even temporarily *déclassé*.

We had, rather to our annoyance, this experience on the evening we arrived, when we went in to dinner and were shown to our table by the waiter in charge. As a table, it had nothing against it, save that we had already fixed our eyes upon those on the veranda beyond, built out over the water, where little red-shaded lamps glowed—and there were still some tables empty, though it was as full as the dining room within. The children went into raptures at the festive sight, and without more ado we announced our intention to take our meals by preference in the veranda. Our words, it appeared, were prompted by ignorance; for we were informed, with somewhat embarrassed politeness, that the cosy nook outside was reserved for the clients of the hotel: *ai nostri clienti*. Their clients? But we were their clients. We were not tourists or trippers, but boarders for a stay of some three or four weeks. However, we forbore to press for an explanation of the difference between the likes of us and that clientele to whom it was vouchsafed to eat out there in the glow of the red lamps, and took our dinner by the prosaic common light of the dining-room chandelier—a thoroughly ordinary and monotonous hotel bill of fare,

be it said. In Pensione Eleonora, a few steps landward, the table, as we were to discover, was much better.

And thither it was that we moved, three or four days later, before we had had time to settle in properly at the Grand Hotel. Not on account of the veranda and the lamps. The children, straightway on the best of terms with waiters and pages, absorbed in the joys of life on the beach, promptly forgot those colorful seductions. But now there arose, between ourselves and the veranda clientele—or perhaps more correctly with the compliant management—one of those little unpleasantnesses which can quite spoil the pleasure of a holiday. Among the guests were some high Roman aristocracy, a Principe X and his family. These grand folk occupied rooms close to our own, and the Principessa, a great and a passionately maternal lady, was thrown into a panic by the vestiges of a whooping cough which our little ones had lately got over, but which now and then still faintly troubled the unshatterable slumbers of our youngest-born. The nature of this illness is not clear, leaving some play for the imagination. So we took no offense at our elegant neighbor for clinging to the widely held view that whooping cough is acoustically contagious and quite simply fearing lest her children yield to the bad example set by ours. In the fullness of her feminine self-confidence she protested to the management, which then, in the person of the proverbial frock-coated manager, hastened to represent to us, with many expressions of regret, that under the circumstances they were obliged to transfer us to the annex. We did our best to assure him that the disease was in its very last stages, that it was actually over, and presented no danger of infection to anybody. All that we gained was permission to bring the case before the hotel physician—not one chosen by us—by whose verdict we must then abide. We agreed, convinced that thus we should at once pacify the Princess and escape the trouble of moving. The doctor appeared, and behaved like a faithful and honest servant of science. He examined the child and gave his opinion: the disease was quite over, no danger of contagion was present. We drew a long breath and considered the incident closed —until the manager announced that despite the doctor's verdict it would still be necessary for us to give up our rooms and retire to the *dépendence*. Byzantinism like this outraged us. It is not likely that the Principessa was responsible for the willful breach of faith. Very likely the fawning management had not even dared to tell her what the physician said. Anyhow, we made it clear to his understanding that we preferred to leave the hotel altogether and at once—and packed our trunks. We could do so with a light heart, having already set up casual friendly relations with Casa Eleonora. We had noticed its

pleasant exterior and formed the acquaintance of its proprietor, Signora Angiolieri, and her husband: she slender and black-haired, Tuscan in type, probably at the beginning of the thirties, with the dead ivory complexion of the southern woman, he quiet and bald and carefully dressed. They owned a larger establishment in Florence and presided only in summer and early autumn over the branch in Torre di Venere. But earlier, before her marriage, our new landlady had been companion, fellow-traveler, wardrobe mistress, yes, friend, of Eleonora Duse and manifestly regarded that period as the crown of her career. Even at our first visit she spoke of it with animation. Numerous photographs of the great actress, with affectionate inscriptions, were displayed about the drawing room, and other souvenirs of their life together adorned the little tables and *étagères*. This cult of a so interesting past was calculated, of course, to heighten the advantages of the signora's present business. Nevertheless our pleasure and interest were quite genuine as we were conducted through the house by its owner and listened to her sonorous and staccato Tuscan voice relating anecdotes of that immortal mistress, depicting her suffering saintliness, her genius, her profound delicacy of feeling.

Thither, then, we moved our effects, to the dismay of the staff of the Grand Hotel, who, like all Italians, were very good to children.

Our new quarters were retired and pleasant, we were within easy reach of the sea through the avenue of young plane trees that ran down to the esplanade. In the clean, cool dining room Signora Angiolieri daily served the soup with her own hands, the service was attentive and good, the table capital. We even discovered some Viennese acquaintances, and enjoyed chatting with them after luncheon, in front of the house. They, in their turn, were the means of our finding others—in short, all seemed for the best, and we were heartily glad of the change we had made. Nothing was now wanting to a holiday of the most gratifying kind.

And yet no proper gratification ensued. Perhaps the stupid occasion of our change of quarters pursued us to the new ones we had found. Personally, I admit that I do not easily forget these collisions with ordinary humanity, the naïve misuse of power, the injustice, the sycophantic corruption. I dwelt upon the incident too much, it irritated me in retrospect—quite futilely, of course, since such phenomena are only all too natural and all too much the rule. And we had not broken off relations with the Grand Hotel. The children were as friendly as ever there, the porter mended their toys, and we sometimes took tea in the garden. We even saw the Principessa. She would come out, with her firm and delicate tread, her lips emphatically coral-lined, to look after her children,

playing under the supervision of their English governess. She did not dream that we were anywhere near, for so soon as she appeared in the offing we sternly forbade our little one even to clear his throat.

The heat—if I may bring it in evidence—was extreme. It was African. The power of the sun, directly one left the border of the indigo-blue wave, was so frightful, so relentless, that the mere thought of the few steps between the beach and luncheon was a burden, clad though one might be only in pajamas. Do you care for that sort of thing? Weeks on end? Yes, of course, it is proper to the south, it is classic weather, the sun of Homer, the climate wherein human culture came to flower—and all the rest of it. But after a while it is too much for me, I reach a point where I begin to find it dull. The burning void of the sky, day after day, weighs one down; the high coloration, the enormous naïveté of the unrefracted light—they do, I dare say, induce light-heartedness, a carefree mood born of immunity from downpours and other meteorological caprices. But slowly, slowly, there makes itself felt a lack: the deeper, more complex needs of the northern soul remain unsatisfied. You are left barren—even, it may be, in time, a little contemptuous. True, without that stupid business of the whooping cough I might not have been feeling these things. I was annoyed, very likely I wanted to feel them and so half-unconsciously seized upon an idea lying ready to hand to induce, or if not to induce, at least to justify and strengthen, my attitude. Up to this point, then, if you like, let us grant some ill will on our part. But the sea; and the mornings spent extended upon the fine sand in face of its eternal splendors—no, the sea could not conceivably induce such feelings. Yet it was none the less true that, despite all previous experience, we were not at home on the beach, we were not happy.

It was too soon, too soon. The beach, as I have said, was still in the hands of the middle-class native. It is a pleasing breed to look at, and among the young we saw much shapeliness and charm. Still, we were necessarily surrounded by a great deal of very average humanity—a middle-class mob, which, you will admit, is not more charming under this sun than under one's own native sky. The voices these women have! It was sometimes hard to believe that we were in the land which is the Western cradle of the art of song. *"Fuggièro!"* I can still hear that cry, as for twenty mornings long I heard it close behind me, breathy, full-throated, hideously stressed, with a harsh open *e,* uttered in accents of mechanical despair. *"Fuggièro! Rispondi almeno!"* Answer when I call you! The *sp* in *rispondi* was pronounced like *shp,* as Germans pronounce it; and this, on top of what I felt already, vexed my sensitive soul. The cry was addressed to a repulsive young-

ster whose sunburn had made disgusting raw sores on his shoulders. He outdid anything I have ever seen for ill-breeding, refractoriness, and temper and was a great coward to boot, putting the whole beach in an uproar, one day, because of his outrageous sensitiveness to the slightest pain. A sand crab had pinched his toe in the water, and the minute injury made him set up a cry of heroic proportions—the shout of an antique hero in his agony—that pierced one to the marrow and called up visions of some frightful tragedy. Evidently he considered himself not only wounded, but poisoned as well; he crawled out on the sand and lay in apparently intolerable anguish, groaning *"Ohi!"* and *"Ohimè!"* and threshing about with arms and legs to ward off his mother's tragic appeals and the questions of the bystanders. An audience gathered round. A doctor was fetched—the same who had pronounced objective judgment on our whooping cough—and here again acquitted himself like a man of science. Good-naturedly he reassured the boy, telling him that he was not hurt at all, he should simply go into the water again to relieve the smart. Instead of which, Fuggièro was borne off the beach, followed by a concourse of people. But he did not fail to appear next morning, nor did he leave off spoiling our children's sand castles. Of course, always by accident. In short, a perfect terror.

And this twelve-year-old lad was prominent among the influences that, imperceptibly at first, combined to spoil our holiday and render it unwholesome. Somehow or other, there was a stiffness, a lack of innocent enjoyment. These people stood on their dignity—just why, and in what spirit, it was not easy at first to tell. They displayed much self-respectingness; toward each other and toward the foreigner their bearing was that of a person newly conscious of a sense of honor. And wherefore? Gradually we realized the political implications and understood that we were in the presence of a national ideal. The beach, in fact, was alive with patriotic children—a phenomenon as unnatural as it was depressing. Children are a human species and a society apart, a nation of their own, so to speak. On the basis of their common form of life, they find each other out with the greatest ease, no matter how different their small vocabularies. Ours soon played with natives and foreigners alike. Yet they were plainly both puzzled and disappointed at times. There were wounded sensibilities, displays of assertiveness—or rather hardly assertiveness, for it was too self-conscious and too didactic to deserve the name. There were quarrels over flags, disputes about authority and precedence. Grown-ups joined in, not so much to pacify as to render judgment and enunciate principles. Phrases were dropped

about the greatness and dignity of Italy, solemn phrases that spoilt the fun. We saw our two little ones retreat, puzzled and hurt, and were put to it to explain the situation. These people, we told them, were just passing through a certain stage, something rather like an illness, perhaps; not very pleasant, but probably unavoidable.

We had only our own carelessness to thank that we came to blows in the end with this "stage" —which, after all, we had seen and sized up long before now. Yes, it came to another "cross-purposes," so evidently the earlier ones had not been sheer accident. In a word, we became an offense to the public morals. Our small daughter—eight years old, but in physical development a good year younger and thin as a chicken—had had a good long bath and gone playing in the warm sun in her wet costume. We told her that she might take off her bathing suit, which was stiff with sand, rinse it in the sea, and put it on again, after which she must take care to keep it cleaner. Off goes the costume and she runs down naked to the sea, rinses her little jersey, and comes back. Ought we to have foreseen the outburst of anger and resentment which her conduct, and thus our conduct, called forth? Without delivering a homily on the subject, I may say that in the last decade our attitude toward the nude body and our feelings regarding it have undergone, all over the world, a fundamental change. There are things we "never think about" any more, and among them is the freedom we had permitted to this by no means provocative little childish body. But in these parts it was taken as a challenge. The patriotic children hooted. Fuggièro whistled on his fingers. The sudden buzz of conversation among the grown people in our neighborhood boded no good. A gentleman in city togs, with a not very apropos bowler hat on the back of his head, was assuring his outraged womenfolk that he proposed to take punitive measures; he stepped up to us, and a philippic descended on our unworthy heads, in which all the emotionalism of the sense-loving south spoke in the service of morality and discipline. The offense against decency of which we had been guilty was, he said, the more to be condemned because it was also a gross ingratitude and an insulting breach of his country's hospitality. We had criminally injured not only the letter and spirit of the public bathing regulations, but also the honor of Italy; he, the gentleman in the city togs, knew how to defend that honor and proposed to see to it that our offense against the national dignity should not go unpunished.

We did our best, bowing respectfully, to give ear to this eloquence. To contradict the man, overheated as he was, would probably be to fall from one error into another. On the tips of our tongues we had various answers: as, that the word "hospitality," in its strictest sense, was not quite the right one, taking all the circumstances into consideration. We were not literally the guests of Italy, but of Signora Angiolieri, who had assumed the role of dispenser of hospitality some years ago on laying down that of familiar friend to Eleonora Duse. We longed to say that surely this beautiful country had not sunk so low as to be reduced to a state of hypersensitive prudishness. But we confirmed ourselves to assuring the gentleman that any lack of respect, any provocation on our parts, had been the furthest from our thought. And as a mitigating circumstance we pointed out the tender age and physical slightness of the little culprit. In vain. Our protests were waved away, he did not believe in them; our defense would not hold water. We must be made an example of. The authorities were notified, by telephone, I believe, and their representative appeared on the beach. He said the case was *"molto grave."* We had to go with him to the Municipio up in the Piazza, where a higher official confirmed the previous verdict of *"molto grave,"* launched into a stream of the usual didactic phrases—the selfsame tune and words as the man in the bowler hat—and levied a fine and ransom of fifty lire. We felt that the adventure must willy-nilly be worth to us this much of a contribution to the economy of the Italian government; paid, and left. Ought we not at this point to have left Torre as well?

If we only had! We should thus have escaped that fatal Cipolla. But circumstances combined to prevent us from making up our minds to a change. A certain poet says that it is indolence that makes us endure uncomfortable situations. The *aperçu* may serve as an explanation for our inaction. Anyhow, one dislikes voiding the field immediately upon such an event. Especially if sympathy from other quarters encourages one to defy it. And in the Villa Eleonora they pronounced as with one voice upon the injustice of our punishment. Some Italian after-dinner acquaintances found that the episode put their country in a very bad light, and proposed taking the man in the bowler hat to task, as one fellow-citizen to another. But the next day he and his party had vanished from the beach. Not on our account, of course. Though it might be that the consciousness of his impending departure had added energy to his rebuke; in any case his going was a relief. And, furthermore, we stayed because our stay had by now become remarkable in our own eyes, which is worth something in itself, quite apart from the comfort or discomfort involved. Shall we strike sail, avoid a certain experience so soon as it seems not expressly calculated to increase our enjoyment

or our self-esteem? Shall we go away whenever life looks like turning in the slightest uncanny, or not quite normal, or even rather painful and mortifying? No, surely not Rather stay and look matters in the face, brave them out; perhaps precisely in so doing lies a lesson for us to learn. We stayed on and reaped as the awful reward of our constancy the unholy and staggering experience with Cipolla.

I have not mentioned that the after season had begun, almost on the very day we were disciplined by the city authorities. The worshipful gentleman in the bowler hat, our denouncer, was not the only person to leave the resort. There was a regular exodus, on every hand you saw luggage carts on their way to the station. The beach denationalized itself. Life in Torre, in the cafés and the pinetas, became more homelike and more European. Very likely we might even have eaten at a table in the glass veranda, but we refrained, being content at Signora Angiolieri's—as content, that is, as our evil star would let us be. But at the same time with this turn for the better came a change in the weather: almost to an hour it showed itself in harmony with the holiday calendar of the general public. The sky was overcast; not that it grew any cooler, but the unclouded heat of the entire eighteen days since our arrival, and probably long before that, gave place to a stifling sirocco air, while from time to time a little ineffectual rain sprinkled the velvety surface of the beach. Add to which, that two-thirds of our intended stay at Torre had passed. The colorless, lazy sea, with sluggish jellyfish floating in its shallows, was at least a change. And it would have been silly to feel retrospective longings after a sun that had caused us so many sighs when it burned down in all its arrogant power.

At this juncture, then, it was that Cipolla announced himself. Cavaliere Cipolla he was called on the posters that appeared one day stuck up everywhere, even in the dining room of Pensione Eleonora. A traveling virtuoso, an entertainer, *"forzatore, illusionista prestidigitatore,"* as he called himself, who proposed to wait upon the highly respectable population of Torre di Venere with a display of extraordinary phenomena of a mysterious and staggering kind. A conjuror! The bare announcement was enough to turn our children's heads. They had never seen anything of the sort, and now our present holiday was to afford them this new excitement. From that moment on they besieged us with prayers to take tickets for the performance. We had doubts, from the first, on the score of the lateness of the hour, nine o'clock; but gave way, in the idea that we might see a little of what Cipolla had to offer, probably no great matter, and then go home. Besides, of course, the children could sleep late next day. We bought four tickets of Signora Angiolieri herself, she having taken a number of the stalls on commission to sell them to her guests. She could not vouch for the man's performance, and we had no great expectations. But we were conscious of a need for diversion, and the children's violent curiosity proved catching.

The Cavaliere's performance was to take place in a hall where during the season there had been a cinema with a weekly program. We had never been there. You reached it by following the main street under the wall of the *"palazzo,"* a ruin with a "For sale" sign, that suggested a castle and had obviously been built in lordlier days. In the same street were the chemist, the hairdresser, and all the better shops; it led, so to speak, from the feudal past the bourgeois into the proletarian, for it ended off between two rows of poor fishing-huts, where old women sat mending nets before the doors. And here, among the proletariat, was the hall, not much more, actually, than a wooden shed, though a large one, with a turreted entrance, plastered on either side with layers of gay placards. Some while after dinner, then, on the appointed evening, we wended our way thither in the dark, the children dressed in their best and blissful with the sense of so much irregularity. It was sultry, as it had been for days; there was heat lightning now and then, and a little rain; we proceeded under umbrellas. It took us a quarter of an hour.

Our tickets were collected at the entrance, our places we had to find ourselves. They were in the third row left, and as we sat down we saw that, late though the hour was for the performance, it was to be interpreted with even more laxity. Only very slowly did an audience—who seemed to be relied upon to come late—begin to fill the stalls. These comprised the whole auditorium; there were no boxes. This tardiness gave us some concern. The children's cheeks were already flushed as much with fatigue as with excitement. But even when we entered, the standing-room at the back and in the side aisles was already well occupied. There stood the manhood of Torre di Venere, all and sundry, fisherfolk, rough-and-ready youths with bare fore-arms crossed over their striped jerseys. We were well pleased with the presence of this native assemblage, which always adds color and animation to occasions like the present; and the children were frankly delighted. For they had friends among these people—acquaintances picked up on afternoon strolls to the further ends of the beach. We would be turning homeward, at the hour when the sun dropped into the sea, spent with the huge effort it had made and gilding with reddish gold the oncoming surf; and we would come upon bare-legged fisherfolk standing in rows, bracing and hauling with long-drawn cries as they drew in the nets and harvested in dripping baskets their catch, often so scanty, of *frutta di mare*. The children looked on, helped to pull, brought out their little stock of Italian words, made friends. So now they exchanged nods with the "standing-room" clientele; there was Guiscardo, there Antonio, they knew them by name and waved and called across in half-whispers, getting answering nods and smiles that displayed rows of healthy white teeth. Look, there is even Mario, Mario from the Esquisito, who brings us the chocolate. He wants to see the conjuror, too, and he must have come early, for he is almost in front; but he does not see us, he is not paying attention; that is a way he has, even though he is a waiter. So we wave instead to the man who lets out the little boats on the beach; he is there too, standing at the back.

It had got to a quarter past nine, it got to almost half past. It was natural that we should be nervous. When would the children get to bed? It had been a mistake to bring them, for now it would be very hard to suggest breaking off their enjoyment before it had got well under way. The stalls had filled in time; all Torre, apparently, was there: the guests of the Grand Hotel, the guests of Villa Eleonora, familiar faces from the beach. We heard English and German and the sort of French that Rumanians speak with Italians. Madame Angiolieri herself sat two rows behind us, with her quiet, bald-headed spouse, who kept stroking his mustache with the two middle fingers of his right hand. Everybody had come late, but nobody too late. Cipolla made us wait for him.

He made us wait. That is probably the way to put it. He heightened the suspense by his delay in appearing. And we could see the point of this, too—only not when it was carried to extremes. Toward half past nine the audience began to clap—an amiable way of expressing justifiable impatience, evincing as it does an eagerness to applaud. For the little ones, this was a joy in itself—all children love to clap. From the popular sphere came loud cries of *"Pronti!" "Cominciamo!"* And lo, it seemed now as easy to begin as before it had been hard. A gong sounded, greeted by the standing rows with a many-voiced "Ah-h!" and the curtains parted. They revealed a platform furnished more like a schoolroom than like the theater of a conjuring performance—largely because of the blackboard in the left foreground. There was a common yellow hat-stand, a few ordinary straw-bottomed chairs, and further back a little round table holding a water carafe and glass, also a tray with a liqueur glass and a flask of pale yellow liquid. We had still a few seconds of time to let these things sink in. Then, with no darkening of the house, Cavaliere Cipolla made his entry.

He came forward with a rapid step that expressed his eagerness to appear before his public and gave rise to the illusion that he had already come a long way to put himself at their service—whereas, of course, he had only been standing in the wings. His costume supported the fiction. A man of an age hard to determine, but by no means young; with a sharp, ravaged face, piercing eyes, compressed lips, small black waxed mustache, and a so-called imperial in the curve between mouth and chin. He was dressed for the street with a sort of complicated evening elegance, in a wide black pelerine with velvet collar and satin lining; which, in the hampered state of his arms, he held together in front with his white-gloved hands. He had a white scarf round his neck; a top hat with a curving brim sat far back on his head. Perhaps more than anywhere else the eighteenth century is still alive in Italy, and with it the charlatan and mountebank type so characteristic of the period. Only there, at any rate, does one still encounter really well-preserved specimens. Cipolla had in his whole appearance much of the historic type; his very clothes helped to conjure up the traditional figure with its blatantly, fantastically foppish air. His pretentious costume sat upon him, or rather hung upon him, most curiously, being in one place drawn too tight, in another a mass of awkward folds. There was something not quite in order about his figure, both front and back—that was plain later on.

But I must emphasize the fact that there was not a trace of personal jocularity or clownishness in his pose, manner, or behavior. On the contrary, there was complete seriousness, an absence of any humorous appeal; occasionally even a cross-grained pride, along with that curious, self-satisfied air so characteristic of the deformed. None of all this, however, prevented his appearance from being greeted with laughter from more than one quarter of the hall.

All the eagerness had left his manner. The swift entry had been merely an expression of energy, not of zeal. Standing at the footlights he negligently drew off his gloves, to display long yellow hands, one of them adorned with a seal ring with a lapis-lazuli in a high setting. As he stood there, his small hard eyes, with flabby pouches beneath them, roved appraisingly about the hall, not quickly, rather in a considered examination, pausing here and there upon a face with his lips clipped together, not speaking a word. Then with a display of skill as surprising as it was casual, he rolled his gloves into a ball and tossed them across a considerable distance into the glass on the table. Next from an inner pocket he drew forth a packet of cigarettes; you could see by the wrapper that they were the cheapest sort the government sells. With his fingertips he pulled out a cigarette and lighted it, without looking, from a quick-firing benzine lighter. He drew the smoke deep into his lungs and let it out again, tapping his foot, with both lips drawn in an arrogant grimace and the gray smoke streaming out between broken and saw-edged teeth.

With a keenness equal to his own his audience eyed him. The youths at the rear scowled as they peered at this cocksure creature to search out his secret weaknesses. He betrayed none. In fetching out and putting back the cigarettes his clothes got in his way. He had to turn back his pelerine, and in so doing revealed a riding-whip with a silver claw-handle that hung by a leather thong from his left forearm and looked decidedly out of place. You could see that he had on not evening clothes but a frockcoat, and under this, as he lifted it to get at his pocket, could be seen a striped sash worn about the body. Somebody behind me whispered that this sash went with his title of Cavaliere. I give the information for what it may be worth—personally, I never heard that the title carried such insignia with it. Perhaps the sash was sheer pose, like the way he stood there, without a word, casually and arrogantly puffing smoke into his audience's face.

People laughed, as I said. The merriment had become almost general when somebody in the "standing seats," in a loud, dry voice, remarked: *"Buona sera."*

Cipolla cocked his head. "Who was that?" asked he, as though he had been dared. "Who was that just spoke? Well? First so bold and now so modest? *Paura,* eh?" He spoke with a rather high, asthmatic voice, which yet had a metallic quality. He waited.

"That was me," a youth at the rear broke into the stillness, seeing himself thus challenged. He was not far from us, a handsome fellow in a woolen shirt, with his coat hanging over one shoulder. He wore his curly, wiry hair in a high, disheveled mop, the style affected by the youth of the awakened Fatherland; it gave him an African appearance that rather spoiled his looks. "*Bè!* That was me. It was your business to say it first, but I was trying to be friendly."

More laughter. The chap had a tongue in his head. "*Ha sciolto la scilinguágnolo,*" I heard near me. After all, the retort was deserved.

"Ah, bravo!" answered Cipolla. "I like you, *giovanotto.* Trust me, I've had my eye on you for some time. People like you are just in my line. I can use them. And you are the pick of the lot, that's plain to see. You do what you like. Or is it possible you have ever not done what you liked—or even, maybe, what you didn't like? What somebody else liked, in short? Hark ye, my friend, that might be a pleasant change for you, to divide up the willing and the doing and stop tackling both jobs at once. Division of labor, *sistema americano, sa'!* For instance, suppose you were to show your tongue to this select and honorable audience here—your whole tongue, right down to the roots?"

"No, I won't," said the youth, hostilely. "Sticking out your tongue shows a bad bringing-up."

"Nothing of the sort," retorted Cipolla. "You would only be *doing* it. With all due respect to your bringing-up, I suggest that before I count ten, you will perform a right turn and stick out your tongue at the company here further than you knew yourself that you could stick it out."

He gazed at the youth, and his piercing eyes seemed to sink deeper into their sockets. "*Uno!*" said he. He had let his riding-whip slide down his arm and made it whistle once through the air. The boy faced about and put out his tongue, so long, so extendedly, that you could see it was the very uttermost in tongue which he had to offer. Then turned back, stony-faced, to his former position.

"That was me," mocked Cipolla, with a jerk of his head toward the youth. "*Bè!* That was me." Leaving the audience to enjoy its sensations, he turned toward the little round table, lifted the bottle, poured out a small glass of what was obviously cognac, and tipped it up with a practiced hand.

The children laughed with all their hearts. They had understood practically nothing of what had been said, but it pleased them hugely that something so funny should happen, straightaway, between that queer man up there and somebody out of the audience. They had no preconception of what an "evening" would be like and were quite ready to find this a priceless beginning. As for us, we exchanged a glance and I remember that involuntarily I made with my lips the sound that Cipolla's whip had made when it cut the air. For the rest, it was plain that people did not know what to make of a preposterous beginning like this to a sleight-of-hand performance. They could not see why the *giovanotto,* who after all in a way had been their spokesman, should suddenly have turned on them to vent his incivility. They felt that he had behaved like a silly ass and withdrew their countenances from him in favor of the artist, who now came back from his refreshment table and addressed them as follows:

"Ladies and gentlemen," said he, in his wheezing, metallic voice, "you saw just now that I was rather sensitive on the score of the rebuke this hopeful young linguist saw fit to give me"—*"questo linguista di belle speranze"* was what he said, and we all laughed at the pun. "I am a man who sets some store by himself, you may take it from me. And I see no point in being wished a good-evening unless it is done courteously and in all seriousness. For anything else there is no occasion. When a man wishes me a good-evening he wishes himself one, for the audience will have one only if I do. So this lady-killer of Torre di Venere" (another thrust)

"did well to testify that I have one tonight and that I can dispense with any wishes of his in the matter. I can boast of having good evenings almost without exception. One not so good does come my way now and again, but very seldom. My calling is hard and my health not of the best. I have a little physical defect which prevented me from doing my bit in the war for the greater glory of the Fatherland. It is perforce with my mental and spiritual parts that I conquer life—which after all only means conquering oneself. And I flatter myself that my achievements have aroused interest and respect among the educated public. The leading newspapers have lauded me, the *Corriere della Sera* did me the courtesy of calling me a phenomenon, and in Rome the brother of the *Duce* honored me by his presence at one of my evenings. I should not have thought that in a relatively less important place" (laughter here, at the expense of poor little Torre) "I should have to give up the small personal habits which brilliant and elevated audiences had been ready to overlook. Nor did I think I had to stand being heckled by a person who seems to have been rather spoilt by the favors of the fair sex." All this of course at the expense of the youth whom Cipolla never tired of presenting in the guise of *donnaiuolo* and rustic Don Juan. His persistent thin-skinnedness and animosity were in striking contrast to the self-confidence and the worldly success he boasted of. One might have assumed that the *giovanotto* was merely the chosen butt of Cipolla's customary professional sallies, had not the very pointed witticisms betrayed a genuine antagonism. No one looking at the physical parts of the two men need have been at a loss for the explanation, even if the deformed man had not constantly played on the other's supposed success with the fair sex. "Well," Cipolla went on, "before beginning our entertainment this evening, perhaps you will permit me to make myself comfortable."

And he went toward the hatstand to take off his things.

"Parla benissimo," asserted somebody in our neighborhood. So far, the man had done nothing; but what he had said was accepted as an achievement, by means of that he had made an impression. Among southern peoples speech is a constituent part of the pleasure of living, it enjoys far livelier social esteem than in the north. That national cement, the mother tongue, is paid symbolic honors down here, and there is something blithely symbolical in the pleasure people take in their respect for its forms and phonetics. They enjoy speaking, they enjoy listening; and they listen with discrimination. For the way a man speaks serves as a measure of his personal rank; carelessness and clumsiness are greeted with scorn, elegance and mastery are rewarded with social éclat. Wherefore the small man too, where it is a ques-

tion of getting his effect, chooses his phrase nicely and turns it with care. On this count, then, at least, Cipolla had won his audience; though he by no means belonged to the class of men which the Italian, in a singular mixture of moral and aesthetic judgments, labels *"simpatico."*

After removing his hat, scarf, and mantle, he came to the front of the stage, settling his coat, pulling down his cuffs with their large cuff-buttons, adjusting his absurd sash. He had very ugly hair; the top of his head, that is, was almost bald, while a narrow, black-varnished frizz of curls ran from front to back as though stuck on; the side hair, likewise blackened, was brushed forward to the corners of the eyes—it was, in short, the hairdressing of an old-fashioned circus-director, fantastic, but entirely suited to his outmoded personal type and worn with so much assurance as to take the edge off the public's sense of humor. The little physical defect of which he had warned us was now all too visible, though the nature of it was even now not very clear: the chest was too high, as is usual in such cases; but the corresponding malformation of the back did not sit between the shoulders, it took the form of a sort of hips or buttocks hump, which did not indeed hinder his movements but gave him a grotesque and dipping stride at every step he took. However, by mentioning his deformity beforehand he had broken the shock of it, and a delicate propriety of feeling appeared to reign throughout the hall.

"At your service," said Cipolla. "With your kind permission, we will begin the evening with some arithmetical tests."

Arithmetic? That did not sound much like sleight-of-hand. We began to have our suspicions that the man was sailing under a false flag, only we did not yet know which was the right one. I felt sorry on the children's account; but for the moment they were content simply to be there.

The numerical test which Cipolla now introduced was as simple as it was baffling. He began by fastening a piece of paper to the upper right-hand corner of the blackboard; then lifting it up, he wrote something underneath. He talked all the while, relieving the dryness of his offering by a constant flow of words, and showed himself a practiced speaker, never at a loss for conversational turns of phrase. It was in keeping with the nature of his performance, and at the same time vastly entertained the children, that he went on to eliminate the gap between stage and audience, which had already been bridged over by the curious skirmish with the fisher lad: he had representatives from the audience mount the stage, and himself descended the wooden steps to seek personal contact with his public. And again, with individuals, he

fell into his former taunting tone. I do not know how far that was a deliberate feature of his system; he preserved a serious, even a peevish air, but his audience, at least the more popular section, seemed convinced that that was all part of the game. So then, after he had written something and covered the writing by the paper, he desired that two persons should come up on the platform and help to perform the calculations. They would not be difficult, even for people not clever at figures. As usual, nobody volunteered, and Cipolla took care not to molest the more select portion of his audience. He kept to the populace. Turning to two sturdy young louts standing behind us, he beckoned them to the front, encouraging and scolding by turns. They should not stand there gaping, he said, unwilling to oblige the company. Actually, he got them in motion; with clumsy tread they came down the middle aisle, climbed the steps, and stood in front of the blackboard, grinning sheepishly at their comrades' shouts and applause. Cipolla joked with them for a few minutes, praised their heroic firmness of limb and the size of their hands, so well calculated to do this service for the public. Then he handed one of them the chalk and told him to write down the numbers as they were called out. But now the creature declared that he could not write! *"Non so scrivere,"* said he in his gruff voice, and his companion added that neither did he.

God knows whether they told the truth or whether they wanted to make game of Cipolla. Anyhow, the latter was far from sharing the general merriment which their confession aroused. He was insulted and disgusted. He sat there on a straw-bottomed chair in the center of the stage with his legs crossed, smoking a fresh cigarette out of his cheap packet; obviously it tasted the better for the cognac he had indulged in while the yokels were stumping up the steps. Again he inhaled the smoke and let it stream out between curling lips. Swinging his leg, with his gaze sternly averted from the two shamelessly chuckling creatures and from the audience as well, he stared into space as one who withdraws himself and his dignity from the contemplation of an utterly despicable phenomenon.

"Scandalous," said he, in a sort of icy snarl. "Go back to your places! In Italy everybody can write—in all her greatness there is no room for ignorance and unenlightenment. To accuse her of them, in the hearing of this international company, is a cheap joke, in which you yourselves cut a very poor figure and humiliate the government and the whole country as well. If it is true that Torre di Venere is indeed the last refuge of such ignorance, then I must blush to have visited the place—being, as I already was,

aware of its inferiority to Rome in more than one respect—"

Here Cipolla was interrupted by the youth with the Nubian coiffure and his jacket across his shoulder. His fighting spirit, as we now saw, had only abdicated temporarily, and he now flung himself into the breach in defense of his native heath. "That will do," said he loudly. "That's enough jokes about Torre. We all come from the place and we won't stand strangers making fun of it. These two chaps are our friends. Maybe they are no scholars, but even so they may be straighter than some folks in the room who are so free with their boasts about Rome, though they did not build it either."

That was capital. The young man had certainly cut his eye-teeth. And this sort of spectacle was good fun, even though it still further delayed the regular performance. It is always fascinating to listen to an altercation. Some people it simply amuses, they take a sort of kill-joy pleasure in not being principals. Others feel upset and uneasy, and my sympathies are with these latter, although on the present occasion I was under the impression that all this was part of the show—the analphabetic yokels no less than the *giovanotto* with the jacket. The children listened well pleased. They understood not at all, but the sound of the voices made them hold their breath. So this was a "magic evening"—at least it was the kind they have in Italy. They expressly found it "lovely."

Cipolla had stood up and with two of his scooping strides was at the footlights. "Well, well, see who's here!" said he with grim cordiality. "An old acquaintance! A young man with his heart at the end of his tongue" (he used the word *linguaccia,* which means a coated tongue, and gave rise to much hilarity). "That will do, my friends," he turned to the yokels. "I do not need you now, I have business with this deserving young man here, *con questo torregiano di Venere,* this tower of Venus, who no doubt expects the gratitude of the fair as a reward for his prowess—"

"*Ah, non scherziamo!* We're talking earnest," cried out the youth. His eyes flashed, and he actually made as though to pull off his jacket and proceed to direct methods of settlement.

Cipolla did not take him too seriously. We had exchanged apprehensive glances; but he was dealing with a fellow-countryman and had his native soil beneath his feet. He kept quite cool and showed complete mastery of the situation. He looked at his audience, smiled, and made a sideways motion of the head toward the young cockerel as though calling the public to witness how the man's bumptiousness only served to betray the simplicity of his mind. And then, for the second time, something strange happened, which set Cipolla's calm superiority

in an uncanny light, and in some mysterious and irritating way turned all the explosiveness latent in the air into matter for laughter.

Cipolla drew still nearer to the fellow, looking him in the eye with a peculiar gaze. He even came half-way down the steps that led into the auditorium on our left, so that he stood directly in front of the trouble-maker, on slightly higher ground. The riding-whip hung from his arm.

"My son, you do not feel much like joking," he said. "It is only too natural, for anyone can see that you are not feeling too well. Even your tongue, which leaves something to be desired on the score of cleanliness, indicates acute disorder of the gastric system. An evening entertainment is no place for people in your state; you yourself, I can tell, were of several minds whether you would not do better to put on a flannel bandage and go to bed. It was not good judgment to drink so much of that very sour white wine this afternoon. Now you have such a colic you would like to double up with the pain. Go ahead, don't be embarrassed. There is a distinct relief that comes from bending over, in cases of intestinal cramp."

He spoke thus, word for word, with quiet impressiveness and a kind of stern sympathy, and his eyes, plunged the while deep in the young man's, seemed to grow very tired and at the same time burning above their enlarged tear ducts— they were the strangest eyes, you could tell that not manly pride alone was preventing the young adversary from withdrawing his gaze. And presently, indeed, all trace of its former arrogance was gone from the bronzed young face. He looked open-mouthed at the Cavaliere and the open mouth was drawn in a rueful smile.

"Double over," repeated Cipolla. "What else can you do? With a colic like that you *must* bend. Surely you will not struggle against the performance of a perfectly natural action just because somebody suggests it to you?"

Slowly the youth lifted his forearms, folded and squeezed them across his body; it turned a little sideways, then bent, lower and lower, the feet shifted, the knees turned inward, until he had become a picture of writhing pain, until he all but groveled upon the ground. Cipolla let him stand for some seconds thus, then made a short cut through the air with his whip and went with his scooping stride back to the little table, where he poured himself out a cognac.

"*Il boit beaucoup,*" asserted a lady behind us. Was that the only thing that struck her? We could not tell how far the audience grasped the situation. The fellow was standing upright again, with a sheepish grin —he looked as though he scarcely knew how it had all happened. The scene had been followed with tense interest and applauded at the end; there were shouts of *"Bravo, Cipolla!"* and *"Bravo, giovanotto!"*

Apparently the issue of the duel was not looked upon as a personal defeat for the young man. Rather the audience encouraged him as one does an actor who succeeds in an unsympathetic role. Certainly his way of screwing himself up with cramp had been highly picturesque its appeal was directly calculated to impress the gallery—in short, a fine dramatic performance. But I am not sure how far the audience were moved by that natural tactfulness in which the south excels, or how far it penetrated into the nature of what was going on.

The Cavaliere, refreshed, had lighted another cigarette. The numerical tests might now proceed. A young man was easily found in the back row who was willing to write down on the blackboard the numbers as they were dictated to him. Him too we knew; the whole entertainment had taken on an intimate character through our acquaintance with so many of the actors. This was the man who worked at the greengrocer's in the main street; he had served us several times, with neatness and dispatch. He wielded the chalk with clerkly confidence, while Cipolla descended to our level and walked with his deformed gait through the audience, collecting numbers as they were given, in two, three, and four places, and calling them out to the grocer's assistant, who wrote them down in a column. In all this, everything on both sides was calculated to amuse, with its jokes and its oratorical asides. The artist could not fail to hit on foreigners, who were not ready with their figures, and with them he was elaborately patient and chivalrous, to the great amusement of the natives, whom he reduced to confusion in their turn, by making them translate numbers that were given in English or French. Some people gave dates concerned with great events in Italian history. Cipolla took them up at once and made patriotic comments. . . .

When fifteen numbers stood in a long straggling row on the board, Cipolla called for a general adding-match. Ready reckoners might add in their heads, but pencil and paper were not forbidden. Cipolla, while the work went on, sat on his chair near the blackboard, smoked and grimaced, with the complacent, pompous air cripples so often have. The five-place addition was soon done. Somebody announced the answer, somebody else confirmed it, a third had arrived at a slightly different result, but the fourth agreed with the first and second. Cipolla got up, tapped some ash from his coat, and lifted the paper at the upper right-hand corner of the board to display the writing. The correct answer, a sum close on a million, stood there; he had written it down beforehand.

Astonishment, and loud applause. The children were overwhelmed. How had he done that, they wanted to know. We told them it was a trick, not easily explainable offhand.

In short, the man was a conjuror. This was what a sleight-of-hand evening was like, so now they knew. First the fisherman had cramp, and then the right answer was written down beforehand—it was all simply glorious, and we saw with dismay that despite the hot eyes and the hand of the clock at almost half past ten, it would be very hard to get them away. There would be tears. And yet it was plain that this magician did not "magick" —at least not in the accepted sense, of manual dexterity—and that the entertainment was not at all suitable for children. Again, I do not know, either, what the audience really thought. Obviously there was grave doubt whether its answers had been given of "free choice"; here and there an individual might have answered of his own motion, but on the whole Cipolla certainly selected his people and thus kept the whole procedure in his own hands and directed it toward the given result. Even so, one had to admire the quickness of his calculations, however much one felt disinclined to admire anything else about the performance. Then his patriotism, his irritable sense of dignity—the Cavaliere's own countrymen might feel in their element with all that and continue in a laughing mood; but the combination certainly gave us outsiders food for thought.

Cipolla himself saw to it—though without giving them a name—that the nature of his powers should be clear beyond a doubt to even the least-instructed person. He alluded to them, of course, in his talk—and he talked without stopping—but only in vague, boastful, self-advertising phrases. He went on awhile with experiments on the same lines as the first, merely making them more complicated by introducing operations in multiplying, subtracting, and dividing; then he simplified them to the last degree in order to bring out the method. He simply had numbers "guessed" which were previously written under the paper; and the guess was nearly always right. One guesser admitted that he had had in mind to give a certain number, when Cipolla's whip went whistling through the air, and a quite different one slipped out, which proved to be the "right" one. Cipolla's shoulders shook. He pretended admiration for the powers of the people he questioned. But in all his compliments there was something fleering and derogatory; the victims could scarcely have relished them much, although they smiled, and although they might easily have set down some part of the applause to their own credit. Moreover, I had not the impression that the artist was popular with his public. A certain ill will and reluctance were in the air, but courtesy kept such feelings in check, as did Cipolla's competency and his stern self-confidence. Even the riding-whip, I think, did much to keep rebellion from becoming overt.

From tricks with numbers he passed to tricks with cards. There were two packs, which he drew out of his pockets, and so much I still remember, that the basis of the tricks he played with them was as follows: from the first pack he drew three cards and thrust them without looking at them inside his coat. Another person then drew three out of the second pack, and these turned out to be the same as the first three —not invariably all the three, for it did happen that only two were the same. But in the majority of cases Cipolla triumphed, showing his three cards with a little bow in acknowledgment of the applause with which his audience conceded his possession of strange powers— strange whether for good or evil. A young man in the front row, to our right, an Italian, with proud, finely chiseled features, rose up and said that he intended to assert his own will in his choice and consciously to resist any influence, of whatever sort. Under these circumstances, what did Cipolla think would be the result? "You will," answered the Cavaliere, "make my task somewhat more difficult thereby. As for the result, your resistance will not alter it in the least. Freedom exists, and also the will exists; but freedom of the will does not exist, for a will that aims at its own freedom aims at the unknown. You are free to draw or not to draw. But if you draw, you will draw the right cards —the more certainly, the more willfully obstinate your behavior."

One must admit that he could not have chosen his words better, to trouble the waters and confuse the mind. The refractory youth hesitated before drawing. Then he pulled out a card and at once demanded to see if it was among the chosen three. "But why?" queried Cipolla. "Why do things by halves?" Then, as the other defiantly insisted, "*E servito*," said the juggler, with a gesture of exaggerated servility; and held out the three cards fanwise, without looking at them himself. The left-hand card was the one drawn.

Amid general applause, the apostle of freedom sat down. How far Cipolla employed small tricks and manual dexterity to help out his natural talents, the deuce only knew. But even without them the result would have been the same: the curiosity of the entire audience was unbounded and universal, everybody both enjoyed the amazing character of the entertainment and unanimously conceded the professional skill of the performer. "*Lavora bene,*" we heard, here and there in our neighborhood; it signified the triumph of objective judgment over antipathy and repressed resentment.

After his last, incomplete, yet so much the more telling success, Cipolla had at once fortified himself with another cognac. Truly he did "drink a lot," and the fact made a bad impression. But obviously he needed the liquor and the cigarettes for the replenishment of his energy, upon which, as he himself said, heavy demands were made in all directions. Certainly in the intervals he looked very ill, exhausted and hollow-eyed. Then the little glassful would redress the balance, and the flow of lively, self-confident chatter run on, while the smoke he inhaled gushed out gray from his lungs. I clearly recall that he passed from the card tricks to parlor games—the kind based on certain powers which in human nature are higher or else lower than human reason: on intuition and "magnetic" transmission; in short, upon a low type of manifestation. What I do not remember is the precise order things came in. And I will not bore you with a description of these experiments; everybody knows them, everybody has at one time or another taken part in this finding of hidden articles, this blind carrying out of a series of acts, directed by a force that proceeds from organism to organism by unexplored paths. Everybody has had his little glimpse into the equivocal, impure, inexplicable nature of the occult, has been conscious of both curiosity and contempt, has shaken his head over the human tendency of those who deal in it to help themselves out with humbuggery, though, after all, the humbuggery is no disproof whatever of the genuineness of the other elements in the dubious amalgam. I can only say here that each single circumstance gains in weight and the whole greatly in impressiveness when it is a man like Cipolla who is the chief actor and guiding spirit in the sinister business. He sat smoking at the rear of the stage, his back to the audience while they conferred. The object passed from hand to hand which it was his task to find, with which he was to perform some action agreed upon beforehand. Then he would start to move zigzag through the hall, with his head thrown back and one hand outstretched, the other clasped in that of a guide who was in the secret but enjoined to keep himself perfectly passive, with his thoughts directed upon the agreed goal. Cipolla moved with the bearing typical in these experiments: now groping upon a false start, now with a quick forward thrust, now pausing as though to listen and by sudden inspiration correcting his course. The roles seemed reversed, the stream of influence was moving in the contrary direction, as the artist himself pointed out, in his ceaseless flow of discourse. The suffering, receptive, performing part was now his, the will he had before imposed on others was shut out, he acted in obedience to a voiceless common will which was in the air. But he made it perfectly clear that it all came to the same thing. The capacity for self-surrender, he said, for becoming a tool, for the most unconditional and utter self-abnegation, was but the reverse side of that other power to will and to command. Commanding and obeying formed together one single principle, one indissoluble unity; he who knew how to obey knew also how to command, and conversely;

the one idea was comprehended in the other, as people and leader were comprehended in one another. But that which was *done*, the highly exacting and exhausting performance, was in every case his, the leader's and mover's, in whom the will became obedience, the obedience will, whose person was the cradle and womb of both, and who thus suffered enormous hardship. Repeatedly he emphasized the fact that his lot was a hard one—presumably to account for his need of stimulant and his frequent recourse to the little glass.

Thus he groped his way forward, like a blind seer, led and sustained by the mysterious common will. He drew a pin set with a stone out of its hiding place in an Englishwoman's shoe, carried it, halting and pressing on by turns, to another lady—Signora Angiolieri—and handed it to her on bended knee, with the words it had been agreed he was to utter. "I present you with this in token of my respect," was the sentence. Their sense was obvious, but the words themselves not easy to hit upon, for the reason that they had been agreed on in French; the language complication seemed to us a little malicious, implying as it did a conflict between the audience's natural interest in the success of the miracle, and their desire to witness the humiliation of this presumptuous man. It was a strange sight: Cipolla on his knees before the signora, wrestling, amid efforts at speech, after knowledge of the preordained words. "I must say something," he said, "and I feel clearly what it is I must say. But I also feel that if it passed my lips it would be wrong. Be careful not to help me unintentionally!" he cried out, though very likely that was precisely what he was hoping for. *"Pensez très fort,"* he cried all at once, in bad French, and then burst out with the required words—in Italian, indeed, but with the final substantive pronounced in the sister tongue, in which he was probably far from fluent: he said *vénération* instead of *venerazione,* with an impossible nasal. And this partial success, after the complete success before it, the finding of the pin, the presentation of it on his knees to the right person—was almost more impressive than if he had got the sentence exactly right, and evoked bursts of admiring applause.

Cipolla got up from his knees and wiped the perspiration from his brow. You understand that this experiment with the pin was a single case, which I describe because it sticks in my memory. But he changed his method several times and improvised a number of variations suggested by his contact with his audience; a good deal of time thus went by. He seemed to get particular inspiration from the person of our landlady; she drew him on to the most extraordinary displays of clairvoyance. "It does not escape me, madame," he said to her, "that there is something unusual about you, some special and honorable distinction. He who has eyes to see descries about your lovely brow an aureola—if I mistake not, it once was stronger than now—a slowly paling radiance . . . hush, not a word! Don't help me. Beside you sits your husband—yes?" He turned toward the silent Signor Angiolieri. "You are the husband of this lady, and your happiness is complete. But in the midst of this happiness memories rise . . . the past, signora, so it seems to me, plays an important part in your present. You knew a king . . . has not a king crossed your path in bygone days?"

"No," breathed the dispenser of our midday soup, her golden-brown eyes gleaming in the noble pallor of her face.

"No? No, not a king; I meant that generally, I did not mean literally a king. Not a king, not a prince, and a prince after all, a king of a loftier realm; it was a great artist, at whose side you once—you would contradict me, and yet I am not wholly wrong. Well, then! It was a woman, a great, a world-renowned woman artist, whose friendship you enjoyed in your tender years, whose sacred memory overshadows and transfigures your whole existence. Her name? Need I utter it, whose fame has long been bound up with the Fatherland's, immortal as its own? Eleonora Duse," he finished, softly and with much solemnity.

The little woman bowed her

head, overcome. The applause was like a patriotic demonstration. Nearly everyone there knew about Signora Angiolieri's wonderful past; they were all able to confirm the Cavaliere's intuition—not least the present guests of Casa Eleonora. But we wondered how much of the truth he had learned as the result of professional inquiries made on his arrival. Yet I see no reason at all to cast doubt, on rational grounds, upon powers which, before our very eyes, became fatal to their possessor.

At this point there was an intermission. Our lord and master withdrew. Now I confess that almost ever since the beginning of my tale I have looked forward with dread to this moment in it. The thoughts of men are mostly not hard to read; in this case they are very easy. You are sure to ask why we did not choose this moment to go away—and I must continue to owe you an answer. I do not know why. I cannot defend myself. By this time it was certainly eleven, probably later. The children were asleep. The last series of tests had been too long, nature had had her way. They were sleeping in our laps, the little one on mine, the boy on his mother's. That was, in a way, a consolation; but at the same time it was also ground for compassion and a clear leading to take them home to bed. And I give you my word that we wanted to obey this touching admonition, we seriously wanted to. We roused the poor things and told

them it was now high time to go. But they were no sooner conscious than they began to resist and implore—you know how horrified children are at the thought of leaving before the end of a thing. No cajoling has any effect, you have to use force. It was so lovely, they wailed. How did we know what was coming next? Surely we could not leave until after the intermission; they liked a little nap now and again—only not go home, only not go to bed, while the beautiful evening was still going on!

We yielded, but only for the moment, of course—so far as we knew —only for a little while, just a few minutes longer. I cannot excuse our staying, scarcely can I even understand it. Did we think, having once said A, we had to say B—having once brought the children hither we had to let them stay? No, it is not good enough. Were we ourselves so highly entertained? Yes, and no. Our feelings for Cavaliere Cipolla were of a very mixed kind, but so were the feelings of the whole audience, if I mistake not, and nobody left. Were we under the sway of a fascination which emanated from this man who took so strange a way to earn his bread; a fascination which he gave out independently of the program and even between the tricks and which paralyzed our resolve? Again, sheer curiosity may account for something. One was curious to know how such an evening turned out; Cipolla in his remarks having all along hinted that he had tricks in his bag stranger than any he had yet produced.

But all that is not it—or at least it is not all of it. More correct it would be to answer the first question with another. Why had we not left Torre di Venere itself before now? To me the two questions are one and the same, and in order to get out of the impasse I might simply say that I had answered it already. For, as things had been in Torre in general: queer, uncomfortable, troublesome, tense, oppressive, so precisely they were here in this hall tonight. Yes, more than precisely. For it seemed to be the fountainhead of all the uncanniness and all the strained feelings which had oppressed the atmosphere of our holiday. This man whose return to the stage we were awaiting was the personification of all that; and, as we had not gone away in general, so to speak, it would have been inconsistent to do it in the particular case. You may call this an explanation, you may call it inertia, as you see fit. Any argument more to the purpose I simply do not know how to adduce.

Well, there was an interval of ten minutes, which grew into nearly twenty. The children remained awake. They were enchanted by our compliance, and filled the break to their own satisfaction by renewing relations with the popular sphere, with Antonio, Guiscardo, and the canoe man. They put their hands to their mouths and called messages across, appealing to us for the Italian words. "Hope you have a good catch tomorrow, a whole netful!" They called to Mario, Esquisito Mario: *"Mario, una cioccolata e biscotti!"* And this time he heeded and answered with a smile: *"Subito, signorini!"* Later we had reason to recall this kindly, if rather absent and pensive smile.

Thus the interval passed, the gong sounded. The audience, which had scattered in conversation, took their places again, the children sat up straight in their chairs with their hands in their laps. The curtain had not been dropped. Cipolla came forward again, with his dipping stride, and began to introduce the second half of the program with a lecture.

Let me state once for all that this self-confident cripple was the most powerful hypnotist I have ever seen in my life. It was pretty plain now that he threw dust in the public eye and advertised himself as a prestidigitator on account of police regulations which would have prevented him from making his living by the exercise of his powers. Perhaps this eye-wash is the usual thing in Italy; it may be permitted or even connived at by the authorities. Certainly the man had from the beginning made little concealment of the actual nature of his operations; and this second half of the program was quite frankly and exclusively devoted to one sort of experiment. While he still practiced some rhetorical circumlocutions, the tests themselves were one long series of attacks upon the will power, the loss or compulsion of volition. Comic, exciting, amazing by turns, by midnight they were still in full swing; we ran the gamut of all the phenomena this natural-unnatural field has to show, from the unimpressive at one end of the scale to the monstrous at the other. The audience laughed and applauded as they followed the grotesque details; shook their heads, clapped their knees, fell very frankly under the spell of this stern, self-assured personality. At the same time I saw signs that they were not quite complacent, not quite unconscious of the peculiar ignominy which lay, for the individual and for the general, in Cipolla's triumphs.

Two main features were constant in all the experiments: the liquor glass and the claw-handled riding-whip. The first was always invoked to add fuel to his demoniac fires; without it, apparently, they might have burned out. On this score we might even have felt pity for the man; but the whistle of his scourge, the insulting symbol of his domination, before which we all cowered, drowned out every sensation save a dazed and outbraved submission to his power. Did he then lay claim to our sympathy to boot? I was struck by a remark he made—it suggested no less. At the climax of his experiments, by stroking and breathing upon a certain young man who had offered himself as a subject and already proved himself a particularly susceptible one, he had not only

put him into the condition known as deep trance and extended his insensible body by neck and feet across the backs of two chairs, but had actually sat down on the rigid form as on a bench, without making it yield. The sight of this unholy figure in a frock-coat squatted on the stiff body was horrible and incredible; the audience, convinced that the victim of this scientific diversion must be suffering, expressed its sympathy: "*Ah, poveretto!*" Poor soul, poor soul! "*Poor soul!*" Cipolla mocked them, with some bitterness. "Ladies and gentlemen, you are barking up the wrong tree. *Sono io il poveretto.* I am the person who is suffering, I am the one to be pitied." We pocketed the information. Very good. Maybe the experiment was at his expense, maybe it was he who had suffered the cramp when the *giovanotto* over there had made the faces. But appearances were all against it; and one does not feel like saying *poveretto* to a man who is suffering to bring about the humiliation of others.

I have got ahead of my story and lost sight of the sequence of events. To this day my mind is full of the Cavaliere's feats of endurance; only I do not recall them in their order —which does not matter. So much I do know: that the longer and more circumstantial tests, which got the most applause, impressed me less than some of the small ones which passed quickly over. I remember the young man whose body Cipolla converted into a board, only because of the accompanying remarks which I have quoted. An elderly lady in a cane-seated chair was lulled by Cipolla in the delusion that she was on a voyage to India and gave a voluble account of her adventures by land and sea. But I found this phenomenon less impressive than one which followed immediately after the intermission. A tall, well-built, soldierly man was unable to lift his arm, after the hunchback had told him that he could not and given a cut through the air with his whip. I can still see the face of that stately, mustachioed colonel smiling and clenching his teeth as he struggled to regain his lost freedom of action. A staggering performance! He seemed to be exerting his will, and in vain; the trouble, however, was probably simply that he could not will. There was involved here that recoil of the will upon itself which paralyzes choice—as our tyrant had previously explained to the Roman gentleman.

Still less can I forget the touching scene, at once comic and horrible, with Signora Angiolieri. The Cavaliere, probably in his first bold survey of the room, had spied out her ethereal lack of resistance to his power. For actually he bewitched her, literally drew her out of her seat, out of her row, and away with him whither he willed. And in order to enhance his effect, he bade Signor Angiolieri call upon his wife by her name, to throw, as it were, all the weight of his existence and his rights in her into the scale, to rouse by the voice of her husband everything in his spouse's soul which could shield her virtue against the evil assaults of magic. And how vain it all was! Cipolla was standing at some distance from the couple, when he made a single cut with his whip through the air. It caused our landlady to shudder violently and turn her face toward him. "Sofronia!" cried Signor Angiolieri—we had not known that Signora Angiolieri's name was Sofronia. And he did well to call, everybody saw that there was no time to lose. His wife kept her face turned in the direction of the diabolical Cavaliere, who with his ten long yellow fingers was making passes at his victim, moving backwards as he did so, step by step. Then Signora Angiolieri, her pale face gleaming, rose up from her seat, turned right round, and began to glide after him. Fatal and forbidding sight! Her face as though moonstruck, stiff-armed, her lovely hands lifted a little at the wrists, the feet as it were together, she seemed to float slowly out of her row and after the tempter. "Call her, sir, keep on calling," prompted the redoubtable man. And Signor Angiolieri, in a weak voice, called: "Sofronia!" Ah, again and again he called; as his wife went further off he even curved one hand round his lips and beckoned with the other as he called. But the poor voice of love and duty echoed unheard, in vain, behind the lost one's back; the signora swayed along, moonstruck, deaf, enslaved; she glided into the middle aisle and down it toward the fingering hunchback, toward the door. We were convinced, we were driven to the conviction, that she would have followed her master, had he so willed it, to the ends of the earth.

"*Accidente!*" cried out Signor Angiolieri, in genuine affright, springing up as the exit was reached. But at the same moment the Cavaliere put aside, as it were, the triumphal crown and broke off. "Enough, signora, I thank you," he said, and offered his arm to lead her back to her husband. "Signor," he greeted the latter, "here is your wife. Unharmed, with my compliments, I give her into your hands. Cherish with all the strength of your manhood a treasure which is so wholly yours, and let your zeal be quickened by knowing that there are powers stronger than reason or virtue, and not always so magnanimously ready to relinquish their prey!"

Poor Signor Angiolieri, so quiet, so bald! He did not look as though he would know how to defend his happiness, even against powers much less demoniac than these which were now adding mockery to frightfulness. Solemnly and pompously the Cavaliere retired to the stage, amid applause to which his eloquence gave double strength. It was this particular episode, I feel sure, that set the seal upon his as-cendancy. For now he made them dance, yes, literally; and the dancing lent a dissolute, abandoned, topsy-turvy air to the scene, a drunken abdication of the critical spirit which had so long resisted the spell of this man. Yes, he had had to fight to get the upper hand —for instance against the animosity of the young Roman gentleman, whose rebellious spirit threatened to serve others as a rallying-point. But it was precisely upon the importance of example that the Cavaliere was so strong. He had the wit to make his attack at the weakest point and to choose as his first victim that feeble, ecstatic youth whom he had previously made into a board. The master had but to look at him, when this young man would fling himself back as though struck by lightning, place his hands rigidly at his sides, and fall into a state of military somnambulism, in which it was plain to any eye that he was open to the most absurd suggestion that might be made to him. He seemed quite content in his abject state, quite pleased to be relieved of the burden of voluntary choice. Again and again he offered himself as a subject and gloried in the model facility he had in losing consciousness. So now he mounted the platform, and a single cut of the whip was enough to make him dance to the Cavaliere's orders, in a kind of complacent ecstasy, eyes closed, head nodding, lank limbs flying in all directions.

It looked unmistakably like enjoyment, and other recruits were not long in coming forward: two other young men, one humbly and one well dressed, were soon jigging alongside the first. But now the gentleman from Rome bobbed up again, asking defiantly if the Cavaliere would engage to make him dance too, even against his will.

"Even against your will," answered Cipolla, in unforgettable accents. That frightful *"anche se non vuole"* still rings in my ears. The struggle began. After Cipolla had taken another little glass and lighted a fresh cigarette he stationed the Roman at a point in the middle aisle and himself took up a position some distance behind him, making his whip whistle through the air as he gave the order: *"Balla!"* His opponent did not stir. *"Balla!"* repeated the Cavaliere incisively, and snapped his whip. You saw the young man move his neck round in his collar; at the same time one hand lifted slightly at the wrist, one ankle turned outward. But that was all, for the time at least; merely a tendency to twitch, now sternly repressed, now seeming about to get the upper hand. It escaped nobody that here a heroic obstinacy, a fixed resolve to resist, must needs be conquered; we were beholding a gallant effort to strike out and save the honor of the human race. He twitched but danced not; and the struggle was so prolonged that the Cavaliere had to divide his attention between it and the stage, turning now and then to make his riding-whip whistle in the direction of the dancers, as it were to keep them in leash. At the same time he advised the audience that no fatigue was involved in such activities, however long they went on, since it was not the automatons up there who danced, but himself. Then once more his eye would bore itself into the back of the Roman's neck and lay siege to the strength of purpose which defied him.

One saw it waver, that strength of purpose, beneath the repeated summonses and whip-crackings. Saw with an objective interest which yet was not quite free from traces of sympathetic emotion—from pity, even from a cruel kind of pleasure. If I understand what was going on, it was the negative character of the young man's fighting position which was his undoing. It is likely that *not* willing is not a practicable state of mind; *not* to want to do something may be in the long run a mental content impossible to subsist on. Between not willing a certain thing and not willing at all—in other words, yielding to another person's will—there may lie too small a space for the idea of freedom to squeeze into. Again, there were the Cavaliere's persuasive words, woven in among the whip-crackings and commands, as he mingled effects that were his own secret with others of a bewilderingly psychological kind. *"Balla!"* said he. "Who wants to torture himself like that? Is forcing yourself your idea of freedom? *Una ballatina!*

Why, your arms and legs are aching for it. What a relief to give way to them—there, you are dancing already! That is no struggle any more, it is a pleasure!" And so it was. The jerking and twitching of the refractory youth's limbs had at last got the upper hand; he lifted his arms, then his knees, his joints quite suddenly relaxed, he flung his legs and danced, and amid bursts of applause the Cavaliere led him to join the row of puppets on the stage. Up there we could see his face as he "enjoyed" himself; it was clothed in a broad grin and the eyes were half-shut. In a way, it was consoling to see that he was having a better time than he had had in the hour of his pride.

His "fall" was, I may say, an epoch. The ice was completely broken, Cipolla's triumph had reached its height. The Circe's wand, that whistling leather whip with the claw handle, held absolute sway. At one time—it must have been well after midnight—not only were there eight or ten persons dancing on the little stage, but in the hall below a varied animation reigned, and a long-toothed Anglo-Saxoness in a pince-nez left her seat of her own motion to perform a tarentella in the center aisle. Cipolla was lounging in a cane-seated chair at the left of the stage, gulping down the smoke of a cigarette and breathing it impudently out through his bad teeth. He tapped his foot and shrugged his shoulders, looking down upon the abandoned scene in the hall; now and then he snapped his whip backwards at a laggard upon the stage. The children were awake at the moment. With shame I speak of them. For it was not good to be here, least of all for them; that we had not taken them away can only be explained by saying that we had caught the general devil-may-careness of the hour. By that time it was all one. Anyhow, thank goodness, they lacked understanding for the disreputable side of the entertainment, and in their innocence were perpetually charmed by the unheard-of indulgence which permitted them to be present at such a thing as a magician's "evening." Whole quarter-hours at a time they drowsed on our laps, waking refreshed and rosy-cheeked, with sleep-drunken eyes, to laugh to bursting at the leaps and jumps the magician made those people up there make. They had not thought it would be so jolly; they joined with their clumsy little hands in every round of applause. And jumped for joy upon their chairs, as was their wont, when Cipolla beckoned to their friend Mario from the Esquisito, beckoned to him just like a picture in a book, holding his hand in front of his nose and bending and straightening the forefinger by turns.

Mario obeyed. I can see him now going up the stairs to Cipolla, who continued to beckon him, in that droll, picture-book sort of way. He hesitated for a moment at first; that, too, I recall quite clearly. During the whole evening he had lounged against a wooden pillar at the side entrance, with his arms folded, or else with his hands thrust into his jacket pockets. He was on our left, near the youth with the militant hair, and had followed the performance attentively, so far as we had seen, if with no particular animation and God knows how much comprehension. He could not much relish being summoned thus, at the end of the evening. But it was only too easy to see why he obeyed. After all, obedience was his calling in life; and then, how should a simple lad like him find it within his human capacity to refuse compliance to a man so throned and crowned as Cipolla at that hour? Willy-nilly he left his column and with a word of thanks to those making way for him he mounted the steps with a doubtful smile on his full lips.

Picture a thickset youth of twenty years, with clipped hair, a low forehead, and heavy-lidded eyes of an indefinite gray, shot with green and yellow. These things I knew from having spoken with him, as we often had. There was a saddle of freckles on the flat nose, the whole upper half of the face retreated behind the lower, and that again was dominated by thick lips that parted to show the salivated teeth. These thick lips and the veiled look of the eyes lent the whole face a primitive melancholy—it was that which had drawn us to him from the first. In it was not the faintest trace of brutality—indeed, his hands would

have given the lie to such an idea, being unusually slender and delicate even for a southerner. They were hands by which one liked being served.

We knew him humanly without knowing him personally, if I may make that distinction. We saw him nearly every day, and felt a certain kindness for his dreamy ways, which might at times be actual inattentiveness, suddenly transformed into a redeeming zeal to serve. His mien was serious, only the children could bring a smile to his face. It was not sulky, but uningratiating, without intentional effort to please —or, rather, it seemed to give up being pleasant in the conviction that it could not succeed. We should have remembered Mario in any case, as one of those homely recollections of travel which often stick in the mind better than more important ones. But of his circumstances we knew no more than that his father was a petty clerk in the Municipio and his mother took in washing.

His white waiter's-coat became him better than the faded striped suit he wore, with a gay colored scarf instead of a collar, the ends tucked into his jacket. He neared Cipolla, who however did not leave off that motion of his finger before his nose, so that Mario had to come still closer, right up to the chair seat and the master's legs. Whereupon the latter spread out his elbows and seized the lad, turning him so that we had a view of his face. Then gazed him briskly up and down, with a careless, commanding eye. "Well, *ragazzo mio,* how comes it we make acquaintance so late in the day? But believe me, I made yours long ago. Yes, yes, I've had you in my eye this long while and known what good stuff you were made of. How could I go and forget you again? Well, I've had a good deal to think about. . . . Now tell me, what is your name? The first name, that's all I want."

"My name is Mario," the young man answered, in a low voice.

"Ah, Mario. Very good. Yes, yes, there is such a name, quite a common name, a classic name too, one of those which preserve the heroic traditions of the Fatherland. *Bravo! Salve!*" And he flung up his arm slantingly above his crooked shoulder, palm outward, in the Roman salute. He may have been slightly tipsy by now, and no wonder; but he spoke as before, clearly, fluently, and with emphasis. Though about this time there had crept into his voice a gross, autocratic note, and a kind of arrogance was in his sprawl.

"Well, now, Mario *mio,*" he went on, "it's a good thing you came this evening, and that's a pretty scarf you've got on; it is becoming to your style of beauty. It must stand you in good stead with the girls, the pretty pretty girls of Torre—"

From the row of youths, close by the place where Mario had been standing, sounded a laugh. It came from the youth with the militant hair. He stood there, his jacket over his shoulder, and laughed outright, rudely and scornfully.

Mario gave a start. I think it was a shrug, but he may have started and then hastened to cover the movement by shrugging his shoulders, as much as to say that the neckerchief and the fair sex were matters of equal indifference to him.

The Cavaliere gave a downward glance.

"We needn't trouble about him," he said. "He is jealous, because your scarf is so popular with the girls, maybe partly because you and I are so friendly up here. Perhaps he'd like me to put him in mind of his colic—I could do it free of charge. Tell me, Mario. You've come here this evening for a bit of fun—and in the daytime you work in an ironmonger's shop?"

"In a café," corrected the youth.

"Oh, in a café. That's where Cipolla nearly came a cropper! What you are is a cup-bearer, a Ganymede—I like that, it is another classical allusion—*Salvietta!*" Again the Cavaliere saluted, to the huge gratification of his audience.

Mario smiled too. "But before that," he interpolated, in the interest of accuracy, "I worked for a while in a shop in Portoclemente." He seemed visited by a natural desire to assist the prophecy by dredging out its essential features.

"There, didn't I say so? In an ironmonger's shop?"

"They kept combs and brushes," Mario got round it.

"Didn't I say that you were not always a Ganymede? Not always at the sign of the serviette? Even when Cipolla makes a mistake, it is a kind that makes you believe in him. Now tell me: Do you believe in me?"

An indefinite gesture.

"A half-way answer," commented the Cavaliere. "Probably it is not easy to win your confidence. Even for me, I can see, it is not so easy. I see in your features a reserve, a sadness, *un tratto di malinconia* . . . tell me" (he seized Mario's hand persuasively) "have you troubles?"

"*Nossignore,*" answered Mario, promptly and decidedly.

"You *have* troubles," insisted the Cavaliere, bearing down the denial by the weight of his authority. "Can't I see? Trying to pull the wool over Cipolla's eyes, are you? Of course, about the girls—it is a girl, isn't it? You have love troubles?"

Mario gave a vigorous head-shake. And again the *giovanotto's* brutal laugh rang out. The Cavaliere gave heed. His eyes were roving about somewhere in the air; but he cocked an ear to the sound, then swung his whip backwards, as he had once or twice before in his conversation with Mario, that none of his puppets might flag in their zeal. The gesture had nearly cost him his new prey: Mario gave a sudden start in the direction of the steps. But Cipolla had him in his clutch.

"Not so fast," said he. "That would be fine, wouldn't it? So you want to skip, do you, Ganymede, right in the middle of the fun, or, rather, when it is just beginning? Stay with me, I'll show you something nice. I'll convince you. You have no reason to worry, I promise you. This girl—you know her and others know her too—what's her name? Wait! I read the name in your eyes, it is on the tip of my tongue and yours too—"

"Silvestra!" shouted the *giovanotto* from below.

The Cavaliere's face did not change.

"Aren't there the forward people?" he asked, not looking down, more as in undisturbed converse with Mario. "Aren't there the young fighting-cocks that crow in season and out? Takes the word out of your mouth, the conceited fool, and seems to think he has some special right to it. Let him be. But Silvestra, your Silvestra—ah, what a girl that is! What a prize! Brings your heart into your mouth to see her walk or laugh or breathe, she is so lovely. And her round arms when she washes, and tosses her head back to get the hair out of her eyes! An angel from paradise!"

Mario stared at him, his head thrust forward. He seemed to have forgotten the audience, forgotten where he was. The red rings round his eyes had got larger, they looked as though they were painted on. His thick lips parted.

"And she makes you suffer, this angel," went on Cipolla, "or, rather, you make yourself suffer for her— there is a difference, my lad, a most important difference, let me tell you. There are misunderstandings in love, maybe nowhere else in the world are there so many. I know what you are thinking: what does this Cipolla, with his little physical defect, know about love? Wrong, all wrong, he knows a lot. He has a wide and powerful understanding of its workings, and it pays to listen to his advice. But let's leave Cipolla out, cut him out altogether and think only of Silvestra, your peerless Silvestra! What! Is she to give any young gamecock the preference, so that he can laugh while you cry? To prefer him to a chap like you, so full of feeling and so sympathetic? Not very likely, is it? It is impossible—we know better, Cipolla and she. If I were to put myself in her place and choose between the two of you, a tarry lout like that—a codfish, a sea urchin— and a Mario, a knight of the serviette, who moves among gentlefolk and hands round refreshments with an air—my word, but my heart would speak in no uncertain tones—it knows to whom I gave it long ago. It is time that he should see and understand, my chosen one! It is time that you see me and recognize me, Mario, my beloved! Tell me, who am I?"

It was grisly, the way the betrayer made himself irresistible, wreathed and coquetted with his crooked shoulder, languished with the puffy eyes, and showed his splintered teeth in a sickly smile. And alas, at his beguiling words, what was come of our Mario? It is hard for me to tell, hard as it was for me to see; for here was nothing less than an utter abandonment of the inmost soul, a public exposure of timid and deluded passion and rapture. He put his hands across his mouth, his shoulders rose and fell with his pantings. He could not, it was plain, trust his eyes and ears for joy, and the one thing he forgot was precisely that he could not trust them. "Silvestra!" he breathed, from the very depths of his vanquished heart.

"Kiss me!" said the hunchback. "Trust me, I love thee. Kiss me here." And with the tip of his index finger, hand, arm, and little finger outspread, he pointed to his cheek, near the mouth. And Mario bent and kissed him.

It had grown very still in the room. That was a monstrous moment, grotesque and thrilling, the moment of Mario's bliss. In that evil span of time, crowded with a sense of the illusiveness of all joy, one sound became audible, and that not quite at once, but on the instant of the melancholy and ribald meeting between Mario's lips and the repulsive flesh which thrust iself forward for his caress. It was the sound of a laugh, from the *giovanotto* on our left. It broke into the dramatic suspense of the moment, coarse, mocking, and yet—or I must have been grossly mistaken—with an undertone of compassion for the poor bewildered, victimized creature. It had a faint ring of that *"Poveretto"* which Cipolla had declared was wasted on the wrong person, when he claimed the pity for his own.

The laugh still rang in the air when the recipient of the caress gave his whip a little swish, low down, close to his chair leg, and Mario started up and flung himself back. He stood in that posture staring, his hands one over the other on those desecrated lips. Then he beat his temples with his clenched fists, over and over; turned and staggered down the steps, while the audience applauded, and Cipolla sat there with his hands in his lap, his shoulders shaking. Once below, and even while in full retreat, Mario hurled himself round with legs flung wide apart; one arm flew up, and two flat shattering detonations crashed through applause and laughter.

There was instant silence. Even the dancers came to a full stop and stared about, struck dumb. Cipolla bounded from his seat. He stood with his arms spread out, slanting as though to ward everybody off, as though next moment he would cry out: "Stop! Keep.back! Silence! What was that?" Then, in that instant, he sank back in his seat, his head rolling on his chest; in the next he had fallen sideways to the floor, where he lay motionless, a huddled heap of clothing, with limbs awry.

The commotion was indescribable. Ladies hid their faces, shuddering, on the breasts of their escorts. There were shouts for a doctor, for the police. People flung themselves on Mario in a mob, to disarm him, to take away the weapon that hung from his fingers—that small, dull-metal, scarcely pistol-shaped tool with hardly any barrel—in how strange and unexpected a direction had fate leveled it!

And now—now finally, at last —we took the children and led them toward the exit, past the pair of *carabinieri* just entering. Was that the end, they wanted to know, that they might go in peace? Yes, we assured them, that was the end. An end of horror, a fatal end. And yet a liberation—for I could not, and cannot, but find it so!

JENNINGS and CALITRI STORIES

TEACHER'S
GUIDE

INTRODUCTION

This collection of stories is divided into three sections. Part One, "Stories of Impact," consists of twelve very short stories, each to be read and discussed in class within a single class period. Part Two, "Stories of Depth," consists of twelve longer stories, which may be assigned for home reading and discussed in class the following day. Part Three, "Stories to Think About," contains eight optional stories, which abler students may read as they find time, and which may be discussed or not at the discretion of the teacher.

The book also contains seventeen poems, and a verse from the Old Testament, each selected to sharpen the impact of the story to which it is related or to underscore its theme. These may be regarded as complementary to the stories they follow, not as selections to be "taught." Let the student discover them.

All the stories and poems bear the mark of the literary craftsman. Five are works of Nobel Prize winners and seven are works of Pulitzer Prize winners. (Page 6.) All are literature of recognized stature and strong impact.

Impact is two-fold, emotional and intellectual. Neither aspect should be slighted. The reader must honestly and freely express what he feels and what he thinks, for in this double involvement he may best approach that kind of understanding which marks the beginning of maturity.

The teaching plan implicit in the choice and arrangement of these stories may be developed by springboard questions: What do you see? What do you feel? What do you think? Add to the second and third questions their corollaries, the "why's."

The authors prefer not to offer in the text conventional and perhaps constricting study questions. The teacher, who is in direct, daily contact with his pupils, can best help his students to make their way through the two-fold adventure in thought and feeling that constitutes a valid literary experience.

In order for this dual adventure to occur, certain conditions must prevail. Reading is an intensely personal experience. It involves the reaction of the reader to what is read. It is conditioned by the reader's temperament and background, and whatever those two have combined to make him; it is affected by the conditions, both physical and psychological, under which the reading is done; it is directed by the purposes for which the reading is being undertaken; it is mediated by the degree of basic language skill possessed by the reader, although interest will often overcome some of the handicaps of the poor reader. For these reasons, the teacher ideally must provide an atmosphere of informality in the classroom; a receptive attitude that begins with the teacher and spreads through the class; and a respect for the right of each individual to share, or to withhold, personal responses.

Every teacher strives to achieve conditions similar to these, often in the face of adverse elements. The kind and quality of the stories in Part One of this book will be the teacher's ally. Short as they are, they will elicit the kind of response, awareness, and discussion that will prepare the way for more sustained, more difficult, and more subtle stories—the "Stories of Depth." The individual student will then be able to go on to Part Three on his own.

There is no editorial material appended to the stories in this book, nor are any judgments implied. Let each reader arrive at his own judgments. For the teacher, whose time and resources are limited, some suggestions may be useful. Accordingly, the authors present in this manual a short discussion of each story—its theme, the probable trend of the discussion that will stem from it, and procedures that may enhance its effectiveness.

Without concern for any "motivating" experience, place the book in the hands of the student. He will read. And the stories he reads in Part One will of themselves motivate his reading of Parts Two and Three.

Alternate Ways of Using This Book

Not all teachers will want to follow the plan implicit in the table of contents. Some may prefer a thematic approach or a chronological approach. The following suggestions will be helpful in such situations.

A THEMATIC GROUPING

Inner Man: Stories of conflicts within oneself.

Frankau The Duchess and the Smugs	*Hemingway* The Undefeated
	Steinbeck Molly Morgan
Hawthorne The Minister's Black Veil	*Walsh* The Quiet Man
	Faulkner Barn Burning

Man and His Family: Stories of loyalty, insight, and understanding.

Faulkner Barn Burning	*Gale* Bill's Little Girl
Björnson The Father	*Gordimer* My First Two Women
Cather Paul's Case	*Lawrence* The Rocking-Horse Winner
Collier Thus I Refute Beelzy	
Dell The Blanket	*Enright* Nancy
Ford Snake Dance	

Man and His Society: Stories of the neighborhood and social world.

Enright Nancy	*De Maupassant* The Necklace
Bingham The Unpopular Passenger	*Fitzgerald* Bernice Bobs Her Hair
	Frankau The Duchess and the Smugs

Henry After Twenty Years	*Sandburg* A Girl from the Queer
Heyert The New Kid	People
Lardner Haircut	*Hawthorne* The Minister's Black
	Veil

Man and His Emotions: Stories of love, hate, fear, and guilt.

Hawthorne The Minister's Black	*Poe* The Cask of Amontillado
Veil	*Saroyan* Romance
Connell The Most Dangerous	*Steinbeck* Molly Morgan
Game	*West* A Time of Learning
Hemingway The Undefeated	*O'Flaherty* The Sniper

Man and Survival: Stories of strife and the future of man.

O'Flaherty The Sniper	*Dahl* The Great Automatic
Bradbury The Golden Kite,	Grammatisator
the Silver Wind	*Mann* Mario and the Magician
Crane The Upturned Face	*Wylie* The Answer

Stories that appear in two different categories are applicable in more than one way. Note that each category begins with the last story of the preceding group, thus relating themes through a "story bridge."

A CHRONOLOGICAL GROUPING

Before 1900:

Björnson The Father	*Hawthorne* The Minister's
Crane The Upturned Face	Black Veil
De Maupassant The Necklace	*Poe* The Cask of Amontillado

1901–1920:

Cather Paul's Case	*Lawrence* The Rocking-Horse
Dell The Blanket	Winner
Gale Bill's Little Girl	*O'Flaherty* The Sniper
Henry After Twenty Years	

1921–1940:

Connell The Most Dangerous	*Hemingway* The Undefeated
Game	*Lardner* Haircut
Faulkner Barn Burning	*Mann* Mario and the Magician
Fitzgerald Bernice Bobs Her Hair	*Saroyan* Romance
Ford Snake Dance	*Steinbeck* Molly Morgan

1941–1956:

Bingham The Unpopular	*Dahl* The Great Automatic
Passenger	Grammatisator
Bradbury The Golden Kite,	*Enright* Nancy
the Silver Wind	*Frankau* The Duchess and
Collier Thus I Refute Beelzy	the Smugs

Gordimer My First Two Women	*Walsh* The Quiet Man
Heyert The New Kid	*West* A Time of Learning
Sandburg A Girl from the Queer People	*Wylie* The Answer

STORY AUTHORS BY NATIONALITY

American

Robert Bingham	*Elizabeth Enright*	*Ernest Hemingway*	*Carl Sandburg*
Ray Bradbury	*William Faulkner*	*O. Henry*	*William Saroyan*
Willa Cather	*F. Scott Fitzgerald*	*Murray Heyert*	*John Steinbeck*
Richard Connell	*Corey Ford*	*Ring Lardner*	*Jessamyn West*
Stephen Crane	*Zona Gale*	*Edgar Allan Poe*	*Philip Wylie*
Floyd Dell	*Nathaniel Hawthorne*		

English

John Collier	*Roald Dahl*	*Pamela Frankau*	*D. H. Lawrence*

Irish
  Liam O'Flaherty   *Maurice Walsh*

French
  Guy de Maupassant

Scandinavian
  Björnstjerne Björnson

German
  Thomas Mann

South African
  Nadine Gordimer

POETS BY NATIONALITY

American
  Franklin P. Adams   *Robert Frost*
  Rosemary Benét   *Edna St. Vincent Millay*
  Stephen Vincent Benét   *Edwin Arlington Robinson*
  Emily Dickinson   *Carl Sandburg*

English
  William Blake   *A. E. Housman*
  Walter de la Mare   *D. H. Lawrence*
  Thomas Hardy   *Siegfried Sassoon*
  William Ernest Henley

Irish
  William Butler Yeats

HONORS

Nobel Prize Winners

Björnstjerne Björnson   1903
William Butler Yeats   1923
Thomas Mann   1929

William Faulkner   1949
Ernest Hemingway   1954

Pulitzer Prize Winners

Zona Gale   1921
Edwin Arlington Robinson   1922,
        1925, 1928
Edna St. Vincent Millay   1923
Willa Cather   1923

Robert Frost   1924, 1932, 1937,
                              1943
Stephen Vincent Benét   1929, 1944
Carl Sandburg   1940

The Hall of Fame

Nathaniel Hawthorne

Edgar Allan Poe

PART 1

STORIES OF IMPACT

The twelve stories of the first group are simple in structure, each short enough to be read in a fraction of a class period. Each story evokes new insight into human relations or self-discovery. The student will find his sympathies quickly engaged. His spontaneous response will be emotional. How does he feel about what happens? Why?

His more deliberate reactions will be intellectual. Move in discussion from his feelings to his judgments. To make this shift the student must identify and put into words his thoughts and feelings. By the end of Part One he will have learned to handle such concepts as are involved in the following questions: What kinds of conflict are involved? How is the problem resolved? Is the solution reasonable and in keeping with the characters as we know them? Is it equally satisfying to his reason and to his sympathies? If the reader reacts in two ways to the impact of a story, is either way more important than the other? Can a story be good that awakens only one kind of response and not the other?

THE SNIPER
Page 3

by Liam O'Flaherty (1896–   ), Irish novelist and short-story writer. His subjects are almost exclusively Irish, often related to the revolutionary periods of 1916 and 1923.

Theme: In the clash of ideologies and ideals, who dies when we kill?

Discussion: This story is concerned with one simple fact—a man kills his brother. There is no extended characterization, no complexity of plot. Ask these central questions:

1. What happened?
2. What did the story make you feel?
3. Would the story be less moving if the man killed were not the sniper's brother? In a deeper sense, does not man always kill his brother when he kills?
4. Has anyone read Ambrose Bierce's "Horseman in the Sky"? What has the Bierce story in common with "The Sniper"?

Without calling attention to Hardy's poem, "The Man He Killed," which follows this story, wait to see whether students of their own accord will read it and observe the relation of its meaning to the theme of "The Sniper."

Resources for Related Experiences:
Short story collections: *Spring Sowing, The Wild Swan,* Liam O'Flaherty
Novels: *Famine, The Informer,* Liam O'Flaherty
Plays: *The Plough and the Stars, The Shadow of a Gunman,* Sean O'Casey
Films: *Odd Man Out, The Informer*
Recordings: See Victor catalogue for Irish revolutionary songs and ballads such as "The Wearing of the Green" and "The Boys from County Mayo."

BILL'S LITTLE GIRL   Page 11

by **Zona Gale** (1874-1938), American novelist and short-story writer, whose work deals largely with life in small towns and the Midwest.

Theme: A parent's sacrifice for the good of his child; the conflict between emotion and reason.

Discussion:
1. Why is this story particularly moving?
2. Could Bill have done anything else? What?
3. Show how this story represents a conflict between emotion and reason.
4. What other kinds of vital choices do most people have to make involving emotion and reason?
5. What decision of your own can you recall that required a choice between what you wanted and what you knew was best?

Resources for Related Experiences:
  Short story collections: *Yellow Gentians and Blue, The Bridal Pond,*
    Zona Gale
  Novels: *Friendship Village,* Zona Gale; *Dombey and Son,* Charles
    Dickens
  Plays: *Mrs. McThing,* Mary Coyle Chase; *Trifles,* Zona Gale
  Film: *The Champ,* with Wallace Beery and Jackie Cooper

ROMANCE   Page 11

by William Saroyan (1908–   ), American novelist, playwright, and
  short-story writer, whose work celebrates brotherhood and love. Saroyan
  is of Armenian descent. He often chooses a California locale.

Theme: Romance generally may be found wherever there are two persons looking for it. (What is the relation of romance to love?)

Discussion: If students do not react spontaneously, suggest a written
  commentary:
    "Write down exactly what you feel and think. You do not have to
put your name on the paper, and there will be no formal evaluation of
the writing. What we are concerned with here is that you tell *yourself*
what this story means to you."
    Read these notes in confidence. They will represent a broad sampling
of a total class experience. If a large majority of the class seems to be
concerned with a mere retelling of the story, then it can be assumed that
a true reader-writer relationship has not yet been established. Do not
try to force it. If, on the other hand, many of the responses are personal
in nature or are attempts to evaluate the situation, ask permission of
the writers to read aloud some of the more perceptive responses. Free
discussion may follow.
    You may want to make use of this technique again from time to
time. A systematic card file is useful as a record of the responses the
students make to the stories they read.
    1. Each student should have a supply of 3-by-5-inch index cards.
    2. At the end of each story, having closed the book and thought about
what has been read, the student will record spontaneously what he is
thinking and feeling.
    3. The student's card file will be his personal property, accessible to
the teacher for purposes of evaluation, but available for reading aloud
only with the consent of the student.
    4. In class discussion the teacher may refer to good ideas he has noted
in these files only when he does not violate the confidence of the student.
    Students may discover that Edna St. Vincent Millay's poem "Re-

cuerdo," which follows "Romance," might easily be a sequel to Saroyan's story, by carrying the couple into another adventure.

Resources for Related Experiences:
Short story collections: *My Name Is Aram, The Man on the Flying Trapeze, The Human Comedy,* William Saroyan
Plays: *My Heart's in the Highlands, The Time of Your Life,* William Saroyan
Poetry of love: Edna St. Vincent Millay, Elinor Wylie, Sara Teasdale, Dorothy Parker

THE BLANKET   Page 16

by Floyd Dell (1887–   ), American short-story writer, whose best work appeared in the 'twenties.

Theme: Insight into the situation of older people in our society.

Discussion: Our government has established social security since the time of this story. Yet it does not solve all problems. What problems does it not solve?
   William Butler Yeats' "Song of the Old Mother" offers a feminine counterpart of the old man in "The Blanket."

Resources for Related Experiences:
Short story: "One for the Collection" in *The Moment before the Rain,* Elizabeth Enright
Plays: *The Old Lady Shows Her Medals,* James M. Barrie; *The Wooden Dish,* Edmund Morris; *King Lear,* Shakespeare
Poems: "Death of the Hired Man," Robert Frost; "Gerontion," T. S. Eliot; "Rabbi Ben Ezra," Robert Browning; "Sailing to Byzantium," William Butler Yeats
Film: *Good-bye Mr. Chips* from James Hilton's novel of that name

SNAKE DANCE   Page 19

by Corey Ford (1902–   ), American humorist and short-story writer.

Theme: A young man practices deception for his mother's sake.

Discussion: Two aspects of this story may be discussed:
   (A) The ethical problem
   1. What situation leads this young man into an act of deception? What are his motives? In the light of his motives, do you approve his action? If not, why not?
   2. What is the essence of the conflict in this story?

(B) Structure of the story

How effective is the telling of a story through a one-way telephone conversation? What common ways of storytelling are there? (The first person narrative, the observer who shares in the action, the omniscient author, and so on.)

Resources for Related Experiences:

1. Some students may want to try experimental writing. Do not make assignments—be ready to accept what they may be willing to offer. See that there is opportunity for each writer to read his story to the class.

Can students make stories out of the following materials: cancelled checks, a collection of dance programs, crumbs on a table, a worn pair of dress gloves, a broken window on the third floor of an empty house?

Before any of these items becomes a real story, the following elements must be added: characters (people); setting (where the action occurs); motivation (what the people are feeling); action (what the people do); conflict (opposing forces); how it all turns out (resolution of conflict).

2. The collateral reading of students may be discussed. Let students develop their own terminology in critical analysis.

3. Some students may be assigned for individual reading James Thurber's "The Secret Life of Walter Mitty" or other stories that have unusual structure.

THUS I REFUTE BEELZY   Page 22

by John Collier (1901–   ), English-born poet, essayist, novelist, and short-story writer, now living in California. He is a master of fantasy and irony.

Theme: Cruelty gets its just reward. (Art may be better than life!)

Discussion: The father in this story is a sadistic bully. In real life justice might be much slower in coming. Might it finally come? How?

1. Why does the ending of this story take us completely by surprise? (Because Collier has made the story entirely credible up to its climax.)

2. It was Oscar Wilde who pointed out that killing the spirit of another by slow degrees is murder as culpable as a sudden act of violence ("The Ballad of Reading Gaol"). In the light of Wilde's statement, would you say the ending of this story is satisfying?

3. Can you analyze Big Simon's character? Why is he a bully? Is there evidence that he feels insecure himself, or even guilty? Do you pity him?

Resources for Related Experiences: Another story in which the ending takes us off our feet is Shirley Jackson's "The Lottery."

Short stories: "Fancies and Goodnights," "The Touch of Nutmeg,"
John Collier

THE FATHER   Page 27

by Björnstjerne Björnson (1832–1910), Norwegian dramatist, novelist, and
short-story writer; a Nobel Prize winner.

Theme: Pride. Perhaps all that we have is ours by the grace of God and
circumstance.

"I have a son for whom nothing is too good. I have all the money
anyone needs to buy anything, even blessings. Why don't blessings stay
bought?"

Discussion: Before the reading of this story the class may prepare to
keep a running account of their reactions on their index cards, rather
than record a single, final impression. This plan will require a different
kind of reading from the kind students usually do. When they have
finished their reading, some of the students will be eager to read what
they have written. Allow this; then send them back to the story to read
the line or lines that prompted the response.

Much of the discussion will come out of the context of the cards.
However, the following points, if not raised by the class, may profitably
be raised by the teacher:

1. Should one who is especially fortunate in social or economic ways,
or even in health, consider all these things irrevocably his *right?*

2. Why is it possible to assign an undue importance to money in
one's scheme of values?

Of first importance in the understanding of this story is an analysis
of the father's character. Proud even to arrogance, he finally learns hu-
mility. May the experience of great loss ennoble a man's spirit?

Ask the students what words and phrases they know that give them a
language with which to discuss stories (situation, scene, character, conflict, style, and so on).

Resources for Related Experiences: The cry of David after the rebellion and death of his son, Absalom, taken from II Samuel, may lead
students to read the Old Testament story of a father's grief.

THE UNPOPULAR PASSENGER   Page 30

by Robert Bingham (1925–   ), American journalist and short-story
writer; now assistant managing editor of the *Reporter* magazine.

Theme: Understanding people makes us tolerant of behavior that may
otherwise seem offensive.

Discussion: Except for the soldier and possibly the narrator, no character in this story is altogether pleasant. No character is identified by name and yet there is no mistaking one character for another. What is the author's purpose in omitting names? Would passengers on an actual flight know each other by name? Is the author presenting persons as representative types as well as individuals? ("The woman with the fox collar," "the man with the slight stutter," "the man with the big hat," "the man with the deep bass voice.")

After the characters have been identified and understood, a discussion of the moral and ethical elements implicit in human behavior can take place.

1. What character seems most offensive? Why?
2. When do you get an insight into the reasons for his behavior?
3. Does this insight redeem him in any way?
4. Could you imagine any circumstances that might account for the unpleasantness of "the woman with the fox collar"?
5. In your own opinion, does knowing more about a person *always* make us more tolerant of him?

Resources for Related Experiences: Other narratives in which persons are brought together by chance include Chaucer's Prologue to *The Canterbury Tales,* in which persons are going on a pilgrimage; Thornton Wilder's *Bridge of San Luis Rey,* in which five persons whose lives have been separate fall to death together; and Hawthorne's "The Ambitious Guest," in which a family and its unknown guest are trapped by an avalanche.

A GIRL FROM THE QUEER PEOPLE   Page 35

by Carl Sandburg (1878–   ), one of America's foremost poets, great biographer of Lincoln, and author of one novel, *Remembrance Rock,* from which this episode is selected as a self-contained short story.

Theme: The persecution of one who is different, and her rescue by one who knows that "a difference to be a difference must make a difference."

Discussion: The card system of making notes on one's personal reactions may be used again here. The student ought to be able to say, "I suppose that in one way or another each of us has been in a situation of this kind. We may have been the victim of the persecution; we may have been the hero; we may have been the leader of the persecutors; we may have been just one of the followers; or we may have stood by and watched, feeling bad, but doing nothing." Remind the class that girls pick on boys, boys pick on girls, older children haze younger ones, city folk laugh at farm people and vice versa—and then there are the problems of minority groups.

It is important to state here that these assignments, though written, are not to be treated as "written assignments." Their function is to record responses, perhaps lacking in form, or personal experiences recalled as a result of this reading. The students' reactions to the stories must be accepted without "moralizing" or censure.

Resources for Related Experiences:
Novels: *Remembrance Rock*, Carl Sandburg; *Kingsblood Royal*, Sinclair Lewis
Play: *The Diary of Anne Frank*, Frances Goodrich and Albert Hackett
Films: *The Boy with the Green Hair; The Trial*
Recording: "Shine" sung by Louis Armstrong

THE GOLDEN KITE, THE SILVER WIND   Page 41
by Ray Bradbury (1920–   ), leading American science-fiction writer, author of movie scenarios such as *Moby Dick*.

Theme: Co-operation may be better than force.

Discussion: This story is a parable, symbolic of far more than its obvious content. The term "symbolism" must be introduced. Symbols then may be analyzed before the implications of the story are discussed. What may be the significance of the two mandarins? The two towns? The race between them? The solution? Draw from the students real parallels in our modern society: walls in the shape of "iron curtains," inaccessible Open Doors, armament races. The class may discuss competition in business and in society.

May competition be both good and bad? In what ways may it be good? In what ways may it be bad? How may this parable be related to events in the modern world?

This story is in a sense one long figure of speech. How is it related to the figure of speech in the Dickinson poem that follows?

Resources for Related Experiences:
Short story collection: *The Golden Apples of the Sun*, Ray Bradbury
Poetry: *Complete Poems*, Emily Dickinson

AFTER TWENTY YEARS   Page 46
by O. Henry (William S. Porter) (1862–1910), American short-story writer, who wrote of the "common man and woman." His stories have a characteristic surprise ending.

Theme: Conflict between duty and friendship.

Discussion: Does the class approve of the outcome? Should duty interfere with friendship? Are there higher loyalties than one's loyalty to an old friend?

In "Those Two Boys," students may note, Franklin P. Adams uses skillfully in a poem the surprise ending technique that is characteristic of O. Henry's stories.

Resources for Related Experiences: One copy of the complete works of O. Henry in the classroom. What other O. Henry stories does the class know? ("The Gift of the Magi," "The Ransom of Red Chief," "The Cop and the Anthem"?) How do the endings of these stories follow the O. Henry pattern?

THE UPTURNED FACE   Page 50

by Stephen Crane (1871–1900), American novelist, journalist, and short-story writer, who was one of the first American realists.

Theme: Men at war: a "slice of life."

Does a story need a plot to be a great story? Although "The Upturned Face" has no formal plot, reading it is an unforgettable experience. Crane's realism has been imitated by many other American authors.

Discussion: The realistic description, the stark setting, the juxtaposition of words for sound as well as for "meaning," all converge upon the reader to enforce what we call the "literary experience."

1. How many times does the word "plopping" occur in the story? What is its effect?

2. How does the writer make us feel what his characters are feeling?

3. Do you think that wars still feel like this to the men who fight in them?

4. Why is this story more than a newspaper report?

Sassoon, noted poet of wartime experience, suggests reality by an opposite approach, no less vivid, in "The Dreamers."

Resources for Related Experiences:

Short story collection: *In the Midst of Life,* Ambrose Bierce

Novels: *Andersonville,* MacKinlay Kantor; *The Red Badge of Courage,* Stephen Crane

Nonfiction: *Brave Men,* Ernie Pyle

Review of Part 1

Because the accumulated experiences which the students have had under the close guidance of the teacher must now be co-ordinated, a period may well be spent summing up the stories in Part One.

THE LITERARY EXPERIENCE

Start the discussion with a simple question of this sort: "What happens when you read?" According to John Dewey, the occurrence of any event in itself is not to be considered as an experience until the mind has worked it over, has considered it, has seen it as a whole.

What has happened? In some cases the student may have seen himself in one or several stories. He has identified himself with characters. He has shared the conflicts. Let him generalize on the literary experience as an emotional and an intellectual exercise.

CRITICAL TERMS

With a backlog of twelve stories upon which to draw, terms like point of view, characterization, plot, theme, conflict, denouement, realism, fantasy, parable, "slice of life," and symbolism may now be taught inductively.

STYLE

The diction of an author is perhaps the only aspect of style that needs to be considered this early. A writer's vocabulary is a clue to his style. Consider the general vocabulary of O. Henry, Crane, and Sandburg.

IMPACT

Which stories have had the strongest emotional impact? The strongest impact in thought and ideas?

PART 2

STORIES OF DEPTH

The twelve stories in Part Two are more sustained and in general more difficult than those in Part One. Themes are likely to be more complex. Characterization is more subtle and extended, and the conflict is more often a struggle within the mind or a conflict of values. Students may need more guidance with these stories, although a good review of Part One will have alerted them as to what to look for.

The system of using index cards for recording the student's own personal reactions as he reads will pay dividends if you continue it with these longer "stories of depth." Do not discourage students by making the cards the subject of censure; do not use them to provide a mechanical means of checking reading or of marking progress. The cards will provide you with an opportunity to see more deeply into the character and personality of each student. What the notes reveal may be used as "signs" not "means." Keep the confidence of the student. Yet, if the atmosphere is encouraging, expect some students to ask that their responses be read and discussed.

Further Use of Cards

In Part Two the cards may serve for purposes additional to discussion. Let them serve as the raw material for critical written evaluation. They may provide the data and evidence upon which the reader can generalize about the story. Suggest that he focus upon the viewpoint and the theme; or perhaps upon one character and the relationship of the happenings in the story to the kind of person that character is; or upon the symbolism and its meaning. Very able students may wish to analyze structure or style. But the subjective, informal essay is more to be desired than any attempt at formal criticism. The limited reader will be capable of doing no more than retell the story in his own terms. The alert reader will write with some maturity.

THE NEW KID   Page 57

by Murray Heyert (1912–   ), a New Yorker whose vocation is aircraft
  sales and promotion and whose avocation is writing.

Theme: All human beings want to belong. Sometimes a group or a gang
  picks on an outsider. Is it human nature for the outsider to try to get in
  by joining forces against a new outsider?

Discussion: The class will want to discuss what has happened in the
  story. In addition to the immediate response to the events of the story,
  there will be a period of consideration during which each student
  struggles to understand Marty's behavior, censoring it, and explaining
  to himself why he feels about Marty's action as he does.
     Recall the experiences of "A Girl from the Queer People." The stu-
  dent is no longer protected by the perspective of history; this is what
  may happen on any street in any neighborhood. The important point to
  grasp is that the barbarous behavior of youngsters has its adult counterpart in group relations on a community level or even perhaps on a national level. If your class is an urban one, students may be able to point
  out parallels in the behavior of new groups in a community.

Just as Marty's behavior seems regrettable, from a mature point of view, so do some adult group relationships seem regrettable in the light of mature consideration.

Resources for Related Experiences:
  Short story: "That Greek Dog," MacKinlay Kantor
  Play: *The Ins and the Outs,* Nora Sterling

THE UNDEFEATED   Page 68

by Ernest Hemingway (1898–   ), American novelist and short-story writer, who won the Nobel Prize for literature in 1954.

Theme: The passing of greatness is always tragic. Yet man's true greatness lies in his continual struggle against the inevitable.

Discussion: Bullfighting is Manuel's whole life. Apart from his art he is nothing. What is obvious to everyone else, Manuel is unwilling to recognize: that his career is over. Not without this final terrible fight will he yield to the inevitable. It is in his almost senseless courage in the face of odds and in his final defeat that the tragedy of his struggle attains a universal symbolism.

The story contains many technical terms that are concerned with bullfighting. There are no adequate English equivalents. It is as if one tried to translate our football term "huddle" into "The players of the team are in a circle behind the line where they will be playing and they have their arms about each other." Translations are supplied here but the teacher need not "teach" them. The context reveals the general meaning of these Spanish words.

banderillos (*bän'de·rēl'yôs*). Small wooden spears used to cut the shoulder or neck muscles of the bull, forcing him to lower his head as a target for the sword.

barrera (*bärr·ā'rä*). A wood screen behind which bullfighters escape from the bull.

caballos (*ḳä·vä'lyôs*). Horses.

cogida (*ḳô·hǐ'dä*). A "kill."

coleta (*ḳô·lä'tä*). The pigtail of a bullfighter.

corridas (*ḳôr·rē'däs*). Bullfights.

corto y derecho (*ḳôr'tô ē dä·rä' chô*). Short and straight.

cuadrilla (*ḳwa·drēl'yä*). A troop of bullfighters.

duros (*doŏ'rôs*). Spanish coins, each worth five pesetas.

faena (*fä·ā'nä*). A full turn, either as the bull passes, or in parade about the bull ring.

Madrileños (*mä'drē·län'yôs*). Natives of Madrid.

monos (*môn'ôs*). Monkeys.

muleta (*moŏ·lä'tä*). The small cape used to conceal the sword.

novillero (*nô'vēl·yä'rô*). A young bull, or one who is in charge of young bulls.

novillo (*nô·vēl′yô*). A young bull, or a young bullfighter.

pase de pecho (*pä′sä dä pä′chô*). A move in which the bull passes close to the bullfighter's chest.

paseo (*pä·sä′ô*). The march of the toreadors.

peseta (*pä·sä′tä*). Metal money worth about a quarter.

picador (*pĭk′á·dôr′*). A man who fights the bulls on horseback.

quites (*kē′täs*). A defensive move.

recorte (*rä·kôr′tä*). A clipping either of the bull's tail and ears as a sign of great victory, or of the

bullfighter's pigtail as a sign of defeat.

rosinante (*rôs′ē·nän′tä*). A saddle horse, half-packed for protection against the bull.

suerte (*swär′tä*). Good luck.

tercio (*tär′thē·ô*). One-third.

toril (*tô′rēl*). A pen where the bull is kept just before the fight.

varas (*vä′räs*). Short sticks with barbed points.

veronica (*vär·ô′nē·kä*). A bullfighter's cape, or the movement which uses the cape to pass the bull.

"The Undefeated" may require more than one class period. The home assignment may be restricted to the writing of response cards. On the following day, discussion of Manuel's character may precede a written composition. In class discussion introduce terms like "integrity," "inner-strength," and "compassion." Ask students: Do you think Manuel should have entered into this final fight? Why did he attempt it?

Do you think Hemingway is interested in bullfighting entirely for its own sake, or as a kind of theater in which qualities of manhood are dramatically displayed?

What similar qualities of manhood are apparent in Henley's poem "Invictus"?

Resources for Related Experiences:

Novels: *The Old Man and the Sea,* Ernest Hemingway; *The Brave Bulls,* Tom Lea

Autobiography: *Juan Belmonte, Killer of Bulls,* translated by Leslie Charteris

Play: *Androcles and the Lion,* George Bernard Shaw

Films: *Blood and Sand, Matador*

Recording: "Heroes of the Bull Ring," Decca

THE NECKLACE   Page 92

by **Guy de Maupassant** (1850–1893), French novelist and short-story writer, who wrote of Norman peasant life and of the middle-class, fashionable life in Paris.

Theme: Although chance and accident may affect the events of our lives, much of what happens to an individual stems from his own personal system of values—the things he considers important to his pattern of living.

Discussion: The values people choose, consciously or unconsciously, as a philosophy of living should be worth living for and suffering for. Ten years of hard work and misery is a high price to pay for vanity. While we pity Madame Loisel, we cannot really feel compassion, for there is no greatness, nobility, or even dignity in her motivation and character. The pettiness of her aims makes their disastrous consequences more ridiculous than tragic.

Let discussion focus on the kinds of values people live by. Are people always aware of their true goals and motives? What are the important things in life? Money? Clothes? Cars? Fame? Social status? Keeping up with the Joneses? What things are more likely to make for true happiness?

Resources for Related Experiences: Ask students to report on any current television drama in which motivation is small and selfish. How deeply are their sympathies involved? With what more worthy television play may it be contrasted?

THE MINISTER'S BLACK VEIL   Page 99

by **Nathaniel Hawthorne** (1804–1864), American novelist and short-story writer, whose work is marked by its symbolism and psychological insight.

Theme: The face of man hides, even from those he loves, the secrets that are within him, and of which, rightly or wrongly, he may be ashamed.

Discussion: Hawthorne provides a footnote, which we have transferred from the text to this guide, so that it may be employed by the teacher after the story has been read. It reads as follows: "A Parable: Another clergyman in New England, Mr. Joseph Moody, of York, Maine, who died about eighty years since, made himself remarkable by the same eccentricity that is here related of the Reverend Mr. Hooper. In his case, however, the symbol had a different import. In early life he had accidentally killed a beloved friend; and from that day till the hour of his own death, he hid his face from men."

This note provides a basis for a discussion of Hawthorne's symbols. Recall the symbols of that other parable, "The Golden Kite, the Silver Wind," and also introduce the idea of Manuel of "The Undefeated" as a symbol of certain qualities in man. Both the mask and the minister become symbols in "The Minister's Black Veil."

Questions bearing on symbolism:
1. What makes the minister different from other men? (Not just the veil; the courage, honesty, and Puritan sense of guilt or sin that cause him to wear it.)
2. What is his purpose in wearing the veil?
3. What are some of the invisible veils men wear?
4. The story looks like realism. Is it truly realistic writing?

Resources for Related Experiences:
Short stories: "The Great Stone Face," "The Ambitious Guest," "Rappacini's Daughter," "Dr. Heidegger's Experiment," Nathaniel Hawthorne
Novels: *The Scarlet Letter, The House of the Seven Gables,* Nathaniel Hawthorne

NANCY   Page 110

by Elizabeth Enright, Chicago-born illustrator for children's books, who turned to writing for children (Newbery Award winner) and now writes mainly for adults (O. Henry Award winner).

Theme: People have fundamental needs. A wealthy and well-regulated home may lack the ingredients for happiness that are sometimes to be found in haphazard households.

Discussion: Have students keep a running written record of their reactions. Notes will vary greatly, but will probably reveal that the class is divided between those who resent the "high-toned" attitude of the nurse and those who are horrified by the earthiness of the family Fiona visits.
The discussion may begin with what the reader sees and what he makes of what he sees. For this purpose the following questions:
1. What happens in this story?
2. What are the differences between the two ways of life described in the story?
3. Why does the writer make this contrast? Does she exaggerate?
4. Why may Fiona be forever changed because of her experience?
5. Would you be changed by a similar experience?
6. Can you think of any totally new experience in your own life which has changed you in some way?
Sandburg's poem "Happiness" expresses the essence of the needs of all human beings. How are Fiona's needs very much of a piece with these?

Resources for Related Experiences:
Short story collections: *The Moment before the Rain, Borrowed Summer and Other Stories,* Elizabeth Enright

THE GREAT AUTOMATIC GRAMMATISATOR Page 123

by **Roald Dahl** (1916–), who was born in Wales of Norwegian parents. He is a short-story writer generally concerned with the fantastic and macabre.

Theme: Satire on automation: Is the machine the master or the tool?

Discussion: This story may be read more thoughtfully if the following questions are asked *before* the reading:
   1. When the telephone rings, do you have to answer it?
   2. When television is on, do you have to watch?
   3. Many factory workers identify themselves as, "I'm turret lathe number five"; sailors call to each other with, "Turret number three, answer." In many ways do we seem to cede our identities to the machines *we serve?*
   With these three things in mind, read the story.
   After the reading, the discussion may return to the orienting questions, resolving with:
   1. What do you think might be the result of a civilization of "grammatisators"?
   2. How do you think this result could be prevented?
   3. Should we destroy all machines to avoid the danger?
   4. Can you write a story on the same theme?
   Have the students note whether "Nightmare Number Three," which follows, treats the subject in the same tone as does Dahl's story.

Resources for Related Experiences:
   Short story: "The God in the Dynamo," H. G. Wells
   Novels: *Erewhon,* Samuel Butler; *Looking Backward,* Edward Bellamy; *Brave New World,* Aldous Huxley
   Science fiction: *The World of Non-A,* A. A. Vogt
   Play: *The Adding Machine,* Elmer Rice
   Films: *The Shape of Things to Come, Metropolis, Modern Times*

THE QUIET MAN Page 141

by **Maurice Walsh** (1879–), Irish author now living in Dublin. As a customs officer he traveled widely, establishing a reputation in the United States in the 'thirties as a contributor to the *Saturday Evening Post* and other magazines.

Theme: The virtues of restraint and self-contained power as they achieve victory on both the moral and the physical levels.

Discussion: This is the story of a "good guy," a "bad guy," and the problem between them. Oversimplified it would be grist for the "Horse

Opry" Western story. There is more to it than that, however, and it is the added depth which gives it importance.

The card responses may be relatively simple, devoted to remarks urging the hero to fight back and to hisses for the brother-villain. Now and then there may be a student who will have wanted the hero to keep the money. A few will understand the nature of the moral victory, and it is upon them that the teacher must rely. Ask students:

1. What do you think of a man who burns money?
2. Which was the bigger victory, the fight or the shaming?
3. What characters from the other stories we have read have qualities in common with the chief character of this story?
4. Can you support the view that this story is especially successful in characterization?

Let students observe in what way the ideal of manhood expressed in Hawes' poem "The True Knight" is representative also of "The Quiet Man."

Resources for Related Experiences:

Novels: *Blackcock's Feather, The Spanish Lady, Trouble in the Glen,* Maurice Walsh

A TIME FOR LEARNING

Page 156

by Jessamyn West, a contemporary Californian, who was born in Indiana of Quaker parentage. Her short stories are modern classics and have won numerous awards.

Theme: Learning how to get over disappointment and even disillusionment is a necessary part of growing up. Often the experience helps one to find himself—to become a mature person.

Discussion: Students will identify with Emmett, the "unrequited lover"; there will probably be some who have had their own experiences of a similar kind. Ask the class:

1. Why is the experience that Emmett goes through an important event in his life? (It leads him to put forth his best efforts and ultimately to know that he has truly the ability to fulfill himself as an artist.)

2. Do you think Emmett was really in love or merely infatuated? What ways are there of telling the difference?

3. Where in the story was there a foreshadowing of the outcome?

4. Why is Oral important in the story?

5. Would Emmett have felt better if he had followed his first impulse and painted a mean, spiteful picture on the barn?

The Housman poem echoes the theme of the story. Let students discover it for themselves.

Resources for Related Experiences:
Short story collection: *Love, Death, and the Ladies' Drill Team,* Jessamyn West
Novels: *Cress Delahanty, The Friendly Persuasion, The Witch Diggers,* Jessamyn West
Poems: *A Shropshire Lad,* A. E. Housman

THE CASK OF AMONTILLADO   Page 169

by Edgar Allan Poe (1809–1849), American poet, critic, and short-story writer. He was the inventor of the detective story and the horror story.

Theme: Poe, who could enter the mind of the mentally deranged, gives us a masterly psychological study of vengeance.

Discussion: Let the class analyze the qualities that make Poe a master craftsman.
   1. How is the writing of this story different from the writing of most of the stories we have read so far?
   2. What is the purpose of the author? If this is a story of violence, then how is it inherently different from "Thus I Refute Beelzy," "The New Kid," and "The Undefeated"?
   3. Is Poe concerned with the moral aspects of evil?
   4. To what extent are your sympathies involved?
   5. Count the number of times the ending is foreshadowed by double meanings in the speeches of Montresor.
   6. What can you say about the language and the use of words in this story, as compared with the use of language in the story of Stephen Crane, "The Upturned Face"?
   Blake's poem "A Poison Tree" is also a study of vengeance. What psychological principle does it express? (What makes hate grow?)

Resources for Related Experiences:
Short stories: "The Pit and the Pendulum, "The Black Cat," "The Tell-Tale Heart," "The Murders in the Rue Morgue," "The Gold Bug," Edgar Allan Poe
Poem: "My Last Duchess," Robert Browning
   Readers of contemporary murder mysteries and crime fiction may make comparisons with Poe (plot, suspense, atmosphere, characterization, style).

THE MOST DANGEROUS GAME
Page 175

by Richard Connell (1893–1949), American journalist and short-story
writer, who also made motion pictures.

Theme: Adventure: the hunter becomes the hunted.

Discussion: The reader will be carried along on this chase and may not be
willing to pause even to make notes. Let him lose himself in the adventure. Then ask him:

   1. Did you foresee the end?

   2. How did the writer succeed in holding you in suspense?

   3. What was the author's purpose?

   4. Which is more important in this story, plot or theme?

   5. What elements present in "The Undefeated," for example, are absent here? (Symbolism, universality.)

   6. Why is this nevertheless a memorable story?

Resource for Related Experiences:
Short story collection: *Apes and Angels,* Richard Connell

HAIRCUT
Page 192

by Ring Lardner (1885–1933), American sportswriter and short-story
writer, whose bitterly humorous sketches of American life are written
in the vernacular of the people portrayed.

Theme: Cruelty is never funny.

Discussion: Ask the class how they feel toward Jim. How do they think
Lardner feels toward Jim? Does the speaker in the story represent the
author's viewpoint? If not, do we know the author's viewpoint? What
is it? Now ask:

   1. Why do people play practical jokes?

   2. What do practical jokes reveal about the character of the joker?

   3. What is true humor?

   4. Is "Haircut" a funny story?

   5. What insight into human nature do you gain from the story?

Resources for Related Experiences:
Short stories: "I Can't Breathe," "Alibi Ike," Ring Lardner
Short story collection: *Round Up,* Ring Lardner

THE DUCHESS AND THE SMUGS
Page 202

by Pamela Frankau (1908–   ), English writer now living in America,
who has moved from light fiction into solid and serious writing.

Theme: Becoming an adult involves the painful process of assessing the values by which people live.

Discussion: Two ways of life are contrasted here. The Bradleys are an ordered but overprotected family. Penelope's life is random, creative, unfettered, and artistic. Gradually the events and opinions of the characters in the story arouse conflict in Penelope. She makes a tentative choice in favor of propriety, security, and order, a choice she must revoke with the dawning realization that conventional values may be artificial. Being true to her own deepest feelings is more important. She chooses her own values—integrity, honesty, self-reliance.

Out of such a discovery comes a new feeling of joy and perhaps even satisfaction. And for this reason the death of the Duchess is the beginning of womanhood for Penelope.

Resources for Related Experiences:

Short story collection: *A Wreath for the Enemy*, Pamela Frankau

Novels: *Thunder on the Left*, Christopher Morley; *Damien*, Herman Hesse; *How Green Was My Valley*, Richard Llewellyn; *Great Expectations*, Charles Dickens

Review of Part 2

DEVELOPING CRITERIA FOR CRITICAL JUDGMENT

A period may be spent inductively developing criteria for the evaluation of the short story. What are the essential standards by which we judge merit? (Let students list these on the board.) May the same standards be applied to all types of stories? Do different readers have different standards? Have your own standards for judging stories undergone any changes as a result of your reading the stories in Part Two?

CONSOLIDATING GAINS

Further discussion may focus around such questions as these:

1. How does a good short story require the reader to "read between the lines"?

2. What purposes may writers have in mind in creating a short story?

3. When an author includes incidents that at first seem trivial, what is likely to be the reason?

4. Is the author's viewpoint always the same as that of the teller of the story?

5. Which stories in Part Two seem to you to have universal themes?

6. In which stories did you find the symbolism thought-provoking?

7. From which did you feel that you gained new insights into human behavior?

WRITTEN EVALUATIONS

Any of the questions listed above may be selected to stimulate the writing of informal essays. Students should be urged to refer to specific examples to support their statements.

PART 3

STORIES TO THINK ABOUT

The end of Part Two may mark the end of guided class work. Part Three may be used in any of several ways. Interested students may read these stories on their own initiative. Better readers may be assigned particular stories and asked to report to the class. A third plan is to continue the study of the short story as intensively as, or even more intensively than, in Parts One and Two. The needs of your class will govern your decision.

Students will approach these final stories with a conscious awareness of what is happening to them as they read, applying the critical perceptions they have developed in their study of the preceding twenty-four stories.

Let students assume the responsibility for their own creative reading without clues and direction from you. The result may be a free exchange of ideas and judgments, teacher and students participating on equal terms. Some students may wish to continue the card system of making notations from which to write, discuss, or report. An optional culminating experience may be a written critical evaluation of one story from this final group.

PAUL'S CASE   Page 239

by Willa Cather (1876–1947), American novelist and short-story writer known for her studies of character and of life in the Middle West.

Theme: Dreams help us to build our lives, but there is no total escape from the real world without tragedy.

Discussion: This story relates to every boy or girl who feels that no one understands, and in one way or another, that means every boy or girl at some time of life. Here are the dreams and the wish-fulfillments. This is perhaps a test story for the maturing reader. You will be able to evaluate the teaching and learning that have been going on in the preceding twenty-four stories by response to "Paul's Case." There will be students who will reject the main character here, feeling no sympathy for him whatsoever. There will be others who understand him and will be able to bring insight to those who do not.

1. What was wrong with Paul's life that he should be forced to create a substitute life? Was the trouble actually with his life or with his *view* of his life?

2. How much blame for the tragic outcome can we place on society and family?

3. How does Willa Cather make subtle use of symbols? (The carnation in the snow, for example.)

4. Willa Cather is considered a great artist in characterization. What instances do you find that illustrate her skill?

5. Do the events of the story go with one another, so that there is no moment when you say to yourself, "This couldn't happen"?

6. Is this realism? Do you come away from the story with the feeling that you have been through an experience that was worth while? What insights have you gained?

Although Richard Cory must have lived a very different kind of life from Paul's, are there any insights gained from "Paul's Case" that may be applied to Cory's case?

Resources for Related Experiences:
Novels: *O Pioneers, My Antonia, Shadows on the Rock, Death Comes for the Archbishop*, Willa Cather

BARN BURNING   Page 257

by **William Faulkner** (1897–   ), American novelist and short-story writer, winner of the Nobel Prize in 1950. His locale is the South.

Theme: Every individual must sooner or later assume responsibility for thinking for himself and making his own decisions. It is never easy, but it is hardest of all if one must choose between honor and family loyalty.

Discussion: Capture the spontaneous reactions of students before conducting a discussion. Tell the class, "Just as soon as you have finished reading this story, put down the book and start to write a composition about 'Barn Burning.' Write what you are feeling and thinking, without taking the time to reason it out."

Class discussion will grow out of these compositions. Consideration of moral and spiritual values will follow naturally when the class touches upon the choices faced by young Snopes. You may prime the pump with these questions:

1. What do you think the following statement does to young Snopes: "I reckon anybody named for Colonel Sartoris in this country can't help but tell the truth, can they?"

2. How is the boy affected by this statement: "You got to learn to

stick to your own blood, or you ain't going to have any blood to stick to you."

3. What do you think made young Snopes' father a "barn burner"?

4. If there is a universal truth in this story, what is it?

Resources for Related Experiences:

Short stories: "The Bear," "Turn About," "Two Soldiers," William Faulkner

Novel: *Intruder in the Dust,* William Faulkner

MY FIRST TWO WOMEN   Page 273

by Nadine Gordimer (1923–   ), who was born and has always lived in South Africa, although many of her stories have first appeared in such American magazines as *Harper's* and *The New Yorker.*

Theme: A subtle psychological study of a child with two mothers, yet none.

Discussion: Treat this story as objectively as possible, for there is a probability that at least some of the students will have undergone similar experiences and they will not want to talk about them. An objective study will induce insights that can help all young persons in thinking about marriage, the family, and the home. Marriage is seldom like the movies, and family relations are not often ideal. But this is an area in which vicarious experience can help young persons to a constructive and realistic attitude.

"My First Two Women" is as difficult and challenging a story as "Paul's Case." Understanding human behavior and establishing sound values are two of the greatest objectives to be gained through reading the short story. To this story the student must bring the kinds of perception that he has been developing all along. The class may want to make comparisons with many of the preceding stories.

Some guides to discussion:

1. At what moment in the story are you aware that the child is a boy?

2. What kind of woman is the real mother?

3. What kind of woman is the stepmother?

4. Does the child see them as you, the reader, see them?

5. What does the boy mean when he says he will never forgive his stepmother?

6. What does this story make you think about families?

7. What in this story made you think about "Paul's Case"?

Resources for Related Experiences:

Short story collections: *The Soft Voice of the Serpent, Six Feet of the Country,* Nadine Gordimer

MOLLY MORGAN
Page 284

by John Steinbeck (1902–   ), American novelist and short-story writer. Exponent of the modern school of realism. Pulitzer Prize winner, 1940.

Theme: The romantic daughter of a romantic father rejects reality as he has done, refusing to face up to life.

Discussion: There are many ways of running away from life. Molly's father has chosen one way; she has chosen another. Running away is an act of weakness. Steinbeck has made it possible for us to sympathize with Molly, to will her strength, perhaps, but also to accept her final act as in character. He has left us, however, with a hope that some day she will have the strength to stop running.

Ask students:
1. How does Steinbeck develop character?
2. How has he given the story universality?
3. How has he made use of symbolism?
4. What qualities do you observe in the author that contribute to his literary stature?

Resources for Related Experiences:
Short story: "Flight," John Steinbeck
Novelettes: *The Red Pony, The Pearl,* John Steinbeck
Novel: *The Grapes of Wrath,* John Steinbeck
Poetry collection: *Spoon River Anthology,* Edgar Lee Masters

THE ROCKING–HORSE WINNER
Page 298

by D. H. Lawrence (1885–1930), English poet, short-story writer, and novelist of the modern school of realism.

Theme: Lawrence is depicting here the fierce sense of responsibility assumed by a child in a world of irresponsible and selfish adults.

Discussion: It is not that no one cares what happens, for there is love in the house. But there is blindness, too; no one can see because the curtain of self is dense, impenetrable. The father thinks only of the pressures which are making him old. The mother sees only the incessant struggle to maintain social status. The uncle seeks an end to incessant lending. The groom sees only the miracle of picking a winner each time he bets. But the children have ears, perhaps are cursed with ears, because only they can hear the house crying, "There must be more money." And so there is.

One may ask:
1. Is it possible that a child can see with terrible clarity what is concealed from an adult?

2. What difference does Paul's sacrifice make in this family?

3. Can we argue that the story is symbolic?

In "Piano" the student will note again Lawrence's ability to recreate the intensity of childhood impressions.

Resources for Related Experiences:
  Fairy tale: "The Emperor's New Clothes," Hans Christian Andersen
  Play: *Three Men on a Horse*, John Cecil Holm and George Abbott

BERNICE BOBS HER HAIR
Page 311

by F. Scott Fitzgerald (1896–1940), American novelist known for his studies of youth in the Jazz Age.

Theme: The problems of growing up in the "roaring 'twenties" were perhaps different only in externals from the problems of today.

Discussion: Although the time of this story is the early 'twenties and the language is "dated," Bernice struggles with the same personal problems that confront the teenager of today: What are the ways to popularity? Are they in harmony with the preservation of status? The dignity of the individual is precious to the adolescent. This story offers an excellent opportunity to identify some of the perennial problems of youth.

Ask the class to think of contemporary parallels for the situation, for the characters, and for the final act of violence. Then ask: In your opinion how is this story important as a "period piece"?

The role of the literary artist in evoking the image of a person or of a period now gone is underscored by Walter de la Mare's "An Epitaph."

Resources for Related Experiences:
  Short story collection: *The Stories of F. Scott Fitzgerald*, Malcolm Cowley, ed.
  Novel: *The Great Gatsby*, F. Scott Fitzgerald
  Nonfiction: *Only Yesterday*, Frederick Lewis Allen
  Biography: *The Fair Side of Paradise*, Arthur Mizener

THE ANSWER
Page 332

by Philip Wylie (1902–   ), American writer of popular fiction, science fiction, and biting satire. Most of his short stories have appeared in popular magazines.

Theme: For survival mankind must accept a full realization of the concept, "Love one another." Man must close the gap between his faith and his acts.

Discussion: The problem of the hydrogen bomb and the insecurity of the human race forces a reconsideration of a very old and very sound religious precept. Wylie seems to be saying that, where all men are concerned in a common problem, none can avoid sharing the responsibility and the guilt for its existence.

Fantasy here makes reality painfully real. Some symbols and situations may seem to students extremely obvious. Ask students:

1. How does Wylie use symbols?
2. Do any characters seem to be symbols?
3. Which characters are "flesh and blood," and what makes them so?
4. How does Wylie's literary style compare with that of other writers of fantasy?
5. What does the title mean?

Frost in "Fire and Ice" suggests the alternative men face if they will not "love one another."

Resources for Related Experiences:
Short story: "By the Waters of Babylon," Stephen Vincent Benét
Essay: "On Being Human," Ashley Montague
Novels: *Brave New World*, Aldous Huxley; *The Shape of Things to Come*, H. G. Wells; *1984*, George Orwell; *Hiroshima*, John Hersey

MARIO AND THE MAGICIAN   Page 358

by **Thomas Mann** (1875–1955), German. One of the foremost novelists and short-story writers of this century. Nobel Prize winner, 1929.

Theme: The surrender of the will and of human dignity—whether by an individual or by a people—is a debasing spectacle.

Discussion: This story can be read on several levels. Mann's story is laminated, from the polished surface of a vacation adventure, through the supporting strata of socio-political, psychological, and philosophical meanings, to the heart of man's struggle for an intelligent and dignified existence. It is only by seeing this surface and depth nature in a story that we can answer questions such as:

1. Why does the magician seem to be more than a state entertainer?
2. What events in modern European history can you relate to the symbolism here?
3. How does Mann keep you constantly aware that this story is an "orchestration"?
4. What philosophical and political statements do you find in the story?
5. What happens to us as we watch Cipolla make an animal out of Mario?
6. How can liberation come out of violence and death?

This is the last story in the collection because it requires all the skills developed by the study of earlier stories. Criteria by now developed and tested by each student will serve, not only for evaluation, but also for depth reading. (See Naomi Gill on "Depth Reading," *The English Journal*, September '53 and December '55.)

Resource for Related Experiences:
Novel: *The Magic Mountain*, Thomas Mann

Review of Part 3

The eight stories in Part Three afford a seminar in human relations: the conditioning of a child ("The Rocking-Horse Winner," "My First Two Women," "Barn Burning"), the problems of growing up ("Paul's Case," "Molly Morgan," "Bernice Bobs Her Hair"), the moral obligations of man in the modern world ("The Answer," "Mario and the Magician"). The plan of review and evaluation you follow will depend on whether the whole class has read all the final group or whether individuals have read various stories, by choice or assignment.

ORAL EVALUATION

Individuals who have read different stories may make up a panel, interpreting the purpose, the insights, the symbolism, and the universality of each story. If several persons have read a given story, they may present a symposium, briefing the listeners first with an account of characters and events, and moving into interpretation of underlying meanings.

WRITTEN EVALUATION

Critical written reports may be assigned on particular stories. It may be well to let the individual choose the story that has most deeply moved him or that has stimulated his thinking into new channels. Fundamental to any good critical evaluation is a statement of the intention of the author. "What is his thesis? What are his views? His beliefs? Why do I think so? (What is the evidence?) To what extent do I agree?"

An alternative written assignment, perhaps on a simpler level, may be developed from the question, "What have I learned about human behavior from the reading of this story?"

If any student wishes to analyze style, he may choose Faulkner or Thomas Mann as distinctive.